THE KING'S MIDWIFE

THE
KING'S MIDWIFE

A HISTORY AND MYSTERY
OF MADAME DU COUDRAY

NINA RATTNER GELBART

University of California Press
Berkeley · Los Angeles · London

University of California Press
Berkeley and Los Angeles, California

University of California Press, Ltd.
London, England

Library of Congress Cataloging-in-Publication Data

Gelbart, Nina Rattner.
  The king's midwife: a history and mystery of Madame du Coudray /
Nina Rattner Gelbart.
    p.   cm.
  Includes bibliographic references and index.
  ISBN 0–520–21036–0 (alk. paper)
    1. Le Boursier du Coudray, Angelique Marguerite, 1714 or 5–1794.
  2. Midwives—France—Biography.   I. Title.
RG950.L4G45   1998
618.2'0233
[B]—DC21   97–8421
                                                                    CIP

Printed in the United States of America

9 8 7 6 5 4 3 2 1

For my parents,
David and Henriette Rattner

I long to speak out the inspiration that comes to me from the lives of strong women. They make of their lives a Great Adventure.

Ruth Benedict

There is no history. Only fictions of various degrees of plausibility.

Voltaire

Women—when they are old enough to have done with the business of being women and can let loose their strength—must be the most powerful creatures in the world.

Isak Dinesen

A fact is like a sack. It won't stand up if it's empty. To make it stand up, first you have to put in it all the reasons and feelings that caused it in the first place.

Luigi Pirandello

Contents

Prologue

Who Is Mme du Coudray?

1. The Portrait

Paris, Summer 1985

Angélique Marguerite Le Boursier du Coudray fixes me with one eye, a direct stare. The other seems trained on the beyond. It is not just her gaze that captivates, half here, half elsewhere. She alone, as the extraordinary note beneath her portrait explains, is "pensioned and sent by the King to teach the practice of midwifery throughout the Realm" (fig. 1). Louis XV might have designated a whole corps of women to undertake this task of nationwide birthing instruction, but it was given only to her. I am dealing here with a singular phenomenon, the royally commissioned expert deliverer; you do not ignore such a person once you meet her.

She smiles slightly. From this first encounter, as she appraises me with amused interest, she seems to know I am spellbound. Well pleased with herself in her generously upholstered frame, she sits squarely, a person of large presence, double chin proudly high, forehead unfurrowed, decked in secular, feminine garb, velvet band about her neck, bow and flowers along her plunging neckline, fur ruff draped over her shoulder. This is how she, the artist's consensual subject, chose to be remembered: corpulent, spirited, and sure of herself. She dressed up for the occasion! Most other midwives of her day looked grim and meek, as if reluctant to pose at all, somberly dressed and nunlike, hooded heads bent, almost apologetic expressions on their faces, eyes often averted. These diffident contemporaries of hers humbly thanked the Almighty, in poems and prayers beneath their portraits, for whatever skills he bestowed upon them. But du Coudray, the national midwife of France, requests no special blessings, shares credit with no god.

Evidently thriving in a big job in a man's world, she does not look in this magisterial portrait like she has paid dearly, or even at all, for her unconventional life. There she sits in a frame rich with emblems: the fasces of power, the full heraldic crest with faithful hound, cornucopia, and jewels. Yet could things really have been as smooth as all that? I suspect not, and my curiosity surges. Something in the midwife's candid solidity discourages worship. This is not a flattering likeness, but matter-of-fact and frank. Here is a robust *bourgeoise*, however adorned she may be with insignia and pageantry. I sense

Figure 1. This portrait first appeared as the frontispiece in the new edition of Mme du Coudray's textbook in 1769, by which time she was already a very important person.

from the first that she is beckoning her beholder to learn and tell her story, that she has designs on me. Above her picture is emblazoned the energetic command that animated her: "AD OPERAM," she seems to order me—"to work."[1]

Actually, I already knew her a bit by reputation. She is featured in numerous eighteenth- and nineteenth-century collections on *femmes célèbres* that I consulted for my earlier work on female journalists. The short notices in these volumes all recount how Mme du Coudray had written a book about childbirth, had invented an obstetrical mannequin on which she demonstrated delivery maneuvers to facilitate instruction, had traveled throughout France teaching the art of midwifery to thousands of peasant women for over a quarter of a century as the monarchy's emissary, and had awakened and mobilized the nation in a fight against infant mortality. What a story! This woman, I remember thinking, must have played a major role in the dramatic demographic recovery of the second half of the eighteenth century. Surely a thorough scholarly biography of her had by now been written. . . .

But when I looked I found no full-length study about her at all. Instead I was strongly encouraged to write one myself. Shelby McCloy, in his work on public health in Enlightenment France, states, "Historians have little remembered the work that Mme du Coudray performed. Nevertheless, she charmed her contemporaries, and many an intendant [king's man] wrote eulogistically of her work. That there were still a large number of quack midwives on the eve of the Revolution reveals the magnitude of the task she faced." In a footnote McCloy remarks, "There appears to be no biography of her, not even an article in a learned journal."[2] These comments were made in 1946. Since then Mme du Coudray had been mentioned in some articles and a book by Jacques Gélis, but still no substantial work on her had appeared.[3] In 1982 Dr. Bernard This suggested that her journey must have been full of excitement and romance, that the details "merit an exhaustive study. What novelist will be able to write this vibrant and passionate life?"[4]

Well, I thought, Mme du Coudray needs no novelist. She needs a historian. The tale of this seemingly indefatigable medical missionary and royal ambassadress did not sound to me like it required any fictional embellishment whatsoever. Hayden White might stress the porosity of the membrane between "facts" and authorial creation, and Roland Barthes might call biography a novel that dare not speak its name, but I still sensed a distinction between these genres. I wondered what evidence remained of du Coudray's teaching stints throughout France, what archival sources I might mine. I contemplated setting out in pursuit of those numerous eulogies McCloy mentioned. But first, and easiest, I would examine her published textbook at the Bibliothèque nationale. And the day I did that I saw her portrait, the book's frontispiece, before I even glanced at a word she wrote. Her look, at once steady and searching, feminine yet framed in such formidable authority, reached me and quickened my interest. From that moment on I was committed to writing this book.

So I began. First I sent letters to the ninety-odd departmental archives of France, explaining that I hoped to reconstruct my midwife's voyage. (Yes, I already thought of her as mine.) I knew that correspondence between the minister of finance and the royal intendants, men chosen by the king and stationed throughout the country to implement his bidding, can be found in the C series of ancien régime provincial records, and I asked the archivists to check inventories for any dossiers on du Coudray's teaching in their region. Many of the replies were positive. Yes, they said, she was here. Some even suggested other municipal or communal documents I might consult, as well as records of provincial academies, agricultural societies, medical schools, local parishes, and philanthropic organizations. I was particularly excited to discover that hundreds of letters by du Coudray herself still exist, and of course numerous others to her and about her. Because each archival response I received told me either the dates of du Coudray's stay in areas where she *did* teach or that she did *not* go to certain other areas, I was eventually able to rough out an approximate map of her route.[5]

The vision that emerged was astounding. For nearly three decades she systematically covered the nation, skipping only the Midi, the Pyrenees, the outer reaches of Brittany, and Alsace. In all, she taught at more than forty cities (see map). As a portrait sitter du Coudray may be immobile, but as a biographical subject she rarely stayed still. So if I was going to follow her trail I had my work cut out for me.

2. Biography as History and Mystery

Los Angeles and France, 1986–1996

Sabbaticals, leaves, summers, spring breaks, a stolen week here and there. Countless trips during these ten years to libraries and archives

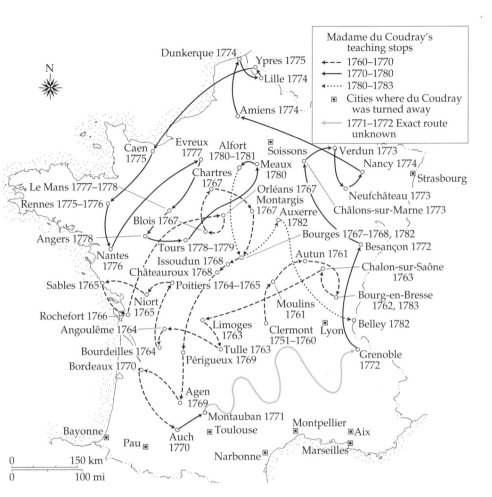

This overall map of Mme du Coudray's teaching travels is divided into three parts: 1760–1770, when she covered much of the center of France; 1770–1780, when she taught mostly in the periphery of the country; and 1780–1783, when she hoped to get the go-ahead to finish the areas she had not yet "done." Because a number of cities in the south turned her away, her exact whereabouts between mid-1771 and mid-1772 are unknown.

in the provinces of France, in Bourges, Caen, La Rochelle, Besançon, Périgueux, Tours, Bordeaux, Rennes, Châlons-sur-Marne, Nancy, Clermont, Rouen, Epinal, Poitiers, and on and on, piecing together bits of Mme du Coudray's works and days. Not a picture, but pictures; not a story, but stories take shape.

She was a bold pioneer in obstetrical pedagogy in the service of France, tirelessly promoting the interests of the government that dispatched her. She was a curse visited upon the traditional village matrons who practiced time-honored ways of birthing and wanted no "help" or instruction disrupting their lives. She was a female upstart usurping the turf of doctors and surgeons who had traditionally presided over all examinations and degree-granting ceremonies for midwives throughout the country. She was a wondrous, brilliant phenomenon. She was a virago. A loyal patriotic servant. A fraud not to be trusted. An ingenious inventor. An outrageous, pretentious quack. A self-sacrificing, devoted teacher. Feminist role model. Traitor to her sex. Savior of the French population. Mere flash in the pan. Boon to humanity. Royal (literally) nuisance. Any and all of the above, depending on your point of view.

I worked through roughly a thousand documents and letters in the official records concerning du Coudray's mission. Her contacts range from lofty—Turgot, Necker, Calonne, and other ministers of Kings Louis XV, Louis XVI, and the empress Maria Theresa—to lowly—obscure country matrons and parish priests—and these exchanges are preserved, along with a massive diffusion of correspondence between her and the royal provincial administrators. There are discussions of her in the letters of her medical contemporaries, references to her in almanacs of the day, petitions and certificates and contracts she signed. I found, in short, an overwhelming amount of material about her ambitious *deeds* in this paper trail.

What I did not find were any personal papers, anything introspective at all. No diary, no *journal intime*, no self-referential writings. In 1834 A. Delacoux, the author of a book on celebrated midwives, mentioned that he saw a collection of "numerous documents left by Mme du Coudray and gathered together by Mme Coutanceau," her niece.[1] Delacoux dismisses these documents in a few offhand sentences, but his comments are enough to reveal that the collection included things that have never been preserved elsewhere and have not been seen since. Perhaps they showed a gentler, less guarded side of her, because Delacoux revised her portrait, divesting her of her masterful frame and credentials, softening and rounding off her edges (fig. 2). Where is that packet of papers now, with its possible clues about du Coudray's interior life? I wrote to three hundred or so Coutanceaus presently living in France in the wild hope that, eight or nine generations later, some distant descendent might still be a keeper of this family flame. To no avail.

But of course, my inability to learn private details about du Coudray was not due entirely to the loss of these papers. It had at least as much to do with her conscious attempt to construct her own reputation, leaving out the personal, concealing her inner self. It is as if she made a bargain with herself to mute the feminine core of her being in exchange for appropriating the prerogatives of male behavior. She tailored, in other words, her own official story, which was one of stunning achievements. Another scholar might find this perfectly satisfying; yet it was only part of the story *I* wished to tell about her. Stubbornly perhaps, I was looking and listening for *her*, refusing to let her get lost within the neat narrative she offered to contain and hide life's chaos. She gave me her doings, but I also sought her feelings. So from the start, because this very public woman was so maddeningly private, we were in a struggle, she and I. This gave rise to several kinds of reflection: on the nature of the historian's craft in general, on the relationship between biographer and biographee, and on my particular subject, a woman who left behind a record at once so full and so spare.

For centuries history was written in an authoritative, detached voice, communicating an illusion of logical progression, objectivity, completeness. It claimed to have discovered "how things really were," to be scientific and factual, and to present a linear, seamless tale. Recently such empiricist presumptions of certainty in the discipline have been attacked; recovery of the past once and for all, the "whole story," now seems a naive and strange conceit. Feminist and postmodernist critics in particular have fought to turn old historical accounts on their ear, to "bring the margin to the center," to "problematize" age-old assumptions, to expose the futility and bankruptcy of searching for absolute answers. Such energetic challenges bring to the field tremendous new vitality and interest, but also considerable discomfort. If we acknowledge that our understanding is at best partial, that our views, far from being objective, are inescapably colored by the concerns of our present vantage point, that evidence itself is subjective, serendipitous, and fragmentary, that our

Figure 2. This much-softened picture, made forty years after Mme du Coudray's death and clearly based on the original in the textbook, flatters her but deprives her of her imposing frame and credentials.

pictures of the past are incurably approximate and full of artifice, that they are constructed by us and not found or given ready-made, *how* then can we distinguish history from fable? How can we convince ourselves that our research leads to anything sound, trustworthy, or accurate?[2] Hayden White has even questioned whether historians, as they assemble their stories, are doing anything fundamentally different than novelists.[3] If there is no "disinterested site from which one can sit back and objectively make unbiased choices and judgments,"[4] what, if anything, can we ever really, responsibly *know?*

With biography, the history of a particular human being, these problems are only compounded. Here the evidence has often been tampered with by the historical subject herself, who may have destroyed some things deliberately, or who may have written an autobiography, a staging of the self, the reliability of which needs to be critically assessed.[5] Biographers have been called "artists under oath" because they must exercise restraint and resist the temptation to invent.[6] Yet such distance is hard to keep, because in life-writing two identities confront each other in an intense, reciprocal relationship. The biographer is unavoidably included in her work, an absent but strong presence. She determines what gets said about her subject; selects, omits, highlights; sets the sequence and pace; changes here and there the velocity of the narrative. But her subject is never the passive victim of such manipulations, for she too is controlling, resisting the inquiry here, cooperating there, a willful agent whose choices to reveal or withhold information ultimately color and shape the whole project. The point is that a "catalytic conjunction" occurs here; writer and subject are in this together, and the interaction is complicated. Explicitly acknowledging this negotiation is not perverse, and can yield surprises.[7]

I realized I could make a virtue of necessity by using Mme du Coudray's case to illustrate these larger issues: the spotty, opaque, incomplete record that all historians have to work with, the tentativeness of answers, the impossibility of closure, and the opportunity for useful storytelling anyway. I want to show the process, not just the product, the recognition that many of the pieces are missing, that the puzzle will be full of holes. That is why this book is arranged by date-line entries, pulses of time, turning points, epiphanies, "liminal threshold" moments.[8] My choice of an episodic rather than a smooth structure seems crucial, to suggest that what happened in between, the connective tissue of reasons and motives, is often unknowable. Historians always have to work with fragments and lacunae, with revelations and secrets. We may crave coherence and synthesis, but because much remains indecipherable we do not get it.

In Mme du Coudray's case the gaps are enormous and impossible to hide even if I wished to. Of the time before her fame she tells us nothing. In her hundreds of letters there is never a single mention of her origins, parents, childhood, siblings, education, young adulthood, training, marriage if there was one, children if she had any, friends outside of her work. But for her death certificate, scribbled in Bordeaux in the midst of the Reign of Terror, which states that she was seventy-nine when she died in 1794 and a native of Paris, I wouldn't even know her place or date of birth. Clearly this biography could not follow the conventional cradle-to-grave pattern. Family cannot be the zero point of origin here, and it is extremely difficult to discover traces of this woman from the years before she, already in her mid-forties, burst into national prominence in 1760. Her teaching mission is then fairly well documented for the next quarter century. She fades from view again after retirement in the mid-1780s and the news of her darkens. How she filled her time in the last decade of her life is anybody's guess. For she is as unconfessional as they come, and I can scarce know the dancer from the dance.

Why does it matter? one could ask. What difference does it make? The story of her work suffices. We know little of Shakespeare's private life, after all, or Chaucer's, but there is still plenty to say about what they did. Du Coudray, too, *did* a great many noteworthy things. She was a woman with dazzling accomplishments to her credit who has been overlooked by historians. On the strength of that she should be a new star in the feminist work of retrieval and rescue of powerful (and therefore threatening) "foresisters," dubbed by Mary Daly in her invigorating wordplay "crone-ology," "hag-ography," "gyn/ecology."[9] Certainly as a public servant and celebrity du Coudray was not at all shy. *That* story she clearly *did* want told. She always referred to her calling in grandiose terms—she was ensuring nothing less than the "good of humanity"—and to her midwifery book and obstetrical mannequins as "monuments to posterity for centuries to come." She wished to be remembered for her mastery.

Yet the fact that she was a woman with an interior life cannot be escaped, however much she downplayed it, so my challenge was to thicken the texture of her tale by keeping that fact in view. For gender, that "overarching category of human identity similar to race in its immutability and contestably more primary than class," is quite simply central to an understanding of any woman, even a woman who does not make an issue of it.[10] Mme du Coudray defied the normal pattern by making a mission, not a man, the focus of her being, having no home where I might discover her "inwardness" or "bridge her silences," never settling with a person in a place.[11] Indeed, there seems to be an unbridgable chasm between her and others of her sex. This paradox of the singular, idiosyncratic woman who follows a "quest plot" instead of a "marriage plot" has been aptly summed up by Caroline Heilbrun: "Exceptional women are the chief imprisoners of nonexceptional women, simultaneously proving that any woman could do it and assuring, in their uniqueness among men, that no other woman will." Du Coudray reached a level of achievement not commonly excusable in a female self.[12] And yet she accepted for her approximately ten thousand students subordinate positions in the hierarchy of medical practitioners. Like Florence Nightingale, du Coudray did not seek stardom for her female disciples.[13] Of course, there *is* something undeniably transgressive, if not truly subversive, about her mission, focused as it was on providing professional training to large numbers of women (she called them "my women"). They learned and laughed and struggled and cried together, bonded in unprecedented ways, got a sense of themselves as a valuable group, pictured new plotlines for their lives. Du Coudray didn't put it that way, of course. If her mission was to succeed, she could not engage in female advocacy; instead she must convey a sense of harmony with male practitioners and present herself as a loyal patriot.

Whatever she might have said, though, medical practice *is* a battleground, fiercely contested by the men entrenched in the profession, and she was a trespasser. It was my task, therefore, to develop the confidence to sometimes override her self-assessment, to interrogate rather than embrace her rosy picture. She wanted her version of the story accepted; I want it examined. I would explore just how the *woman* du Coudray composed her life, carved out her own special place in the world, formulated her agenda, negotiated herself into a position to do something great.[14] What drove her to such creative efforts? What conditions did she have to accept? How did she adapt and adjust to changing political regimes and to the modernizing trends in Enlightenment medicine to advance her career? When did public and private intersect in her trajectory? Why in midlife did she create a new script for herself? Where is what Virginia Woolf calls the "iridescence" of her personality, what Phyllis Rose calls her "central spine"?[15] By crafting and shaping the narrative in a way that leaves room for such inquiries and thus gives it meaning for me, I suppose I am committing "fiction" in Natalie Davis's sense of the term.[16] But then I like to think that du Coudray would sympathize with some of these moves. She was herself a great creator of fictions, as we will see, playing with different names and identities, fashioning as she went along what real life failed to provide. So I should not settle for appearances, since things are seldom as they seem.

The subjects about which du Coudray said little held a special fascination for me. Eking out meaning from such reticence is hard, but then, when I agreed to work with her, she never promised it would be easy. For example, she disdained sightseeing. She focused in her numerous letters on the business she was doing, not on cathedrals or fountains, not on peasants pegging up their wash or drawing well-water, not on the weather. And she rarely spoke of the decades-long journey itself, whether bone-bruising or picturesque. Not for her the frivolous travelogues of the chatty. Yet the woman crisscrossed and saw the entire country! If we squeeze the letters for all they can possibly yield, we learn that she loved to eat—she traveled with a cook—and read—even the newspapers—and go to the theater and entertain—her rented houses were always outfitted with a service for large parties. One official commented: "It would surely be easier to quarter a company of cavalry than to furnish the lodgings for Mme du Coudray and her students"; another observed: "She demands a house fully equipped from *cave* to attic."[17] Du Coudray, as her portrait shows, was no misanthrope. She had a strong sense of fun, and certainly did a lot of living in the many places she visited. I wanted to reconstruct some of that experience, even though she didn't help much.

So as I spent time in the archives of these places, I learned where she lived during her stay, I wandered in her neighborhood, I smelled the waxy interiors of churches where she baptized babies, I strolled along the rivers where water coaches sometimes carried her baggage, I ate regional specialties that she must have enjoyed, I explored numerous *hôtels de ville* (town halls) where she gave her lessons in the main hall. In Rouen I actually found one of her obstetrical mannequins, with all of its cloth parts and labels intact. This sole survivor, this last extant model, linked her to me very tangibly; she probably sewed those stitches herself. These are the things I could

see today that make hers what Henry James calls a "visitable past."
The rest I had to imagine: her horsedrawn carriages on rutted dirt
roads, the trumpet fanfare and noisy announcements by town criers
of du Coudray's upcoming courses, the commotion of mobs of barefoot women hastening to town to hear her, the grave diggers scav-
enging bones to be used in the anatomical demonstrations, the re-
lay watering posts along the routes where she and her horses took
hurried refreshment during day stops, the moats and locked town
gates, the extreme poverty of much of the countryside.

Du Coudray discovered or developed a taste for forging into the
shadowy unknown to shed her light. She makes it all sound so pur-
poseful, so directed, because all this activity was heading her *toward* something she had pledged to accomplish. But I could not
help thinking that her strenuous exertions were also moving her
away from something else. Was the fierce ambition for public success a kind of compensatory flight from some private failure? For
what reason did she place herself safely beyond the risks of intimacy, into a life where competence and achievement took its place?

From the first it struck me as the ultimate irony that this national
midwife was herself childless. The only heirs she had were ones she
created late in life by adoption. Without this maneuver she would
have left no progeny, appearing a pathetic figure in a culture that
so valued fertility. Was her avoidance of what Adrienne Rich calls
"pairing and bearing" the stimulus for her boundless commitment,
indeed her passion, to save babies for her *patrie*?[18] Having shunned,
by choice or necessity, the traditional role of childbearer and mother,
was she driven to transcend from the personal to the patriotic arena,
to make her work fruitful though her body had not been, to propa-
gate both the *bien de l'humanité* and the *biens* of the French state, to
literally deliver the good(s), to make human life on a grand scale
her very business?

3. The National Midwife's Mission Statement

Clermont, 1 August 1760

Monsieur,
Monsieur the Controller General desired that I have the honor
of sending you a copy of the little work I composed on childbirth. It is perhaps even more useful because I was determined

to make it simple; I have assembled in it all that is most essential in this art, and most accessible to those least schooled in this matter.

The infinite calamities caused by ignorance in the countryside and which my profession [*état*] has given me occasion to witness moved me to compassion and animated my zeal to procure more secure relief for humanity. Drawn to Auvergne, I invented there a machine for demonstrating delivery. Monsieur de la Michodière [former intendant of Auvergne] realized its utility and his intention was to benefit from it, but he left the province. Monsieur de Ballainvilliers, who succeeded him, was equally supportive, and these first successes encouraged me to present it at Court and to the Academy of Surgery. The advantages of this invention are immediately apparent. The academy approved it and the king accorded me a certificate [*brevet*] permitting me to teach throughout the realm. M. de Ballainvilliers wished to be the first to obtain this help for his region. And I was eager to give my first attentions to the inhabitants of the province where the machine was born. The magistrate, whose name will always be blessed among the people of Auvergne, formed an establishment to make these instructions permanent. He distributed a machine in each of the most populous cities of the province; able and zealous surgeons came for fifteen days to study closely with me and learn its workings; the machines were entrusted to them, and they in turn are now committed to instruct at no charge, as I did, the country women who will be sent to them by the subdelegates. In three months of lessons a woman free of prejudice, and who has never had the remotest knowledge of childbirth, will be sufficiently trained. We have the advantage of students practicing on the machine and performing all the deliveries imaginable. Therein lies the principal merit of this invention. A surgeon or a woman who takes the sort of course available until now will learn only theory, [and will expect] the situations encountered in practice to be uniform, or at least not very varied. The course no sooner finished, [these] young surgeons and women, rushing to benefit from a profession they know only superficially, spill out all over the countryside. But when difficulties arise they are absolutely unskilled, and until long experience instructs them they are the witness or the cause of

many misfortunes, of which the least terrible is the death of
the mother or the child and even both. Nothing is sadder than
being deprived of the use of one of our limbs. How many poor
wretches seem born only to excite the pity of a public that is
impotent to relieve them. These subjects could have been useful to the state, and mothers often would not have to lose their
fertility in the flower of youth; one learns on the machine in
little time how to prevent such accidents.

Love good works, Monsieur; procure them through inclination and through love for the people who regard you as their
father. It is your daily occupation and to second you I have
the honor of proposing an establishment like that which M. de
Ballainvilliers has set up in Auvergne. Monsieur the controller
general who watches over the good of the state and the multiplication of subjects useful to the king has approved all the expenses that have been necessary. I am delighted to be able to
cooperate. My zeal showed me the way, and the same motive
animates me to share it. I am with respect, Monsieur, your very
humble and very obedient servant,

Le Boursier du Coudray[1]

By any measure, an arresting letter. Who is this person, that she addresses each of the king's royal administrators, the thirty provincial
intendants, as an equal, indeed as a somewhat superior political ad-
visor? How has she earned her posture of moral rectitude? This is
her first exercise in mass self-promotion, yet the deft argumenta-
tion seems to come so naturally. She is having many copies made of
this letter by secretaries and sent around the country, informing His
Majesty's men that there is now a national midwife commissioned
to serve and rescue the state, for it is widely believed that France is
becoming depopulated. Except for the deferential closing—a mere
formality—her letter is strong, almost imperious. She begs no pardon, as a female, for advertising her worth and importance. On the
contrary, with the king and the minister of finance behind her, she
is above needing to make even the usual opening bow; she has dispensed with the *monseigneur*—my lord—commonly used for the intendants. The controller general himself is simply *monsieur!* In other
ways too she has crossed the threshold into the male world of in-
strumentality and control, penetrating with unrehearsed familiar-
ity, treating men as her peers.

Her opening sentence announces without apology that she has written a birthing textbook, thus matter-of-factly invading the patriarchal province of medical print culture, taking for granted her right to make a valuable contribution to knowledge. That she introduces her book even before she introduces herself is a hint of what a central role this volume, and her authorship, will play in her mission. Her very act of writing and publishing is audacious, a refusal to accept subordination to learned males, and she sends a copy of her textbook to every intendant with this letter.[2] It is her passport to legitimacy, in a sense. Now we can talk, she seems to be saying; because I have produced a volume, you must take me seriously. Her pared-down work, as she points out, will have especially wide appeal because it can reach and benefit many whom the writers of erudite treatises generally ignore. Targeting an audience overlooked by the elite custodians of culture, she further attempts to bridge this gap between city and country, high and low, by inventing a prop, an obstetrical mannequin on which to demonstrate birthing techniques. Miniature anatomical models of wax, glass, ivory, and wood had existed for some time, but life-size, malleable ones made of fabric, leather, and bone, and used so aggressively for practice, are of her own devising. Mme du Coudray's introduction of the palpable body into medical instruction on such a grand, innovative scale constitutes nothing less than a revolution in pedagogy.[3] By reducing infertility, infant and maternal mortality, and disabling accidents at birth, she and her radiating network of students and trained teachers can end the peacetime massacre of innocents. They can regenerate France.

But this letter does much more than advertise her services. It calls upon the reader to react, shaming the recipient out of his complacency. It sets up an equality, not just in its forcefulness but in its reciprocity, its demand for a reply, its challenge to the status quo. The receiver will now need to become a sender of his own letter; the "you" will become the active "I" of a decisive response.[4] All the royal intendants will feel compelled to write back, to endorse and join the obstetrical enlightenment of the countryside. They have never received such a letter from a woman before, but that she is female is not emphasized, indeed, it is not even mentioned. It is beside the point. She steps forward with unselfconscious ease, takes these men into her confidence, and simply assumes that she and they

are all together in this crusade. Their common foe is ignorance—
not incompetent village crones, not mean-spirited surgeons, but the
absence of the proper training that, with the intendants' support
and assistance, she will now be able to provide. This midwife is
proposing to teach numerous men as well as women (the noncha-
lant offer to instruct surgeons coolly topples the age-old medico-
political hierarchy, which always placed males on top), and the issue of any professional or gender rivalry between midwives and
surgeons is not even hinted at. The critical thing is the call to joint
action, the shared gesture of revolt against fatalism.

She has shaped her language for this group of addressees, devising for them a particular rhetorical formula. Her letter, entirely relaxed in its stylistic imperfections, longwindedness, and inconsis-
tent tenses, is designed to convey energy and an innate sense of
authority, to give a picture of activity already under way, to make
her readers feel responsibility for preserving this momentum, and
to gain obedience. The king has chosen her for this job; only unco-
operative, passive, benighted intendants would allow its failure. If
on the other hand they facilitate her mission, she assures them, they
will be more loved by their people than ever. The midwife knows
how to flatter and cajole. Despite her assertiveness—she has "composed" a book, "invented" a machine, "presented it at court"—she
seems to recognize that these men must ultimately feel in control.
As if they, not she, had had the idea of inviting her to teach in their
region, she agrees to "second" them, to back up their interests. Together they will carry out the king's bidding, the "multiplication of
subjects" for the crown. She wants to be seen not as a dangerous
woman making public mischief but as a dedicated servant of the
state who can count on other enlightened individuals to vanquish
ignorance and bring about much-needed reforms.

A word about the signature. The midwife plays name games.
This is her only letter, of hundreds that still exist, signed "Le Boursier du Coudray." Both the letter and the book date from a transi-
tional period of just a few years during which she used this long
version of her name. Earlier communications of hers say simply "Le
Boursier," later ones simply "du Coudray." In more ways than one,
then, this letter of 1760 marks a watershed. A metamorphosis is taking place. Its middle-aged sender has been gradually giving up one
persona for another much more public one, seeing fit to assume a

new name—with the coveted noble particle—and a new identity.[5]
She is reinventing herself, leaving behind her private life as Dem-
oiselle Le Boursier, a maiden lady, and giving herself flat out to
France as Madame du Coudray, an expert matriarch.

She is forty-five years old. Is this an awesome manifestation of
what Margaret Mead calls "post-menopausal zest," that hidden resource of energy and vitality tapped into by women in their later
years?[6] Du Coudray becomes now something of a secular saint, but
she is also the king's trusted emissary soldiering in his service. No
other woman in her day of whom I am aware devoted herself exclusively to public service in this manner, sacrificed herself entirely
to the *bien public*. And du Coudray makes clear her uniqueness. She
credits no mentors, claims no ancestral help. If she descends from
the great seventeenth-century midwife Louise Bourgeois Boursier,
she does not tell.[7] She betrays absolutely no attachments, no tethers.

Does she even know her origins? Was she perhaps one of the
enormous number of abandoned children—more than 40 percent
of all born in eighteenth-century France—raised in foundling hospitals?[8] Does she hide some painful emptiness, some distant shame?
Certainly she displays particular sensitivity to the indigent and to
unwed *filles-mères* with their misbegotten offspring.[9] She devotes
herself to a profession whose business is saving lives regardless of
rank or fortune. Her contemporary, the philanthropist Piarron de
Chamousset, believed that foundlings were truly the most faithful
enfants de la patrie, deeply beholden to the state that reared them.[10]
Was she one of those anonymous children, who, not knowing her
own roots, vowed to define herself anew, to forge a lone path and
pay back her debt to France in this spectacular way?

Either life has stripped her of conflicting loyalties, or she never
had them. She seems totally unencumbered by marriage or motherhood. The practice of inventing husbands is not unheard of among
enterprising females of the day, and in her case it comes in especially handy. She is a consummate role-player who uses pseudonymity creatively, who sees it as enabling.[11] Her new marital status
is her first of many improvisations. And this husband is even dis-
posable, for almost immediately she becomes *veuve* du Coudray. Widowhood is of course still more useful, affording many legal advantages in business transactions. By sheer force of character and an
acute political sense she makes her skill in midwifery into a national

institution. She is shouldering this responsibility for and by herself, and she takes charge fully, splendid in her autonomy.

But when, where, why, and how did she develop the taste for it? As we follow her we must be careful not to view each action as a step toward some manifest destiny; even so, we must ask whether, early in her career, she recognizes in herself some special gift. What makes her separate, pull away from the others, spark to do something out of the ordinary? Is there an awakening? She writes this exceptional letter before she actually begins her famous mission, but after decades of development and growth of a different kind. To track things from the first trace we have of her (because we know nothing of her biological birth, her professional birth must serve as our beginning), we need to go back another twenty years.

From Private Practice
to Public Service

A PARISIAN MIDWIFE

4. Hanging Her Shingle

Paris, 22 February 1740

A clerk inscribes in the register of the Châtelet police court today that Marguerite Le Boursier, mature maiden, is officially received "mistress matron midwife of the city and *fauxbourgs* of Paris."[1] She is twenty-five years old. Five months ago she completed her three-year apprenticeship with Anne Bairsin, *dame* Philibert Mangin, and passed her qualifying examinations at the College of Surgery. This was a major expense—169 livres and 16 sous—and involved a hair-raising test administered by a panel composed of the king's first surgeon or his lieutenant, a number of Paris surgeons, various deans of the medical faculty and royal surgical school, the four sworn midwives of Paris attached to the Châtelet, and receivers, provosts, class masters, and council members.[2] An intimidating ordeal, an awesome rite of passage, but she survived it. She had then submitted letters of capacity and mastery of her art with a request to be formally accepted by the city's court.

Before approving her they must get character references as is customary, but they do not hurry. It has taken this long for police officials to organize interviews with her parish priest and various other neighbors and acquaintances. Those questioned might have been shoemakers, goldbeaters, innkeepers, or tailors who lived nearby, or professors of surgery or doctors regent of the medical faculty with whom she had contact. Whoever they were—the records identifying them are not preserved in her case—they responded affirmatively to the rather formulaic questions asked. Just last week, on the seventeenth and nineteenth of February, they gave sworn depositions that Le Boursier upholds the Catholic, apostolic, and Roman religion, lives an upstanding life, and demonstrates fidelity in the service of the king and of the public.[3] Now that a favorable report has come in, she simply needs to "take the oath required in these cases" to be legally admitted to the ranks of Paris midwives, swearing never to administer an abortive remedy and always to call masters of the art to help in difficult cases.[4] And she must pledge to honor one further obligation.

On the first Monday of every month, if it is not a holiday, all sworn midwives are expected to attend holy services at the church of St. Côme and, afterward, pay "pious and charitable visits" to indigent women still inconvenienced by present or past pregnancies.[5] The church, dedicated to the martyrs Côme and Damien, patron saints of surgery, sits on the corner of rue de la Harpe and rue des Cordeliers on the Left Bank, halfway between the river and the Luxembourg Gardens. Next to the church is a cemetery surrounded by charnel houses, and beyond the cemetery is the school of surgery, familiarly known also as St. Côme. For centuries the sick have flocked here on the first Monday of each month to be tended for free. It is a scene at once morbid and heartening. The cemetery keeps its ditch open until it has received its full complement of corpses; the dead who cannot be accommodated there are buried in the church or surrounding walls. Often the bodies and bones are used in surgical demonstrations. Since 1664 surgeons have been giving lessons to midwives in the charnel house on the western border of the cemetery, which abuts the church, although seven years ago the courses were moved to the college's amphitheater. Over the cemetery's south wall there is a granary and storehouse, where the poor find provisions. They are comforted, once a month, to be in the helping hands of healers.[6]

Le Boursier will become part of this world now. Perhaps she knows it well already, and even as an apprentice has attended courses there with her teacher. What sort of relationship do they have? She never once mentions Anne Bairsin in her textbook or letters. Yet Delacoux reported that her packet of private papers contained several memoirs on extraordinary deliveries and cesarean sections written, "with precision and exactitude," by Bairsin, "which show her to have been a practitioner both able and learned [*instruit*]."[7] So Le Boursier held on to these writings by her teacher all her life, valuing them enough to keep them (and keep track of them) throughout all her travels. They may have guided her hand in certain circumstances, or served some more sentimental purpose. Might she have collected other manuscripts or case studies by female colleagues, and saved them too over the years? Such unacknowledged debts are probably numerous, for she begins to hone her skills now as an official member of the group of Paris midwives, busy women with vast experience, sources of much shared wisdom and lore.

Louis Sébastien Mercier, the famous chronicler of Paris, estimates that each of the two hundred or so midwives of the capital delivers about one hundred babies each year.[8] Such an average is misleading; some of these women are surely much more in demand than others. But there is no doubt that, for one with a good reputation, this is a strenuous and full life. Mercier describes the *tavaïolle*, a large muslin and lace cloth the midwife wraps every baby in, rich or poor, for the trip to church, a kind of "spiritual frock coat that attends all baptisms, the principal and most conspicuous garment of a midwife. If this cloth is not sanctified, then none in the world can be, because this one gets blessed sometimes as often as four times a day." The midwife also uses it to carry the many candies and sugar-coated almonds [*dragées*] she receives as tokens of thanks from mothers, fathers, godparents, and guests at each birth, perhaps two to three pounds of these goodies at a time. "The *armoire* of such a midwife rivals the boutique of a confectioner on the rue des Lombards."[9]

Because he always has an eye for the sensational and scandalous, Mercier stresses another important role that city midwives play. They do not just officiate at family births; many of them help conceal unwed girls in their apartments, and they are as skilled in diplomacy as in delivery. As a result, hardly anyone seeks an abortion. A girl who finds herself pregnant, though she may concoct a story that she's leaving for the country, need only go around the corner or across the street to the local midwife to hide until she gives birth. Total secrecy is maintained in these apartments, which no one can enter without superior orders. They are divided into many discretely curtained partitions. For two or three months the inhabitants of these cells might converse, but they might never see or know one another. In the capital these wayward girls have privacy; while confined they can look out onto the roofs of their unsuspecting parents' home. In country towns, however, there is no such anonymity, and often a great scandal instead. The city midwife takes care of everything, has the baby baptized, gives it to a wet nurse or to the foundling hospital depending on the fortunes and desires of the parents. Midwives charge a lot to provide these services for fugitive girls (Mercier calls it usury because his sympathies lie with the young lovers, "victims of their sweet weakness"), often as much as twelve livres a day for the room, board, delivery itself, and of course the confidentiality. Justifying the high cost, they remind everyone that their discretion preserves reputations and saves many from utter ruin. The priest, however, knows that if a midwife unaccompanied by a parent presents a baby for baptism, it is a love child born out of wedlock. He is not particularly happy to see her coming alone; bastards deprive him of the customary fee paid for his services by proud mothers and fathers. Anyone who wants to hear anecdotes about the ruses and the courage love inspires (in which the true identities of the adventurers is, of course, never revealed)—such a person need only get to know four or five midwives. They can tell tales for all classes: women of the people, *bourgeoises*, courtesans, *grandes dames*.

The truly poor, those with no resources to pay for a private midwife, deliver at the general hospital, the Hôtel Dieu, infamous for its high death rate and its cramming of five or six to a bed in the main wards. But this hospital's separate maternity clinic, the *salle des accouchées*, is superbly administered; the critical Mercier even goes so far as to say it is "beyond reproach." Thanks to this establishment, and to the public orphanages, the once rampant crime of infanticide is almost unheard of in the capital these days. Delivering in secret and giving the baby to the foundling hospital, however, has become a widespread practice, and the law has looked the other way. Probably only one in a hundred girls who give birth clandestinely even knows that an edict of King Henry II, now fallen into desuetude, once made their action punishable by death.[10]

Le Boursier and her colleagues have numerous other functions besides assisting married women at births and harboring unwed girls during their pregnancies. Juries of midwives are consulted on capital crimes. They are frequently used as expert witnesses in legal battles, sometimes called upon to ascertain whether a woman is a virgin. (Here Le Boursier points out that occasionally the hymen is still intact even if the person in question has "endured [*souffert*] the approaches of the male," and is thus "not an absolute proof of her purity," but that in general its presence allows the midwife to "presume advantageously" for the girl.)[11] They are often asked by parties in a legal dispute to establish whether a pregnancy is true or false and make, if necessary, a *déclaration de grossesse* to a doctor, surgeon, or directly to police authorities.[12] And their presence is usually requested to determine whether a dead baby expired in the womb or was killed after birth. The famous lung test is used to establish a mother's veracity when accused of infanticide. A baby in the womb does not breathe air, but of course it does once it is born. If a piece of the baby's lung sinks when thrown into water, so the theory goes, it proves that the child never experienced respiration, that it was stillborn. If the piece of lung floats, however, it is because air has gotten into it. "This circumstance would condemn the mother," Le Boursier explains, no matter how much she insists that her child was born dead, being a proof that air penetrated its lung, consequently that it was once, however briefly, alive.[13] The judgments rendered by midwives are regarded as essential, and sometimes even shape the evolving legal system.[14] They are called in on cases of suspected rape, contraceptive use, or abortion. They question seduced and abandoned women during labor, urging them to identify the child's father, thus ensuring the filiation of bastards. Their word is considered sworn testimony. In a very profound sense, then, the law recognizes them and trusts their verdicts. A doctor writing on medical jurisprudence calls their profession "one of the most important in society."[15] Men, in short, often need and depend on their expertise.

Yet for all their importance—indeed, *because* of it—relations between midwives and authorities, whether religious or secular, have been strained throughout history. These women are powerful; they have special skills, and knowledge of hidden and forbidden mysteries involving conception, blood, death, and passion. Some have practiced illegally and given their profession a bad name, infamous abortionists like Lepère, la Voisin, and Manon, who toward the end of the 1600s were tortured and either burned alive or strangled for their iniquities.[16] This trade is still rife with risks and dangers. Occasionally midwives are blamed for causing the monstrous defects of deformed babies that spew forth into their hands, blamed for somehow conjuring the creatures they merely catch. Even now rumors of sorcery and witchcraft hover around any one of them who behaves bizarrely. Their petty thefts are punished especially severely, as if they, of all people, custodians of the newly born, should know better. One such, "just a poor midwife," accused of stealing copper candlesticks from a wine shop, is whipped and sent for three years to the prison of the Châtelet, then for longer to the Conciergerie, where she now languishes in chains. Protesting this unduly harsh treatment, she says she is afraid she will die.[17]

Originally the church supervised and controlled midwives, since their work involves them in baptism, in the saving of lives, or at least of souls. An ordinance declared that Protestant women could never exercise this art because they could not be trusted to *ondoyer* the child, to assure its eternal life if it was dying too fast to get to the priest.[18] Gradually, the secular state had been taking over surveillance of this group, monitoring it closely. Royal edicts in 1664 and 1678, advertised on huge posters, and numerous parlementary injunctions against particular midwives are evidence of the government's seriousness. In 1717 the art of midwifery was declared of the highest value, and dire sentences were announced for those practicing illegally, "read and publicized in loud and intelligible voice with trumpet fanfare" by the king's official criers "in all usual and accustomed places" so no one could claim ignorance of the law.[19] Midwives, then, obviously get a great deal of attention, both good and bad. "The policing of childbirth," says a contemporary, "is an object of the greatest importance in the administration. It interests humanity; upon it depends the health and life of citizens. Abuses that slip in [to this field] are not private misdemeanors; they are public crimes."[20]

Yet Le Boursier and her colleagues, despite efforts to oversee them, continue to function outside the sphere of male control. They gather a loyal clientele without any external help, simply by word of mouth among their female acquaintances. They select apprentices on their own. They are privy to more secrets about lineage and legitimacy than anyone else. It always seems to the authorities that despite their overt cooperation, midwives are first and foremost deeply loyal to the women they serve. For this reason midwives have constantly been denied the right to form a guild, to organize themselves into an autonomous corporation. No official bonding is permitted among these masterless women; they already seem conspiratorial enough. Doctors and surgeons are relieved that midwives have no recognized channels for grouping together, asserting themselves, seeking legal redress, or voicing grievances.

Independently, however, these women play powerful roles in the greatest drama of life.

5. A BIRTH

Paris, January 1744

This baby is finally coming, ready now to make its dive into the world—with the help of an *accoucheuse*, of course.[1] For months Le Boursier, a robust woman of twenty-nine, has been looking in on the mother-to-be, providing oils and liniments to keep the growing breasts and belly elastic: white pomades of melted pork fat purified with rose water, others of calves' foot marrow, the caul of a baby goat, goose grease, linseed oil, almond paste, and marsh mallow. She counseled the use of supporting bandages recently as the stomach really began to sag, and suggested the woman sleep on one side so that the opening of her womb, a bit off kilter, would be pulled by gravity into alignment with the vagina.[2] To keep the bowels moving and avoid constipation, which only exacerbates the inevitable hemorrhoids, enemas have been administered regularly—mixtures of bran, oil, butter, and river water.[3] There was a false alarm in the seventh month when the baby, who had been sitting up, suddenly turned a somersault and reinstalled itself upside down. The woman had feared she was in labor, but the midwife, upon examination, knew better.[4]

Bloodlettings have been performed at least once a month throughout the pregnancy—whenever the woman felt short of breath or nauseous, got dizzy, bled from the nose, or presented varicose veins in the legs—to relieve tension in the organs and prevent premature delivery. Once before this woman had been pregnant, but lost the baby because another midwife had not known to bleed her.[5] At least she has not needed purgings of manna, rhubarb, cassia, and senna, because she has been spared the bad breath, livid skin tone, and bilious vomiting that many others suffer and for which such remedies would be indicated.[6] The midwife has cautioned her to avoid excessive passions and to coif herself with care, combing and styling to get rid of vermin and to keep herself decent and presentable despite her fatigue. She may powder her hair—nothing with a strong fragrance, though—and put on a bonnet so she won't need to fuss with it for twelve to fifteen days and so her head will stay warm.[7] Walking is recommended, to keep the sinews strong and resilient. Cleanliness is not mentioned—only women of pleasure wash and bathe frequently—but clothing is to be loose and comfortable, the bed firm and dry, the diet moderate. No ragouts, sauces, fatty meats, or *aliments de fantaisie.*[8]

Now a few female friends, neighbors, and relatives have gathered, responding to the baby's quickening. They will help the midwife, as their familiar faces afford comfort; but if anyone's presence upsets or inhibits the mother, that person is quickly removed. The room is fresh and airy; it must not be allowed to get too hot.[9] The patient (*la malade*), as the birthing mother is called, has been put to bed and will stay there through the delivery. She has only light covers over her. Incontinent these last few days from her great womb pressing on her bladder, she is now, instead, retaining her urine, because the baby has moved down, squeezing the neck of the bladder almost shut. By introducing a hollow tube, an *algalie*, up into the urinary passage, the midwife quickly relieves that discomfort and watches the bright yellow fluid gush out.[10] This obstruction cleared, the labor pains come more often now. The midwife's greased fingers skirt around the neck of the womb, normally the size of a fish snout or the muzzle of a small dog, and feel the opening growing larger. When it has dilated to the size of a large coin, an *ecu de six livres*, the serious ministrations begin. On a strong contraction the midwife breaks the waters, piercing the mother's taut membranes with a large grain of salt; and to ease the breathing, lessen engorgement, and soften the cervix so it will stretch and open more easily, she bleeds her from the arm.[11]

The mother strains now, rolling and rocking. A more comfortable position will work better, head and chest raised, legs spread, heels planted against her buttocks, knees held apart by a helper. She is a slight woman with a narrow pelvis, and it is a big baby, a boy from the way the frame feels, although the midwife cannot be sure. Hours have gone by; the cervix is quite open, and still the head has not crowned. A malpresentation certainly, but just how bad is it? If any part other than the head presents, the delivery will have to be breech. The midwife checks the extent of dilation, speaking in comforting, affectionate terms to the mother, encouraging her, assuring her that she is not in danger, telling her honestly that things will still take a long time, for unrealistic expectations and impatience could make her tense, worsening the pain.[12] There is no point in trying to rush nature; the birth will progress in due course.

All along, under the bed linens, the midwife is continuing her tactile exam with fingers and full hand. Mucous, blood, and the waters provide natural lubrication. She hardly needs to look, and it would only offend the mother's modesty. A less experienced midwife could make a terrible mistake right about now. Desperate to hurry things along, she might put a finger into the mother's rectum to push the baby down, but this can ulcerate the anus and destroy the separation between the bowel opening and the vagina, rendering the woman "very disgusting."[13] Too much vaginal meddling is bad too: it can inflame the bladder. The best thing is to wait patiently, alert to all cues. The mother pushes a little, blows into her hand, and the midwife gently rubs her stomach, speaking in soothing tones.

Changes now. The baby is coming faster. She feels a bulge, not hard enough to be the head, too big and round for an elbow or a knee or a foot. It is almost surely the baby's bottom. She feels the crack between the soft buttocks, and up higher the fold of his thigh. Refraining from probing any further, for fear of releasing the black, tarlike meconium from the baby's rectum, she must move quickly before he engages too low.[14] Inserting a well-greased hand and following the rear, thigh, knee, and lower leg, she takes a foot down into the birth passage, then goes back in for the other one so the knee doesn't get caught. To do this between the womb's powerful contractions the midwife's arms must be very strong. Slowly, with the mother's help as she pants and pushes, she pulls the two feet together, evenly, steadily, out through the vagina. She wraps them in a soft, dry cloth so they won't slip out of her hands. Once the knees are out she must flip the baby, because he is coming with his chin facing up toward his mother's navel, and in this position his jaw will catch and get stuck on the pubic bone. She continues pulling gently on the little legs as she turns the baby around so his nose is now facing down toward his mother's backside. Straightening and bringing down the arms doesn't deliver the head as it usually does, so Le Boursier asks one of the women to hold up the half-born child, thus freeing both her hands. Deep inside the mother now, she seizes the baby's lower jaw and slides the index finger of her left hand into his mouth, while her right hand pushes down on the back of the baby's head to release it. With both hands she tucks and pulls the head out and up toward her while another assistant, at the same moment, coaxes out the big shoulders. None too soon, for the ordeal has left the mother completely exhausted.[15]

The newborn baby boy's cord is tied in two places and cut between the ligatures with a blunt scissors. He seems rather weak; there are faint sounds but no robust wailing. The women wrap cloths soaked in strong wine or eau-de-vie around the cord stump and over his head, chest, and stomach. Some liquor in his mouth, some crushed onions near his nostrils, bring him around dramatically. He lies briefly against his mother's private parts, nesting and squirming. After a few minutes, since he is out of danger, the women take him and wash him in lukewarm wine and fresh butter to remove the muck. Soft worn cloths soaked in oil envelop the cut cord, and a bandage around his middle holds this compress in place to prevent umbilical hernia when he cries, which he is doing a lot now. They bundle him up in toasty linen.[16]

The midwife turns back to the mother, who is relieved and spent, but her work is not finished yet. She must push another time or two to help the placenta out. When some gentle coaxing on the cord still doesn't deliver the afterbirth, Le Boursier goes in with her whole hand to explore, but it is stubbornly adhering. She injects into the womb some mallow, pellitory, linseed, and fresh butter, gives the mother a drink of lukewarm cinnamon water, syrup of artemisia and almond oil, tries an infusion of couch grass with syrup of sour lime, adds orange juice to the bouillon. None of this is working and too much time has gone by, so the method of last resort comes into play. The woman stands up in a tall vat of hot water. She pushes while the midwife rubs vigorously downward on her thighs until finally, all intact, the "secondine" is expelled. Once the attendant women have examined it and determined that it is complete, the mother lies down again, covered and protected from cold. Finally she can rest.[17]

Attention turns now once again to the baby, who has been slumbering on his side. He gets another wash in warm water and fresh wine, and then he is swaddled again, this time with his legs free to kick. This is far better, the midwife boasts, than the tight wrapping and binding that prevail in some other countries; few French babies are bandy-legged as a result.[18] Once he seems to be comfortable, the mother becomes the focus again. She is helped with her toilette and

the bed is prepared so that she can sleep. Luckily there are no signs
of unusual lethargy or convulsions, or a doctor would need to be
called in.[19]

Le Boursier will watch the mother closely over the next days, to
make sure all is well. As soon as she is strong enough, a trip
will be made to church for the baby's baptism. The midwife will
make all the necessary arrangements with the *curé*, or parish priest.
She, rather than someone else, must present the baby because her
word is trusted to certify its sex. If a domestic were to present the
baby, he would need to be undressed and examined for visual veri-
fication, and this is considered indecent in church.[20] The midwife
has also lined up a wet nurse (*nourrice*). For the first twenty-four
hours of his life, while he is getting rid of phlegm, the baby drinks
warm wine with sugar, syrup of chicory with rhubarb, or boiled and
strained honey water to get his digestion going. At first it had seemed
a surgeon might need to be called to open a membrane across the
baby's anus, but now the bowels are moving freely.[21] Tomorrow he
will begin to suckle at the breast of his *nourrice*. May she not roll
over and crush him in her sleep![22]

Because this mother is of a "delicate complexion" and will not
nurse her own baby, a regimen is prescribed to prevent milk fever.
Breast milk is believed to be nothing other than menstrual flow that
rises in the body, fades in color, and is transformed. The *garde*, hired
to stay with the mother, will bring her bouillon every three hours; it
mustn't be made from veal, which causes diarrhea. If she is terribly
hungry, she may have a soup of soaked white bread cut thin and
small, easy to digest. She should also drink infusions of couch grass,
or lukewarm water with a little wine, or syrup of maidenhair fern.
In five or six days she will be allowed some poultry in the morning,
but not in the evening until she is walking and exercising. The *garde*
must check the mother's *chauffoir*, a kind of diaper, for blood clots
and a flow that is bright red and normal. If it stops or becomes pale,
it means too much milk is still going up to the breast. Then a bouillon of chervil will be called for, with *arcanum duplicatum* or Glau-
ber's salt dissolved in it, and the breasts, kept covered and warm,
will need to be treated with an unguent of marsh marigold or olive
oil with tow of flax, or honey, to prevent engorgement.[23]

The new mother is suffering because her parts are somewhat
torn. Embarrassed, she reluctantly confesses this to the midwife,

who tells her she must help along the healing by bathing herself in a soothing lotion of milk and herbs. A mixture of water and vinegar and some hot wine alleviate the itching. Her diarrhea can be calmed with an enema of milk, egg yolk, and sugar, changing after a few days to a potion of equisetum and pomegranate peel with an egg yolk twice a day.[24] The diet of good bouillon must continue, and she can eat some jelly. Because she is still bleeding, cloths soaked in oxycrate, a mix of water and vinegar, are wrapped around her thighs and placed under her back. Some powdered Spanish wax, about a hazelnut's worth, dissolved in six spoonfuls of water, should be swallowed, followed by a second dose. A brew of wild chicory, orange blossoms, syrup of *diacode*, and *capillaire* will help too. She must sniff cloth soaked in Queen-of-Hungary water, which will strengthen her heart, as will drinks made from comfrey root and rice, and sap of purslane. And she continues to be bled from her arm.[25]

Soon the midwife will give some vaginal injections and fit the mother with a pessary made of cork and layers of wax to hold her womb where it belongs. Its ligaments have been loosened by the strains of childbirth, and it might prolapse completely without support. If the pessary gets dislodged, it needs to be dipped in wax again, and again, until the added hardened layers enlarge it sufficiently to stay in place. A hole in the center allows the woman to conceive.[26]

And so the whole cycle will begin anew.

6. The Petition

Paris, 17 May 1745

For many, it is a day like any other in the tumultuous capital, with its unique mix of luxury and filth, of magnificence and obscenity, its changing cacophony of sounds. Heavy spring showers have for weeks now sent rainwater gushing from the roofs of the many-storied buildings, making rivers of mud in the narrow, packed streets below, where people jostle, shove, and splash one another. Enterprising Auvergnats run about with planks to improvise bridges whenever they spot well-dressed pedestrians who might be willing to pay to keep their feet dry. Huge shop signs made of wood or heavy iron depicting the various trades—cobblers, glovemakers, perfumers, butchers—protrude high above the storefronts, creaking ominously in the wind. Midwives' signs usually show a cradle or a child leading a pregnant woman and carrying a candle. Scents of wet stone, ashes, wax, leather, soap, bread, sage, wine, grease, damp straw, fish, rotting apples, feces, and blood from the slaughterhouse near the Châtelet permeate the air. Shrill voices resound—merchants hawking their wares, town criers bellowing out royal edicts— filled in by the background shouts of bargemen floating west on the brown-gold Seine, the din of the blacksmiths' hammers, the clatter of carriage wheels and horses' hooves, and the tintinnabulating bells of a hundred churches. Sturdy women plant themselves on the corners, rain or shine, carrying on their backs large tin canisters of café au lait, which they serve, with little or no sugar, in earthenware cups for two sous.

A habitual sequence of events unfolds in Paris. At 7 A.M. gardeners with empty baskets on decrepit horses return to their little plots having sold their goods wholesale to the market during the dawn hours. At nine wigmakers scurry to coif and powder their clients, while young horsemen followed by their lackeys go for a practice gallop on the boulevards and make fools of themselves falling off. At ten there is a parade of black-robed justices going to the courts with plaintiffs running after them. Noon brings the money men to the Bourse, and solicitors of all stripes to the quartier St. Honoré, where financiers and men of rank have their dwellings. By 2 P.M. the carriages are in great demand as everyone scrambles to find a ride; passengers often come to blows, and police have to intervene. Three ushers in a peaceful spell; few are in the streets, for everyone is eating. Quarter past five, on the other hand, is truly infernal. There are crowds everywhere—on the way to the theater or to the promenades—and the cafés are overflowing. By seven it is calm again, although as night falls criminals come out of hiding and honest citizens must watch their step more carefully. Now carpenters and stonecutters head back to the outskirts of the city, whitening the streets with sawdust and plaster from their feet. As these laborers turn in after a long, hard workday, the marquises and countesses are just rousing themselves to begin their toilette! Nine is noisy. Theaters let out, many make their way to dinner engagements, prostitutes solicit potential clients. By eleven supper is finished, cafés disgorge. At one in the morning six thousand peasants arrive at Les Halles on their exhausted mounts, bringing vegetables, fruits, and flowers from the surrounding countryside. After

these produce deliverers come the fishmongers, then the wholesale egg merchants with their precariously balanced pyramids of
baskets. A similar scene takes place on the quai de la Mégisserie,
but here instead of salmon and herring there are straw cages full of
hares and pigeons. The rest of the city sleeps through most of this.
At 4 A.M. only brigands and poets are awake. At six the bread gets
delivered from the *boulangeries* of Gonesse; laborers rise from their
straw pallets, gather their tools, and go to their workshops, stop-
ping on the way for café au lait, their breakfast of choice. Libertines
stumble out pale and rumpled from the whorehouses, gamblers
emerge into the brutal light of day, many hitting themselves in the
head and stomach, looking heavenward in desperation. And then
everything starts over again.[1]

Babies, however, are born any hour of the day and night, so Le
Boursier is on call around the clock. There are no set rhythms or patterns to her schedule, although its very unpredictability in a sense
becomes routine.

For her, though, today is special. She is one of forty midwives
who have just signed a petition urging the Faculty of Medicine of
the University of Paris to provide them with instruction. Her name
appears near top center of the signatures (fig. 3), immediately after
those of the four official sworn midwives of the city, *jurées* whose
job—bought and usually passed down within a family—is to oversee the craft, make known infringements, collect fines, and expel of-
fenders. If Le Boursier has not spearheaded this rally among sister
practitioners, she was at least one of the first to approve it.[2] A few of
her cosigners demonstrate a fluid, easy hand; many more make
quirky scrawls and seem to find writing awkward, as though they
rarely have occasion or need to join letters together, and one who
cannot write at all marks the document with an *X*. Le Boursier's
manner of signing, though not flamboyant, seems sure and practiced among the clumsy ones. She has been a midwife in the capital
for many years and is no stranger to writing her name.[3]

Organizing for this petition was not easy. Midwives are deliberately kept as subordinate members of the guild of surgeons, "to
whose policing they must submit," and have historically been deprived of a separate, recognized voice. There is "absolutely no community among them," gloats the surgeon Louis in the *Encyclopédie* with obvious relief, reassuring himself and his readers, as if an
independent consorority of these women would be a nightmare.[4]

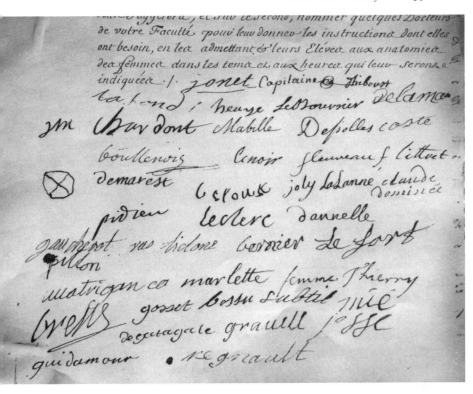

Figure 3. A rare look at the handwriting of forty midwives on a protest petition. One cannot sign, some obviously sign rarely and with difficulty, some have a fluid, confident signature. Le Boursier (as Mme du Coudray was known in Paris) puts her name near the top.

Lacking a corporation of their own, they have no meeting house, no built-in avenues for sociability, no established network of communication. They are excluded from academies, ignored by the press, never eulogized after death as are male practitioners. Even annuals like the *Almanach royal* in these years leave them out of the lists of health officials. So solidarity and camaraderie among them are not fostered, do not come naturally.

There are, however, some old rules that encourage a kind of interdependency. Midwives cannot be approved for their licenses until authorities learn about their lifestyles, so they are sometimes asked questions about their colleagues.[5] Do they live wholesome lives, eschew profanity, practice discretion? As far back as 1580 statutes and regulations forbade midwives to use any dissolute words or gestures or to speak ill of each other, unless it was to expose anyone among them who conspired to help women "kill their fruit."[6] Back then, in the late sixteenth century, Paris had only sixty midwives, and it may have been easier for them to know one another, whether personally or by reputation. But ever since then there has been enormous migration to the capital, and the expanding population has naturally swelled the demand for midwives. These days there are about two hundred of them scattered around and out into the burgeoning *faubourgs*.[7] Presumably they see each other monthly at the first-Monday services at the church of St. Côme, although it is not clear how rigorously they attend.

Yet something has occurred recently to pull forty of the most enterprising among them together. Disenfranchised though they may be, they have a shared grievance now, and they have mustered the stoutness of heart to initiate a protest. Since 1733 midwives have been admitted to classes at the school of surgery on the rue des Cordeliers. César Verdier was the demonstrator for anatomy, Sauveur-François Morand for dissections and surgical operations.[8] Recently, however, these lessons were closed to them, and the women are now turning to medical doctors, the surgeons' age-old rivals, for help. Doctors, with their Latin, their robes and bonnets, and their university schooling, have always fancied themselves greatly superior to surgeons, whose roots lie in the more practical artisanal tradition, so the women request their intervention. Exactly how many midwives have actually been attending these lectures is not known, but the forty who assemble today to complain about their recent exclusion obviously feel debarred from what had become, at least for them, an accustomed right.

Not only are the midwives intellectually deprived; they fear that their very profession is in jeopardy. The petitioners complain that for the past two years the normal testing and reception of aspiring midwives by Paris surgeons has also been suspended. The "dangerous consequences of such a cessation" are now rampant. Many women, finding the credentialing examination at St. Côme unavailable, have simply been setting up shop without it. The city's sworn, official midwives have forced such illegal practitioners to "take down their shingle," but these are put right back up again, the defiant matrons claiming that they have studied and therefore deserve to profit from their vocation, and that it is not their fault if surgeons refuse to test them. These women, though they have broken the rules, at least boast some training. But others—their names are provided in the petition—upon hearing there are no more formal receptions, have begun to practice without any background experience whatsoever. Expectant mothers seeking help from *these* unscrupulous characters court, according to the signers, the gravest peril.

The petitioners go on to demand instruction in reproductive anatomy, which will replace the classes now suspended by the surgeons. Understanding the "parts used in generation," far from being "vain curiosity," allows them to serve their clients better than the purely empirical training they have received as apprentices. In particular, they feel unsure about when to call for help; some are too secure, nearly foolhardy, others overanxious and lacking in confidence. The group now formally asks that doctors provide regular demonstrations for them and admit them and their students to all dissections of female corpses.

In response to this pressure the members of the medical faculty, unaware that the situation had gotten so out of control, move very quickly. They promise to prepare and distribute a yearly list of officially approved midwives, which should put an end to the anarchy and help regulate the profession. They assign one professor, Exapère Bertin, to teach bone structure, and another, Jean Astruc, to teach delivery, both for free and in an accessible form—in French, not Latin—in their school amphitheater on rue de la Bûcherie. The classes are to start immediately. They even try to get some cadavers from the hospital administrators, despite the fact that between 1 May and 1 September, because of putrefaction in hot weather, autopsies are not allowed. In an effort to persuade, the doctors boast about their latest facility, a beautiful rotunda with a dome built just last year, magnificent and modern: "Our amphitheater is new and cool. The demonstrator will prepare the [cadaver] parts with spirits of wine and aromatic essences and take all precautions so that his work will cause no foul smells . . . in neighboring houses." Despite this plea, a response to the medical dean from the chief of police denies the request for bodies because of the season; the lecturers continue anyway, doing the best they can using skeletons. Twenty-three lessons are given, to which "the midwives most in demand [*les plus employées*]" and their apprentices flock in large numbers.[9]

Why are the doctors so eager to help out? And why since 1743 have surgeons turned their backs on their teaching and licensing duties? Perhaps because on 23 April of that year the king gave a great boost to the status and prestige of surgeons, separating them squarely from any demeaning past association with barbers and wig-makers, putting them now on the same lofty footing with doctors, their historic enemies. The year 1743 was the beginning of the personal reign of Louis XV, who was very much under the influence of his first surgeon, La Peyronie.[10] The chronicler Barbier predicted then that, because the science of doctors was merely conjectural, surgeons with their combined practical experience *and* book learning would soon be the only experts needed.[11] Do the newly favored surgeons, imbued suddenly with a fresh sense of importance, simply believe the approval of midwives to be beneath their dignity? Or do they wish to squeeze out female practitioners completely, thus eliminating any competitive and menacing alternative to the male surgeon *accoucheurs* already fashionable in high social circles?

The midwives suspect the latter. They feel cheated because the "masters of their community" who owe them instruction are withholding it. They soon complain again to the medical faculty, that "the more carefully they watch the conduct of master surgeons toward them the more they are persuaded that they wish to destroy them in the [eyes of the] public even though they are part of the same community." They thank the doctors for responding to their request for instruction with such "clarity and precision." Surgeons have apparently complained that Paris has too many midwives already. The petitioners protest vociferously. There are fewer than two hundred they say, some of whom are far too elderly to practice. New ones take a long time to train, as private apprenticeship lasts three years. And now the Hôtel Dieu, which forms midwives much more quickly in several months of intense clinical training, is distributing most of its graduates outside of the capital into the provinces.[12] As a result, only six or seven new Parisian midwives present themselves each year, while at least that many retire. "Such a small number in a city as extended and as populated as the city of Paris shows that, far from being overabundant, [the supply] is not even sufficient." The timely reception of new, legitimate midwives must be reinstituted. Surgeons, the petitioners now claim unequivocally, "are trying to deprive midwives, against order and the public good, of the fruits of a profession." The group urges doctors, magistrates, and the lieutenant of police to *force* surgeons to recognize their error and resume their duties as instructors and examiners.

The doctors seem ready to do anything to embarrass their professional rivals, including the forging of this temporary alliance with the midwives. And the women do not hesitate to exploit the traditional animosity between the two groups of male practitioners, whose polemics have been at fever pitch for the last two years, if it means achieving their aim of better training and regulation. The surgeons, however, despite their scorn for their female underlings, seem unready to relinquish control of them, and vow to put a stop to the doctors' encroachment. The midwives must not fancy that they can go over to the other camp permanently. "You will never escape from our *corps*, whatever entreaties you make. Alert your companions, because no matter what you try you will only be the dupes."[13] And indeed, the doctors' lessons soon cease.

Being caught in this crossfire, pawns in this game, is humiliating for the midwives. Surgeons are busy making a display of their new professional and academic status; doctors are busy doing anything and everything to protect their traditional prestige. Both groups are far more concerned with their personal interests and privileges than with helping the midwives. They give hollow, false promises at best. The petitioners seem overworked, insecure, forsaken. That they band together and demand more thorough education shows they possess at least some sense of a shared work identity. But what is driving them is not chiefly female pride. A large part of the grievance here is against female quacks practicing blind, murderous routines. "It is to the mercy or rather the rashness of such women that the life of other women and children is surrendered." These petitioners do not experience—or at least do not express—the indignities they suffer at the hands of surgeons as affronts to their sex, but rather as professional usurpations. Job-related alliances like this petition doubtless offer some consolation, but there is little sense of sisterhood under such circumstances. The issues here are not framed in terms of women defending themselves against men.[14]

Le Boursier signs the petition beside one Heuzé, with whom she will exchange an apprentice several years from now. Perhaps they are friends who afford each other mutual support. For now, though, they are only two of many midwives whose collective work is not properly appreciated, not receiving adequate recognition. They are lost in the crowd, their reputation suffering because charlatans masquerade as colleagues. To observers commenting on the group, the superior practitioners are indistinguishable from the others. One doctor, musing on the fact that midwives were once highly esteemed in Greece and Rome, laments: "To see the low opinion of midwives in Paris, one is tempted to say 'past honors are only a dream.' But we must focus on individuals who practice this profession and not on the profession itself. . . . There are many who should be excepted, even singled out with high praise; but we have often seen crime obscure the virtue that walks beside it."[15] Is the future of Paris midwifery imperiled, even for this enterprising group of petitioners who crave learning in addition to technique? Could Le Boursier already be thinking she must break away if she is ever to shine?

Whatever her thoughts may be at this point in her career, she is making the best of it in Paris. She and Heuzé may even have been designated or have assumed the role of unofficial leaders of Parisian midwives, for their signatures are the first after the pro forma list of *jurées*, women who have inherited the title but are not necessarily good at rallying the group. That Le Boursier denounces as abusive the threat posed by surgeons and quacks to her livelihood, that she organizes or joins others who regard it also in that light, is perhaps an early indication of her strong sense of self. It is impossible, naturally, to do your best work when such obstacles are thrown in your path. There are things about the Paris scene that are irksome, even mortifying. If the surgeons think she will be cowed by their snub, waiting submissively for the affair to blow over, her activism for the petition shows otherwise. What satisfaction there would be in turning the tables on them some day!

And there is all this new talk, especially at the Hôtel Dieu, about well-trained midwives being so sorely needed in the provinces right now. Might this be when the idea of leaving and setting out on her own first takes root in Le Boursier's mind? Whether it is or not, for a while still she will stay here in Paris, biding her time.

7. Apprentices and Associates

Paris, 22 January 1751

Today Le Boursier takes on a new apprentice. It would have made no sense to have one these last six years because all that time the surgeons stayed on strike, refusing to resume their duties.[1] It finally took royal intervention to halt the conflict, and only lately have things begun to pick up again, so there is quite a backlog. The petitioners had estimated that six or seven apprentices usually finish each year. Now, to make up for the lost time, twenty-five women sign up to begin three years of training with mistress midwives throughout the city. The ranks must be replenished.

Angélique Marguerite Le Boursier seems still to be unmarried, for the notary who draws up the arrangement, scrupulously thorough about such details, mentions only the marital status of her apprentice. Madeleine Françoise Templier, widow of the baker Fourcy, has for the last four months been apprenticed to Marie Anne Heuzé, but quite recently she moved to rue St. Croix de la Bretonnerie, where Le Boursier lives. She no doubt finds it more convenient to have a near neighbor for a teacher. In any case, she now makes a new contract reflecting the change. Three hundred livres will be paid to Le Boursier for three years of training, during which the midwife will "show and teach [her apprentice] all that her profession involves." The student will live in her own home and dress and eat at her own expense, but she will come to Le Boursier's residence, or accompany her on rounds elsewhere, whenever needed.[2]

This is a very advantageous contract for Le Boursier. Such a student is an important source of income, and indeed, Heuzé loses no time finding another for herself, just six days later, negotiating similar terms.[3] These two women drive a hard bargain. Most midwives charge their apprentices considerably less, give them considerably more, and spell out precisely just what the conditions will be. Le Boursier's contract, however, is sketched in abbreviated terms, as if working with a midwife of such distinction and reputation is enough in itself.

Usually, contracts made by Le Boursier's colleagues are elaborate, and mutual obligations intense. One midwife pledges "to show her whole art . . . without hiding or disguising anything, and to alert and call" her student to come with her everywhere. The aspirant, for her part, will "learn with all possible attention the art of delivery, agree to all that can contribute to her instruction, do for mothers and for children all that a midwife should, and generally listen to and practice all" that she is shown, "day or night."[4] Most midwives promise to "feed, sleep, lodge, warm, and light" their students, even wash their laundry—towels, sheets and clothes—in addition to teaching them, thus taking on a maternal role. Most students stipulate that they will "enhance the profits" and "prevent the damage" of their teacher, that is, warn and protect her against injury to her reputation. They also swear "never to leave or work elsewhere during the three years" and, in case of flight, to submit to finishing out their obligations after being hunted down by the searchers dispatched to find them.[5] Some midwives commit themselves to teach about medicines and remedies, bandages, fomentations and fumigations, as well as about childbirth itself. Some students specify that they will follow the midwife faithfully as long as she is trustworthy, "obey her in all she asks that is honest," "reasonable," and "licit."[6] The reciprocal agreement is for the exchange of ethical attitudes as well as skills. Whereas most preprinted apprenticeship contracts, kept handy by the notaries with blanks to be filled in, talk of learning a "trade" (*métier*), midwife contracts are worded differently. They call this line of work an "art."[7]

Arrangements vary considerably. One woman from Meudon puts her sister into apprenticeship for only three months, because she will practice in the countryside where regulations are quite lax, in some regions nonexistent.[8] Another provincial, from Champagne, the wife of a master founder, is determined to take the full three-year course. She pays 250 livres for this apprenticeship.[9] It is curious that she is willing to spend long years away from her hometown, but perhaps she has been urged to do so, even subsidized, by the authorities of her region, who are zealous about securing thoroughly trained practitioners.[10] Most provincials study for a much shorter time, although such truncated training limits their marketability, obliging them to keep their practice outside the capital forever.[11]

A few contracts involve family members. Two sisters-in-law have an arrangement in which one instructs the other "without a single sou being exchanged."[12] But even within families some considerable sums are paid for instruction, with all manner of guarantees and collateral stipulated to make the obligation binding. The wording can be dramatic. The husband of one apprentice pledges "solidly" to pay the necessary fees, or lose all his earthly goods.[13]

A midwife might agree to teach a next-door neighbor for free, simply taking her around to watch and help during a three-year period. In one such case on the rue des Fossés de Monsieur le Prince, the apprentice is single, the midwife married to a master perfumer.

Perhaps his income is sufficient for his wife not to be preoccupied by gain.[14] Others may simply enjoy the company and assistance. Usually neighbors do exchange money, 100 livres, 200 livres.[15] Le Boursier's 300 livres for such an arrangement, however, where no hospitality is offered, no responsibility assumed for the apprentice short of the instruction itself, is very high. She must already consider her teaching of sufficient quality and value to command a superior price without providing any fringe benefits for her pupil. And she is apparently uninterested in having a boarder, companion, or surrogate daughter as do so many of her colleagues. Life can sometimes get rough for apprentices; they can be a burden. One midwife will take an apprentice from the provinces who, when seduced and abandoned by an old doctor promising to help her advance in her career, exposes him and creates a public scandal. Though the apprentice wins a good financial settlement, her reputation is ruined and the whole affair is most unpleasant.[16] Le Boursier avoids these sorts of entanglements.

Apprentices frequently present themselves alone, of their own volition; others are brought before the notary by husbands, older sisters, or parents who wish to prepare them for a secure profession. One seventeen-year-old orphan is presented by the guardians who have cared for her since age four.[17] Midwifery continues to be regarded as a valuable, worthy female trade, despite the dire scenario foreseen six years ago by the petitioners, in which they would be irreparably sabotaged by the surgeons. Dancing masters, financial administrators, clerks, cobblers, prisonkeepers, printers, pastry chefs, caterers, locksmiths, and journeymen all willingly pay large sums for women in their family to acquire expertise in the art of delivery.[18]

One midwife, *dame* Bresse, requires an all-around helper, a woman to serve as domestic and personal secretary. So her twenty-year-old apprentice pays her no money for the three years of training but agrees in exchange to see to the "needs" and "personal affairs" of her teacher, to be generally "at her service."[19] Quite a number of midwives have responsibilities managing the household accounts and so seek clerical help.[20] One brings to her marriage a dowry of several thousand livres.[21] Another has been part owner of some property in Fontenay.[22] Another brings only 500 livres but marries a man with nearly 10,000 and many investments.[23] One midwife, widowed after twenty-eight years of marriage and the mother of seven children, decides to apprise her eldest son, a soldier, of their estate. The current value of everything after the ebb and flow of life for nearly three decades—itemized down to the gold buttons on some sleeves—is now 4,213 livres, 2 sous, 3 deniers. When all is said and done, each of the seven children will get a rather paltry inheritance, but it must be accurately calculated nonetheless.[24] Severe economic reversals can occur quite suddenly with widowhood. One midwife whose surgeon-husband dies abruptly needs to sell all her belongings to pay three months' back rent for the apartment she sublets. The inventory of this sale shows she occupies several rooms cluttered, indeed overflowing, with possessions—numerous feather beds, straw mattresses, cots, serge curtains, wall hangings, and armoires.[25] Almost surely the many furnishings and tapestries have been used in the private partitions described by Mercier. What will she do, even with her back rent paid, in this suddenly empty apartment, once the scene of much activity, the temporary refuge of numerous pregnant clients over the years, now stripped and bare?

Le Boursier's colleagues are scattered all over the city, although some very populous quarters seem to have more midwives than others. According to records from the 1770s (no lists for earlier periods have been found), several of the Right Bank neighborhoods, teeming with inhabitants, have as many as twenty-three, sometimes even a few clustered on the same street. Le Boursier's quarter, St. Avoie, near the graceful recreational boulevards and full of grand homes and gardens, has only two.[26] Has she expressly chosen to be a big fish in a smaller pool? Does this put her in greater demand and ensure her a healthy, wealthy practice and singular reputation even before she enters public service? Or is it that her presence discourages others with lesser reputations from establishing themselves there? The Marais, where she lives, once an aristocratic bastion, still has many nobles, magistrates, and others of distinction. Rue St. Croix de la Bretonnerie, her street, is itself the home of several provincial intendants, royal ministers, and bankers.[27] It is quite likely that Le Boursier has gotten to know during these years some prominent and powerful neighbors, whose financial support and political assistance will soon become important to her.

She also frequents and befriends colleagues in the medical field. She has been acquainted with the surgeons Morand and Verdier since their lectures at the anatomy courses for midwives at St. Côme.

Old-timers who have been practicing since 1724, they were probably on her jury when she completed her apprenticeship and took her qualifying examination. They seem not to hold a grudge from the petition days of accusation and recrimination, and will facilitate things for Le Boursier later on. Morand will do this in his capacity as royal censor. He seems to take particular interest in sponsoring talented women, and has given special encouragement also to a Mademoiselle Bihéron, who fashions precise anatomical models out of a secret lifelike wax substance. A former midwife who now devotes herself entirely to this "artificial anatomy," she holds weekly visiting hours in her home *cabinet*, where these pieces are on exhibit, so realistic, it is said, that only the smell is missing. She is presently preparing a collection of models commissioned by Catherine of Russia to be sent to hospitals and displayed in the museums of St. Petersburg, and Morand is lending her his patronage. Le Boursier, typically, never mentions Bihéron, but these wax models of pregnant women might well have been the inspiration for her own later mannequin made of cloth. Verdier, a peerless lecturer and close friend of Morand, will later pen some obstetrical "observations" to be published alongside Le Boursier's textbook.[28] She is also acquainted with the Sües, a veritable dynasty of influential medical men, three of whom, a father, a son, and a first cousin, will come to the midwife's aid in a variety of ways.

But Le Boursier's most important contact from the Paris years is the maverick lithotomist Jean Baseilhac, known internationally by his nickname Frère Côme, for this celebrated surgeon is a monk. He is a fascinating character in his own right, as his swashbuckling portrait seems to bear out (fig. 4); a native of Tarbes in the south of France, he has recently discovered and perfected new techniques for cutting out stones, and for curing cataracts. Special instruments of his own devising are made for him by a favorite cutler on the rue Galande, and he tries them out on patients at the Hôpital de la Charité. He also experiments on corpses. Though a great humanitarian, so intense is he in his research, so enthusiastic about his findings, that he is said to have lamented the recovery of a person whose cadaver he was particular curious to dissect! An expansive and generous man, he is devoted to healing the poor, for whom he has set up a number of free medical clinics, but constantly sought out by the rich and famous, especially many in the king's immediate

Figure 4. Frère Côme, the famous medical monk, assisted Mme du Coudray and managed her mission in various ways behind the scenes. Photograph courtesy of the Académie Nationale de Médecine, Paris.

entourage. In the mid-1740s his virtuosity came to the attention of the king's first surgeon, La Peyronie, and ever since he has been a darling at Versailles. Superior orders forced the Paris surgical community to accept him into their fold, but his unorthodox methods and the favoritism shown him at court have made most of the members of the Academy of Surgery too resentful to welcome him.

He has a deep, genuine commitment to the destitute, an enormous talent, a colorful personality, and an entirely unique and very powerful position in the medical landscape, won by skill, of course, but also furthered by people in high places. Le Boursier will develop along these same lines, and perhaps he foresees this potential in the gifted, ambitious midwife. He probably teaches her how to exploit good connections, how to use letter writing to her own ends, how to generate a network of supporters and gather their written testimonials, how to create and enjoy special idiosyncratic freedoms. He has perfected and used these methods for years, and she is much influenced by his example. He will later claim to have groomed her for her great task.[29]

In any case, Frère Côme is to become her principal fan and impresario. His unflagging support for her, which will last until his death in 1781, is a mixed blessing. That she has a strong, influential man working behind the scenes to sustain her during three decades is not bad. That he is a flamboyant personality who gets distracted by his own exciting projects and makes as many enemies as friends is not good. The famous Rouen surgeon Le Cat, for example, hates Frère Côme and calls him Frère Coupe-Chou because he lacks the usual university credentials and behaves in such an earthy manner. Another medical colleague, the eye specialist Daviel, who peddles a rival cataract procedure, refers to his own method as Davielique and to Frère Côme's as Comique in an unsuccessful attempt to reduce the monk to a laughing stock. There are also far more insidious attacks on his reputation, and even physical assaults on some of his disciples. He survives all this, his energy undiminished, and remains steadfastly loyal to the midwife, raving about her wherever he goes. And he travels widely. He does enough for Le Boursier's reputation through his solicitations that doctors and surgeons both at court and far beyond know well who she is and marvel at her abilities.[30]

Frère Côme realizes as well as anyone the desperate need for good midwives in the provinces. An *enquête* back in 1729 revealed the woeful state of rural delivery practices, one panicky priest near Laon estimating that more than 200,000 country babies were dying each year.[31] The monarchy responded, and since 1735 the Hôtel Dieu has been training provincial midwives almost exclusively.[32] This hospital's maternity ward, an alternative route for apprentices who have neither the time nor the money to study privately with the likes of Le Boursier and her mistress colleagues, used to train women from all over Europe—Sardinia, Denmark, Spain—and of course Parisians, but they are now being turned away in favor of those from the French countryside. This training is of the highest quality. It is an exhausting, intensive, round-the-clock three-month session, presided over by one midwife who devotes herself entirely to this responsibility, living like a nun, dressing modestly, eating with her apprentices—no meat—spending all her nights at the hospital, accepting no tips for deliveries and baptisms, receiving no guests in her room, earning a mere 400 livres a year. The teacher committed to this "assiduous and sedentary" engagement demands that same kind of devotion from her apprentices, of whom she takes only four at a time.[33] These students get extraordinary clinical practice: each year 1,400 to 1,600 women give birth at the Hôtel Dieu, and some nights as many as a dozen deliveries take place.[34] Not only is this education superb and efficient, but it is also a bargain. It costs only 180 livres, and includes the fee for the qualifying examination and certification when the three-month session ends. City apprentices, by contrast, in addition to their lessons, which can cost several hundred livres, must bear the further expense of the grueling qualifying exam.[35] Le Boursier and her Paris colleagues endured the private apprenticeship, but provincial women opt, understandably, for the cheaper, shorter training at the Hôtel Dieu.

There is a problem, however. Even the three-month session in Paris is stressful for many who do not want to be away from home so long. Although provincial wigmakers, valets, coachmen, sculptors, shoemakers, notaries, surgeons, masons, millers, sheriff's officers, and wine merchants from all over France respond to the Hôtel Dieu recruitment program and hasten to sign up their wives, the women themselves are often reluctant. They comply at first with their husbands' bidding but, once inscribed, prove to be unready for the commitment. It is too rigorous and fatiguing. The registers of the hospital's maternity ward make note of these ambivalent pupils: "paid but has not shown up to enroll"; "paid and we have accepted her but she no longer wishes to come"; "paid—we have searched for her—nobody knows where she is"; "does not wish to learn, does not want to come." Some women try to get refunds of their deposit after changing their mind.[36] Obviously this system of enlistment is not really working. There is more and more talk in high circles of better, alternative ways to train midwives for the provinces. Recently a few regions have employed an experienced Parisian woman to come teach the locals, but the fledgling efforts have been sporadic and there are very few trainees.

Soon a wealthy philanthropic seigneur from Auvergne comes to Paris looking for someone to instruct the peasant women on his estates in the art of childbirth. He may be considering sending one or two of them to study at the Hôtel Dieu, for he feels the situation is urgent. He and his wife make inquiries. Frère Côme seems to know that Le Boursier is restless, that she would gladly reassign her new apprentice to someone else and break free, that she is just waiting for an opening. The quickening pace of intrusion by surgeons into the professional space of midwives has displeased her for some time, but there is apparently more. She wants to leave *now*. Maybe some private drama has taken place in her life, to which Frère Côme is privy, though we cannot be because all correspondence between him and the midwife is lost. In any case, the monk dissuades the seigneur from looking any further. Once the man hears of Le Boursier in such glowing terms, he will stop at nothing to lure her south to his *terres*.[37]

8. Break to the Provinces

Thiers-en-Auvergne, 1 October 1751

So eager to make her breakaway, the midwife has left precipitously, arriving in Thiers far ahead of schedule. Nothing is ready. She will have to be put up at the inn for a few days while her residence is prepared.[1] What has made Le Boursier quit Paris in such a hurry, has made her rush to accept this call? Some sudden trauma? A need, building slowly but abruptly felt, to escape from the relentless ritual of city birthing? The wish to test herself? One can cut oneself adrift, take refuge in a journey. It is evidently not hard for her to leave things behind when she has been singled out and summoned for a purpose out of the ordinary. She seems to have lost interest in what is within easy reach; it is as if she has been waiting to spring loose, to be given a challenge, a change, a chance. Indeed, she craves adventure, if her early appearance here is any indication.

The voyage from Paris has taken her along a route that follows the great river valleys, where it can, but that passes through the forests of Fontainebleau and Montargis with their assorted dangers, and bumps along elsewhere over brush-covered, scrubby bogs and rocky hills with an occasional dappled goat. A contemporary guidebook of France classifies only the last part of the trip, south of Moulins, as offering "good roads." This has no doubt been a long, hard journey, the carriage creaking and lurching on these broken routes, but the autumn climate is bracing and the destination lovely and we hear no complaints. Thiers, full of steps and narrow zigzag streets, is situated on a jog of the rollicking Durolle River, which laps at its walls. It is a densely populated commercial center where boats come and go, cleaving the water beside the paper mills and the tilt-hammers where knife blades are forged.[2]

Le Boursier's apprentice back in Paris, having given her teacher 200 livres already, was supposed to pay the balance of her fee, another 100 livres, at Easter of next year, but the midwife has collected it instead on 17 September,[3] and with this early payment has embarked on her travels. She seems to have dutifully made some private arrangement with another midwife to continue teaching the apprentice, perhaps for free; her student does finish her contracted training on schedule and does become a full-fledged Parisian *sage-femme* in 1753.[4] Meanwhile, Le Boursier turns her back on the capital without apparent remorse, and although she will make numerous trips to this center of power and influence, it will never again be her home. She has walked away from one life to begin another. She has broken free.

Auvergne's intendant, La Michodière, is especially progressive and has for some time been concerned about the perceived depopulation crisis. He is therefore keen to provide his region with good obstetrical care, even corresponding with Voltaire on the matter.[5] As early as 1746 he recruited a Paris midwife, a Madame Berne trained at the Hôtel Dieu, who settled in Riom just north of Clermont, was paid a salary of 500 livres, worked hard, and sang Italian cantatas. The husband of this "gracious lady," however, could not find a satisfactory job, so in short order the family returned to the capital. Next came a Madame Bailly; she lasted five years at her job, but grew to feel she was inadequately recompensed to sustain her ever-growing family, and left at her husband's urging. At the moment of Le Boursier's arrival in Thiers, in nearby Brioude a male surgeon is doing all the deliveries because of the difficulties in keeping Paris-trained midwives in that town. The last one, discouraged, had returned home to her husband, "to the bosom of her family where she could find comfort."[6] For these reasons the Auvergne authorities might be pleased to find that the newest Parisian midwife in their midst is unattached, that she has no husband pulling her away.

Right now Le Boursier is here on a private arrangement. Although the intendant knows of her, she has been invited to Thiers by the local seigneur and philanthropist, Monsieur de Thiers himself. He is vacationing in Tignes, but has alerted his men to her coming. Le Boursier's premature arrival, however, has thrown everything off balance. A Monsieur Merville, judge and journalist in the town, is trying desperately to smooth the path for her. Almost immediately a conspiracy of surgeons and local matrons forms and vows to undermine the efforts of the new recruit, to treat her as if she came unbidden, to turn the townswomen against her and ensure her ostracism. They experience her presence among them as an invasion, a violation. Merville laments a few days later that already a mother and child have died unnecessarily for stubbornly refusing her services. The new midwife "feels all this, although she doesn't know the extent of it," explains Merville, who believes she will be entirely justified if she, too, chooses to leave the region.

Le Boursier, meanwhile, is watching, listening, taking everything in and learning a great deal. This encounter with blatant hostility is a new experience for her. She handles herself with dignity and restraint, telling Merville that despite all this she is glad to be away from the hustle and bustle of Paris. He, unable to contain his distress, pleads with regional authorities to help him muster support for this "poor outsider, whose merit, spirit of charity, and sound judgment are infinitely touching." Merville works himself into a fury trying to sell the virtues of this highly trained Parisian midwife to his "ignorant" and "undeserving" townsfolk. He contacts the intendant himself, apologizing for the futility of his efforts, and goes on dramatically to despair for the whole unenlightened nation. France is "ungrateful. . . . I thought I knew her. I was wrong, and I swear, she is worse than I dared believe."[7]

If an onlooker is this upset, what is Le Boursier herself thinking? Calm and seemingly unperturbed, she is nonetheless not at all sure she can overcome the obstacles in Thiers. Or that she wants to. But she needs no pity. Shrewdly assessing her chances, she is already sending her papers and recommendations ahead to the much bigger city of Clermont, where the principal mistress midwife has just died. It is a coveted post, and she perseveres. She offers to submit to any new examinations the Clermont surgeons care to give her if her Paris credentials are for any reason insufficient or unacceptable. She volunteers to teach four apprentices.[8] Le Boursier is, instinctively, designing a strategy that will serve her well. Unfailingly gracious to those, like Merville and de Thiers, who appreciate her, she tries not to be discouraged by the others. Far from making anyone regret that some of their efforts on her behalf fail, she commiserates with them about how difficult it is to change habits, to break from old, familiar ways, to overcome inertia. All the while, though, this energetic woman is doing what she must on the practical front for herself, so that her talents will not go to waste in some obscure backwater of Auvergne. She has not left Paris to molder and fade into oblivion here. A strong sense of self-preservation propels her forward. If supporters, however obliging, are too few or timorous or ineffectual, she will go elsewhere, press on, not squander time reproaching them. She is cut out for nobler ventures. Let other midwives summoned to the provinces retreat to Paris, licking their wounds, seeking tranquillity. No amount of possible peril will deter her; for her there will be no turning back.

Why would she want to go back anyway? The atmosphere in the capital grows increasingly unwelcoming to midwives. The much-anticipated first volume of the *Encyclopédie* has appeared, and it is the talk of the town. Its article "Accoucheuse" is nothing short of defamatory, quoting the philosopher La Mettrie as saying, "It would be better for women . . . if there were no midwives. I advise . . . to repress these reckless *accoucheuses.*" The author of the article, a doctor named Pierre Tarin, claims to have gone out of curiosity to watch a *sage-femme* do a delivery. "I saw there examples of inhumanity," he reports, "that would be almost unbelievable among barbarians. . . . I therefore invite those in charge of watching over disorders in society to keep an eye on this one." The preceding article, "Accoucheur," sums up the prevailing view: "A surgeon delivers better than a midwife." The article "Accouchement," all about childbirth itself, does not even mention midwives at all, and has only men presiding.[9] Demoralizing to be sure for Le Boursier's former colleagues. She is less inclined than ever to look back with nostalgia. Her aim is to move ahead.

Soon she receives a license from the community of master surgeons in Clermont and moves on to that city.[10] She will remain there for the next decade, fashioning and slowly implementing a brave and mighty plan.

9. "The Stories They Told Me"

Clermont, 9 May 1755

Today at the St. Pierre parish church is the baptism of "Marguerite Guillaumanche, legitimate daughter of François and Aimable Parcou his wife, inhabitants of Talende, born the 4th of this month in our parish and presented by Helène Desson, midwife, godfather Jean Crouseix, godmother Marguerite Crouseix, inhabitants of this city, who did not sign."[1] Talende is a little town about twenty kilometers due south of Clermont. The parents of this baby were visiting the big city when she was born, but had they come expressly to give birth here or were they taken by surprise? The little girl may well have been premature, for five days have elapsed between birth and baptism, suggesting that the baby was too weak or sickly to be taken to the church until now. The parents, godparents, and midwife are evidently all illiterate, for they cannot put their signatures to the baptismal act.

Le Boursier is nowhere in the picture, evidently not involved in this birth in any way, neither as family member, nor as godparent, nor as presiding midwife, although she has been living, teaching, and practicing in Clermont for four years already. Her surnames bear no resemblance to those of the principals here. She might not even be aware of this event when it occurs. Yet this newborn girl, by some quirk of fate, will become her "niece," will be raised by her, taught by her, and declared her sole heir. Orphaned early, Marguerite Guillaumanche will become the itinerant midwife's only known "family," in one of several acts of self-styling by which, it seems, the midwife finds or invents for herself what life itself has not provided.

But while she appears right now to have no connection with this particular peasant family, Le Boursier has gotten to know many others just like them. Living and teaching in Clermont these past years has gradually transformed her. Ladies of the local nobility place their confidence in her, as did her elite clients in the capital, but there is something different now. She finds herself increasingly drawn to the indigent women of the countryside and moved deeply by their stories. They have become the real focus of her attention.

Auvergne is a rough, isolated part of France where winters are harsh, the snow blanketing the volcanic massifs and reluctant soil during many months of the year. Summers are heavy and hot, cultivation and plowing thankless, poverty rife. The rural women from the surrounding villages whom the midwife befriends have been toughened by the realities of life in huge, hungry families so poor that husbands go out on the road for up to nine months out of twelve seeking work as seasonal migrants. These traveling Auvergnats rarely make enough to send or bring home more than a few pocketfuls of seed, but at least they "eat away from home" and so do not need to be reckoned in for food.[2] When they return, the pregnancies that result are often unwelcome; every new mouth to feed is something of a calamity.

Worse yet, birthing leaves many of these women permanently impaired, or so the midwife reports. They complain to her of constant disabling pain, uterine prolapse, private parts hideously mangled by village practitioners who don't know what they are doing. Not only that, but many of their babies, if they survive at all, suffer injuries that last a lifetime, a fate worse even than death. Misshapen heads squeezed, then clumsily remolded by some desperate matron (the number of village idiots is very high); useless shrunken limbs; broken backs; eyes rendered sightless by a jagged dirty nail during delivery—such tales, told repeatedly, touch the midwife's soul.[3] Since coming here she has encountered for the first time the climate of terror and dread that hangs over childbirth in the countryside, the constant menace of pain and death.

How does she hear and understand the stories? These rustic matriarchs have qualities that quickly win her respect, though with their rough ways and crude talk they could as easily arouse aversion as liking. The more shocking she finds their revelations, the more frightful and strange their experiences sound, the more determined she is to help. In Paris she had been safely insulated from all this, had never been exposed to the blood, gore, and butchery these women report, or to their world of supernatural signs and symbols, powers and threats. She interviews them tirelessly. But then an interesting process takes place as she transforms their tales into terms she can comprehend, filters out much of their color and drama in an effort to gain some control. Their narratives of ghosts, spirits, all manner of unseen forces and dangers, are recast by her into rational medical language. The result of this superimposition, of her reductive laundering of their magical popular stories, is the depiction of childbirth as a mechanical problem to be solved.[4] That is what she offers to these women, who are both patients and pupils. She heals them and gives them free advice and free lessons. Then she begins to formulate, especially for them, a new pedagogy, a special teaching aid to relieve their suffering.

The Parlement of Paris has just this year ruled that midwives are not authorized to use obstetrical forceps. The encroaching surgeons rave about this innovative technology as a new conquering tool that can and will change the medical landscape and make midwives obsolete. Watching her female colleagues belittled and diminished in this way gives Le Boursier pause, then resolve. She would pioneer as a special kind of teacher, so as not to be bound by such rules and constraints. Inspired by this contemplated freedom, she begins to reconfigure her own sphere of competence. This is yet another opportunity for her ingenuity, and she takes full advantage of it. She will create a device of her own, one that women can use and that will help them immeasurably: not an instrument for extracting babies like the forceps, but one that will make forceps unnecessary. It is her way of fighting back, staking a claim, securing a piece of the action. There will be something in it for her women, and there will be something in it for her.

10. The "Machine"

Paris, 13 May 1756

After learning in the capital the art that I profess, and having practiced for sixteen years, destiny led me to the provinces. To earn the marks of esteem shown me by those who called me there, I announced that I would gladly give my advice to poor women who needed it. I cannot say the number who opened up to me about their sad situation, most of whom were afflicted with a loosening of the womb. I made them go into detail about their deliveries, and by the accounts they gave me I could not doubt that they attributed their infirmities to the ignorance of the women to whom they had recourse, or to that of some inexperienced village surgeons. My zeal therefore determined me to offer to give free lessons to these women. I made this proposition to the subdelegate, who, charmed to procure such a great benefit, accepted my offer. The only obstacle I found to my project was the difficulty of making myself understood by minds unaccustomed to grasping things except through the senses. I took the tack of making my lessons palpable by having them maneuver in front of me on a machine I constructed for this purpose, and which represented the pelvis of a woman, the womb, its opening, its ligaments, the conduit called the vagina, the bladder and *rectum intestine*. I added a model of a child of natural size, whose joints I made flexible enough to be able to put it in different positions; a placenta with its membranes and the demonstration of waters that they contain; the umbilical cord composed of its two arteries and of the vein, leaving one half withered up, the other inflated, to imitate somewhat the cord of a dead child and that of a live child in which one feels the beating of the vessels that compose it.

I added the model of the head of a child separated from the trunk, in which the cranial bones are caved in on each other. I thought that with a demonstration this tangible, if I could not make these women very skilled, I would at least make them feel the necessity of asking for help soon enough to save the mother and child, help that cities do not lack, but that would be very necessary in the countryside, where the skill of a surgeon called too late is often useless, and he can only be the spectator of two expiring victims for whom his art and his zeal are by then fruitless. Thus my project was to have these women recognize the diverse dangers to which their incapacity exposes the mother and child.[1]

Large groups. Collective teaching. Students whose mental universe is quite distant. Here is the new challenge, very different from training a single apprentice whom you know well. So a palpable, concrete technique must be designed, one that features hands-on experience and practice, not theory and principles. Dealing with this new audience of rustics whose thoughts and worries are so alien, the midwife realizes that "it is to their eyes and their hands that [I] needed to speak."[2]

This, then, is the origin of the midwife's famous anatomical model, her upholstered "machine" with its womb and extractable baby doll (fig. 5). Upon this mannequin her students can practice, practice, and practice. The skin and soft organs are made of flesh-colored linen and pliant leather—some parts are redder and some paler—stuffed with padding, and the pelvic basin and various bones are at this point made of real skeletons, although later wood and wicker frames will be used. The different parts of the machine are numbered, and an accompanying table identifies all the anatomical names. Besides the main mannequin, as the midwife explains, there are many detached pieces, exhibits that allow a closer look at, for example, "the membranes showing the void filled with water in the middle of which the child swims."[3] The model is meant mostly for maneuvers that, as others confirm, allow her students to gain confidence, be "encouraged, and succeed perfectly."[4] Delivering babies from every conceivable position and presentation will prepare her students for all eventualities. But other auxiliary exhibits are meant also to warn and alarm, hence the flattened, shriveled umbilical

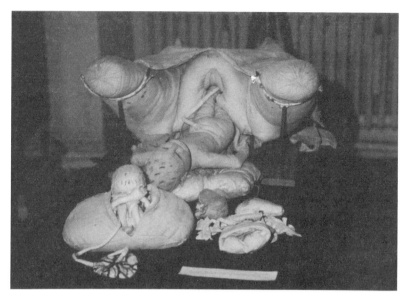

Figure 5. The only known extant example of Mme du Coudray's obstetrical "machine," made of wicker, fabric, leather, stuffing, and sponges. She produced hundreds of these, but the others must have disintegrated with use. This one is preserved in the Musée Flaubert, Rouen.

cord of a lifeless baby and the severed head with crushed cranium. This machine, as the midwife's followers will continue to testify, makes an "impression that can never be erased," "an advantage all the more essential because this class of surgeons and these women [of the countryside] do not have the resource of reading . . . [so] these daily continual maneuvers . . . [must be] vividly impressed on their senses."[5]

Today in Paris two distinguished surgeons, the midwife's old acquaintance Verdier and his colleague André Levret, "named by the Royal Academy of Surgery to examine a machine invented by la Dame du Coudray, Maîtresse Sage-Femme licensed in Paris, established in Clermont in Auvergne, to demonstrate the practice of delivery," approve it in a "very advantageous report."[6] She journeyed to the capital in April to show it to La Martinière, La Peyronie's successor as the king's first surgeon, whom she no doubt knows from her last years practicing in Paris, and he suggested she show it to the academy. It is an age when such innovations are recognized and prized; they sometimes even reap financial rewards in the form of royal pensions, and she has been led to believe she might be entitled to one of these. Officials in Auvergne tell Versailles about the good works she has done in their region which make her deserving of recompense, stressing especially her "spirit of charity that leads her to seek out the poor."[7]

But what is happening to this "spirit of charity"? The midwife has been motivated, she explains, to develop this device out of *pitié*.[8] This sentiment, however, is not simply sympathy or compassion. It is, as the books of the day and the *Encyclopédie* explain, a generous natural feeling brought out in the relatively prosperous by the sight of those who suffer or live in misery.[9] There is, in other words, a latent condescension embedded in the concept. Somehow, the midwife's genuine calling to help these country women has reinforced her sense of superiority. The city-trained, modernizing midwife responds to the flocks of women who divulge to her their secret distress, and she gains their trust. But she then imposes on them a sophisticated diagnosis. As she sees it, ignorance is the culprit, and she with her mechanistic explanations of anatomy will serve as a vector of science, of progress. She seems increasingly shaped by the spirit if not the letter of the *Encyclopédie*, five volumes of which have now appeared. This influential work, so scathingly critical of midwifery as "superstitiously" practiced, may be inspiring her to create a very new and different image of her trade, one that is not folkloric but simple and free of danger, not secretive but transparent, not haphazard but professional. To promote her craft and win over its critics, she is reframing it using their conventions and language. She is always evolving new strategies.

That she refers to her obstetrical mannequin as a "machine" is telling. This is not an idiom that would naturally occur to her students, "mes femmes," as she calls them. They do not have, until they work with her, a mechanical view of birthing. The midwife is speaking here the language of enlightenment and reform, one well understood by the men she seeks to impress, but altogether foreign to her female pupils. Although she is grateful to the women for opening her eyes to a problem, for giving her a raison d'être, her own motives and agenda are shifting. Requesting unabashedly the reward she believes is her due for this invention, voyaging to Paris to defend her interests and make known her own new technology, the midwife puts a new spin on things. Her original altruistic devotion and a newer entrepreneurial zeal are conflating now. Thus far in her career her allegiance has been to the women, the mothers who seek her help and expertise, share confidences, bond with her. That was true in Paris, and has continued in her Clermont practice so far.

But with the introduction of the machine, by which she hopes to profit, some separating has necessarily begun. She is working on a different plane here, generalizing about bodies in the most impersonal terms. Since Descartes, writers in France have assumed that lack of freedom is inherent in all mechanical devices. He equated the animal body with an automaton, but to explain human free will he depended on his theory of the soul.[10] Where, then, is the soul in the midwife's mechanical teaching? What kind of message is communicated by the objectified pelvis she now deploys on such a grand scale? The animate individual, the person in the patient, the organic whole could start to fade from view if she is not careful. Does she realize any of this as, armed with the male establishment's official approval of her machine, she heads back to Auvergne?

11. Early Lessons

Clermont, July 1757

The midwife's lessons, developed in Auvergne over the last many years, are assuming an order and form that she will preserve, with only minor variations, throughout the decades of her teaching career, because she is finding that this method works. She reaches her students, makes herself understood, builds their confidence, and believes that by the end of her course she has imparted to them knowledge and techniques of real value. Her lofty self-assessment is shared by the subdelegate, who has eagerly accepted her offer to teach for free and is, as she puts it, "charmed to procure such a great good." There are about forty lessons. Each takes a day, so with weekends off the course lasts approximately two months.[1]

She begins, always, with a discussion of the qualities necessary in those women who mean to practice the art of delivery. Christianity is familiar terrain for her rustic students; she therefore starts out sounding more like their parish priest than the worldly Parisian expert that she is. There is a back-and-forth, give-and-take rhythm comfortably reminiscent of a catechism. Speaking in the inclusive *nous*, she talks as one of them, a member of their group, joined with them in a career of devotion and service. This immediate identification, this bonding in a common cause, at once relaxes them and makes them proud. "Penetrated by our Religion . . . we must do good works . . . care for the poor women who need our help . . . satisfy the commandment of loving God in his members."[2] The destitute, who fill the countryside, should never be abandoned for wealthier clients, should never be made to pay, should never be treated with bad grace or coldness. They must know that charity will keep their midwife by their side however long the labor might take. "Let us calm their fears, sympathize with their situation; it is the only way to console them. Let us endure a thousand inconveniences and all the disgust we encounter in their thatched huts; the recompense that God grants should give us the force and the courage to withstand all of it."[3]

These words might shock and even insult many of her students, who are themselves from humble hovels, but they have distinguished themselves by coming forth to complain about traditional rural delivery practices, by opening up to her, so the midwife has already elevated them into a select group deserving of her help. Yet that does not spare them further admonition. On the contrary, it allows her to be particularly hard on them, to speak plainly, and to spell out very firmly the high standards of conduct to which they will now be held. She warns once more against being seduced by the rich or rushing a birth for which there will be no payment just to get it over with. These, she says, are "hideous crimes," for negligence and haste often kill both mother and child. "Do we not know that these two victims were dear in the eyes of God, useful to their family, necessary to the State? They were a deposit entrusted to us. Can we, in sacrificing them to vile interest, not tremble at the exact reckoning we will need to give one day to [the creator] who gave them being?"[4] Another "crime" matrons sometimes commit ("that they try vainly to justify with virtuous-sounding sophisms") is refusing aid to a girl who gets pregnant out of wedlock. "We abandon her, and reduce her to despair; we force her, deprived of confidence and consolation, to kill an innocent whose mother's crime does not render unworthy of our attention." But it is not their place to be judgmental. Such self-righteousness, which would "leave nothing to divine vengeance," is unacceptable among midwives, who must instead "scorn prejudices so contrary to religion and humanity" and help these unfortunate girls and their illegitimate babies as much as possible.[5] The teacher will not tolerate intolerance. Even the misbegotten are precious.

God is featured rather centrally in this opening discussion, but the midwife sees her task as a secular one, and the tone of the lessons becomes now less pious and more practical. She moves on to the next pressing issue. "It should not be necessary to advise women never to become overly fond of wine, but midwives must be even more careful about this than others, as they can be called at all hours and must have a clear head so as not to expose the mother or the child to any danger."[6] *Bonnes mœurs* (high morals) are essential to win and to deserve the confidence of those who will need their services. With sober seriousness would-be midwives must undertake the conscientious learning of "things essential for the profession": the parts of the human body—at least those involved in delivery—and knowledge of the practice of the art. Such learning can be acquired four ways: by the thoughtful reading of good books containing all the precepts; by watching able people practice; by practicing oneself; and finally, by attending, as often as possible, anatomical dissections.[7] Here the teacher betrays her distance from these unlettered students, most of whom will never realistically have the opportunity to do either the first or last recommended step; she means, however, to impress them with the gravity of their chosen course. If they cannot read, or study anatomy in city classes, they are at a disadvantage and must be aware of their inadequacies and limitations. Nevertheless, she adds encouragingly, with the benefit of her lessons they can progress enormously, and be of great service.

This introduction to professional ethics behind her, the teacher now turns to the body itself. Here she alters her voice and tone; she is lecturing *to* them as an expert to novices. The next lessons concern basic anatomy, for which she uses large posters with pictures. One day is devoted to the womb, its muscular, membranous makeup and its situation in the pelvis between the bladder and the large intestine (this she also gives the common name, *gros-boyau*, by which her students know it). All the bones are named and discussed—some of them spread apart a bit during birth, some do not—as are ligaments and the endpoints to which they attach.[8] The womb must be demystified, understood, respected, treated gently; it is an anatomical organ, not a curse. Ignorant village matrons call it the "mother" and see it as the root of all evil, but that, says the teacher, is nonsense. Next the fleshy vagina is described, its length measured in thumbs. Students learn about the intact hymen and what it looks like after rupture. The lips, the clitoris, the *fourchette* (the area between the vagina and anus), and the perineum become familiar terms, as do the fallopian tubes and ovaries.[9]

There follows a brief and difficult lesson on theories of generation, in which the teacher introduces several technical terms and puts forth her view that the whole baby is preformed in miniature in the mother's egg and that with fertilization it begins to grow to a size and strength at which it can be born.[10] Although the midwife does not dwell on this notion because it has little practical import, she has, however unobtrusively, introduced an idea of considerable ideological significance. By placing herself squarely in the ovist camp, she has taken sides in a controversy over generation that is currently raging. The more popular position among her male contemporaries is the spermatist or animalculist view, which gives all the credit for reproduction to the male sperm swimming about in semen, discovered in the 1600s by Leeuwenhoek with the aid of his microscope. Misogynists tend to think of women as nothing more than a receptacle, whereas the midwife's ovist position, by privileging the egg, casts women as the life-producing force. We should not make too much of this, because she doesn't, but it is worth noting that her statement here is unequivocal and that if her students reflect upon this matter at all, they could feel a certain pride.

Discussion of the fetus, placenta, and umbilical cord come next, of circulation through arteries and veins, of systole and diastole, of amniotic membranes, of animal spirit in the nerves. All of this information on anatomical structure and physiological function is completely new to these students.[11] How to distinguish real from false pregnancy is the next lesson, followed by a very important one on the technique called "touching," "the touch," or palpation, with hands and fingers under the sheets, by which an aspiring midwife must learn to do most of her vaginal exploration and diagnosis. Indeed, a good midwife should be able to do an entire examination and birth blindfolded.[12] The need to bleed the pregnant woman is the next subject. Here the teacher goes along with the view, popular in obstetrics since the Renaissance, that bloodletting from the leg, arm, and neck at regular intervals is salubrious, relieving an excess of this humor.[13] The need for systematic bleeding, purging, and dosing to get rid of other surpluses in the body, and an introduction to the midwife's arsenal of herbal remedies, take up the next lesson. There are numerous cures, brews, poultices, potions, enemas, bouillons, and compresses that her students must learn how to administer. The last two classes on this introductory material concern tumors or other kinds of uterine growths—"a chaos with no mark of a child"[14]—that detach and get automatically expelled during the first three months, and miscarriages (called "abortions"), often caused by the failure to administer bleedings, or by straining at stool, violent coughing, anger, dancing, falls, blows, carrying heavy loads, riding in bouncing carriages, exercising too vigorously. There is, of course, no discussion at all of women willfully aborting their babies. In the case of a stillbirth, all attention is focused on checking for blood clots and making sure all parts of the dead child including the placenta are out so that the mother, at least, can survive.

Now the students are prepared to move on from foundations to the actual techniques of delivery. The teacher devotes the remainder of the course to developing the skill and dexterity of her students on the machine. Proceeding almost as if they were children, she patiently explains, repeats, then shows, and shows again, helping them to feel and visualize everything so that they will have the moves indelibly etched in their memories. First they spend several days on the normal presentation and easy delivery of the baby, with its head down and facing toward the mother's back. "Although great science is not necessary in natural delivery . . . there are still plenty of precautions to take during labor to ensure that favorable beginnings do not end badly."[15] Techniques for facilitating the baby's slippery exit from its "prison" are explained,[16] as are others for tying the cord. Lots of anecdotes keep the students interested, mostly concerning feats and rescues performed by famous Parisian *accoucheurs*.[17] After explaining the delivery of the placenta, the teacher focuses the students' attention briefly on the newborn child, the kind of care it requires, then back to the new mother, whose diet, hygiene, and toilette are all important for her speedy return to normal life.

Lest this process become entirely mechanical, the students *are* reminded now and then that they will be dealing with human beings, not cloth mannequins. "You must console [the woman] as affectionately as possible: her distressing state obliges you to; but you must do it with an air of gaiety that gives her no fear of danger. Avoid all whisperings [in the ears of others], which can only make her nervous and make her worry about bad things. You must speak to her of God, and engage her in thanking him for putting her out of peril. Avoid letting her do anything that will depress her. If she has recourse to relics, persuade her that they are just as effective on the bed beside her as on her body, where they might constrict her."[18]

The last half of the course is devoted to *l'accouchement contre nature*, malformations of the mother and malpresentations of the baby, whose unusual positions can result in tragedy if the practitioner does not know some basic anatomy and design her maneuvers accordingly. By now, the midwife's students have a good understanding of the pelvic basin, both its bony and soft components, so they know that extracting babies from many positions is physically, mechanically impossible. The child must therefore be moved around so that it *can* be delivered safely. Numerous lessons teach the students how to turn the baby, through a combination of external and internal pressures after detecting by means of touch that it is presenting abnormally—a shoulder, elbow, stomach, chest, heel, hand, knee, or chin. Nearly all of these presentations require podalic version and footling breech delivery. With the proper manipulations and positioning, a baby can almost always be safely extracted. And it is in that positive, activist spirit that the students work away at the machine, engineering the right lifts, twists, and turns.

But what about twins? Here one must be particularly careful.

Any time a student feels a left foot and a right foot presenting, before pulling them out she must check that they both belong to one baby. If instead she is holding one foot of each twin, it would be futile and fatal to pull. She will need to push them back in and search around until she is confident that she has found two feet of the same child.[19] Nothing can be assumed, everything must be verified. She also learns what to do if the cord comes out first, if the womb comes out, if the placenta detaches too early.[20] All of these reduce to clever, dexterous, speedy, confident maneuvers. The teacher reminds her students that in the villages from which they come, matrons and surgeons who lack this experience watch many children perish and "need to separate the head, or use hooks and ladles to go in and get the rest of the body out in pieces."[21]

The lessons end, as they began, on a sober, even pious note, away from the mechanics of birthing and back to issues of conduct, professional ethics, and morality. There are certain, very grave conditions that can follow a birth, such as lethargy ("a weakening of the whole animal economy"), convulsions, fevers, and hemorrhage, for which an able surgeon or doctor *must* be called in, to help the midwife or to take over completely. She should never fancy that she can handle such emergencies alone. Instead she prepares a full report of events leading up to the crisis and passes it on to the summoned expert. The teacher assures her students that with this deferential attitude they will win the cooperation of male practitioners. "I have found myself many times in . . . cases where, having called *habiles gens* [skilled men], I could ensure that no woman died [of the complications] and even that I often delivered their children alive."[22] As the lessons come to a close, the students are told that their final obligation is to secure a good wet nurse if they cannot persuade the mother to feed her own baby, which is best for all concerned. The nurse's character traits will almost surely be passed on to the baby she suckles, so she needs to be upstanding and without vice. "We should neglect nothing in informing ourselves about all these circumstances," and above all must refuse to accept bribes to influence the choice, which would be a "very great crime." All sorts of inquiries should be made in the little villages wet nurses come from, where gossips will gladly provide information about them. Every precaution must be taken so that, at the critical juncture when the midwife surrenders responsibility for the baby, she will have nothing to reproach herself.[23]

This, then, is what the teacher passes on to her numerous disciples. The course has a clear shape, a symmetry, beginning with the serious duties a midwife must assume, moving through the skills and techniques, and finishing with the rigorous, careful choice of a *nourrice* to whom the new life will be entrusted. Whether they can read or not, the students receive written copies of these lessons so that they or a literate person of their acquaintance can review them whenever necessary.[24] Throughout the course the word *accoucher* has been used, a transitive verb meaning "to deliver." Students have been taught, in other words, that they need to intervene and *do* things to the mother, deliver her safely with the aid of the art rather than assist her in delivering herself.

Yet, as the much more commonly used reflexive verb *s'accoucher* connotes, self-delivery is the deeply ingrained habit of the women these students will now go home to serve. They return to their villages armed with two months' worth of new theory and practice; but are they prepared to face the inevitable clash with centuries of country tradition? Do they or their teacher honestly imagine that they will be welcomed with open arms either by the matrons who, as part of a convivial team of mutually aiding friends and confidants, assist birthing mothers, or by those very mothers themselves, who take pride in controlling their own deliverance from nine months of bondage?

12. A FUTURE HERO

Chavaniac, 7 September 1757

Yesterday a baby was born here in the great château on the slope with its long flat front two stories high and its circular towers at either end. They say the birth took place in a chamber of the western turret that commands the valley and faces the violet rim of mountains on the horizon. The child's name is Marie Joseph Paul Yves Roche Gilbert du Motier. He is held at the baptismal font today by Paul de Murat, grand vicar of Sens, almoner of the dauphine, abbé of nearby Mauriac.[1] But it seems the midwife who delivered him yesterday was none other than du Coudray. She is a celebrity in Auvergne and must have been summoned all the way from Clermont, fifteen leagues northwest of here, because of her great reputation. Despite complications, she brought the child safely into the world. She has not stayed to preside at the baptism; no doubt the pressing business of her teaching called her back to the big city. But her niece will one day declare that du Coudray saved this baby's life. Had she not done so, he would not have grown up to become the marquis de Lafayette.[2]

13. TEXTBOOK AS PATRIOTISM

Clermont, January 1759

Le Boursier du Coudray's textbook, the *Abrégé de l'art des accouchements*, has just been printed in the capital. It is published on the rue St. Jacques by the widow Delaguette, official printer/bookdealer of the Royal Academy of Surgery, with royal approbation and privilege, and sells for 50 sous, or two and one-half livres. This is a momentous occasion; plans for the book have been in the works for years. Some ambivalence about the audience for the volume is evident in its full title (fig. 6): *Abridgment of the Art of Delivery, in which we give the necessary precepts to put it successfully into practice. We have joined to it several interesting Observations concerning singular cases. A work very useful to young Midwives, and generally to all Students of this Art who wish to become skilled in it.* The work is supposedly for women, but it is also for men; it is an abridged, practical manual, but it has added to it some stories of curiosities and freaks. For whom is this book intended? Why has the midwife chosen to write a book at all, when the vast majority of her country pupils cannot read?[1] Why has it suddenly appeared now, a year and a half after permission was first granted to print it?

An interesting series of events has led up to the midwife's decision to go public, to bother publishing, to become an author. Her successes in Auvergne have gradually emboldened her: the support of the intendant, the favorable reception of her machine in Paris, the popularity of her innovative lessons and demonstrations, her broadening fame. Yet her repeated requests for a pension, despite professed appreciation for her teaching and her invention in Versailles, have gone unheeded. Since France's 1756 entry into war with England the midwife has envisioned a larger role for herself, a grander kind of recognition. She has employed more and more the language of political significance to describe her work, has come to

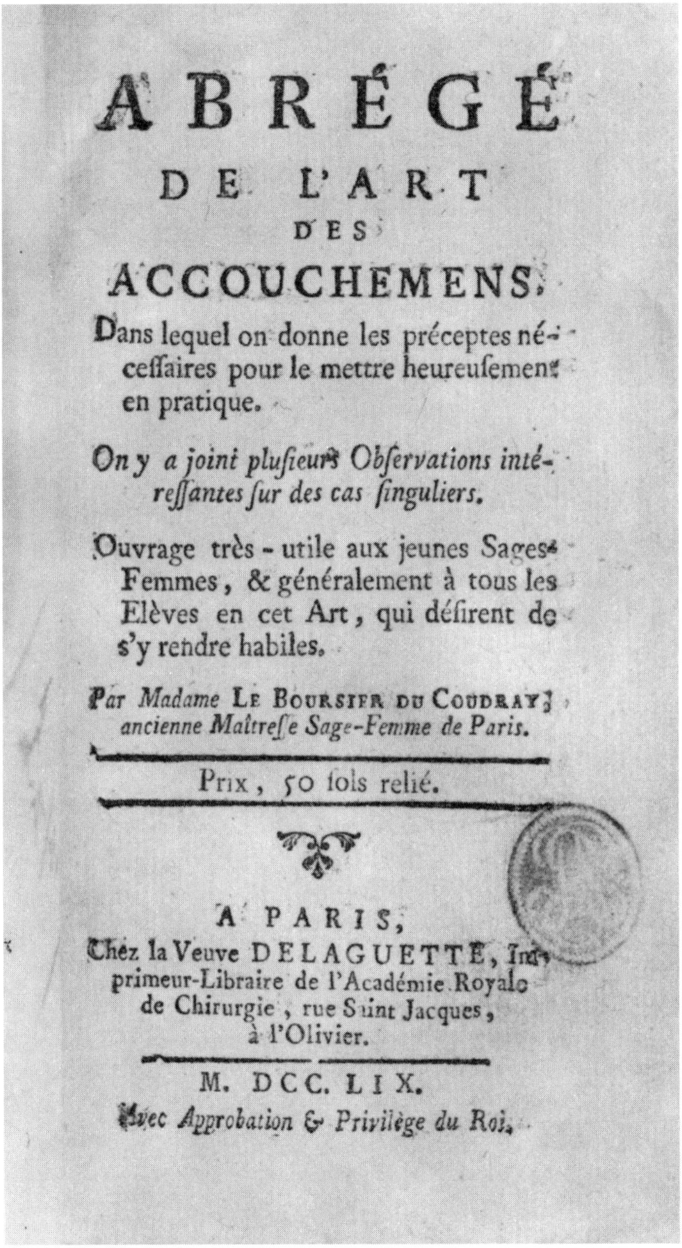

ABRÉGÉ

DE L'ART

DES

ACCOUCHEMENS,

Dans lequel on donne les préceptes néceffaires pour le mettre heureufement
en pratique.

On y a joint plufieurs Obfervations inté-
reffantes fur des cas finguliers.

Ouvrage très - utile aux jeunes Sages-
Femmes, & généralement à tous les
Elèves en cet Art, qui défirent de
s'y rendre habiles.

Par Madame LE BOURSIER DU COUDRAY,
ancienne Maîtreffe Sage-Femme de Paris.

Prix, 50 fols relié.

A PARIS,

Chéz la Veuve DELAGUETTE, Im-
primeur-Libraire de l'Académie Royale
de Chirurgie, rue Saint Jacques,
à l'Olivier.

M. DCC. LIX.

Avec Approbation & Privilège du Roi.

Figure 6. Title page for the first edition of Mme du Coudray's textbook (1759). This one had no illustrations and was published in
the 12° format to be inexpensive. There would be five subsequent
editions. Photograph courtesy of Special Collections, University of
Maryland Libraries.

see it as her patriotic duty to make her expertise more widely available. Saving future soldiers and cultivators of the earth for France is now crucial. Gradually she has reframed birthing as a matter of state.

In mid-1757 the midwife, who had already been writing up her lessons for some of her students, assembled them into a textbook and took them to Paris. She saw a new opportunity for her work. This was a difficult moment for the crown. Since the beginning of the war the Parlement had been resisting the new taxes necessary to finance it. The resulting disorder in the royal treasury had led to near chaos, and Damien's attempt to kill the king on 5 January 1757 only added to the sense that the monarchy's authority was disintegrating.[2] The midwife's book could perhaps make a small contribution to shoring it up. Presenting it in this light shortly after the regicide threat, she obtained approval to print the manuscript from the royal censor Morand, one of her former anatomy professors, on 2 July. That same month she wrote to the controller general reiterating her interest in a pension, this time placing her machine and now her book in the rhetorical context of patriotism and the war effort.

Apparently her timing was good, for suddenly things began to move. On 26 July Versailles informed the intendant of Auvergne that, although the financial demands of war made a regular pension for the midwife impossible, a handsome gratification would be forthcoming.[3] A month later, in connection with the imminent publication of the book, a gift of 400 livres was promised.[4] Although the actual appearance of the *Abrégé* has been held up this last year and a half—during which time her other old teacher, Verdier, added a set of notes and observations to her text, without attribution—the censor and *accoucheur* Süe has just last month given his enthusiastic approval to this longer version of the book.[5] And a flurry of correspondence has begun that will soon see the gratuity for the new author raised to 700 livres.[6] At the end of this year she will be charged by the king to launch a nationwide teaching tour. And as we already have seen, the bold "mission statement" letter she then writes to the intendants features the *Abrégé* centrally; in it she announces her authorship of a book on birthing before even explaining what the monarch expects her to accomplish on her travels.[7]

The *Abrégé*, then, is pivotal in the fashioning of the midwife's special part in the obstetrical mobilization of the country. She and the authorities in Versailles agree that the book is a passport granting her agency, absolutely necessary if she is to function in a more public capacity and figure not just locally but nationally in the modernization and medicalization of France. Participation in literate culture seems a sine qua non; it will enhance the professional status of her art. "It is to be hoped that *la dame* Du Coudray will send her book to the intendants as she promised me," reads one ministerial directive. As if to confirm the special validating impact of her text, one intendant, upon receiving it, will claim to his subdelegates that it is "imbued with all the authenticity necessary for meriting complete confidence in the lessons she gives."[8] There is no question that the book makes possible her navigation in the public sphere.

The midwife's transformation through authorship from a humanitarian into a political actor can be seen immediately in the book's opening dedication to the intendant of Auvergne, Ballainvilliers:

A little work of this nature will doubtless seem very strange and inappropriate for the important affairs you administer to so much praise. Nonetheless, I do not hesitate at all in offering it to you; everything that has some utility earns an author the right to your goodness and protection. You understood in an instant, Monseigneur, the advantages of the machine that I invented to facilitate the Art that I treat. Your love for the *bien public* encouraged my zeal, and I perfected an invention that pity made me imagine. The students you gave me occasion to train already prove in the countryside the usefulness of my machine . . . [and] many subjects worship the protector of the art who saved them from falling victims to ignorance. Your name, Monseigneur, at the head of this book will never tarnish the brilliance of eulogies posterity will owe you. It is no less glorious to watch over the conservation of His Majesty's subjects in the bosom of his realm, than to chase from his frontiers and destroy the enemies of his State.[9]

Thus support for the midwife's work is as significant as victory in battle. She is up there in loyalty and importance with military generals, sustaining and defending her country. They kill foes, while she repairs, restores, preserves life. They do warfare, she does welfare. In the "Avant Propos" she continues the same argument: "I have put together these lessons and am venturing to publish them today less out of presumption, which twenty years of experience might have inspired in me, than out of the desire to make myself more useful to my *Patrie* in this manner."[10] She claims, in a seeming contradiction, that "compassion alone made me an author," that empathy and identification with other females inspired her,[11] but she tries to reconcile that with her newer purpose. What began in Auvergne as genuine sympathy for the "pauvres malheureuses" (poor unfortunate women) has evolved into an understanding that the safe delivery of their offspring, of healthy future citizens, is of immense value to the nation.[12] France must be abundant and prosperous; children are an investment in that renewal. By the time the *Abrégé* appears in print, the midwife's focus has shifted significantly from mother to baby, her tone from sentimental to soldierly.

Some rather patronizing passages were added as the midwife assembled the book. In the lessons themselves she speaks as one with her students, but the printed *Abrégé* has numerous sections in which she speaks *about* them. "My whole object is to include in a few words the true principles of this Art and to present them from a point of view comprehensible to women of little intelligence. How many of these there are, who, without foreseeing any problem, meddle in childbirth, and how many unfortunates become the victims of this ignorance. . . . Since I do not write for the enlightened, I cannot err in expressing myself simply."[13] She consequently begs her readers not to pay attention to faults they might notice in her "diction," implying that her foremost desire is to convey useful information to these deprived rustics.[14] At the same time, she knows the book may be picked up by "more intelligent people likely to be interested in more extended instruction." For them she has added particular remarks (and the editor has added erudite footnotes) so the book can be read with "more satisfaction" and "more fruit."[15] After all, she is the bearer of city wisdom, of the latest obstetrical knowledge, which she will spread to *petits endroits* (small localities) but also way beyond.[16]

The midwife is trying to please many publics at once, including doctors, surgeons, and apothecaries. Seeking harmony with male practitioners, she acquiesces willingly to them, most of the time pointing the finger of blame at inexperienced or incompetent *bonnes femmes*.[17] The *Abrégé* is activist, interventionist, bold, but for all her confidence the midwife admits several times in the book to mistakes she nearly made, and praises the triumphs of great men in her field.[18] She has no airs, alienates no one, creates no sense of danger. Quite the contrary. She writes:

I ask the grace that I not be accused of passing myself off as a Doctor. I speak here only from a pure zeal for unfortunates deprived of all aid, either because the distance of the villages does not permit a doctor or able surgeon getting there in time, or because the poverty of these women prevents them from paying the suitable fees. It is in these pressing cases that I hope country midwives will be capable of giving the necessary help to women in danger. I cannot exhort them too strongly never to overestimate their supposed knowledge, and to be docile to the wise advice of experienced persons.[19]

Thus the author artfully constructs the image of midwives obedient to male medical authorities whom they will never challenge or compete with.

The Church must be placated too, of course. One of the first lessons her students learn is "the necessity of procuring baptism as soon as possible for those [babies] who seem ready to die."[20] She provides elaborate instructions for baptizing the child by syringe if getting it out alive seems impossible. "Child, if you are living, I baptize you in the name of the Father, the Son, and the Holy Ghost." Baptism must be given preventively to any child in abnormal presentation. "The time it will take to do this delivery could deprive the child of eternal happiness. We would reproach ourselves greatly if we neglected to do this." If all goes well and the baby survives to be taken to church, the priest must be informed that the private baptism (*ondoiement*) has already taken place.[21] Thus any ecclesiastical authorities looking over the *Abrégé* should be sufficiently convinced of the midwife's piety.

Most of all, she strives to write a book that bridges from group to group. She is female, but not antagonistic to men; Parisian, but adaptable to the provinces. She is superior, but never scornful of her students, conveying to them her conviction that they can learn to do what needs to be done to save numerous babies from the jaws of death. She is schooled, but not so urbane that she cannot appreciate the robust earthiness of peasants. She can use the common terms for body organs as fluently as the learned ones, and does. She can use units of measure from town or country, describing cervical dilation by the size of a coin here, the size of a fish's open mouth there. The midwife's book, as she says on the first page, is not an obstetrical treatise. Of these there have been many, full of theory, Latin terminology, and ponderous references to authorities from antiquity. The *Abrégé* is an abridgment, a different, new genre, a practical how-to manual, possibly the first of its kind in France. In fact, this text will generate a fad: short, clear, accessible childbirth booklets, often in question-and-answer catechism form, proliferate during the rest of the century.[22]

Journalists recognize immediately the usefulness of such a volume, reviewing it in the papers of the day. They sense the incongruity of the footnotes and the "Observations," which, written in a scholarly idiom and offer a titillating bit of the grotesque—dead babies that allegedly stayed in the unsuspecting mother several years, fetal bones found in a woman's excrement—really do not seem to fit with the practical text. (The editor of the *Abrégé* must have realized this himself, because after placing recondite notes in chapters 4, 9, and 10 he abandoned the idea completely.) The *Année littéraire* says the *Abrégé* contains nothing new for the learned but is helpful for those incapable of profound thought, and therefore it is good for humanity. It also recognizes how essential the publishing of a book is for the midwife if she aspires to practice her art nationwide.[23] The *Mercure de France* and the *Journal de médecine* herald the *Abrégé*'s appearance,[24] and Grimm's *Correspondance littéraire* remarks, "Here is the title of a useful work."[25] The *Censeur hebdomadaire* thinks it is wonderful, written with great precision. The tone is pleasing; the author writes "with a modesty that is the constant companion of true understanding, stripped of any vain parade of erudition." The work will surely help France, for midwifery is an "important function on which depends the hope, the strength, and the support of states."[26] The most enthusiastic review is in the *Annales typographiques*, a journal edited by three doctors. It explains in detail the great things du Coudray has been doing in Auvergne, including her ingenious machines. Prophetically, the reviewer hopes her "establishment" will spread everywhere and have many imitators. The book, a précis of her lessons, is "clear and methodical" and "contains all that is essentially useful in the art of delivery." The "Observations," on the other hand, which he recognizes instantly to be by a different writer, are "too erudite for the people for whom the *Abrégé* is intended."[27]

The *Abrégé*, then, has certainly attracted attention. In a time when women writers are mostly ignored and denied the courtesy of a reply, male reviewers at least do the midwife the honor of critiquing her. Hers is a fresh voice—something of a curiosity, but worthwhile.

Later, when she is on her mission and famous, when the novelty has worn off, newspapers will be far less charitable. Many will enter the lists against her.

The *Abrégé* is to become a key player in du Coudray's odyssey, a central character whose carefully timed appearances, in the form of five new editions over the next twenty-six years, will signal important developments in her life. This little volume serves its readers, but it definitely serves its author as well, now by establishing her reputation and catalyzing her mission, eventually also as a source of considerable revenue. She writes so as never to be dismissed as an empiric. Rather, she is an authority worthy of publicity and posterity, enhancing the ability of her readers, be they women or men, high or low.[28] Parts of it may appear to wildly flatter and overestimate her peasant audience, but she is aiming also at other publics, and she is being widely heard.

Of course, not everyone likes what they hear.

14. Protest from a Village Matron

Plauzat, 12 June 1759

The matron of this village near Clermont, one Brunet, has a mounted policeman banging at her door, a *cavalier* of the *maréchaussée*, serving her with an official warning from the intendant.[1] A spectacle of public embarrassment! What next?

About a month ago the king's man told the *curé* that only du Coudray's trainee should be allowed to practice in this town.[2] Ridiculous! says Brunet. That woman cranks out students from her classes in the big city; after a mere two months and some lessons on a cloth doll, they think they know everything! Jeanne Cureyas, handpicked by the *curé* Biron, attended the course in Clermont to profit from the new-fangled instruction and has just returned with a special diploma. Together the priest and the girl are trying to rob Brunet of her loyal following, she who has been helping mothers deliver themselves of babies in this parish for more years than she can even count. Because she won't bow down to a certificate, a stupid piece of paper, they call her a "rebel" and say she has ganged up on Cureyas, organized a "faction . . . cultivated in these parts by surreptitious practices and by secret calumnies."[3] Such fancy words!

A surgeon friend of Brunet's told her of these accusations. He understands, of course, that the parish women know and trust her, and he is not so fond of du Coudray himself; after all, her students get away without the exams and approval normally given to midwives by village surgeons. So he has written out a license of his own for Brunet allowing her to claim *she* is the one practicing legally, to turn the tables and make the young trainee look like the impostor.[4]

Oh, how Brunet resents that Cureyas woman. She had no business seeking out the class in the first place, complaining about village ways as crude and empirical, betraying her peasant stock. She has polluted the air, made sour feelings. And now she's always carrying around a book by her teacher. Probably she's just *pretending* she can read it. Or maybe, even worse, she really *does* read, and knows forbidden things. Maybe it's full of spells. After all, Cureyas managed a few tricky births when she first got back from her classes; it seemed almost like magic what she could do! Brunet wouldn't be surprised if she *was* a witch, with her nose in that book all the time, and plenty of other folks around here think so too. So now nobody's asking her for help anymore. To Biron the priest, who's completely on the girl's side, it seems unfair that she has no business. He pities and protects the pathetic creature. He blames her, Brunet, for turning everybody against Cureyas, reports to his higher-ups that the poor thing is "terribly afflicted," "leaves her house no more than a recluse," and is reduced to misery.[5] To Brunet's mind it's the girl's own fault. What did she and her big-shot teacher from Paris expect? What does that du Coudray woman know of our country ways anyhow? She carries on about the "ignorance" of us *femmes de campagne*, but we have traditions that date back ages and routines that work just fine much of the time without any help, thank you.

Brunet is not alone. Almost every parish in France has at least one matron (or *preneuse* [taker], *attrapeuse* [catcher], or *ramasseuse* [picker upper]), a trusted and familiar figure, secret keeper, sometime matchmaker, who helps mothers deliver the local children— or as they put it, "make new feet"—often with success. After all, these matrons have had numerous babies of their own, have experienced in their own flesh these labors. Sometimes they are paid by the village, like the shepherd. Usually they practice for a period of thirty to thirty-five years.[6] When the baby presents abnormally, or the woman's pelvis is too narrow, mother or child or both will die, but there is widespread resignation about death as a part of the birth process. The matron helps with that too, if need be, laying out the corpse, easing the eyes shut, dressing and preparing the body for burial. Among peasants there is an acceptance of things others might call tragic. More often than not, though, the birth works out all right. In spite of the hardships and dangers, most women want to get pregnant and have children. Everyone in the parish expects this, watches, waits, celebrates. Having babies is a normal life-cycle event, not a medical procedure. Of course there are anxieties and fears, but nobody here thinks of calling the expectant mother *la malade* (the patient), as du Coudray and her students do. From beginning to end, country pregnancies are marked by rituals and rhythms that evolved over hundreds of years and that feel comfortable, natural, right.

A clove of garlic slipped into the vagina tells a woman if she is with child or not. The next morning, if her breath smells of garlic, she believes she is not pregnant: a fetus would have blocked the diffusion of the characteristic odor. Sweet breath means there must be an obstruction and that she has conceived. Another woman consults a *uromancer*, a seer of waters, another listens for particular bird songs, another checks phases of the moon. Many wear amulets to prevent their baby from plunging into the world prematurely, and they try to avoid intense maternal desires and yearnings, which can scar the unborn. *Envie*, after all, is a common word for birthmark. To avoid the untimely birth of an "unripe fruit" or "dough not cooked long enough in its oven" women stay away from funerals, make sure their feet touch the floor when sitting, and refrain from working on the baby's layette. Prayers and vows to the Virgin safeguard the pregnancy, and pilgrimages are made to the shrines of Saint Margaret—they are numerous and scattered throughout France—where women walk around the baptismal fountain, press their naked navels to the statue, then continue to wear a cord or piece of clothing that has touched the holy relic. Some just soak a symbolic garment in a spring that is thought to be blessed. Many town churches have fertility stones that wishful mothers rub. The one outside Le Mans cathedral is especially famous, its hollowed pits worn by myriad fingers over the ages.[7]

During pregnancy peasant women take other precautions as well.

Most cannot afford cosmetic pomades to avoid stretch marks, but they slather themselves with animal-fat concoctions of their own devising. They continue to wear their usual clothes and wooden sabots (if they even have shoes) but try to get as comfortable as possible. To keep the bowels moving they prefer diet to enemas, eating combinations of leeks, spinach, honey, and prunes. Intercourse during pregnancy is thought to be the father's way of molding and imprinting the child, giving his stamp to the otherwise shapeless mass. Women long for a pink, hale, blond, curly-haired child with good complexion and bright eyes. They want sons, mostly, and it is amusing sport for friends and neighbors to divine if the baby is male or female. Is the mother rosy and merry, carrying high, with red, hard, raised nipples and her right breast firmer than the other? Then she will have a boy. If she is pensive, of dry and hot temperament, with paler, drooping nipples oozing dilute milk, then she must, alas, be about to give birth to a daughter.

Many country women work in the fields to the end and, surprised by the onset of labor, give birth unassisted right then and there. Others prepare more gradually and arrange to deliver at home. When the hour approaches, the communal room of the low-ceilinged dwelling (often the only room) is darkened and closed up tight against cold and evil spells. The birth takes place usually in front of the hearth. Bright flames from the fire scare away the night, when the souls of dead ancestors, attracted by the newborn's cries, beckon the baby to join them. Straw scattered before the fireplace absorbs excretions. It can be burned afterward, and if there is excessive blood, ashes conveniently soak it up. Numerous female relatives, neighbors, and friends surround the laboring mother in the warm, moist room, chattering, advising, exchanging recipes, drawing and heating water, supporting the woman, washing, sponging, drying linen. Later they will be there to hold and care for the baby, to sing it lullabies and ward off demons, to prepare cordials and broth. Each of these women has her own stories to tell: most are mothers themselves, and they try to calm their agitated friend as she labors. Unmarried girls are rarely allowed in; decency and custom dictate that virgins stay away. Only very exceptionally is the husband admitted to this collective drama, and if he is it is usually a bad sign, for these are cases where his extra strength is required, to push or pull more than is necessary in a smooth, normal birth. In extreme circumstances he may even mount his laboring wife to lubricate and open passages, to "shake the baby out" if it just won't come. Husbands, though generally excluded from the scene, have their own moods and sometimes do the *couvade*, going to bed themselves for attention, getting fussed over and waited on.[8]

The mother keeps an armory of comforts and puts her favorite talismans nearby or actually on her abdomen or thigh. The eagle stone shaped like a pigeon egg, which contains other smaller stones rattling safely inside it, symbolizes when worn high on the neck or arm a secure pregnancy and the certainty that the baby has been held in and carried to term. When pains start it is moved lower, to the thigh or foot, so its magnetic effect can now coax the baby down and out. A snakeskin belt is sometimes tied high up about the left leg, or a snakeskin broth might be sipped; since the snake sheds its skin with ease, it is hoped that this birth too will be easy. When labor begins the mother's hair must be styled; village women are convinced that the outcome of delivery is greatly influenced by how carefully they are coiffed.[9] The woman opens her mouth wide to let out the pain, to scream, grunt, cry, if it relieves her fears or makes her more comfortable. The father's hat, turned inside out, is placed upside down on the woman's stomach or vulva. The inversion signifies a reversal of the process whereby the man put the baby into the mother months earlier. She may clutch a mysterious, unopenable "birthing bag," containing saints' lives and prayers, secret, sacred, and safe like the womb itself. A dried Rose of Jericho placed in water near her swells and unfolds as it gets wet—a sort of vegetable vagina. This will, it is hoped, cause the cervix to dilate.

Various positions are assumed as the contractions intensify: sitting, crouching, kneeling upright or on all fours, standing, leaning forward with elbows on a table, reclining in a chair. Vertical positions are the most natural, the most instinctive; gravity seems to aid and hasten the birth. Squatting on her haunches or standing gives her an awareness of her body's pulses and changes, a way of watching the process, of helping the baby come down, even of welcoming the child as it emerges between her taut, sweating legs. She sees what's going on, and she can actively deliver herself. Lying high up on a bed is far less natural. Hardly practiced at all in the countryside, it removes the happening from the mother's control, restricts her freedom of motion; besides that, it fouls a set of bedclothes. Some women half sit, half lie on a straw mattress in front of the fire on the floor, supported under the armpits by a sister or friend, but this is rare because it is so awkward and uncomfortable for the birthing attendants. Mostly, such horizontal positions distance country mothers from the event in which they desire to have a major role.[10] They far prefer to be upright, and are often encouraged to climb stairs, walk around a table, even bounce, so that the baby will "fall into the world" like fruit from a tree.

The mother does not want to be captive any more to this pregnancy. The circle of women speak now of the baby as a parasite to which the mother has devoted more than enough time and energy. Her moment has come for relief, for freedom. If anything goes wrong with this birth, it is the baby who's guilty. The mother deserves now to help in her own liberation. With her long, hard pushing she makes a steady rhythm of rolling, heaving, guttural sounds. To hasten this last spreading of the flesh and bones, she is given drinks of wild herbs and roots. The matron works the parts, trying to subdue the womb, keep it from its wanderings, seduce it into place with perfumes, or egg yolks on the navel, or sweat from the husband's testicles rubbed into the vulva.

Finally everything gives, and the head appears, hairy, wet, long, lopsided, and shiny. One more push and the rest slides out, covered with its silvery, slippery, sweet-smelling film. Even once the baby is out, attention continues to focus on the mother. The placenta is actually called "the delivery," or "deliverance"; experience has shown that only with its complete expulsion is the woman out of danger. Peasants believe the fate of the placenta must never be left to chance. Animals generally eat their own afterbirth, and while few country women go that far, they certainly keep close track of it. Some bury it in the garden to ensure future fertility of the family and of the crops. Some save it, dry it, grind it into powder, and use it for medicine.[11] In many huts it seems to be fussed over more than the newborn!

And what of the baby? If it is born with the amniotic membrane, or "divine skin," draped over its head, there is wild rejoicing. The umbilical cord of a child so blessed must be saved, for it will bring its bearer every conceivable kind of luck. The ordinary child, not so lucky, is considered still unformed, its head, nose, hands, limbs malleable, adjustable. So it is pushed, stretched, flattened, and molded aggressively. If it is a girl, its nipples are pulled, pinched, and twisted, and its cheeks are pressed and poked where dimples should go. If it is a boy, its umbilical cord is left longer to encourage the penis to grow "to good measure." The baby is swaddled tightly and left for days at a time in the same wrap, still caked with its white, cheesy coating. This covering, combined with sweat, urine, and excrement, is naturally protective, it is thought, and creates a warmth that prevents crying.[12]

Village women practice this kind of mutual assistance or communal aid, helping one another in a constant exchange and crisscrossing network of favors. Usually the matron is presiding, though she is just one member of the group, a familiar, sturdy person with little or no formal training but lots of children of her own and thus plentiful firsthand experience. For her service she is paid, if at all, some eggs or cakes, a bread, a capon, some soup, fruit, or lard, some firewood or faggots, and of course hospitality and food as long as the confinement lasts. She comes whatever the hour or weather to tell reassuring stories. However robust, she is known for her nimble, supple, graceful hands. These matrons believe a birth should go quickly. If it's too slow, the mother will get exhausted and complications will ensue.[13] So they manipulate and stretch her parts, patting her vulva, massaging and pressing on her abdomen, rolling her from side to side, having her walk or even jump to dislodge the baby, keeping her active and involved so that she can deliver herself of her burden. Vomiting and diarrhea are induced to speed things along, to bring the woman through safely and fast. Loyalty is always to the mother. If a choice needs to be made between her and the child in a complicated birth, almost always the baby is sacrificed. Either it is born mutilated or dead, or it gets stuck in the birth canal and needs to be gone in after with spoons, knives, and hooks to be removed piecemeal. But this is almost never considered the matron's fault. The child was somehow just not meant to be.

Matrons like Brunet know what they know because they have watched and learned by doing, over the years. They might lack *savoir* but they have ample *savoir faire*; without any lectures or demonstrations on a model, they have figured things out for themselves. Situations, not theories, dictate their behavior. They have imitated and matched maneuvers their elders performed, at first helping in little ways, then, and most important, continuing to absorb and understand more fully as they grew up. Delivering babies is less a job than a way of life for them. Gradually they assumed new responsibilities, took over bigger parts of the workload from the older women, who showed them the way. They didn't have to ask a lot of questions because they were learning all the time, driven simply by what needed to be done. As years go by they become competent in longer stretches of the process, more central, complex jobs. Their elders have guided their hands, so that they *feel* the baby somersaulting in the abdomen, *feel* the head crowning, *feel* the life flowing from the mother through the pulsating cord. No need to be praised or blamed; they know how they measure up.

There is much talk, always, but these women offer stories, not lectures. At difficult births they relate similar cases they've seen or experienced themselves, pooling suggestions, deciding collectively what's best to try next. Stories bind this community of women together, but they also serve to identify and legitimize the matron, move her out of the shadows toward recognition in her own right as the wisest one. She must inspire confidence; it cannot be imposed. Then, even though mothers mean to do the big work of birthing themselves, they want her to be there.[14]

Brunet has earned her following in just this way. But now along comes du Coudray with her students to turn the matron's world upside down. Have these girls learned as they grew up, do they work out of connectedness with the women of the village? Of course not. They've had a government training course, that's all. And they have picked up some pretty crazy ideas, calling the mother the "sick one," making her lie down passively and surrender to her deliverer, caring far more about the survival of the *child* than the woman! They pretend to know all about anatomy and mean to charge for their services. But really they have just memorized a bunch of rules, manipulated a rag doll, gotten a piece of paper, and that's the sum total of their experience. Cureyas is one of them. She is young, has done nothing to win the trust of the village women. She has never heard their lamentations, welcomed their offspring, escorted them to the baptism at church, advised them about teething or how to wean the baby when the time comes. She has no knowledge of any of these repeated rituals and life passages. Yet for this upstart Brunet is supposed to step aside.

The king's man and the priest threaten her with "various penalties" for just going about her business, doing what she is and always has been expected to do.[15] It sounded pretty vague to her at first, and she doesn't take it seriously—until today, when she is told by the horseman at her door that if she persists in delivering babies she will have to pay a fine of twenty livres. And it gets still worse. If she temporarily complies, and then tries to start working again when the whole fuss blows over, they will throw her in jail for "recidivism"! They'll know, of course, that she has resumed her activities if she shows up at a baptism, for who else presents a child at church but the one who catches it?[16] So she's trapped for the moment, hands tied (almost literally), and furious at du Coudray for ever coming to Auvergne.

2

Saving Babies for France

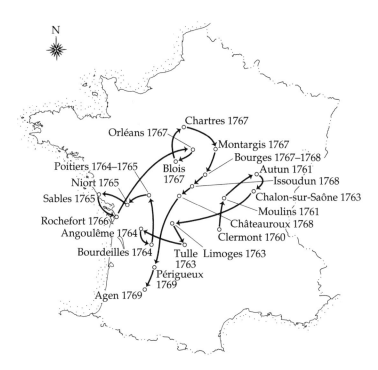

15. Royal Brevet: "Sent by the King"

Versailles, 19 October 1759

France is still in the midst of the devastating series of battles eventually to be known as the Seven Years War, and the government is obsessed, as always in a military crisis, with how badly it needs soldiers. But this time the problem is felt acutely. Whereas the War of the Austrian Succession had ended in something of a stalemate with England in 1748, now France is losing its possessions and influence throughout the world. The king's troops are dying in Canada, India, Minorca, Hanover, Westphalia, Senegal, the Mississippi basin, the Caribbean. Mutilated, crippled veterans, the pathetic survivors who return, are an increasingly common sight. The war, an utter rout, is pushing up both debt and taxes, pushing down morale. It is a catastrophe.

Since the Regency, the nation has been alarmed about what it perceives as a rapidly plummeting population. Montesquieu's *Persian Letters* in 1721 had dealt at some length with this matter. Many reasons have been suggested for the decline: the celibacy of Catholic priests, the "fanaticism" that forced Protestants to flee after the revocation of the Edict of Nantes, slavery in the colonies, the waste of lives in war, the debauches of luxury, the fact that most domestics in the cities do not marry, the neglect of agriculture, the impossibility of divorce and re-pairing.[1] But high on the list is infant mortality, the flagrant waste of human life at its very start. This, it is agreed, must be stopped. Women's bodies have as a result gradually come to be thought of as a kind of national property, somehow coming under the stewardship and use rights of the state, counted on to ensure the regular fecundity of society. Married women are considered morally obliged, patriotically bound to perform the public function of producing citizens. The fertility patterns and reproductive capacity of the country poor in particular are under close surveillance. Children are now discussed almost as commodities, building blocks of the state's prosperity, their safekeeping a central economic concern. Raulin's *De la conservation des enfants* is one of several best-sellers on the subject. The death of babies is viewed more and more as a public crime, a form of lèse-majesté.[2]

Today, in this connection, the king officially launches the mid-wife's nationwide teaching mission. He issues his *Brevet en faveur de la Demoiselle Boursier du Coudray sage-femme*, a special reward for her fine practice of midwifery, her machine, the great success of her work in Auvergne, all of which make her richly deserving of His Majesty's protection. But he has much more than mere thanks in mind. He now desires that her zeal, her talent, her knowledge, be "liberally distributed" throughout France, under royal patronage and protection. She is to travel freely wherever she judges appropriate, "without encountering, for any reason, trouble from any person or under any pretext whatsoever." Intendants, *commissaires départis*, officers, *justiciers* and all other administrators must see to the execution of this brevet. The king signs, to show this is his will and it must be obeyed.[3]

For nearly a decade the royal ministers have heard reports of the midwife's uncommon gifts, and since the outbreak of hostilities with England in 1756 they and Frère Côme and the intendant of Auvergne seem almost to have been readying her for this national task. Le Boursier du Coudray has cooperated fully. Her work teaching huge numbers of midwives in the Clermont region, already legendary, fits right into this pronatalist program. The king knows of her dedication, loyalty, and special talents. And he makes what turns out to be a smart bet on her ambition and herculean energy. Is it any wonder that he would select her to enlighten all of France and press her into service for the crown?

The royal brevet is both less and more than the midwife expected. Although she has hoped for years to be promised some ongoing monetary pension, the king still does not give her that regular salary. But the brevet *is* a veritable consecration of her work, turning her skill into a national institution. It recognizes officially the moral and political value of what she is doing, safeguarding her and her students, at least in principle, against the kinds of problems they have just encountered in Plauzat. Not that one can legislate emotions. But the spirit of the brevet is to clear the way for this mission and to signal and warn anyone who would openly, flagrantly, thwart it. A grand destiny has just been sanctioned for the midwife "demoiselle" by the monarch himself. And she will not let anyone forget it.

It is worth pausing on this, because the men with whom the

midwife deals, unaccustomed to receiving directives from a woman, will naturally have mixed feelings about her. They admit her skills, some graciously, some grudgingly, but all want to be sure that she doesn't somehow escape from their control, that she remain linked to them or beholden to them in some permanent way. An autonomous woman is unthinkable in this period, a massive threat to the corporate structure, and their willingness to accept and cooperate with her at all comes from their confidence that they can rein her in when necessary, can maintain mastery. This preoccupation is seen at every turn. Even Frère Côme needs to boast that it is he who superintends and manages her travels.

Examples of attempts to circumscribe her abound. The *Abrégé* itself was held up until a former teacher of hers, Verdier, could attach to it his thirty-five-page "Observations sur des cas singuliers." The first censor of the original manuscript, Morand, had been supportive but with qualifications, saying of the book only, "I think it very useful to midwives of the countryside incapable of more extensive instruction."[4] With the additions by Verdier—the "Observations" refer to seventeen famous obstetrical authorities and cite many books, scholarly journals, and proceedings of learned academies—the second censor, Süe, a master surgeon and *accoucheur* himself, can say not only that the work is useful to provincial and city midwives, but that it has been raised to a loftier plane.[5] In fact, between the time of Süe's approval and the actual pressing, the male editor had decided to bind the "Observations" in the *front* of the volume. The midwife has been encouraged by men to write her book, but they want to have the last (or in this case, first) word.

Other men, similarly, do not want the midwife to get away from them, to slip beyond their grasp. On the ministerial level Silhouette, the controller general, and two other ministers of state, Bertin and Ormesson, have repeatedly explained that because of military expenses no regular yearly payment to the midwife from the Royal Treasury is possible. "The problem is that the time and circumstances are not propitious for obtaining new favors at cost to the state."[6] But this is only part of the reason for the denial. She might start to take her position for granted. Ormesson in particular feels this way. "It would be appropriate to vary this bonus each year according to greater or lesser service this woman gives to the province . . . so that [the payments] are always regarded as graces which, however small they may be, must nevertheless continually be earned."[7] Ormesson is going to make her sing for her supper, now and later.

The king's first surgeon, La Martinière, has the same desire to simultaneously approve and check her, and to reaffirm his superiority. If she is not sufficiently diffident to surgeons, he warns, she will be perceived by the profession as a menace, and ruined. "Her machine has its merits for speaking grossly to the eyes of women from the countryside who would not be able to obtain more solid instruction. But in the opinion of the masters of the art, it lies always far below the knowledge furnished by good theory."[8] The intendant of Auvergne, the marquis de Ballainvilliers, who understands the midwife quite well and knows how good she is, has quipped to Versailles that surgeons are clearly threatened by her or they would not seek to disparage her. But even he believes she must be reminded of her place. He is genuinely supportive of her and extremely proud to initiate in his province this pilot program. As one of the first architects of her planned road show, however, he introduces a decisive twist that will have lasting impact. From the beginning he stipulates that the midwife must teach not only village women but regional surgeons as well. The king's brevet mentions nothing about the training of men, but Ballainvilliers has decided men would be safer depositories for the machine, better able to perpetuate her method. Otherwise a vast, controlling corps of exclusively female teachers would be created. Male surgeons learn faster than women, he asserts, and so should be guardians of the obstetrical models, which they will use when they in turn become demonstrators after the midwife's departure.

Ballainvilliers has certainly finessed this. Female students will now learn to practice, but never to instruct. The true professors, the ultimate possessors of the spoils, will thus always be men. A copy of the mannequin must be kept untouched in the Hôtel de Ville of each town where a surgeon disciple plans to give his courses. This will serve as an enduring reference, for the demonstration models suffer wear and tear and will need to be repaired and rebuilt according to the pristine original. To the suggestion from a doctor in Brioude that this system might fail, that women might hesitate to take lessons from a "garçon," Ballainvilliers replies impatiently: "Those who know and truly love the good will not sacrifice it to a displaced modesty and will go in search of it wherever it is."[9]

He is wrong. The courses set up by surgeons for midwives in nearby Ambert, Arlanc, Aurillac, Brioude, Mauriac, St. Flour, and Thiers attract mostly male students, and not very many of them either. Within a few years these classes will die out completely.[10]

What is the effect on Le Boursier du Coudray of all this engineering of her mission by men? She seems not to be bothered in the least. If she wants to call attention to gender imperatives in her personal or professional development, this would be the time. She could parlay her prominence into something more, defend midwifery from encroachments by men, engage in the period's major debates on education and women's intellectual capacity. Still a "demoiselle" according to the brevet, she could celebrate economic independence and alternatives to marriage. But doing so would destroy her chances for success. Why frighten precisely those people who give her this unique opportunity? Far from flaunting her spinsterhood, she pretends to be married, renaming herself "Madame" to conform to a familiar image and set men at ease. To preserve this unprecedented place for herself in public life, she can easily accept a few conditions. She is, of course, the ultimate beneficiary of this strategy, and she knows it. Compliance will earn her the freedom to do something singular. The royal brevet authorizes her, as no other woman has ever been, to represent Louis XV's will throughout the kingdom. It gives her carte blanche to travel freely "wherever she judges appropriate." From now on she sees herself as a man of action. She is not at odds with male domination in medicine and politics—as long as some very special room is made for her, as it now seems to be. She will make history.

Over the last decade, then, a profound metamorphosis has been taking place. The midwife seemed restless in Paris, but during these Clermont years she has honed old skills and discovered new ones, developed a courageous vision and a strong sense of calling. Her evolution has led from private practice to public service, from monotonous routine in Paris to mobility and adventure in the countryside, from personal mentoring of an occasional apprentice to group teaching of hundreds by means of an innovative pedagogy, from relative obscurity to celebrity as the trusted agent of His Majesty. Once a neighborhood healer, she is about to become a national star.

Ascendant now, she need no longer address the king's men as "Monseigneur" the way she did Ballainvilliers in the *Abrégé*'s dedication, but simply as "Monsieur." She and they are patriots, doing the monarch's bidding together. Hence her unquestioned assumption, that we have already seen in her earliest known letter announcing her mission in 1760 to all the intendants of France, that she is unassailably their equal.

16. Traveling for His Majesty

Moulins, November 1761

Mme du Coudray—she has now shed her former name—has just finished her first invited teaching visit in her new capacity as the king's official emissary, one hundred kilometers north of Clermont in Moulins. This Bourbonnais region feels harmonious in late autumn, with its low-roofed farm houses and narrow snaking valleys. Over the centuries Moulins's imposing chateau has attracted numerous kings of France, perched high as it is above the rich town. A grandiose stone bridge, one of the greatest engineering feats of Trudaine's administration, attaches the city to its *faubourgs*.[1]

The midwife has been here since the beginning of the year, at the enthusiastic invitation of the intendant Le Nain, who learned a lot about the childbirth courses and about du Coudray herself in an exchange of letters with Ballainvilliers.[2] (Such intense lateral correspondence between intendants is noteworthy in this supposedly centralized administration, and in the case of the midwife will become a common practice during the next twenty-five years as they jockey for positions on her itinerary.) Le Nain appreciates her enormously. Enthralled by her talent and person both, he feels lucky and proud to be among the first to secure her services, for every intendant has by now received the letter in which she presented herself to the world. He has had the perspicacity to snatch her up before she gets too far afield, has even housed her as his guest in his own official residence,[3] and has printed a *Mémoire sur les cours publics d'accouchements*. Together they are sending this brochure around to all his colleagues, as a model for how her teaching in each new region should be organized. It is the first endorsement in her portfolio, and she will continue to use it to introduce her method of instruction for many years to come.

Le Nain's *Mémoire* is a detailed advertisement for du Coudray's work in the "conservation of citizens."[4] It first describes the unnecessary loss of productive subjects caused by ignorant midwives, the death of mothers and babies, the huge number of maimed children and women so mangled in their first delivery that they are incapable of bearing children again. "It was very easy to feel the extent of this evil, but very difficult to find a remedy," for most highly trained midwives who might have been helpful refuse to live in the "miserable countryside." But du Coudray, as "inventress" of a teaching machine, came to the rescue. Here in Moulins, Le Nain writes, "the infinite good she has brought has far surpassed our hopes." He offers himself as a consultant for anyone who wishes to learn more about du Coudray's services and his successful formula for the running of the course. The midwife's stay, including rest periods before and after classes, lasts about three months. The king pays only for the establishment of the course itself. Communities must provide for their own students; lords, parish priests, subdelegates, and magistrates in charge of each town should all actively recruit suitable candidates to come profit from the "bountifulness of the king."

All this is not, however, as easy as it sounds. Here Le Nain betrays the typical intendant's condescension for his rural charges. "We know only too well the indolence of the provinces even for the most obvious good, if it requires the slightest expense." One must insist, never give up, write letter upon letter, until the money is finally raised. Such repeated efforts on Le Nain's part brought eighty subsidized students to du Coudray's first course in Moulins; the second, with seventy, was slightly smaller because the timing conflicted with harvesting and many women were not free to leave their farms. Thirty-six or forty livres amply support such simple women during the course and even pay for their certificates at the end. Some students show no aptitude and are sent home; a few truly stand out. The majority learn just the basics, but this suffices to make them extremely useful in their villages. The teacher works them hard, yet she has realistic expectations and does not intimidate. Classes take place six days a week all morning and all afternoon and last two months, so that every student has plenty of time to listen to the lectures and then practice each maneuver repeatedly on the machine. There is even some training in live births as well; indigent women of the town, attracted by the midwife's enterprise, volunteer to be delivered by the best in the class while the teacher comments and the others look on. The midwife will, of course, not allow any woman to graduate whom she finds inadequate to the task.

"The gentleness and patience of Madame du Coudray, the singular talent she possesses to make herself loved, is what contributes the most to spreading the fruits of her lessons." Le Nain is struck by how these young women are drawn to her, how she can attract and spellbind. He adds a further incentive: prizes for the three best students. Graduates leave the course armed with a special license to practice as midwives, approved by the Moulins surgeons for a tiny fraction of their customary charge. Le Nain is especially grateful to these men for cooperating, not a thing to take for granted; the tender vanity of surgeons will be an ongoing problem.

Du Coudray herself has been paid 300 livres for each month of her teaching, and Le Nain suggests an additional 600 as a bonus at the end. Each machine costs 300 livres to construct, which some towns pay to the midwife not in silver but in the form of a gift worth a still higher price. Le Nain says that "these presents please her much more than money, because she regards them as emblems and as testimonies of her successes." He suggests that provinces with an easier tax burden, the *pays d'états*, should be even more generous to du Coudray when her travels take her there. Her motive, "not interest, but . . . an ardent zeal for humanity," should be encouraged. All must work together "to conquer the indifference of people for anything without instant results. . . . It is true that M. Le Nain made it a capital point to support this establishment, that he neglected nothing to encourage the Mistress and her Disciples, that he barely let a day go by without appearing at the course; this method succeeded for him, and he thinks it essential to follow."

The *Mémoire* is a disingenuous maneuver on Le Nain's part. It does indeed promote the midwife's work, but it accomplishes two other significant things as well. First, it unabashedly flaunts, to authorities at Versailles and elsewhere, this intendant's good behavior. He has been totally attentive to the fledgling mission, rallying loyally to the king's wishes. Second, it states baldly that women are entirely to blame for the population crisis, conjuring up the specter of filthy peasant crones and superstitious mutterings. Du Coudray's *Abrégé* had been somewhat more evenhanded, implicating foolhardy surgeons as well as matrons in the carnage. But she has not been forceful on the issue of protecting women, having acquiesced with no sign of struggle to Ballainvilliers's idea of making male surgeons the exclusive depositories of her machine. Now, once again without apparent objection from her, Le Nain has placed her in an adversarial role against other women, has worded things in such a way that du Coudray seems co-opted into the patriarchal camp.

Why has the midwife agreed to this? In order to generate support she must distinguish herself from the feminist midwives of her day, whose polemics have reached fever pitch lately. Just last year the Englishwoman Elizabeth Nihell, who trained in the early 1730s under Mme Pour at the Hôtel Dieu in Paris, published her *Treatise on the Art of Midwifery: Setting Forth Various Abuses Therein, Especially as to the Practice with Instruments*. An impassioned attack on male obstetricians, this book is creating a huge stir in London and now, ever since its review in the *Journal encyclopédique*, is much talked about in France as well.[5] Nihell is deeply convinced that men have no place in the birthing business, that they are in it only for greed and gain. She is particularly hostile to their use of forceps and other instruments, their rash, rough, rushed approach. She witnessed two thousand births during her training at the Hôtel Dieu, all but four safely concluded without the help of any man.[6] *Accoucheurs* are, she claims, a "band of mercenaries who palm themselves off upon pregnant women under cover of their crochets, knives, scissors, spoons, pinchers, fillets, speculum matrices, all of which and especially their forceps. . . . are totally useless."[7] Nihell makes venomous personal attacks against some very distinguished surgeons of the day. Far more deaths, she argues, are attributable to the presumption, interference, and clumsiness of men than to the ignorance of women.[8] Midwives must reclaim their "ancient and legitimate profession." They should never even teach men their art because these men will turn and betray them; male hearts are as "false as they are ungrateful."[9] The English author speaks of a powerful female bonding, "a certain shrewd vivacity, a grace of ease, a hardiness of performance, and especially a kind of unction of the heart, . . . that supremely tender sensibility with which women in general are so strongly impressed toward one another in the case of lying-in." Male practitioners—"cold," "awkward," "stiff," "unaffectionate, perfunctory"—work like technicians *on* women, whereas midwives work *with* women—this is what the word literally means— guiding, caring, boosting morale.[10]

Nihell's sarcasm and anger contrast markedly with the silence of du Coudray, whose instincts have told her from the beginning not to defend a separate professional space for women. It is of course true that by training women she enables them to move from marginal means of subsistence to greater financial security and social esteem, but du Coudray never says so. Such fighting words would only alarm. Instead she pledges to train any and every person willing to join the government's drive against infant mortality. This is the language to which administrators of the monarchy will listen and rally. Her avoidance of explicit female advocacy, her apparent denial of such identification, certainly seem to compromise her feminist credentials. But that she might be seeking similar goals by other means has to be considered. Remember that long before her celebrity she freely chose a profession that brought her intimately close to other women. They are never very far from her mind, and the bonds are there, articulated or not. By using skill, not gender, as the key to her image as a practitioner, by stressing competence and control as criteria that elevate her students above the rest, she is suggesting that obstetrical ability can be cultivated in *any* person. The leveling implications of this message are powerful, and may serve "her women" better in the long run than Nihell's belligerence.

Du Coudray, then, allows Le Nain to shape and reinforce her role. Invigorated by this first experience performing for such large numbers of students, 150 in all, she presses on now, entirely committed to the nationwide tour. Le Nain's is the kind of enlightened local support she realizes she will need but will not always find. Meanwhile this intendant, truly smitten, never stops praising her—always mindful, of course, that by supporting her the king's administrators can help not only the country but also themselves. Even years later when taking the waters at a thermal spa where he meets a colleague, he will rave about her mission, inspiring the other man to invite her to *his* region immediately upon returning home.[11]

17. Boasts, Rebuffs, and Boutin

Chalon-sur-Saône, 19 March 1763

Monsieur,

Monsieur the Controller General, attentive to all that contributes to the good of the state, especially to conserving its subjects, orders me to have the honor to write to you about the establishment of educated midwives for the security of villages. I am sending you the Mémoire of M. Le Nain, which is as interesting as it is instructive and which will spare me having to tell you all the details of this establishment. I have completed all the engagements I had with M. de Villeneuve, whose happy successes have brought him as much admiration as gratitude from the citizens. I am free, Monsieur, and I urge you to give me an answer as promptly as possible. I know the secretary of state desires that I bring the good that I do particularly to your province. I must give him an accounting of the time I spend fulfilling his wishes. He does not permit me to waste any. He would even want me to be everywhere if that were possible. You see, Monsieur, that your delay in replying would make me lose time that is too dear to the good of humanity, and I would worry that the minister of state who honors me with his benevolence and with his confidence will suspect my zeal of a slackening of which I am not capable.

I have the honor to be, with respect, Monsieur, your very humble and very obedient servant

du Coudray[1]

It is spring. The midwife, writing today to the intendant of Bordeaux, has spent the last year and a half traveling and teaching in Burgundy, the region administered by J. F. Dufour de Villeneuve. Courses have gone well in Autun, with its Roman gates and theater; in Bourg-en-Bresse, with its unique timber-built farmsteads and "saracen" chimneys; and now at Chalon-sur-Saône.[2] This city, where Peter Abelard famously died—the locals talk of it still—has been an important market town since the Middle Ages; each year before Mardi Gras the fair attracts trappers from all over to trade in pelts. Extraordinary wines, cultivated for centuries by Cluniac and Cistercian monks, enhance this region's fame.[3]

Du Coudray is very pleased with herself, indeed elated. During the six invited courses taught in this region she has trained more than four hundred students.[4] Some, just recently examined by the surgeons of Dijon, passed their tests with flying colors.[5] She sees already what a difference her teaching makes, how highly she is regarded. Increasingly privy to information and directives from Versailles, she is not always as tactful as she might be in handling these confidences. It is thought, for example, that the Bordeaux region is unusually backward in its practice of midwifery. Upon learning this, the midwife decides she should hasten there next, even though it is far away. In this overzealous letter du Coudray therefore foists herself rather boldly on Boutin, the intendant of Bordeaux, crowding him, rushing him to answer, insinuating that he requires her services more than do others, brandishing Le Nain's *Mémoire* so that she need not bother to explain herself, anticipating how much Boutin's hesitation will inconvenience her, blaming him in advance for slowing down her mission of salvation, almost threatening to report him. Carried away by her increasing importance, heady from the authority vested in her, she makes her first diplomatic blunder.

Deeply affronted, the administration of Bordeaux reacts badly to this woman's imperious tone, her brazen self-promotion. Is it because a female presumes to speak for the government? Is it her insulting suggestion that Bordeaux is in worse shape than other areas of the country? Boutin does not feel it is for her to judge, and finds her display the height of insolence. The intendant's secretary responds that they will not be needing her services, thank you. "We can very well do without Mme du Coudray at Bordeaux."[6]

It is not as simple as that, however. What Boutin fails to realize is that one does not refuse the services of the king's midwife and get away with it. Just last month the Treaty of Paris put an end—albeit a humiliating one—to the Seven Years War; ministers can therefore pay more attention to domestic issues now. France, licking her wounds, her international prestige severely damaged, is determined to put at least internal affairs in order. The controller general Bertin immediately defends du Coudray and presses Boutin to explain his reasons for snubbing her. What has caused his embarrassing stance against the royal midwife? Has some ill-informed party prejudiced him against this worthy woman?[7] Reprimanding him and urging him to see the situation clearly, the minister suggests Boutin try straightway to undo the damage of his rebuff.

And the damage is great. Du Coudray is coming to see her work and the good of the nation as one and the same. She experiences Boutin's slight as both a personal rejection and evidence of the man's political obtuseness. He is trying to obstruct the *bien de l'humanité*, a phrase she first uses in this letter but which is to become her rallying call, a synonym for her mission. As she does not suffer fools gladly, she will hold a grudge against Boutin for years. It will give her enormous satisfaction to humble him as an object lesson for others who might neglect to pay her the proper respect.

18. TURGOT

Tulle, 29 December 1763

Rather than put up with the indignity of trying to go where she is not wanted, du Coudray has accepted an eager invitation from Turgot, the energetic thirty-six-year-old intendant of the Limousin, and traveled to the capital city of Limoges in late spring. This land is a mosaic of greens with its meadows, grass, dense forests, and fern fronds, yet it is a poor, backward area for agriculture; most live on a coarse bread made from buckwheat, rye, or barley oats. The only plentiful crops are chestnuts and coleseed.[1] Turgot is pressing hard to introduce a new food, the potato, but so far it is not catching on.

In this intendant du Coudray has found someone whose zeal surpasses even her own. Already now, more than a decade before he will become controller general of France, Turgot is undertaking numerous reforms in the area over which he presides, initiating new farming methods and improving roads, bridges, and mail transport, but especially making such taxes as the *taille* and the *corvée* less burdensome for the poor. He has brought du Coudray here to his region with great fanfare, first to Limoges, an old city of mud-wall houses whose roofs jut out so far that one can barely see the noonday sun. The locals, however, are not known for politeness or openness to new ideas. A contemporary guidebook even comments that the intendant, who has his main residence in this town, will, alas, not be much enriched by his contact with the Limousins.[2]

And at times his task *is* thankless, but Turgot is not one to give up. In August he had bristled at the small turnout for du Coudray's first course, castigating his underlings for not advertising her coming or organizing things properly, berating the "deplorable nonchalance" of subdelegates, priests, and parishioners who had failed to find enough students to take advantage of this stellar opportunity. He shared his impatience with officials in Paris. "I will not hide from you that I am afflicted that they did not profit from the important service I wished to render. I want, however, to make it available again so they may make up for their negligence."[3]

Realizing then that a favorable welcome for the midwife could not be taken for granted, Turgot has ever since been relentlessly shaming both secular and religious leaders of surrounding towns into raising enough money—he estimates a mere 28 livres can support a student in town for two months—to send women from as many parishes as possible to the courses. When du Coudray moved from Limoges to Tulle to begin teaching a new group of students on 15 November, the intendant had been careful to anticipate and compensate for the notorious stinginess of this town.[4] Tulle residents have a reputation as quibbling, peevish, and disobedient.[5] Turgot has decided to entice students by promising them exemption from taxation on all extra earnings from their future profession as midwives.[6] This time he is determined that the course succeed, and he will brook no argument. It is not, however, the midwife's feelings that are paramount in his mind. As he phrases it in his letter, her courses are an "important service I wished to render." If they go badly, in other words, it is a reflection upon him. That is his prime motivation.

Meanwhile, Boutin in Bordeaux, who had initially wanted nothing to do with du Coudray and her courses, is paying dearly for his "shortsightedness" and is obliged now to gather information about her and attempt to bring her to his region after all. It is winter, and Turgot is on his rounds touring the area near Angoulême when he receives a letter of inquiry about the midwife from the once-reluctant, now repentant, Boutin. Turgot answers with this assessment:

> I believe her work extremely useful and her manner of teaching the only one accessible to country women. You will perhaps find her person rather ridiculous with the high estimation she has of herself, but this will probably seem to you, as it does to me, quite unimportant. The essential thing is that she gives useful lessons, and hers are very useful. Her sojourn in the province is a bit expensive, because I give her 300 livres of stipend each month, not including the cost of her voyage and the transport of her trunks. I also have the cities provide her with lodging, wood, candles, and household utensils. Add to this the purchase of some of her machines in order to establish perpetual courses that I will entrust to some surgeons. I figure all of this will cost the province about 8000 livres, but I consider them well spent.[7]

Why, despite his recognition of her exceptional work, does Turgot depict du Coudray as a ludicrous character? Is this merely a misogynistic reaction to a self-confident woman? Or is the midwife behaving in an exaggeratedly boastful manner at the moment? Probably both. Turgot shares, almost surely, the deeply assimilated prevailing assumption that a strong, capable woman proclaiming her own worth somehow transgresses the bounds of normalcy. But the fact is that du Coudray is also tooting her own horn excessively right now. Gravely wounded by Boutin's rejection of her services, she has recently been hit by yet another worry: the war may be over, but the Treasury is overwhelmed with debts, and there has been a major shake-up at Versailles. Will the new ministers in power, whoever they are, regard her mission favorably and continue to facilitate things for her? Her protector Bertin is being replaced. Will her cause be forgotten with his departure? She has been corresponding with him lately about her fears and preoccupations in this regard.

Today, as the new year is about to begin, she unburdens herself to her original supporter, Ballainvilliers in Auvergne. Writing at Bertin's suggestion, she is in a state of agitation. Misspellings are rampant, and the hand is shaky:

> Receive please the remembrance of all the best wishes I feel for you. You could never doubt their sincerity, since so many sentiments come together to form them and lead me to assure you of them. . . . You will, Monsieur, contribute to the decision of my fate by please providing me with a certificate for the good works that my students did in Auvergne. The circumstance is most essential, according to what M. Bertin tells me. His retirement at first frightened me, but he was good enough to inform me that I must send him as soon as possible certificates from all the provinces where I set up this establishment and that then my future would be secure. If, Monsieur, the new Controller General is known to you, I hope you will be kind enough to speak to him in my favor. I always count on your goodness.[8]

Suddenly du Coudray senses her vulnerability in the shifting political winds. In some ways she believes she holds the upper hand. The intendants, though at the top of the provincial hierarchy, seem in no way superior to her. They are removable, and she knows they can be reassigned or dismissed, and often are, when they fail to do their job properly. If she reports administrative obstacles thrown in her path or relays an unfavorable impression of her stay in a particular region, it could be very damaging for these men. The public embarrassment of Boutin is a case in point. But now everything seems much more tenuous and complicated. Bertin has advised her of new measures she must take to guarantee the security of her position. She will have to solicit testimonials of her accomplishments and successes from these very intendants. She, in other words, is now as dependent on them as they are on her. She needs enthusiastic endorsements from each province she services, valorizations of her efforts that will henceforth constitute a written dossier assuring her of future teaching engagements. Bertin believes such a portfolio of praises is necessary and will protect her.

What this means, of course, is that her work as a teacher, however outstanding, is not enough. She must impress during her time off as well. The pressure on her to promote herself, especially after Boutin's rejection and Bertin's disgrace, is enormous. What if other intendants get it into their heads to turn her down also? She must persuade them of her merits, must advertise her superb record thus far. The parading and strutting that Turgot balks at is thus something rather new, a function of her uncertainty about continued sponsorship and of her dawning awareness that despite the King's brevet, she will need ceaselessly to muster support for herself. Because in her patriotic zeal she believes her job so consequential, it seems beneath her to have to ask for help or indulgence. Yet she is now beholden to these men for their accolades. However impatient she might be with some of their prevarications or obtuseness, she must be solicitous and humor them.

This, then, is the delicate balance of power to be negotiated between the midwife and the intendants. It will be a complex dynamic, resulting often in mutual adjustment and cooperation.

Though not always.

19. "Her Unendurable Arrogance"

Angoulême, 30 July 1764

Du Coudray has been teaching within the ramparts of this hilltop city for many months. The surrounding countryside is luminous and misty now in summer. She came from Tulle over the soft rolling heather-covered hills and marshlands in a stagecoach drawn by four horses. The official in charge of her stay here has been watching her closely. They do not get along; she suspects him of having been the one who turned Boutin against her in the first place. He is both fascinated and disturbed by this powerful, complicated woman. The tardily penitent Boutin is now desperately trying to make amends and create a strategy for wooing the midwife to Bordeaux, and she enjoys watching him grovel. Having contemplated Turgot's response to his inquiry, he has next asked the subdelegate of Angoulême to fill him in on du Coudray's work and on her present frame of mind. Today the man obligingly writes his answer, with attempted fairness and objectivity, "as a good citizen and without any prejudice." She has angered him—"I have reason to be personally very unhappy with the conduct of this woman"—but he gives credit where it is due and grants, reluctantly, that she has great "experience, devotion. . . . to her profession, and natural gifts."[1]

The journey, he explains to Boutin, was expensive, as each of the four horses cost 6 livres a day and their return trip must be paid too. The midwife requires two months for the course itself, fifteen days to prepare before it begins and another fifteen to rest after it is over, so the town pays 900 livres in bonuses for the three months, and another 600 for lodging. Four machines cost 1,200 livres, and a copy of her book is "indispensable" for each student. She sells the book directly for 40 sous a copy, but he proposes that an "economy" printing of two thousand could be done—he has of course not consulted her on this—so that each one would only cost 5 sous. Thus a little over 3,000 livres, he estimates, will pay for du Coudray to train eighty women and twenty surgeons. On the subject of her "very ingenious" obstetrical model he somehow feels more inclined to respect her proprietary claims than in the case of her book. He explains about the model: "being of her own invention and composition, she seems to have an exclusive right to make it and distribute it." Imitations are inferior anyway, and "it would be a kind of larceny against her to deny her the considerable profit she makes on the sale of her machines." There is no substitute for du Coudray herself either; the "honest truth" is that only she really knows how to go about this teaching properly.

So much for the work. Now the person herself. "The difficulty will be to find out if, still today, the vanity of Mme du Coudray, humiliated by your refusal to receive her in your generality when she counted on going there, won't lead her to the stupidity of rejecting the invitation that you would make. For she has her imagination so full of the superiority of her talents that she often puts to the test the most resolute patience by the explanation she is always ready to make of her merits and by the recitation of her honors. I am understating, because one must even speak to her of the homage she claims was rendered to her in the cities she passed through, so that whoever does not render her similar homage appears in her mind as a mere automaton, having nothing human but the shape."

It is, the writer continues, du Coudray's firm conviction that Bordeaux, like all other generalities, is contracted to receive her, and that Boutin's refusing her was a breach of faith, a "breaking off" of that solemn engagement. He now recommends strongly that Boutin charge someone else with the negotiations so as not to compromise himself. He even suggests a particular person whom the midwife trusts. She might then give in. "Despite her unendurable arrogance, she knows she needs to teach to live, and I have seen her here reduced to great embarrassment when resources for the voyage . . . were lacking. She maintained that she wanted nothing more than to be able to return to Paris, but at the same time she was writing and having people write for her far and wide to find some region where they would welcome her." If she has something lined up as a result of this feverish correspondence, in other words, "she might play hard to get [*faire la difficile*]. But if she has nothing else, she might consider herself lucky to come to you." Boutin should, the letter ends, get someone new to approach and flatter her, to butter her up by explaining that they have finally persuaded him of her indispensability.

Here, then, is how one critic sizes her up. Clearly put off by her pushiness, he finds nothing admirable in her vigorous proselytizing and dislikes her histrionics. Yet he perfectly understands how essential her work is, and even sympathizes to some extent with her desire to protect her financial interests. He paints a poignant picture of her neediness, her temporary loss of will, her confusion. Just a few years into her traveling mission, he believes he has detected some faintness of heart. He knows it would be best for both Boutin and du Coudray if, still saving face, they could come to terms. Hers is the greater vanity, it seems, the noisier bravado, but in this man's estimation it is really a thin and rather fragile facade.

20. The Thrifty Laverdy

Fontainebleau, 16 October 1764

Louis XV moves around often between his many palaces in the Paris region—Compiègne, Fontainebleau, Choisy—taking with him his council of ministers and other advisors. It is outrageously costly to maintain all these royal households, and there are rumblings everywhere about the monarch's extravagance. The ministers in charge of finances can scarcely keep their heads amid the whirl of hunting parties and feasts, but they try to stay focused on the needs of the country, try to tame royal excesses, try to support worthy causes.

The new controller general, Laverdy, has been told all about the midwife, and he is impressed. She must have gathered and forwarded to him, as Bertin suggested, many rousing recommendations written by officials in the towns where she has taught so far. Laverdy is a stern and frugal Jansenist, rather partial to the *parlements* in their battle against royal spending. But the war is now over, financial constraints have relaxed slightly, and this reform-minded man means to translate his admiration for du Coudray into a more stable financial arrangement for her. Today he sends to all intendants a letter stressing her generosity in traveling so extensively for the cause. Not given to hyperbole, Laverdy nonetheless casts du Coudray's mission in grand terms: she does far more than save subjects for the king; she preserves the whole human race.[1]

Laverdy, a keen mathematician and crisp administrator, plans efficiently. He wants the midwife to be guaranteed 8,000 livres a year. He cannot, any more than his predecessors, commit the Royal Treasury to this, so he wants the money raised by the provinces, as it is they that reap the fruits of her labor, the benefits of her instruction. This is an artful argument, of course, because the monarchy is the big winner no matter what Laverdy says. In fact a great struggle is brewing between the crown and the countryside. The controller general, as an agent of the monarch, is pressing for the provinces to shoulder this fiscal responsibility, because the crown, by sending the midwife around, has done its share. Each province need give only 270–280 livres to the common fund, a small price for this invaluable training. A diligent du Coudray should manage to complete what remains of her *tour de France* in six or seven years, Laverdy figures; she requires three months for each course, so she should be able to "do" four provinces each year.[2]

But wait. Laverdy may be good at arithmetic, yet the midwife is not a ticking mechanical clock. He is dealing with a human being, and an opinionated, demanding one at that, who is willing to work very hard but insists on her rest in between and on everything being set up exactly to her specifications. Hers is a grueling job, and she goes about it in her fashion, proceeding without undue haste. Being used to major hardships, she expects minor comforts by way of compensation. If anyone were to tell Laverdy that she would still be traveling on her mission two decades from now, that he has grossly underestimated the time it will take, the thrifty man would be horrified. As it is, he will have trouble accepting even the shortest delay or extra expense. He supports her, but finds upsetting any vicissitudes of life that muddy his careful calculations. And the business of birthing is notoriously incalculable.

Also, this amount of 8,000 livres is merely a hope, not a promise. And it is unrealistic. Laverdy is counting, naively, on provincial cooperation to arrive at that substantial sum. Just two months ago, in August, he issued an edict whose purpose was to bring more uniformity to the municipal administrations of the realm, to crush the old city oligarchies and reform their finances. Seemingly oblivious to how unpopular these ideas are, he feels he can press the regions to underwrite du Coudray's mission.[3] Here, too, he has seriously miscalculated.

A major rebellion against royal authority has been taking shape in those provinces with a *parlement* and an *états*, or assembly, of their own. Not only does France have privileged groups—the clergy and the nobility—but it has these privileged territories as well, areas that function with considerable autonomy, enjoying special exemptions and rights. These *pays d'états*, as they are called, are therefore often refractory to progress, innovation, and considerations of general interest. The intendants there are having great trouble trying to implement the will of the king and his ministers, as the experience of Le Bret, intendant of Brittany, demonstrates. He wants to oblige Laverdy and support the monarch's midwife but is clearly intimidated by the local *états*, who have endorsed instead a male surgeon. Du Coudray, he explains, will need to jump through hoops, will need to come in person and do a dazzling demonstration before the *états* will even consider her. And there are still no guarantees after this trial; rather, he sees a large chance of rejection. He knows the *états* will object to the 270 livres Laverdy is requesting. All he can do, despite his supposed influence, is "mediate."[4]

So the plot thickens. The midwife will of course continue to court and cultivate ministers and royal administrators, but she will soon realize that no matter how fervently they support her, a whole new set of political obstacles will need to be surmounted. And often they can't be. Provincial bodies now actively contest the crown's authority, aggressively seek to destabilize and desacralize the monarchy's effective and symbolic center. Nothing is sure or steady in this job, when being "sent by the king" turns out sometimes to be as much a curse as a blessing. Her own loyalties do not waver, but it is a shocking discovery for her nonetheless that His Majesty is not everywhere revered.

21. SOUNDING HER MOOD

Bourdeilles, 12 December 1764

As a special favor to the former minister Bertin, du Coudray has gone to teach the women on his estates in this magical town in Dordogne, where the river flows beneath a Gothic bridge and the seigneurial mill juts out defiantly like a boat's prow, the château anchored above to an enormous rock shelf. Even here—or perhaps especially here, among the cliffs and valleys of Périgord—the hapless Boutin is pursuing the midwife, for she is now very close to Bordeaux and he does not want her to elude him.

This chase has become a matter of pride and political survival. Boutin has, through his inquiries, actually come to value the training du Coudray offers, but mostly he is now just obsessed by the need to clear up the mess he has made, to erase all trace of his earlier insubordination, to no longer stand out as the one intendant too dense to recognize her importance. He knows she will refuse to come directly to him no matter how much he tries to ingratiate himself, as he has explained wearily in a summer letter, but perhaps he can begin to win her over by enticing her next to the town of Sarlat a bit further south, and thence to Bordeaux. She is presently planning to go north to Poitiers, and he hopes to intercept her before she slips away. But to ensnare her before her departure, subterfuge will be necessary. She must never know the request comes from him.[1] He asks a friend of his in Bourdeilles to casually suggest Sarlat to her and "take a sounding of whether she is disposed to it." In the meantime Boutin wants to procure her props to use in his region, even if he cannot get her in person. He instructs his contact to buy one of her "ingenious machines" and "the greatest number that you can of copies of her book, again without her suspecting that this purchase is being made for me. It must be done by an intermediary. I have reasons for this that it would take far too long to explain."[2] This, then, is the plan.

Except it does not work. Du Coudray sees through this scheme immediately. She turns the Sarlat proposal down flat and gives all her energies to teaching the students in Bourdeilles and overcoming the antagonism of the local surgeons. She knows she has the new controller general's endorsement, and today Bertin informs her that he too still stands fully behind her, however diminished his role may be. He is particularly touched that she is giving her precious time to his townspeople, and vows to do all in his power to insulate her from detractors. "It would not be possible, or even fair, that you make war at your own expense. It is sufficient that you give your time and your pain, and we should all be most grateful."[3]

Probably because of this heartening reiteration of support, du Coudray figures she can afford to shun Boutin a little while longer. Delighted to be the unattainable prize in his quest, to leave his increasing need for her unrequited, she is perhaps taking things a bit too far. But keeping such men in check is part of her mission, for she must have their cooperation. She is not frivolous, merely eager to test the extent of her power with the intendants—which is considerable if Boutin's conduct is any indication. Rather than ignore her or give up in exasperation, he persistently keeps track of her movements and moods, involves numerous others in the subtle orchestration of his pursuit, plans continually new ways to obtain her. That she must relent eventually and go to Bordeaux is a foregone conclusion. Even the keenest acrimonies are apt to fade. For now, though, she can hold out at no cost to her. If anything, her recalcitrance increases her prestige. Boutin's predicament is getting to be a famous story.

22. Delivering "Like a Cobbler Makes Shoes"

Poitiers, February 1765

Du Coudray is no longer alone but is now traveling with an entourage of four. If she was accompanied before, none of the observers reporting on various aspects of her mission has so far mentioned the fact. Now, however, her arrival with her company has created a sufficient stir and spectacle to be noticed.[1] They have had to climb steeply to reach Poitiers, this awkward, poorly built high platform of a city, and it proves too much of a strain for the full coach. It is easy to watch and count visitors if they empty out of the carriage to lighten its load on the flank of the pitched slope, and walk beside it for the last part of the ascent.

This strange town actually has some workable land within its Roman walls.[2] The intendant, de Blossac, had difficulty initially in rounding up students for the first course despite numerous posters and printed circulars.[3] He had found lodgings for du Coudray in a vacant house that was formerly used for recruits going to the colonial islands. Frightening rumors buzzed at first, fanned by the jealous surgeons, that students attending the midwife's courses there would be trapped, kidnapped, and shipped off to Cayenne! This misconception has been cleared up, however, and eighty have taken the first course, with still more clamoring to attend the second. The intendant is providing funds for those who travel far, though not for others who already reside and cultivate the land in Poitiers. Eighty is about the maximum du Coudray thinks she can teach at a time, for each woman needs a long turn manually operating the machine under her close supervision. At the start of the lesson every student receives a number, and they come up to work with her in that order. During breaks, or at the end of the afternoon, a *répétitrice* drills them orally on what they've learned.[4] The intendant is struck by how the midwife focuses on the product, the baby; only a few very general lessons are devoted to caring for the mother. The students, he reports, "know how to deliver like a cobbler knows how to make shoes; that's all that's necessary." They are taught to do good by producing goods.

In general the intendant is very pleased. Reflecting and congratulating himself, in a now familiar trope, on the great service he has procured for his province, he advises his friend and colleague Le Bret, the intendant of Brittany, to have du Coudray come there as soon as possible no matter how refractory "your interminable *états*." She seems too good to be true, he muses. Wintering now in "horribly cold" Paris, huddled by the fire with fever, feeling sorry for himself because he is missing various festivals and concerned about his children who have measles, de Blossac is wondering if the midwife too might succumb to any weakness. Will she be spoiled by Laverdy's projections of financial security? A slight note of cynicism creeps in. "I see only one inconvenience about which I'd say that the minister did not think, if it is possible that a minister doesn't think of everything. That is, to be worried whether this woman, seeing her future provided for, won't relax and save herself trouble, unlike when, her well-being and her recompense dependent on our satisfaction with her pains, she spared nothing to satisfy the public." On the chance that the midwife's efforts might soon begin to wane, Le Bret should get her right away before she starts to take it easier and cut corners, "before half-heartedness sets in."[5] But the terrible conflict brewing in Brittany right now between the *parlement* and the crown has escalated, and Le Bret finds his position far too precarious to push any more for the king's midwife at this juncture. He will store the idea, however, and make sure she comes later when the trouble dies down. He has no way of knowing that that will take more than ten years.

Viewing du Coudray's teaching as mostly mechanical, de Blossac seems to think that she, like her machines, may wear out with overuse. In fact, she shows no signs of winding down at all. On the contrary, the midwife is making a lasting impression here, as the local newspaper, the *Affiches de Poitou*, still testifies years later. (She is, by the way, becoming a favorite feature story in the provincial press wherever she goes.) In numerous villages women gather to review her book; those who can read do so out loud, the others listen attentively. They study the lessons and "meditate" on them together, taking the new teachings very seriously. Of course there are some negative reactions too. This reporter has no patience with what he calls the backwardness of small-minded peasant women who "can't imagine that anyone could learn anything outside the boundaries of their parish. . . . They prefer always to rely on midwives in their villages who have no other claim to fame than having made many women and children perish."[6] And a local surgeon will try hard to undermine du Coudray's lessons, claiming consensus among his colleagues that "this woman's courses were more dangerous than useful, as they trained *demisavants* who with no in-depth knowledge believed themselves to be her equals."[7]

The midwife, however, is growing accustomed to such inertias and jealousies and can take them in stride, knowing that her teaching here has made a huge difference, whatever some might say. Women giving birth in this Poitou region, before her arrival, followed the local custom of walking around once the baby's head appeared, a terribly dangerous practice resulting in a high incidence of strangulation.[8] She has shown them the folly of this and many other things, so she is confident that her students here, both male and female, are learning well and enduringly. And this faith is to be borne out. One surgeon she trains here will be using her machine and method well into the Revolution.[9]

23. SURGEONS OF THE KING'S NAVY

Rochefort-sur-Mer, 30 April 1766

More and more surgeons are impressed with du Coudray as she travels now along the Atlantic coast through a series of port cities—Niort, Les Sables d'Olonnes, La Rochelle, Rochefort. When du Coudray teaches in the marshy inland port of Niort after leaving Poitiers,[1] she wins the undying devotion of a M. Saint Paul, surgeon-major in a regiment of the royal cavalry. He will take her course again and again whenever their paths cross. Years from now, after studying with her in Lorraine in 1774, he will reminisce about the "incomparable" du Coudray, "the most celebrated midwife who ever existed," a "divine woman" who "demonstrates so sublimely."[2]

He had not been so sure about her at first. "I confess to you," he tells a friend, "to my embarrassment, that before having seen for myself the astonishing effects I regarded her exclusive mission as an act of favor accorded by the ministers to an ordinary person. . . . Stuck in this prejudice, my regiment in 1765 was sent to Niort . . . where she had just given her course of instruction. Everyone was exalting the sublime talents of this woman; the enthusiasm was unanimous. I still had the weakness to think that people gave more credit to the novelty than to real merit." His regiment, however, had stayed in that area for three years, and he had the chance to witness many deliveries brilliantly executed by her students. They were all youthful and energetic women with no previous training in the art, and therefore "not numbed by habit and infatuated by their would-be worth like the old ones." Training the young, he recognizes, is just one more innovative feature of du Coudray's program. She wants to teach the uninitiated who can be formed by her from scratch. Another reason for targeting the young is that her students will still have before them many "long years of precious service," making the teaching investment worthwhile. It is, Saint Paul emphatically agrees, an efficient way to generate a lasting network of expert midwives.

Du Coudray's reputation has been running ahead of her, her visit eagerly anticipated in these coastal towns. They make her welcome despite hard times, for the main commerce of this area had been with Canada, whose loss just recently in the Seven Years War ravaged the local economy.[3] She handles this series of lessons with particular dispatch. The city of Sables actually raises more money for her stay than can be spent, so swiftly does she complete the training there.[4] Then four months in La Rochelle, and she moves on to set up shop here in the port of Rochefort, a navy stronghold with its gunpowder works and cannon foundry, a center of activity for royal sailmakers, armsmakers, shipbuilders, and ropemakers. The king takes special interest in his naval hospital here and in his Hôtel des Cazernes, where three hundred marine guards are coached in all exercises befitting officers who aspire to serve on His Majesty's ships.[5]

But what a curious place for the midwife to be! Why would she teach here, given that these classes are exclusively male?

Passions are running high just now in favor of the monarchy, so du Coudray rides with pleasure on the current enthusiasm. For the king has at last asserted himself, after two years of repeated humiliations inflicted upon royal authority. Uprisings of *parlements* in the provinces and the capital started in earnest around 1764 and got quickly out of hand, these law courts declaring themselves the united defenders of the fundamental laws of the realm and spokesmen of the nation, remonstrating against all the king's royal edicts, refusing to register them or give them the force of law. Invoking historical precedent, they claimed something like a power of judicial review over royal decrees. Finally provoked, the king just last month, on 3 March 1766, went in person to Paris, solemnly assembled the judges in the Palais de Justice, and gave his *séance de la flagellation*, or scourging session. In this speech, a forceful statement of absolutism, Louis announced that he would tolerate no more disobedience from these intermediate bodies and reaffirmed that all authority in the realm was vested in him alone.[6] The strength of his declaration took everyone by surprise. His powerful words have been ringing throughout France ever since. All this is still new enough that the reaction, the backlash, has not yet organized itself. For the moment, anyway, it is a good time to be the king's midwife, and du Coudray means to make the most of it by choosing to teach here in this royal stronghold.

His Majesty's naval surgeons, who invited the midwife, are extremely solicitous. The lessons here differ markedly from those she offers to women. They deal with obstetrical instruments and cesarean sections, tools and techniques female midwives are never to use, procedures they are never to do or even attempt, on pain of death. Since 1755 laws have effectively denied women access to all new technologies such as forceps and hooks. Surgeons, especially in Paris, are trying more concertedly than ever to exclude women from the cutting edge of the field of childbirth. Ironically, though a woman, du Coudray has special dispensation to reveal her knowledge of this forbidden area and to impart it to these members of the very profession trying to monopolize it.[7]

Today eleven of du Coudray's surgeon disciples compose a letter officially certifying how much they have been taught. "We first learned simple and complicated deliveries, then the way to extract children with the help of instruments in malformations of the pelvic bones, as well as to do cesarean operations, and the puncture of children's heads . . . in cases of hydrocephalus. Mme du Coudray accompanied all her operations with liquids, [to show] loss both of blood and of waters. She has skillfully detailed for us the signs leading to knowledge of pregnancies and miscarriages, and showed us all the infirmities of women, including cancer of the womb, all so well depicted [on her machine] that one could not better imitate nature. Which has perfectly convinced us that she rightly deserves the brilliant praises that are won for her everywhere by her great reputation."[8] The liquids mentioned—dispensed from an elaborate set of sponges, some saturated with clear and others with opaque red fluid—which make things so realistic, seem only to be used for the surgeon classes at this point. Soon du Coudray will adopt them more generally, referring to them as a "supplement" to the machine, and sell them for extra money.[9]

This curriculum, then, is much more concerned with death, with pregnancies that end in extremis, where a dead baby must be extracted from a healthy mother, or a live baby from a dying mother.

It is at this point, usually, that surgeons or doctors are called to the scene, after the midwife realizes too late that her client is in serious trouble. If some cutting or some killing needs to be done, if either mother or baby must be sacrificed to preserve the other, it is the men who intervene and decide which one will be saved. Where women are held criminally liable for making such judgments, male practitioners do it routinely, with impunity. It seems a dubious honor, but such is their prerogative.[10]

Du Coudray finds time to make some side trips. Among them is probably an excursion to nearby Saintes, exceptionally rich in Roman monuments and its cathedral built by Charlemagne.[11] Perhaps she befriends a printer there, because a few years from now a new edition of her *Abrégé* will be published in that town, an unlikely place to pick for book business unless you have some personal connection. The residents of some of the offshore islands, encouraged by her local explorations, have reason to hope she will come their way to teach, however briefly. A surgeon from St. Pierre on the Ile d'Oléron will remember the excitement over her proximity, then the disappointment when she did not visit. Deeply regretful that his isolated area missed out on her tour, he notes that "we received from no one any compensation for this loss."[12] Preachers in surrounding towns thank divine Providence for sending her to their region and know that heaven will grant her lasting prosperity.[13]

The Rochefort surgeons will not be able to sustain the momentum after the midwife leaves, for the local girls refuse to study a matter so private with men.[14] When du Coudray is invited back in 1776 and again in 1781, she resents the fact that her impact here has been so fleeting, through no fault of her own, and attributes the scant success of her activities to the mediocrity of her successors. This is a "a source of annoyance" to du Coudray, and she declines to squander more time where there has been little serious effort at follow-through.[15]

For now, however, she basks in the glow of this hearty fan letter and in the impression, in this case illusory as it turns out, that she has once again left an indelible mark. How wonderful to have the king's royal surgeons gathered around her, hanging on her every word, virtually eating out of her hand. The hostility of surgeons has caused her a good deal of trouble elsewhere. Twenty-one years ago in Paris, when she agitated for instruction and signed the petition, surgeons had come close to undermining altogether the practice of midwifery in the capital. They continue to stifle her former colleagues back in Paris even now. How far away that must seem! And how different things are for du Coudray, at least for the moment. It is something to savor.

24. BREVET NO. 2: THE ROYAL TREASURY

Compiègne, 18 August 1767

Today, the King being in Compiègne, His Majesty, always occupied with the care of procuring for his people the help they need, principally with everything that can tend to their conservation, and well informed of the science and experience that said Dame du Coudray, midwife, has acquired in the art of delivery; wanting, besides, to repay her for the infinite attention she has taken to carry this so useful and so necessary art to a high degree of perfection, His Majesty has appointed her to teach the Art of Midwifery throughout the whole extent of the Realm. In order to obtain for her the means to transport herself . . . His Majesty wants and ordains that, as long as she gives public courses of instruction anywhere in the realm, she enjoy, each year, the sum of 8,000 livres that he accords her as annual gratification; and when age or infirmities no longer permit her to give said courses, [the sum] of 3,000 livres only, to facilitate her life in her retirement. Which sums will be paid to her . . . in future, each year, for her entire life, by the custodians of the Royal Treasury . . . starting this day.[1]

Finally, the coveted royal pension! No more talk of du Coudray needing to prove herself every year, as Ormesson had insisted. No more pipe dreams of the provinces pooling their respective monies, as Laverdy had originally wished. Now the king, while alighting at yet another of his palaces, has committed himself to a steady payment.

For the midwife it is a sort of epiphany. There was no way to enforce Laverdy's initial plan, to *make* the different regions contribute, especially in the climate of hostility to royal directives that had prevailed before Louis's scourging. The *états* of Brittany, where resistance to Versailles was greatest, flatly refused in early 1765 to pay the 270 livres "required" of each province, just as Le Bret had predicted. So did many others.[2] But things have changed since the king reasserted himself. The *états* and *parlements* had wanted a reduction in the number of pensions paid by the Royal Treasury. Defying their wishes, Louis now adds another pension to the list, one supporting his ambassadress of birthing. Her mission is far too important to entrust to the regions, whose position on fiscal matters is historically intractable. From this day forward the central administration will guarantee du Coudray's salary. Laverdy, perhaps to compensate for the failure of his original plan and any anxiety caused thereby, has even arranged for a sum to be paid her in her retirement, a wonderful surprise.

She feels tremendously appreciated, and her expectations soar. Financial security at last! Or so one would think from this proclamation. Around this time she begins to make more grandiose plans. She will soon sit for her magisterial portrait, which, copied as an engraving, will decorate a new edition of her book. She is rejoicing, enjoying a buoyant sense of her new marketability.

But such happy tidings can make a person too prideful for her own good.

25. THE *Bien(s) de l'Humanité*
Montargis, 30 September 1767

Orléans, Blois, Chartres, Montargis—the last eight months have been a flurry of activity in a particularly lovely part of the country. The intendant of this region, M. de Cypierre, has been following du Coudray's travels with interest since 1763,[1] but it took a while for him to placate the surgeons and persuade them that their corporate rights would not be undermined by a visit from her.[2] Now she has come with her growing entourage. Ample furnished lodgings have been found for her whole staff and their paraphernalia, "four or five persons and much equipment."[3] She is teaching one hundred women, the biggest group so far. It is a veritable performance, and the midwife relishes the attention. Her much-heralded entrance into the town and the arrival of her barefoot pupils streaming from the surrounding villages is merely the curtain raiser. The all-day lessons and demonstrations are a spectacle in their own right, culminating in the ceremonious granting of the royal certificates. The dismantling and packing up of anatomical posters and mannequins resembles the striking of a set as each engagement ends and she departs with her supporting cast of assistants for the next booking.

Today du Coudray is busily arranging her next trip, to Bourges. Over three weeks ago she committed herself to going there, name-dropping to the intendant, in a curious postscript, a reminder of her connections: "dear Frère Côme asks me to present to you his re-spects."[4] Evidently she anticipates trouble and believes this extra mention of the famous medical monk's patronage might be required to enhance her prestige there. Now she goes into more detail on her situation and her needs, in particular that whatever teaching space is secured for her be close to her residence.[5] She will require an "apartment nearby, that consists of several rooms furnished with four master's beds and one servant's bed. If it is possible to find in the house where I live a big hall where I could give my lessons, that would be convenient for me, but if all cannot be found together, I will give them at the Hôtel de Ville. The house must contain com-plete kitchen utensils, table linen, sheets, and the city provides wood. My salary is 300 livres each month. . . . The King has just accorded me an 8,000-livre stipend and 3,000-livre retirement pension [for] when my strength no longer permits me to continue the good of hu-manity. This last grace, which I had not expected, is a very particu-lar kindness from the Controller General. I am very moved by it. I am not exactly sure when this salary will begin, so I cannot yet promise to go to Bourges at my own expense."

This money, in other words, is to cover her transport only. Stress-ing again that the city must in any case continue to pay the cost of her lodgings, she had asked for an advance for the travel, which she will reimburse as soon as the Royal Treasury pays her. She has been waiting nearly a month and now wants a go-ahead from the intendant immediately, "in order that I don't lose time so dear to the unfortunate and whose great value you know." She hopes to get to Bourges by 1 November, the holiday of Toussaint, for she needs two weeks to get settled before beginning her "operations and to put in order my machines, which are always disturbed by trans-port." In closing she pushes more, pressuring for an instant an-swer. It seems she has finally relented on the Bordeaux matter and might actually consider going there instead, hence the urgency of her tone. "If you cannot find the possibility of setting up this institu-tion this year, if circumstances oppose your charitable desires for your province, I will accept the invitation from the intendant of Bordeaux, whom I asked to wait while I give you preference. The long trip [to Bordeaux] would become very disagreeable for me at the beginning of winter, especially for my health, which doesn't adjust at all. You will forgive me this indulgence, but I am unfortunately forced."

So du Coudray, fifty-two years old, is now beginning to admit the strain, to economize a bit with her energy, to reveal how much she expends her own strength for her calling. She has never said things like that. Was de Blossac right when he predicted two years ago that she would soon begin to wind down? Of course, it is entirely reasonable that she try to avoid unnecessary detours whenever possible, particularly now that she needs to pay for her own travel. Why swoop down south only to have to come north again so soon? She must carry on with "the good of humanity," a phrase now found in all her letters—but at a price. Her work is "dear," of "great value," she reminds the intendant of Bourges in the same breath that she discusses her salary, conflating as she is increasingly wont to do the moral and monetary worth of the good(s) she disseminates.[6] She is manipulative in other ways as well, playing two invitations off each other and thus creating a sense of lively competition over her services, until she gets the desired result and heads for her chosen destination.

Somehow, however, in her eagerness to flaunt the new brevet with its generous provisions, to broadcast this latest vote of confidence from her monarch, she has boasted overmuch and confused some officials into believing they need provide for her nothing but a classroom. Having bragged too loudly about royal liberality, she now will have to spend much time and effort disabusing various regional administrators of the false impression that she comes entirely for free.

26. THE STUDENTS—"MES FEMMES"

Bourges, All Saints' Day 1767

The midwife targeted this holiday of Toussaint for her arrival here, and Bourges with its huge dark cathedral is bustling. Nearby in the Voiselle Marshes "water rats" (market gardeners) get about in flat-bottom boats. Here, and at other local fairs throughout France today, women sell surplus dairy products and sometimes a fattened cow that would do poorly on the sparse fodder (at best some marsh grass) available in winter. A new cow can be purchased in the spring. Such activities are part of the rhythm of the peasants' year.

Du Coudray's courses, on the other hand, are not part of their seasonal pattern. The midwife means to start her teaching soon. How do country women fit her into their lives? The curés choose girls from their parishes to go and learn for two months from the famous *attrapeuse*. It is hoped that these young women, selected for their alertness, will profit from these lessons. But can the families manage without their daughters even for a short spell? When they are home they help with everything.[1]

These girls' villages generally have about eighty households. On the little farms, women are expected to plow, spread manure, weed, reap, sometimes thresh. They garden, cultivating turnips, radishes, onions, leeks, parsnips, carrots, beets, and of course peas and beans. They look after the animals, milk the cow, bring slop to the pigs. They keep the house swept, gather kindling, tend the fire, watch the cauldron of stew, haul well water in great buckets. Along with their mothers, aunts, and sisters they knit, spin, make lace, mend worn clothes, sew, crochet. They wash and scrub. And of course they care for all the children running around in the house, usually a large rectangular room which all generations share with each other and often with the animals. The good animals, that is, domesticated and useful. Sometimes bad animals come from the forests, like wild boars that trample the crops or wound the livestock, or wolves, foxes, and the untamed hares that eat the cabbages.

The year shapes the changing tasks of these young women. Harvest time is very busy, August and September. They would be most missed then. Whether it's hemp (for rope and sacks) or flax for linen, or barley or rye or wheat, the men do most of the cutting, but the girls and younger women bind the sheaves and collect them and pile them up. They don't generally flail the grain, but they rake and sweep it into bags. On windy days they throw it up into the air to separate wheat from chaff, then take it to the lord's mill to be ground into flour. This they will use all year round to make gruel, porridges, oatcakes, coarse black bread. There are grapes for the picking, hops for brewing, honey to be gathered from the hives. When plowing starts again, the women herd the cattle into the cut field to eat the stubble. In fall, up until Christmas, they prepare food for the winter. They don't kill the sheep or chickens or geese, because the wool and eggs are valuable, eggs especially, which they give to the landlord to keep him happy. But the piglets, born in early spring, are weaned and fattened on nuts from the forest; the litter is then slaughtered usually in November, right about now. From this the women make blood pudding, sausages, and gelatin, and use the hair for brushes or add it to the wall plaster. Salted or smoked pork is made from the meat for the long winter months ahead.

From Christmas to Easter is such a hard time, waiting for the first grains to ripen. Food is scarce, and the winter days are rainy, windy, short, cold, muddy, dark. Many in the villages get sick in this season with fevers and coughs. The men keep busy preparing the fields for spring planting, while the women stay mostly indoors, close around the hearth for heat and light to lengthen the days, making thread, spinning, carding, combing. It is difficult turning raw wool from their sheep, or flax from their fields, into a length of cloth for a cover or a shirt or a tunic, from light fluffy rolls to skeins of thread to the loom. They make clothes, bolsters, covers, and featherbeds, mostly of gray and brown, nature's colors, although sometimes they use dyes from roots and leaves found in the forest. They sing and pray and tell stories to get through these months. Whatever disasters weather or disease might bring, it must be God's will. Meanwhile they do their chores and try bravely to survive.

Finally, with Easter comes spring and excitement. The men sow the fields, but the women do hoeing, weeding, mulching, and join in the anticipation of the summer growing time. They are also very busy with laundry—April is the time of one of the big washings; the other is in October—lightening and whitening with lye from the fire ashes. They put the clothes into vats covered with cinders, add boiling water, the next day beat them with paddles, and then spread them out in the sun to dry and bleach. It is cheesemaking time too. They separate out the cream, sour it, thicken it, press it, let it age. The children love the whey, squealing for it as a special treat. Many of these cheeses, along with milk and butter, are taken to market to sell.

As the midwife explains, mid-November after harvest, about two weeks from now, is a relatively good time for the young women to interrupt their chores and come to her. She recognizes that they are actually indispensable all year long, and of course she needs to teach during the other, less desirable seasons as well. But this late-fall moment, when the great gathering of crops is finished, is the least disruptive of all for her to start her class and be able to count on the students' fullest concentration.[2]

27. "A Furious Disgust"

Bourges, 9 February 1768

Things are not going well here at all, and du Coudray is unable to hide her indignation. To begin with, Laverdy, so supportive until now, is eyeing her suddenly with suspicion. He has explained that the steady pension on the Royal Treasury was awarded last year so that the midwife could "give her time entirely to the instruction she has practiced for a few years,"[1] implying that although she may once have needed to supplement her funds by doing other things besides teaching, such as delivering babies herself privately or selling remedies, she is presently freed of all distractions and should devote herself exclusively to training students. Out of the blue Laverdy is questioning in rather inquisitorial tones her need for her entourage, as housing all these extras seems to him an "excessive and abusive" expense. He queries the intendant of this poor Berry area, Dupré de St. Maur, on "this large number whom you say she is accompanied by. I urge you to examine particularly this matter and to give me your opinion on it." The results of this inquiry surprise the minister, for St. Maur staunchly defends du Coudray's need for her helpers; without them, he argues, she would never be able to teach groups of one hundred students.[2]

Laverdy has a point. Who *are* all these people in the midwife's company, and are they in fact crucial to her operation? They are described as two surgeons, an apprentice who assists with the demonstrations, a "kind of chambermaid," and a lackey. Perhaps du Coudray is coaching the surgeons privately in exchange for their assistance with the class. The "apprentice" is probably the thirteen-year-old Marguerite Guillaumanche, who will later claim to have been "raised" by her "aunt" and must therefore have joined her early on during these years. The two servants are clearly essential in many ways. Someone must carry the ubiquitous chests and trunks, must serve the midwife at inns and way stations, must light her path in the dark. Someone must run the household for her, as her teaching occupies her all day from morning to night. They must bear parcels, clean up, bargain, market, hire menial workers to fix and set up things and prepare the lecture hall, hound debtors and settle scores, admit or turn away visitors, mediate in disputes involving their mistress, keep the world at bay when necessary. They must prepare food, which seems to be important to the stout midwife, for she comments when the menu is boring; later she even adds a cook to her retinue. They must assist in the making and sewing of the machines, an enormous labor. And they must serve as her private secretaries, keeping accounts and writing the letters she dictates in large numbers to organize her travels. Literate and skilled servants can be found if one looks hard enough, and du Coudray absolutely requires them. She has probably selected her staff carefully, for she keeps them by her side. Were she not attached to a particular team of assistants, she would simply hire new help everywhere she goes.[3]

There is something else, too. Du Coudray loves the theatricality of a grand arrival. As a midwife in Paris it is highly unlikely that she had any service help whatsoever. To move about now attended by several disciples and domestics gives her an air of dramatic importance. And there is added status in having a manservant and chambermaid as part of the display: upper servants with specialized functions are associated with the nobility. This crew lends the road show extra prestige. They provide a "theater of rule," a public demonstration of the mistress's superiority.[4]

In addition to the physical need for this company and its importance as public spectacle, du Coudray may require them emotionally. She can maintain control over at least them even when external forces conspire against her, as they do now here in Bourges. She can exercise authority in this private sphere as a "female patriarch" in her household even when command of the outside world begins to elude her.[5]

And what is in it for the servants? Those who voyage with du Coudray must have a somewhat offbeat taste for excitement and adventure, as they could surely find a more stationary, conventional employment. They get bed and board and possibly some clothes. Beyond this, they may get the special satisfaction of feeling needed, since they are the only steady company du Coudray has, her movable space that goes with her from place to place insulating her from loneliness. Servants, who often venture far from their native region to find jobs of any kind—think of the ubiquitous Auvergnat—rarely become absorbed in their new place of work and so experience a strong sense of foreignness wherever they end up.[6] But traveling with du Coudray makes it unnecessary to settle down, thus minimizing the psychic dislocation of conforming to new ways. Adjustments to the outside world can be superficial and temporary, for the entourage always knows they will soon be moving on. Committed to the midwife, they live and journey with her in close physical proximity day and night. Privacy is nonexistent. Du Coudray shares a bedroom with her personal maid and is very attuned to her moods. She trusts her servants, is not quick to accuse them. Only once in her hundreds of letters does she mention any strife within her household, and that will be a very extreme and special case.[7]

No, the midwife's difficulties here in Bourges have nothing to do with her staff, except that their very number has attracted negative attention. Instead she is dealing with a host of much greater indignities than she has never encountered before. The intendant is away. The city officials treat her shabbily; they have not greeted her, and she has had to go seek them out. Worse, their scantness of ceremony betrays a deeper unwillingness to cooperate. They seem to believe that her new expense account from the king covers everything, and refuse to pay her rent, candles, or wood.

Du Coudray is no complainer, but she is driven today to write to the intendant for help, scandalized by this insult to which she can recall no parallel. She of course cannot afford and would never have promised to cover all her own expenses; these officials have misunderstood the letter she wrote from Montargis where she spoke of payment from the king, and are trying to cheat her. They are refusing her heat, and she fears she may literally need to go into a kind of hibernation to preserve her health. Even for her monarch she cannot attempt valorous impossibilities. "I have spared you the first vexations, they were too miserable to repeat, and to avoid greater ones and the unpleasantness of having to just retire to my bed, I yielded to them on light. But on fire I cannot do it. I confess to you, Monsieur, that if all the city *corps* had thought this same way, it would have given me a furious disgust for my mission, it would surely have weakened my resolve." Besides, she is doing new, improved, more costly lessons now, embellished with sponges showing blood and fluids as she had done for the surgeons in Rochefort. The wet machines must be carefully dried to prevent mold. "I begin here my Grand Operations, that is, with all the liquids that accompany childbirth; these expenses are quite considerable in themselves with the detriment to the machines so I cannot incur additional ones, and whatever wish I have to oblige the city of Bourges I cannot permit myself to go beyond the engagements I have the honor to hold with the minister." She has shown her willingness to oblige and compromise and sacrifice, she has not stood on ceremony. But now it is the other side's turn to make concessions. Having said this, lest she leave a negative impression, she ends on a cheerier note: "I could not, Monsieur, be happier with my women, and you have one, especially, for your lands, who will be a truly great subject. She is of a singular intelligence. I am filled, at each lesson, with admiration."[8] This prize student, one Jouhannet, daughter of a surgeon and widow of another, will remain for du Coudray a source of pride and joy for many years to come.

The intendant responds immediately. The provocation of "furious disgust" in this staunch, usually unflappable woman dishonors him and his region. He had no idea how bad things were, how close the midwife came to giving up completely, and is deeply embarrassed by her mistreatment. In the hierarchy of reprimands, just as Bertin had admonished Boutin, St. Maur now fires off a letter to his subordinates ordering them to undo the damage, to make and keep du Coudray happy. "She has experienced in no other place she has gone any similar difficulties. I would be angry if she could justifiably complain about our province and that we be guilty of not doing what we must to derive from this establishment all the advantages we hoped for." As for du Coudray, he simply assures her that the officials of Bourges will henceforth do "all that you desire."[9] Succinct reassurance, but it will do.

How ironic that du Coudray's first stop after her new hard-won brevet is so fraught with difficulties. Just when things should be smoother she finds herself disgracefully strapped. There are other problems too, like illness. The winter is bitter cold; her friend and protector Frère Côme reports that the extremely frigid temperatures have even discouraged many students from attending the first course. Du Coudray was already somewhat under the weather before leaving Montargis; the despicable squabble over heat, so hurtful to her spirit, now also seriously compromises her physical health.[10]

How does the midwife react to what could be a terribly depressing situation? By throwing herself with renewed passion into her work, in several ways. First, as we have seen, she presents more thorough demonstrations than ever, incurring additional expenses for the complicated machines. Second, at this very moment she decides to put out a new edition of the *Abrégé*, and applies for a royal privilege to do so. And third, she commissions twenty-six extremely costly anatomical engravings for this new edition. They will be in color! Far from pocketing funds for herself or trying to enhance her personal comfort, she has reinvested her newly promised pension in her work. It will cost at least 3,000 livres to pay for these illustrations, which use a revolutionary three-color process, the very latest in print technology (fig. 7). "This expenditure," Frère Côme explains, "has already very much inconvenienced and starved her in her finances; more than half of the King's pension since August is already gone."[11]

But of course this is not all altruism. Characteristically, du Coudray thinks of using her book to improve her situation, to restart her, as it had served to propel her forward a decade ago. This book is her faithful ally, and she needs it this time for a very specific purpose. She enjoys the monarch's authority and is today famous, as she was not yet in 1759 when the first version appeared. The moment has evidently come to remind everyone just how important she is, and this new edition is designed to do precisely that. She will charge 6 livres for it rather than the former 50 sous. She will make it bigger, publish it in the more impressive octavo format rather than 12° as before. The "Observations" by Verdier will appear *after* her text, at the end of the book, not at the beginning. The volume will be uniquely beautiful with its colored pictures. And the first thing the readers will see is the author's imposing portrait (see fig. 1), with her qualifications all spelled out. They will be instantly reminded that she is "sent by the King to teach the practice of the art of delivery throughout the realm." Just around the time that things are going so terribly here in Bourges she poses for this plucky, confident picture. A popular copy of the engraving made from this painting circulates separately with flattering doggerel printed beneath it exalting her "wisdom," "glory," "genius," and favoring her work of preserving subjects over men's work of destroying them in military conquest.[12]

In her effort to enhance the book, the midwife has chosen an innovative technique for her pictures, very hard to come by because so few are trained to do this multichrome process, which involves

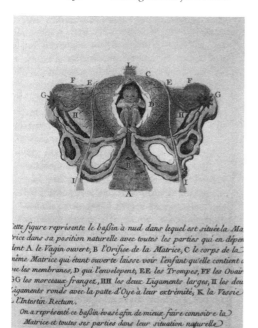

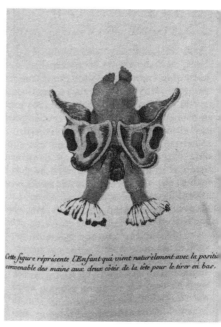

Figure 7. Two illustrations from the second edition of the textbook (1769). These were color engravings, the result of a new and very expensive process never before used in anatomical pictures. The picture on the left labels the various organs; the picture on the right shows the baby in a normal presentation passing between the pelvic bones into the midwife's white-cuffed, waiting hands.

inking successive copper plates in red, yellow, blue, and black and printing the image four times in superposition. Originally invented by Jacques Christophe Le Blon, it has never been employed for obstetrical illustrations before. A disciple of Le Blon's, Jean Robert, has been hired by du Coudray for this job. Robert has been involved in a vicious priority dispute over the color process with an aggressive rival, Gauthier d'Agoty. Years ago, in the spring of 1756, when du Coudray was in Paris seeking approval for her machine from the Academy of Surgery, Robert had published an impassioned plea in the *Mercure de France* that anyone wanting to use this process please contact him directly.[13] So she has gone straight to him for her color engravings, splurging in a way that makes clear how very important these illustrations are to her. They break entirely with all conventions of obstetrical representation used by du Coudray's male predecessors or contemporaries. Her pictures are arresting in their fresh, gentle, watercolor-like tones, almost cartoonlike in their simplicity and accessibility, and very beautiful. She makes this extremely costly choice without hesitation, as Frère Côme explains, to "render her mission luminous and lasting."[14]

Here is what the midwife says about these pictures:

> Commissioned by the King, and overwhelmed by his goodness, to instruct, with the aid of the machine I thought up, women and girls who mean to follow this profession, especially in the countryside, I add to my second edition plates that can remind my students of my own demonstrations; and to render [the students] still more aware [*sensible*], I made [the pictures] in color, so that the different shades give greater clarity to the objects. I am determined to show the impossibility of bad maneuvers performed by people who dabble in the practice of delivery without knowledge of anatomy [*conformation intérieur*]. After presenting the womb in its position, its opening, its dilation by gradation, its contraction and obliquities, I decided that the child alone in the pelvis would become more striking [*frappant*], especially for my students.[15]

The fetus in these pictures is *indeed* striking—unforgettable, in fact. It is fully developed and bright pink, just waiting to be navigated to the safety of the midwife's outstretched hands. These pictures have three people in them, but it is easy to forget the mother. She is only present as an outline of pelvic bones, an obstacle course. Key players are the baby—male, of course—ready to be useful to the state, and the midwife, her trusty hands claiming each new child for France.

So these pictures send out multiple messages. They are obviously designed to highlight du Coudray's patriotism. But they also serve to enhance the esteem of her students. The very inclusion of such pictures in a text for women asserts their right to *see*, to behold rather than be beheld, to play subject as well as object. This is quite daring, because representing women has until now always been considered a male prerogative. Du Coudray's illustrations are decorous, respectful, practical. They have a style and design all their own, foregrounding the midwife's hands, symbol of the artisanal world, which are there to tame, civilize, manage the birth. She is proud of her students, and shows it with these illustrations.

She shows it also whenever she awards them the handsome printed certificates that have been prepared, stating that each recipient "followed exactly my course on childbirth, that she behaved prudently there, that she showed progress, putting her in condition to make correct prognoses in even the most difficult deliveries and soothe women in labor."[16] That the validity of this credential has been and will be repeatedly challenged by jealous surgeons and unschooled village matrons never tarnishes the joy of the day on which, after much hard work, these diplomas are awarded.[17]

Du Coudray knows she will leave here unlamented by the town officials, but she has refused to let them get her down and has instead taken a big forward step. That the published, bound book will not actually appear for another year matters little. What is important is that du Coudray, in extremely troubled times, conceives these pictures, initiates the process of obtaining permission to produce this extraordinary illustrated text, and gets the project under way. Her vision, her activity, dispel whatever "furious disgust" she might have felt—at least for the time being.

28. PRIZE PUPIL

Issoudun, 2 August 1768

Du Coudray is considering quitting, and well she might. She has been here in Issoudun for several months. Her letters dwell on the fact that the king has approved a "pension of 1,000 ecus [3,000 livres] for the rest of my life," as if she is mulling things over in her mind, counting on that retirement pension should she now give up her mission.[1] But these promises of money are precisely the problem, for they are only promises. So far she has received next to nothing of the salary pledged to her in the new brevet, and today she writes to Versailles that surely some mistake has occurred. It is Frère Côme who has been watching over and coordinating her payment, and she wonders what might have happened to this faithful supervisor. "Since I know all his goodness and his punctuality in everything that concerns me, I fear he must be sick." She urgently needs 600 livres to be sent by return post so she can make her next trip, to Châteauroux. The problem, she fervently hopes, is a temporary oversight by Frère Côme rather than an institutional difficulty, some hidden snare in the arrangement. "If the delay is at the Royal

Treasury, this would be very disagreeable for my continual moving about. I have never before been in this position. I knew how, with my meager stipends, never to be in debt to anyone. Many people will vouch for that in the provinces that I have already done. I *will* know what is causing the lateness."[2] Even in distress the midwife is commanding, never spiritless.

And she has good cause to worry. The impact of the *séance de la flagellation* has by now completely worn off, and *parlements* throughout France are once again mounting their collective opposition, making a particularly vehement attack on pensions. D'Aiguillon, the king's commandant in Brittany, has been forced by his dispute with the *parlement* of Rennes to resign—a major mortification for the crown. A new chancellor, Maupeou, has been brought in to try to strengthen the central administration, but he is just getting his bearings and right now the monarchy is looking bad. Laverdy's ministry is weakening by the day. The royal midwife is justifiably concerned about her place in all this.

Meanwhile she is stuck, unable to proceed with her journey. She knows no one well enough to ask a personal favor, in this case a loan so she can travel on as scheduled. Du Coudray speaks now for the first time of how hard it is to be always on the move, to deal with a constantly changing cast of characters, "staying far too little time in each place to have recourse to any friends." She is also costing the next city, Châteauroux, rent for an apartment she obviously cannot occupy because she isn't there, and she fears that her students, already assembled and no doubt squandering living expenses while awaiting her arrival, will use up all their money for nothing. These village girls are having the adventure of their lives in the big town. Totally unsophisticated, they cannot be expected to budget their small allotment in a disciplined fashion. This is normally not a problem because the midwife arrives before her students and can supervise them, but everything is upside down this time. "I feel all this trouble so strongly that it is altering my health."[3]

Communications do seem to have broken down temporarily, but the ever loyal Frère Côme now gets things back on track. He has even somehow managed the miraculous diplomatic feat of smoothing things over in Bordeaux, arranging for her to head there soon. After that he wants her "in my country, which is in the generality of Bordeaux and for which she will have the attraction of gratitude . . . for all my pains for the advantage of the general good seven years in a row." In other words, the only thanks he asks of her is that she grace his native region with a teaching visit. He does a great deal of negotiating in Paris to keep things running as smoothly as possible for his protégée, for he knows she is worth the trouble. Every bit of it. "I have nothing more to get from this world than the salvation of my soul. That is all the fortune I claim for all my effort in behalf of this invaluable affair."[4]

So du Coudray bounces back. The monk's reassurance dispels her doubts, the mood of gloom is gone, and summer ripens into a *belle saison*. The money arrives eventually, preparations for the new edition of the *Abrégé* are moving along,[5] and she gets the go-ahead to proceed to Châteauroux. There she will once again encounter miserly town officials—again in fights over extra coal and wood as winter approaches—but her students and a group of special surgeons sustain her. She orders from Paris a box of surgical instruments worth 200 livres as a gift to these men. Cheerful now that things are looking up, she asks for still "another favor" from the intendant, "for the good of the poor women of Châteauroux. I trained a student there among all the others who gave me all the honor in the world by her success. . . . She is full of charity and I can guarantee to you that she has the trust of the whole city. She would like to have a dozen pairs of sheets and some shirts to change poor women in childbed, and often it is to this precaution that we own the saving of their lives by evading for them all the vapors that putrid linen can occasion. This generosity is of so little consequence in terms of cost and would produce such a great good that it is worthy of you. I really beg you urgently."[6]

This Mme Jouhannet, who had taken the course in Bourges as well, is du Coudray's special triumph, a true soul mate, whose clinic sounds like a rather advanced operation. Teacher and pupil will pair up again fourteen years from now when du Coudray returns to this area, so it is likely that they maintained contact during the interim. They agree on the importance of clean bedding and clothing, sensing that dirt is somehow dangerous. The illustrations in du Coudray's new edition of the *Abrégé* are designed to emphasize this, showing the midwife's cuffs to be bright white. The importance of washing hands, however, does not come up, no doubt because lubrication of the birthing parts with oil or grease precludes any such fastidiousness.[7] It will be another century before a real understanding of germ contamination and the need for sterile technique catches on.

Du Coudray's astonishing recuperative powers show in her letter to the intendant of Berry, who resides in Bourges, where she has had her most depressing moments.[8] She will have done five courses during fourteen months in Berry, and the road has been both emotionally and physically rocky. Deeply bruised, here in Issoudun she vows to accept in future only invitations from people genuinely motivated to do good.[9] But to the intendant she will emphasize the positive, fibbing robustly, calling the stay in Berry a "sojourn that I very much miss because of all the kindnesses extended to me."[10] This last seems an amazing whitewashing of the facts, but it is a testament to du Coudray's psychological health, her mental determination not to succumb. Once she vents her spleen nothing festers, and she refocuses her energy. Then she can remember the successes, refer back brightly to the good memories, and rewrite history in a way more becoming to the legend she will leave for posterity. After all is said and done, she is not stepping down yet.

29. New Edition, Strong Words

Périgueux, 4 September 1769

Back among the limestone cliffs of Dordogne once again, here in the center of Périgord where all roads meet, du Coudray is in a huff. The subdelegate of this town has failed to rouse enthusiasm for her good works. His subjects need their zeal "reheated," but he cannot seem to do it, and the midwife feels he is taking her for granted. Some of the men with whom she is forced to deal seem so incompetent it infuriates her. Is the imminent trip to Bordeaux, which she has successfully avoided for nearly a decade but which Frère Côme has finally set up, making her edgy? She cancels a planned spring visit to Sarlat, disgusted with the subdelegate there for changing his mind about the dates after she has already reserved the carriage. And she alludes to plenty of other problems (*tracasseries*), worries, pesty and fussy things she should not need to be bothered with.[1] The surgeons are awful, and one city official insults her especially by insisting that she reregister her brevet from the king before they will honor it.[2]

Why can't these men be reasonable? Even when things improve, she is still fuming. To the intendant, who does finally intervene, she writes with unusual impudence: "I see, Monsieur, that you have brought the syndic back to his senses." And she downright refuses to do the intendant's bidding when he tells her to offer a copy of the *Abrégé* to this man, who is an important leader of the town. "As regards the book, you are in charge. His tone did not please me enough for me to give it to him."[3] Her book, especially this beautiful new edition, is very precious to her. At six livres, each volume sold represents a sizable profit; she will give one free only as a mark of particular esteem, never to someone undeserving. Laconic to the point of curtness, she is clearly letting things get on her nerves. Some people seem simply asinine, and dealing with them can reduce you to pettiness yourself.

It is especially galling to be snubbed now, when the new edition of the *Abrégé* with its significant changes and additions has at long last appeared. In it, du Coudray has gone to great lengths to redouble and underscore her commitment as a public servant. She has spelled out her mission explicitly under her portrait. She has updated the book, presenting revised techniques and new experiences, reiterating her faith in nature and in the skilled hand.[4] But she has also added large sections of new text, emphasizing the compatibility of her mission with male practitioners, priests, and government officials. Introducing some ideas on breast-feeding, for example, she writes that "doctors do not disapprove of this conduct" and proceeds to show that most of them give the same advice themselves.[5] Elsewhere in the added sections she refers the reader to chapter 14 especially, on tying the umbilical cord, the only chapter where she cites several male authorities—Viardel, Mery, Aubert, de la Motte—and uses them as the basis for her recommendation.[6] She deliberately signals also a rapprochement with churchmen, adding a long discussion of baptism—at the request, she says, of parish priests. And stressing further her devotion to the state, she insists that her students work still harder, that they play an added role in postnatal supervision. "My mission teaches me every day how many children perish after emerging from their mother's bosom, due to lack of care . . . which leads me to go into greater detail."[7] What is the point of engineering a safe birth only to watch the newborn expire? Her new text, in short, is sterner than ever, and she expects the men with whom she works to be appreciative.

Shocking her reader to attention, she graphically describes how many babies, born safely, die in their first moments of life through inattention on the midwife's or wet nurse's part. A weak, motionless baby mistaken for dead will be wrapped up and put away in a corner to spare the mother such a sad sight. Some are buried alive, and without baptism; "witness four such who had been given up on, and whom I had the joy of bringing back to life and having baptized in Church. I found one of these children whose toe had been eaten by a dog without anyone noticing. One can see how painful such negligence is to humanity . . . one must never abandon [a child]."[8] After getting the students riveted on such dramatic stories and inspiring them to see themselves as potential savers and guardians of life, du Coudray goes on to enumerate with renewed vigor the many practical details and responsibilities a midwife must handle. It is she who arranges the visit with the curé and fixes an appointment for baptism. The trip to church must be done promptly and quickly. If the baby is exposed to the "rigors of the season" or becomes fatigued or is mishandled because the party stops to drink en route, it could be ruinous.[9] One should avoid going at night; bad roads, ditches, ice, foul weather, dogs, a false step—all imperil the precious life, the sacred trust, who might die before receiving eternal blessing. In wintertime, the midwife must also remind the priest to warm the holy water so the child does not catch cold and die. At the baptism itself she must hold the child carefully while pins in its bonnet are undone and other wrappings removed so it can receive unction on the chest and between the shoulders. She has a far larger role than the godparents, who only watch and touch. The priest must be told not to splash the water from too high, and not to press too hard on the baby's tender skull.[10] Midwives must also select good wet nurses, because a bad one is a "monster of nature." A pastor in Bugey near Lyon, she comments, actually holds a special church meeting to impress upon wet nurses the preciousness of their charge and the rewards that await them for good works in this life and in the next.

Beyond advising priests and wet nurses, du Coudray's trainees also keep mothers in check. "It is very unfortunate that the State loses so many subjects: but there are still others who also do it no good: that is, the imbeciles, the maimed, the deaf."[11] Here the mothers themselves are often to blame. Everywhere they plead with midwives to "repair defects of nature, to shape the head of the child, to make it rounder, to fix its nose. . . . " Mothers must come to their senses and stop requesting such cosmetic procedures, which end in atrocities, but until they do midwives must categorically refuse to perform these lethal squeezings and moldings. Her pupils receive strict directives on this serious matter.[12]

There is nothing subtle about du Coudray's insistence on the obligations of her students to the little human being newly delivered, in text that is coupled with pictures of cherubic pink babies. Together they give a pronounced twist to the new *Abrégé*. Children are "precious treasures," "treasures of great price," "goods" "dear" to the state.[13] Du Coudray's work, quite simply, enriches the nation.

Why, after all this, do these officials in Périgueux insist on trying to belittle and demean her?

30. The Kindness of Strangers

Agen, 30 November 1769

On her way here Du Coudray has made a fleeting stop in Bordeaux. That city, which she once virtually swore never to visit, now has a new intendant whose first secretary, M. Duchesne, she hit it off with instantly. He is a man of immense warmth and charm, so the place she had dreaded feels unexpectedly comfortable. The strong affection she develops for both Duchesne and his wife, and they for her, is an unanticipated and welcome novelty, a keen pleasure, something she has done without but that now seems, suddenly, a vital necessity. It is for her an almost desperate response to special kindness, to true caring for which she has been starved, so reluctant was she up until now to take others into her confidence. She has worked with some supportive intendants and attentive subdelegates, but this is a real friendship, with a generous man she can count on to listen sympathetically, trust her and lend her money unhesitatingly, be there to lighten her load. Her moods have been erratic lately, so she badly needs Duchesne's calming, healing company. He gives her 600 livres to tide her over and facilitate her journey. She confides in him, they chatter and gossip together, and her joy in the relationship animates her letters. This fortifying boost comes just in time, for where she finds herself now, Agen in the land of prunes, is not an easy place.

The ugly terrain along the banks of the Garonne is quite inhospitable,[1] as du Coudray immediately senses, especially now in the bleakness of winter. Just before her arrival the locals had written to Bordeaux that they were perfectly satisfied with their own practitioners, that therefore "this woman need not be so determined to come here." They are disgruntled by "the pretensions of this woman" and claim to be too busy with more important affairs. The barefoot poor of the region, they say, are also not receptive to anything that fails to provide instant results.[2] As if to confirm this, the first circular sent to parish priests and seigneurs soliciting students has brought no response.[3]

Du Coudray feels she is surrounded by nearly insufferable coarseness. Earlier she reported to Duchesne that her reception in this town has been only "tolerable," and conveyed a sense of the seediness of things, even referring unflatteringly to her students. "I have a big divine house where I can walk my rats with those we have for company. . . . I very much fear I will have plenty of time here to be bored. I will tell you how many students come. That will decide [the timing for] the course in Bordeaux, [a city] I will see again with pleasure. You were right, Monsieur, to think I'd be able to economize here. This life cures the taste for sumptuous fare, and those who live only to eat might as well hang up their teeth. The market consists of a bundle of onions and a cabbage, so one could be just as content with the weeds that grow in the street." In an uncharacteristically personal note, she says she misses him.[4] She is craving her return to civilization and affable company. Having so recently opened herself to friendship, she seems to feel here in Agen a real sense of deprivation and can't wait to get this teaching stint over with.[5]

Today she writes Duchesne again, eagerly looking forward to the end of the course. It will be finished on Christmas Eve, so she asks that her house in Bordeaux be prepared by the end of December. "I am writing this to M. the Intendant, and for my consolation I repeat it to you." She has some doubts about the intendant's effectiveness, for despite his express instructions, Agen has refused to buy a machine and thus, as she forthrightly sees it, to "erect a monument to humanity." She confides to her friend that she has mentioned this refusal to his superior also but has watered down its vehemence, so that he can be spared "the little value given to his orders." She is meanwhile busy training an exciting young surgeon from Mont-flanquin, meeting with the subdelegate of that little town to per-suade him to buy a machine,[6] drumming up business whenever she can. She does not like being idle. And at least the surgeons of Agen do appreciate her and her unsentimental, no-nonsense approach. Seemingly unbothered by the small turnout for her course—only twenty showed up—they write a glowing letter of recommendation, praising her machine, which is "based on the best principles and con-forms to the laws of mechanics and of movement."[7] Given her ea-gerness to leave, she might well be teaching with less feeling than usual, merely going through the rote maneuvers. But that suits the surgeons fine. For these men, the reductive view of childbirth as a physical, quantitative problem is all to the good, a positive develop-ment for which the midwife deserves credit.

These days if du Coudray needs money, she asks for it with no shame. The new system of payment from Paris, which was to have improved her situation, has been a bitter disappointment. In Octo-ber 1768 Laverdy fell from favor, replaced by Mayon d'Invau who seems far less interested in the midwife and may even be encourag-ing others to question her position.[8] Duchesne and the Bordeaux in-tendant are understanding and have been kind, even casual, about loans. Upon arrival here in Agen she took immediate advantage of a letter of credit from Duchesne and cashed it for 25 louis d'or (600 livres).[9] But the local officials here, who have less faith in her, are stingy and keep track of each tiny amount she borrows—even to the tune of 18 sous![10] In the early years she had been humiliated whenever she needed to request help because her money came late, but now she is often short owing to mix-ups in the capital. The Royal Treasury is not forthcoming, and fighting for her payments becomes the rule rather than the exception. As long as she under-stands this as the fault of others rather than any reflection on per-ceived shortcomings of hers, as long as she can persuade herself of that, she will demand what she requires, unabashed.

3

Forging Farther Afield—
Friends, "Family," and Foes

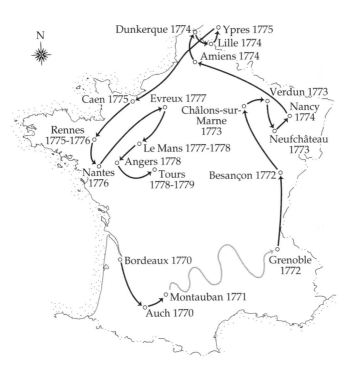

NEW STRAINS, PRIVATE NEEDS

31. Friendship and Fortification

Bordeaux, Spring 1770

This prosperous city with its crescent-shaped tidal port dominates the Guyenne region, whose people have a reputation for being intractable, boastful, and extremely frank.[1] Du Coudray certainly appreciates the frankness, especially in the person of Duchesne, whom she gets to know still better now during a rather quiet and anticlimactic teaching spell here. Things go so smoothly that she really can relax and socialize. Local villages send young women, each with 60 livres generously contributed by the parishioners—nearly twice what Turgot used to give students in the Limousin.[2] One of the midwife's trainees will even become a teacher here in her own right, an extremely rare case of the job of demonstrator being passed to a woman.[3]

Primarily this stop, a watershed in her life, serves the purpose of emotional refueling. Du Coudray has been on the road a full decade; she is fifty-five. She had feared coming here, but now Boutin is gone, and it turns into a delightful occasion instead. Simply being here at last plays something of a cathartic role. In her relief she can take stock of her situation.

About many things she has been absolutely stoic. Her traveling, for example. She has looped north, east, south, west, north again, south again, west again, covering with these tours and detours well over two thousand miles. Often the dusty roads are crowded with noisy farm wagons, heavily laden donkeys, flocks of bleating sheep and full-uddered cows, and of course numerous boisterous voyagers on foot—indigent seasonal migrants, students, peddlers, musicians, traveling players, pilgrims to various religious shrines, *compagnon* artisans on their formative *tour de France*. These latter stroll in merry, often rowdy bands, scattering sometimes to distribute themselves behind or alongside carriages for shelter from the winds.[4]

143

The upper classes journey also, to parties or operas in other towns, adding to the general clutter and congestion.

There are no rules of the road, and frequently the many wagons and carriages jockey for position on routes too narrow even for one of them, capsizing or at the very least listing precariously, careening wildly, shaking up and injuring the passengers. More often than not there are too many creatures and things crammed into the small space, loud snorers, incontinent revelers, mothers with crying children, lap dogs, parrots, and the ubiquitous cloaks, parcels, and umbrellas. It is impossible to find a comfortable position. Horses act up, coachmen get drunk—or grow horn mad or whip crazy and decide to have a race. Wheels, axles, and reins break. On steep hills, as in Poitiers, everyone needs to empty out and walk, or even help to push the still-heavy carriage. These vehicles are uncomfortable, with their oilcloth flaps barely keeping out the elements. They have little suspension and so bump, plunge, creak, and lurch along on roads that in some provinces are little more than rocky dirt paths. Soon Turgot will make some innovations in transportation, such as lighter, spring-cushioned carriages that can reach their destinations faster by traveling through the night.[5] For now, though, because area tolls and regional frontiers are not manned after dark, the distance can be covered by day only and the traveling seems to take forever.

And all over there are beggars—crowds of wretched folks, files of them at inn doors, swarms of them in and around churches, interrupting rests, meals, and even prayers with their importunity.[6] Winter, of course, brings another set of problems, the piercing blasts of cold being the least of them. Mud, ice, floods, and poor visibility greatly increase the number of accidents on the road. Carriages fill with freezing water at every ford. Warm weather has its own drawbacks; sickness of one sort or another routinely follows a ride through pestilential, marshy plains. And there are wolves, especially in the forests that come right up to the roadside. And muggers, smugglers, highway bandits who often kill. "We advise our public," reads a notice in the *Gazette de France*, "that there is no substance to the rumor spread about regarding a robbery of the coach to Lyon and the assassination of its passengers."[7] The fact that carriage companies must so protest to reassure the public about safety reveals the true conditions that prevail. Much apprehension surrounds travel; passengers often prepare their last will and testament before embarking on a long voyage, and some have been known to die of apoplexy.

Of these hazards, which are legion, of the inevitable headaches, sore rumps, bruised or even broken bones, indigestions, fevers, and terrors of the journey, du Coudray says next to nothing. She has borne them with indomitable strength of character. Her consistent demand for two weeks' rest upon her arrival in a town before beginning her class and for another two weeks' rest to fortify herself before setting out on the next trip speaks more eloquently than words of the physical and emotional toll of her travels. But she has kept her feelings to herself, hiding any vulnerability, any scars to her body or spirit. In those few instances where her letters do reveal some distress—at Angoulême, Bourges, Issoudun, Périgueux—she hastens to move on to an upbeat subject, never allowing herself to dwell on problems for long or to leave a dejected impression. Her resolution to establish her mastery of the monumental job entrusted to her has prevailed. She has not dared to falter before admirers or critics. Above all she will not expose herself to accusations of female delicacy. Perhaps she made, long ago, a conscious choice to suppress and silence her personal needs in exchange for the right to function like a man.[8]

Such spartan endurance, however, can turn eventually to exhaustion, such exaggerated self-reliance can change to deep yearning for emotional intimacy. Earlier du Coudray hinted at the loneliness of the nomadic life, the lack of opportunity to make friends. Now in Duchesne she has finally found one, and he becomes a kind of lifeline. She has discovered him just in time, because she will soon be traveling much greater distances than before. Her trip thus far has been mostly in the center of France, in *pays d'élection* where the intendant's influence is most powerful. But she must next reach farther afield to the outskirts, to areas with which she is not familiar, areas added more recently to the country, where the king's influence is therefore less accepted. Feelings of affection, so long pent up, now give her new strength, new energy. If she worried formerly that such ties would "weaken" her, she sees here that she can let down defenses without falling apart or losing momentum. She has confronted this city, exorcised her Bordeaux demon, opened up her heart. She can tackle the tasks of the future honestly and whole now, facing squarely her felt needs, finding balance, acknowledging a kind of hunger she has ignored or refused to admit. It has been said that the first discipline required of a leader is that he or she have no friends, and ever since the start of her mission and the dizzying expansion of her role she has coped alone, steadied herself, kept her own counsel, and proven her professional competence and capacity to lead. But now she senses she can give free rein to these new stirrings of the soul. Her letters will be looser once the floodgates open here in Bordeaux, permitting the midwife's ink to flow more freely.

And there is another change. She has spent the last decade getting, losing, regaining, and maintaining her bearings essentially by herself. Until now this has been very much a solo performance. But here, before leaving, she adds to her traveling team a helper, a Bordeaux surgeon named Coutanceau. She still remains very much in charge, and in fact her extant letters from this period do not mention him at all. Does she yet realize or even begin to imagine the significant part he will play?

32. The Suitor and Other Calamities

Auch, 19 December 1770

Monsieur—Read me when you have the time.

I don't know if you remember a certain marriage proposal to my niece when I was in Bordeaux. It was a fortune offered for her. If you recall, I refused all these advantages. I saw nothing but vices in this young man, and my governess as well as my niece saw nothing but 30,000 livres. The importunities of the mother and of the sister of the young man showed they wanted to pawn off this scoundrel on me. I left even refusing from the mother a pension for Monsieur her son that she offered me to train him further. After so much stubbornness on my part, I suddenly reflected that in the event that I should die, [my niece] would reproach me for having opposed a so brilliant fortune. This idea seized me like an inspiration: What do I risk? say I to myself. His views are monstrous. When people live together, facts strike a young person more than all the advice in the world. I resolved then to put him to the test, supposing that if I was mistaken and that he has more virtue, this could make a suitable engagement. But God who gave me inspiration for this trial was good enough to surpass my expectations. A letter negligently discarded and luckily found, in which he wrote to Mme his mother that he gave up the rest of his legitimate inheritance in exchange for 4 louis, reversed the fortune of my niece, and as the strongest feeling she had for him was interest, you can judge, Monsieur, that this little inclination, or love if you will, took flight immediately. But to join antipathy to disdain, a last stroke brought the whole thing down. He left for Bordeaux at the time of the fair. He stole from my niece a small lined ring box of little value but a treasure more precious to her than that of St. Denis. He came back but the box was lost, and all her jewels. What a flood of tears, what indignation against him, and what joy for me that she could regard him with all the scorn he deserved. The maid, touched by the little one's weeping and affected by the trick he played on her, could have strangled him. I must tell you too, Monsieur, that he took from my cupboard a gold knife with a little lined case of the same metal. This knife, just by chance, I wanted to show to someone, and I couldn't find it at all. Luckily for my staff, I am not hasty to accuse. I wanted to discover it before I punished, but a second inspiration came to me, and I suspected him of taking it away. I stopped all the crying I was causing in the house. I assured them I knew who. I was not wrong. The young man returned, and in a firm and confident tone, fixing him with my eyes: Give me back my knife and my case. He pulled it from his pocket, and [so] happily I did not lose these two little personal effects. Even if he had had for me only the defect of lying, for I don't think there can be a man in the world who equals him, I could never have allowed, you realize, Monsieur, all of these scenes. I could no longer stand the sight of him. However, I was charitable enough, in order to avoid a great scandal, not to throw him out immediately, and I have continued to feed, lodge, and have his laundry done since his return from the fair of Bordeaux. I wrote to madame his mother that it was not possible that I keep M. her son any longer, that his blunders did not suit me, and that, combined with the debts he incurred, I was really always alarmed. You will be good enough, Monsieur, to read Mme Rodes's letter that I'm enclosing . . . [and my notes about] the debts he had and that I paid. You will do the greatest thing in the world, you will be good enough to go find her and to settle this affair. I see no other hope for me than this approach by you. You see what faith I have in your way of thinking. . . . I have every reason to dread on the part of the mother troubles of a different kind from her son's. It's in your hands that I put my interests. I could not do better. With anyone else I would worry that the charms of the young man's sister would outweigh the claims I could inspire, but with you I have nothing to fear. It is enough that my cause is that of justice.

I have yet another story to tell you. The subdelegate of Pau does not want me to bring my good works there. Speaking of the good, M. Esmangart [the newest intendant of Bordeaux] could oblige me if he agreed to. The *états* of Bigorre want two machines as soon as possible. I will send them yours, which are all ready, and will receive for them needed money right away. It is only to you that I tell this, and especially as I am about to go on vacation. . . . Answer me as quickly as you can, a thousand thousand pardons. I am, with all feelings of esteem and veneration, your very humble and very obedient servant.

du Coudray[1]

How complicated and messy things have suddenly become! So the midwife has had a young scamp under her roof since summer, when they all came and set up house here in Auch, not far from Frère Côme's hometown of Tarbes, where the monk has asked her to enlighten the region as a personal favor. Du Coudray has had her share of calamities since her arrival, including an illness she diagnoses as overwork.[2] And she relates them liberally now to her friend Duchesne.

She had written to him earlier in a dither asking for help, because she misplaced a receipt showing she had cleared a debt of 600 livres. Du Coudray is usually remarkably organized and meticulous in her record keeping, despite the fact that nothing has a permanent, stationary filing place, so she is half crazed over the missing slip of paper. Hopeful that officials in Paris will remember her reimbursing them, she tells Duchesne: "if they have the slightest doubts, I will not hesitate for a moment to be accountable." What courage it must take to make this gallant statement when she has absolutely no extra funds, indeed, barely enough to manage at all. "If you only knew my chagrin, I cannot express it to you, and that I cause you problems just makes it worse. I will rest easy only when this matter is settled. I will take great pains not to be careless even as I experience such dismay." Meanwhile, however upset she is, her teaching obligations must be met. "I will use for this meeting the machine made for Agen because mine is soaking wet—my thriftiness in sending my trunks by water transport nearly cost me the total loss of the little I possess. That's another experience! I have many things, Monsieur, to tell you about the reception that I got here, but I am too preoccupied by our cursed matter. May the angels accompany you. I will await your response with all the vivacity of my impatience."[3]

This money matter is satisfactorily resolved by Duchesne, for it is not mentioned again. Either the receipt is found, or the Paris officials let it drop, or Duchesne is a dear enough friend to cover it from his own pocket and never say. He next does another favor and sees to it that every one of the surgeons du Coudray designates as a demonstrator does indeed get his commission—in Agen, Monflanquin, Périgueux—in spite of "all the difficulties that the cabal of the community of surgeons ordinarily gives rise to." She thinks long and hard about who best deserves these coveted appointments, so Duchesne honors her wishes and immediately expedites her orders.[4]

Now comes the biggest crisis, a matter of greed, betrayal, and a fifteen-year-old girl's heartbreak. Du Coudray's household help get very emotionally involved in this drama concerning their mistress's family and the bad seed in their midst. And who is this "niece," Marguerite Guillaumanche, who abruptly appears as such a central protagonist? She is probably first mentioned as the "apprentice" in Bourges. Had her parents, illiterate peasants from Tallende, turned her over to the midwife, or had she recently been orphaned? *Was* there perhaps some very distant relationship?[5] The midwife's clear understanding that preaching self-righteous sermons has no success with adolescents sounds like the insight of a seasoned guardian. Chances are they have had quite a few years together already. Is she also remembering some stubbornness in her own distant past? In any case, du Coudray, playing the maternal role, feels responsible for providing her niece with future security by marrying her off sensibly. And the money *is* tempting.

But the midwife, a keen judge of character, will not be the dupe of this feckless young man. The letter shows that, perhaps for lack of companionship of female equals, she has conversations with herself in the privacy of her brain to decide on a course of action. Unscrupulousness cannot go unpunished; as mistress of the house she must educate them all. For the first time, too, the midwife confronts her own mortality. What will happen to her ward when she is gone?

There is still further cause for alarm—of which she does not speak to Duchesne, though it is deeply disquieting. The administration has decided, unaccountably, to sponsor another midwifery manual, of over 250 pages, by a doctor named Joseph Raulin. That Pau and Bayonne have just rejected her offer to "bring the good there," thus defying Frère Côme's wishes, is bad enough, but now there is this other matter of Raulin's rival publication. His *Succinct Instructions . . . for Midwives in the Provinces*, printed "by the ministers' orders," has immediately sold out in first edition and is already being reprinted in large numbers. What ministers? the midwife wonders.[6] Literate women in the parishes—*dames distinguées*—are being asked to read this work regularly to illiterate women and to engage them in conversation on the subject so that they become familiar with the art of childbirth.[7]

Raulin's book appears to be catching on fast. A new dictionary of the trades declares that his instructions are all that country women need in order to learn to deliver babies properly.[8] His text, like du Coudray's, has pictures, but they are twelve unhelpful illustrations of babies floating in acrobatic positions in unfolded wombs that look like geometric puzzles. These pictures do not compare in utility or beauty to the colored ones in the *Abrégé*. In fact, the rival publication has no particular merit that the midwife can discern. There is a lengthy section on religion and the crucial importance of baptism, all of which can be found in her book too, of course, but Raulin has cleverly devoted to this material a disproportionate number of pages, thus winning the resounding approval of the Paris Faculty of Theology.[9] Is this perhaps a rebuke because du Coudray's text is more secular?

In any case, it is not a good development. Of course, the new book cannot substitute for her actual teaching. Deep down she understands that. It is nonetheless an affront and a scare, for it is no mere private undertaking by Raulin, but a government-supported project. Who exactly commissioned Raulin's book? Politically, things are more turbulent than ever. The king's man d'Aiguillon was actually brought to trial this spring by the Parlement of Paris, a trial that dragged on for several months until the king held a *lit de justice* and quashed the proceedings. Louis's new controller general, Terray, is doing his best to back up the crown, but the chorus of *parlements* protesting royal policy and appealing instead to public opinion grows louder and louder. Just last month Chancellor Maupeou declared, as Louis did four years ago at his famous session of the scourging, that *parlements* are nothing but courts of law, have no legislative authority, and are forbidden to act as one body. This political conflict seems to be coming to a head, and the midwife surely finds it unsettling and confusing to try to follow from afar.

Was it worth spending so much of her personal funds last year on illustrations for her *Abrégé* only to see the book get lost among competitive publications? She is not flattered by the idea of imitators. She does not know Terray. Is he against her for some reason? She must keep her head and monitor this situation carefully. The knife almost stolen from her just now, and reclaimed, seems in some way symbolic of her need to insist on her rights here, to jealously guard what is hers, to arm and defend herself. This knife is no mere trinket, but one of many priceless gifts given in recognition of her extraordinary efforts wherever she has taught, her legacy of successes. In her household she has confronted the foe, recovered the goods, and restored order. She must now do the same in her job, do all she can in the outside world to save her mission.

New tests, new challenges. But just how widespread is this ministerial mutiny? How much trouble is she really in?

33. Coutanceau, "Provost" and Partner

Montauban, Winter 1771

This pink brick city, once a hotbed of Protestantism, is now a center for the manufacture of textiles. In fact, there is so much spinning of wool and hemp, so much weaving, such a spread of these industries even into the countryside, that the peasants sometimes neglect the land.[1] Du Coudray has been impatient to get here early, ahead of the game, so she can start making machines before beginning her lessons. In Auch she was sick for a spell;[2] now she has much catching up to do filling numerous back orders. This is, too, a way to get her mind off her worries. She tells Duchesne she is eager "to put myself to the task."[3] *Ad operam* is indeed a guiding principle for the midwife; lying fallow depresses her, and work seems therapeutic.

We now hear more about the sixth and newest member of her band, thirty-three-year-old Jean-Pierre Coutanceau, a surgeon from a medical family in Bordeaux.[4] Somehow in the short period since he joined them he has assumed a very special role. Du Coudray is for the first time admitting that she needs assistance. Although young enough to be her son, he is treated as an equal, a colleague. She obviously already admires and trusts him, for she sends him to do a course in her stead a bit to the north, in cozy, affable Cahors.[5] They give Coutanceau the perquisite of a few hundred livres that usually goes to the midwife. The two seem to have agreed on this, although it is not clear if he contributes the money for shared household expenses or if it is his exclusively.[6] Du Coudray is regarding him still more appreciatively since the fiasco with her niece's suitor. She counts on Coutanceau, who is as steady and reliable as the younger man was shiftless, calls him her "provost," and passes on to him many demonstration and teaching responsibilities. Having an intelligent and loyal adult along has to be an enormous comfort. Perhaps he can become a permanent fixture, an extra pair of hands she will be able always to rely on.

Such have probably been her thoughts lately, for more and more she treats their relationship as a partnership. Is she instinctively insulating herself from adversity? Never before has she given a helper this kind of status, but now she hesitates to proceed alone. She is heading next into the south of France, an area full of conservative *pays d'états*—Pau, Toulouse, Foix, Perpignan, Montpellier, Aix—where having a male surgeon partner might indeed be an advantage.

But an odd thing is about to happen. Even with Coutanceau's company and cooperation, she will be repeatedly cast out, forced to wander as if in the desert. She disappears now from public view for over a year, her mission seemingly suspended, her whereabouts entirely unknown and unmarked in the official correspondence.

34. "Happy as a Queen"

Grenoble, 16 June 1772

Monsieur—

I write to you almost from the other world. I am in Grenoble happy as a queen: a charming intendant, a secretary worthy of him, inhabitants full of gratitude, and lots of intelligence in the subjects. This has made amends for the ennui in which I found myself in Toulouse, traveling calmly along across six provinces in my carriage. Can it be imagined, I was turned away. I do not know what will be my destination, if I will go to Trevoux or to Besançon, but at least let me find there the same zeal and readiness to receive me [as I find here]. I am writing to M. Esmangart to ask that he please give to M. Brochet, surgeon in the city of Périgueux, the commission I had obtained for M. La Combe who just up and died on me [*qui s'est laissé tout bonnement mourir*]. I am not telling the intendant that I am urged to do this by the demoiselles Bertin, but I am asking you to second me so that such supplicants not be disappointed. So oblige me, Monsieur, and give it your attention as promptly as possible. I count on all your kindness toward me. A ton of fond wishes to Mme Duchesne, please, [and] to your sons. You will favor me with a reply as soon as you've expedited this matter, so that I may report to the demoiselles Bertin. I am for life, with feelings of pure attachment, Monsieur, your very humble and very obedient servant.

du Coudray[1]

Where has the midwife been? For thirteen months she sank from sight and Duchesne has heard not a word. In March 1771 she was still in Montauban,[2] by April 1772 in Grenoble. But in between she had been compelled to keep moving, had been unable to stop anywhere to teach. It was certainly not for want of trying. There was some major problem in Toulouse; as she reports to her friend now with considerable shock, several places actually refused her. Narbonne did. And Montpellier.[3] The latter is perhaps not surprising, for this city has a very strong medical faculty, the great rival of Paris; they do not believe they can use any help from this woman trained in the capital. So there she is, reduced to a fugitive! It is so shameful that she chooses silence rather than attempting to tell Duchesne the details of what happened.

But we can conjecture. Throughout late 1770 the *parlements* had grown flagrantly disobedient and provocative. On the night of 19 January 1771 the chancellor Maupeou effected a coup, a complete purge of the law courts, banishing the recalcitrant magistrates to remote, desolate corners of the country. In June d'Aiguillon, so hated by the refractory *parlements*, was made secretary of state for foreign affairs. Maupeou, Terray, and d'Aiguillon now constitute the so-called triumvirate of ministers, determined to see that the king's will be done, that his edicts be imposed and forced into law. In the eyes of many, not just the privileged nobility, Maupeou's maneuver was an act of naked despotism, and the royal midwife almost surely suffered the resentment and hostility directed toward the monarch.

There were other reasons for her rejection in these southern regions. The intendant St. Priest, in April 1771 and again in November, put du Coudray off as politely as possible, referring to bureaucratic complications with the powerful *états*, suggesting she try again sometime in the future.[4] These areas are in any case notoriously inhospitable to female practitioners. Elizabeth Nihell's fierce attack on *accoucheurs* has just been translated into French, with an updated diatribe against the Frenchman Levret who advocates forceps. The Midi apparently makes no distinction between such belligerent feminist midwives and du Coudray: none of them are welcome. Despite seeing that her slightest attempt to alight provoked such antagonism, the royal midwife was too proud to bow, scrape, and explain herself.

The setbacks during this year of enforced leisure, when she could gain no foothold anywhere, must have raised the specter of her whole mission fizzling ignominiously. But she does not permit herself to wax maudlin in letters. In fact, it would seem she wrote no letters during her wanderings, and resumes contact only now after the humiliation is over and past. Even today she gives just the sketchiest picture of those many months. She will not be seen as the plaintive exile. Some things, some feelings, are beyond description. If they go unreported, however gravely wounding, they can lose their edge and fade away.

Du Coudray somehow again now musters all her ardor for Grenoble. She has been in this capital city of Dauphiné for two months, where the locals, even the most rustic, are known for friendliness to outsiders.[5] Technically this is also a *pays d'état*, but the *états* have not met since 1628 and a much more progressive atmosphere prevails. Here the king's intendant, Marécheval, has considerable influence. He has been truly excited about du Coudray's arrival, writing before she came to both lay and clerical administrators in surrounding towns that they "must be convinced in advance of the utility cities can derive from her intelligence. It should interest citizens of all orders." An *avis* has been printed up and circulated, explaining how her mission came about. It is based on Le Nain's *Mémoire* but much more succinct.[6] Perhaps because of the recent hiatus in her teaching, Marécheval believes it wise to reintroduce her; she has not been lately on people's minds. In response, numerous villages have sent students to take advantage of "this important school."[7] The midwife trains some very talented women here, and being appreciated again is sweet.[8]

Even with Duchesne, du Coudray prefers to display her proud moments and keep low moods to herself. Now that her routine is picking up again she feels like reconnecting, sharing her feelings but also reestablishing her businesslike mode. Duchesne takes care of the favor she asks for the surgeon protégé of Bertin's daughters.[9] She has, of course, much to thank the former minister for; without his help all those years ago her mission might never have gotten going at all. Du Coudray is feeling so much better that she can even speak flippantly of the inconvenient death of one of her demonstrators. Finding replacements for her trained disciples is at best a bother. She is regaining her sense of humor. And she again pushes, however charmingly, for what she wants, returning time after time to the favor she needs and insisting on a reply so she'll know it has been taken care of. Her epistolary pressures are in full swing once more. She is back to her old tricks.

Politically now too, in the summer of 1772, things have settled down considerably. The royalist "triumvirate" has been in power for some time, and the *parlements* have been subdued and replaced by courts more cooperative with the crown. D'Aiguillon, the new minister of foreign affairs, seems sufficiently impressed with the midwife's mission, and especially with Coutanceau, that he grants him permission, even though he is not a military man, to don the surgeon-major's uniform.[10] It was good to bring him along after all.

35. Networks, Newspapers, and Name Games

Besançon, 16 November 1772

Crisp, confident, and vigorous, the midwife has been executing numerous tasks in this capital of Franche Comté, another erstwhile *pays d'état*, land of plentiful, exquisite fish, superb big game, abundant wheat, and wine. But the roads here are known to be dangerous, too closed in by menacing woods, too narrow and rutted, too overgrown.[1] As a consequence the trip from Grenoble, not so far as the crow flies, took an inordinately long seven days.[2]

Du Coudray had pushed herself with unusual aggressiveness on this intendant, La Coré, writing in May from Grenoble with a detailed enumeration of her talents. Dreading another idle spell, she is resolved to preserve her new momentum in a long, strong trajectory. In case La Coré shares the prejudice against *accoucheuses* that she encountered in the south, she stresses her connection with surgeons especially. The awkwardness of the letter shows that she is not relaxed. She has, it seems, almost gone to Besançon once before. This time the trip really must materialize.

> I do not doubt that the sentiments of humanity that you have always held will have you learn with pleasure of my proximity. . . . Your reputation inspires me. . . . I have made such a round of visits but despite the postponement I never forgot about you. I am in Grenoble. Everyone in this province supports the beneficence of M. de Marécheval. He is loved, you are, Monsieur, and you are everywhere, and I can do the same for yours. I thought of doing the Lyonnais, but the impossibility of M. de Flessel setting up this establishment only hastens the satisfaction of being with you. . . . My brevet . . . removes all difficulties. I enclose a recommendation from the surgeons of Rochefort that might make yours interested in seeing operations that so much resemble nature. I have here, as I have had everywhere, a great number of [surgeon-students]. I will await your answer, and I will be painfully afflicted [*douloureusement pénétrée*] if obstacles interfere with your desires and with the eagerness I have to support you.[3]

Du Coudray makes it hard to deny her. Plans have not worked out for her to teach in Trévoux near Lyon,[4] so she simply can't let Besançon fall through, for the memory of her year of rejection still smarts. She is in luck, as it turns out. The subdelegate of Besançon, Ethis, having heard the highest praise for the midwife from Grenoble,[5] is very ready and willing to accommodate her. They have a good working rapport, though no close friendship. She has told him bluntly, "I need time to rest before starting."[6] Without such acknowledgment of her limits, she would soon be irretrievably spent.

Since mid-August she has been living and teaching in a house

on the rue St. Vincent, not far from the square in front of the governor's palace, where there is a fountain in the shape of a nude seated
woman with water spurting from her breasts. Ninety-four students
have come, but Ethis and du Coudray herself have had to advance
nearly all of them money, as their parishes fell far short of covering
their living expenses.[7] This is unprecedented. Ethis will later be
obliged to go in hot pursuit of the funds from these delinquent villages, threatening them with lawsuits and arrests if the responsible
parties do not pay up.[8] The midwife, however, knows full well she
will never again see the sums she "lends" these poor women. Certainly she needs the money, but she is also aware that they are far
worse off than she. Besides, they are an investment for her, in the
immortality of her life's work, in the future (fig. 8).

Something else is new here also. A particularly intense selection
process has taken place, with many letters exchanged between the
midwife and the parish priests. Usually the students are all lined
up for the midwife beforehand, but here the priests consult her on
each choice, addressing her variously as "the very deserving *dame*
du Coudrez approved by the King," "midwife proposed by His majesty for instructing," "established by the King," "his Majesty's dep-
uty in the whole extent of the kingdom," "midwife by special appointment," expecting her to be intimately involved in the shaping
of her class. One girl is "sheepish and timid" and "has never left
her village" but is being sent anyway, "informed of your consideration and kindness toward this sort of person." Another painfully
shy girl is nevertheless "rich in character." Du Coudray interviews
them all, then sends off cheerful and efficient notes to Ethis telling
him her decisions. In one case she has to explain to "surprised"
town officials why she rejects a practicing midwife in favor of her
untrained daughter; she wants fresh, open, malleable minds that do
not need to unlearn bad habits first. Only one pupil is supposed to
be sent from each town, but the curé of Héricourt, embarrassed because his best volunteer is Lutheran, begs du Coudray's "dear person" to accept a Catholic girl as well, to balance things out. Protestant midwives are technically against the law, for it is feared that they
will not baptize babies, yet in this region there are many of them.[9]

One particularly supportive priest is helped by a good word du
Coudray puts in for him with the cardinal. In return she asks for
his assistance making certain that her students get clients and are

Figure 8. On top is a call sent by the subdelegate of Besançon on behalf of the king, recruiting suitable midwifery students from each village, to be carefully selected by the parish priest and financially provided for during the lessons. Below is a typical diploma awarded by Mme du Coudray at the completion of the course.

not squeezed out of their rightful job. She fights aggressively on this point, to make sure *her* system of birthing prevails. Priests in each parish, she suggests, should refuse to recognize any midwife at baptisms except the one trained by her. Mothers so obstinate that "they prefer to die in the hands of ignorant women than to call to their aid the new one" can choose an old matron if they wish, but in du Coudray's system both the mother and the matron will be liable five sous each to pay for the baptism. A shrewd boycott indeed. "Shame and stinginess together" will soon win the village women over to the new trainee. You must sometimes, she explains, force "the good" on a public too backward to recognize it themselves.[10]

The midwife develops a special closeness with her students here in Besançon, perhaps because she protects so strenuously their right to practice. She hears about their bad livers and hearts, traumas with their children, and always their immense gratitude to her, for everything. "As for me, my dear lady," writes one succinctly, "I will never forget you."[11] Another thanks du Coudray for being such a sympathetic listener and sends her a gift she received at a noble baptism. This woman is falsely accused of a crime, and complains that she is at a great disadvantage because her adversaries are "rich and well protected." Her honor and all her earthly goods are at stake, and she begs du Coudray to intercede in her behalf with the intendant, "for which I will not stop being grateful as long as I live."[12] The teacher is as sensitive to her students as she is harsh with the old matrons. The hardship she must cause these "other" women, who have practiced for years and are now being pushed aside by girls with a couple of months' training, is nowhere in her thoughts. Saving babies is her sole goal, and creating a new set of victims in the process does not appear to deter her.

That she is noticeably hardened against the older matrons here might be because she finds more than the usual birthing atrocities in this region. A supporter of hers will later explain that she beheld

> horrible spectacles devised by ignorance and cruelty to deliver a woman with a malpresentation, the account of which makes one tremble. She was called to a poor peasant, exhausted by a long labor: they had sat her on a chair with a chopping block under her thighs, on which they cut with a butcher's knife all the emerging parts of a live child; one stepped on the head and pieces of limbs of this child upon entering the room, and to pull the rest of this victim out of this unfortunate mother's body, they tugged and tore it with handles of soup

ladles and hooks from a scale by turns, under which the woman expired in this sad moment.[13]

Even du Coudray, exposed constantly to upsetting sights, found these abominations too much.

The local newspaper has just carried two extensive articles on her lessons, which are credited with having "ended . . . abuses so contrary to the public good, prevented the shedding of an infinity of tears . . . avoided the extinction of families." She is working longer hours than ever, teaching from eight in the morning to noon and then from two to seven in the evening, with only Sundays off. Including surgeons, she has 120 students. The reporter, waxing rhapsodic, portrays a saintly midwife, nearly beyond recognition.

> Mme du Coudray shuns praise. Her modesty cannot admit it. Let us just say then that she taught with much order, neatness, and precision. Her method employs no hooks or other metal instruments, which are alarming and dangerous, but only the dexterous hand. She has as assistants M. Coutanceau, of ample erudition and experience, and Mlle de Varennes, faithful follower of Mme du Coudray her aunt. All the students, male and female, filled with gratitude, praise the seigneur for having given them this favorable opportunity, and to show him thanksgiving Mme du Coudray in her rare piety thought it appropriate to say, last Sunday . . . at 9 in the morning at the Capucins, a mass with offering of blessed bread. . . . She took the sacrament of the Eucharist along with most of her students.

The intendant, the newspaper reports, has generously prepared and presented special leather-bound copies of the *Abrégé* to each of the graduates.[14]

The second article laments that more men are not willing to study with du Coudray, mistakenly thinking they have nothing new to learn. These men should "banish such vain politics, the fear of blushing," and "base sentiments of misplaced pride" and open themselves to enlightenment.[15] The dean of the University of Besançon's medical faculty, who attended the midwife's course, adds his voice too: "We see only too often enormous mistakes made in childbirth by the very ones who call themselves experts in this profession."[16] This kind of blindness and stubbornness on the part of men, coupled with the rashness of untrained matrons, the dean observes, results in the kind of horror scene the midwife witnessed in the region.[17]

These press reports raise several questions. First, how has Coutanceau been persuaded to stay on permanently as part of the crew? The midwife has been turning over her gratuities to him since Bordeaux. Was that all the coaxing he needed, or did he have other reasons for wanting to stay? Second, why does du Coudray suddenly style her "niece" as "Mlle de Varennes"? Maybe it is part of some aristocratic role-playing to enhance the prestige of the group and wipe out memories of the bruising year of rebuffs. Du Coudray, after all, has seen fit to assume for herself a surname complete with noble particle to suggest a lineage of status, and the younger woman is supposedly her relative. A third question concerns why the midwife thinks Besançon is worth a mass. Is it because, just now when she is eager to wind things up and leave, the province turns out to have no money whatsoever to pay her? A display of piety might help. It certainly didn't hurt her rival Raulin get a lot of support and attention for his birthing manual.

Today, chafing at the bit, she writes to her contact M. St. Etienne at the projected next stop, Châlons-sur-Marne. By happy coincidence, she somehow already knows and likes this man very much. Did they perhaps befriend each other during her hard vagabond year when he was on another administrative assignment in a different region? In any case, he is about to take Duchesne's place as her best confidant. She seems positively giddy at the prospect of their imminent reunion. Delayed here, she must wait a full month for the Treasury to be replenished so she can collect payment for the many machines she is leaving in the Besançon region. "I cannot wait to see you again, and without this reason I would have left immediately. I embrace you always, while waiting to be able to tousle your head, goodbye, hello. I am very respectfully, your little servant, du Coudray. P.S. Dear me how we will gossip!"[18]

Is du Coudray actually flirting? For a woman nearing sixty, this *petite servante* sounds positively girlish. It is impossible to be sure. But St. Etienne is clearly a kindred spirit for whom she feels enormous affection, and she is bursting to tell all. Periods of relief, release, unwinding seem essential to her now to punctuate the grueling routine. Bonds created by chatter, laughter, good times, hilarity even, have become vital necessities. And between her and St. Etienne there is something very special. This is her most ebullient letter to date, a complete change from the self-conscious gravity of some and the breezy efficiency of others. Whatever their relationship is, here in anticipation of their meeting she expresses a boisterous, almost visceral joy.

36. FLIRTATION IN CHAMPAGNE

Châlons-sur-Marne, March 1773

A dalliance perhaps? Certainly an especially good time. Sharing the limelight now with her niece and M. Coutanceau, the midwife has spent the winter in this walled city with its shady canals, situated in a large plain in Champagne.[1] Rouillé d'Orfeuil, the intendant, is solicitous, though he is away on rounds and not here to supervise things himself. His official, St. Etienne, has taken over in his absence, adding several incentives to attract students. The first two—the offer of free lodging in Châlons and an assurance that extra earnings from the practice of their new art will never be subject to the *taille*—have been tried before, but the third—exempting their husbands from the hated *corvée*, the enforced labor on royal roads, as long as the midwives remain professionally active—is an innovation.[2]

Nevertheless, things have not gone entirely smoothly. The fanfare has upset one combative surgeon, who casts aspersions on du Coudray's book and its "sloppy" way of "laying the foundations of this establishment." Luckily, this attack does not sway Rouillé d'Orfeuil from his loyalty to the midwife and her enterprise.[3] But there have been other difficulties as well. Some curés have had trouble recruiting students; one who could not find anyone to volunteer sends a compensatory poem instead, lauding the intendant for his farsightedness on this important issue.[4] The problem in gathering recruits for the courses is perhaps related to how hard women work the land in this area, where the chalky soil would form an almost solid crust, broken only by an occasional black pine, were it not for the combined power of men and women.[5] Those students who do come, though, get printed certificates on which the promise of tax exemption is clearly spelled out.[6]

Du Coudray is so happy. Deeply appreciative of Rouillé d'Orfeuil's support, she writes to him: "One feels in this province all the good you do for it. I will neglect nothing, so that your kind intentions will be carried out. I only regret that I will not have the happiness of seeing you."[7] However much she likes writing and receiving letters, the midwife also looks forward to meeting people in the flesh. In this case, however, there is ample compensation for the intendant's absence. St. Etienne is helping with everything, rounding up more students, selling machines, turning a lackluster beginning into a smashing success for du Coudray. She can relax. He is one conquest already made.

Beyond the likelihood that St. Etienne is unmarried—her subsequent letters to him never include greetings to a wife, as is her custom with Duchesne—we know very little about him, except for the unprecedented coquettishness he inspires on the midwife's part. Nowhere else in her extant letters does she speak or behave this way, loosened up, even playful. He and only he, in her extensive correspondence, will be addressed as "Monsieur and Dear Friend." Perhaps a romance really does blossom between them. But if so, it never sways du Coudray from her path. Aeneas may have slowed down for Dido, but the midwife does not seem to skip a beat. Whatever the nature of this interlude, it gets transformed by her into yet another business relationship, does not make her stray, stay, or even delay. Really, St. Etienne is far more of a facilitator than an obstacle, helping her achieve and indeed surpass her goals. More and more she sees that mixing pleasure with work enhances her effectiveness. She need not take it all so terribly seriously.

And now things are picking up, getting lively. Surgeons in surrounding towns fight for the chance to become her demonstrators, hearing of the midwife's courses through public announcements at the meetings of their guild. Male pride and professional rivalry ensure that initial reactions are rarely enthusiastic, but in the end many compete to be chosen, and sometimes there is acrimonious argument and even foul play as they vie for the coveted assignment. The nearby city of Troyes is a case in point. One Picard, a master surgeon, had with a gesture of irritation read out loud the notice of du Coudray's coming in a scornful tone, stressing that anyone traveling to Châlons to attend the course would lose valuable business on the home front and that, in any case, it is indecent and demeaning to be taught by a woman. Having elicited the desired negative reaction, Picard was dispatched to the mayor of the city to report that nobody was interested. Once there, however, he betrayed the fold, taking advantage of the interview to slip an idea to the town officials:

his own son-in-law would be a willing candidate. Hearing of this deception, the community of surgeons nominated a member of their guild, M. Simon, as well, and Troyes was eventually obliged to send both men. As things stand now, though, only one can officially be named demonstrator. Simon, eager for the designation and disturbed by the irregularities of the procedure, has reminded the intendant that he once sent him some verses, for which an unspecified return favor was promised. Has the time come to make good on that promise? But Picard's relative is a favorite of the subdelegate of Troyes, and in the end it is he who gets the commission and the machine, though only after an intense and ugly struggle. Similar dramas are played out in many towns. Sometimes surgeons literally come to blows in their scramble to be chosen to help bring du Coudray's science to the villages.[8] The *Affiches, annonces et avis divers de Reims et de la généralité de Champagne* reports that some surgeons even join the classes for women to reap additional profit from the "rare talents" of the aunt and niece and the "precision" of Coutanceau.[9]

All in all the stay here ends up a huge hit, thanks to the extra help and encouragement from St. Etienne.[10] Letters from fans inundate du Coudray, and do not abate after her departure.[11] Rouillé d'Orfeuil, who has already given her numerous silver presents as tokens of thanks,[12] also sees to it that the towns in his jurisdiction order twenty-three of her machines—a record for one region and a handsome profit for her.[13] Now that such large numbers of these mannequins have to be produced, du Coudray has begun to make a less expensive, less elaborate version in linen, for which she charges only 200 rather than the previous 300 livres. She is working on other shortcuts, alternative ways of fabricating the models more quickly. She once dreamed of such gigantic orders; now she recognizes that they sap her strength even as they replenish her purse.

Her purse has been replenished in yet another way. A new, third edition of her *Abrégé* has been published here in Châlons-sur-Marne, in response to growing demand for such birthing manuals.[14] Du Coudray realizes she must keep hers available in abundant quantities, saturating the market so that the increasingly popular rival book by Raulin does not jump in to fill the vacuum. Once unique of its kind, her simple text is serving as a model and has inspired a fashionable trend, for others quickly see, as she did years ago, that a new public requires new kinds of reading matter, books that marry word and image and serve as ready reference.[15] These days du Coudray must defend her literary and professional property as never before.

37. "I Cost Nothing"

Verdun, 17 June 1773

Monsieur and Dear Friend,

Finally, thank God, my course is finished, and the machines also. We had 108 students; we are all in collapse. Our sojourn because of our bad health was altogether disagreeable. And by another heap of bad luck I still don't know when I can get out of here. On the faith of what M. de Calonne told me, that all was arranged with M. de la Galazière and the exchange made between them . . . for Verdun . . . [and] Nancy . . . , CRASH [*patatras*] all plans are broken. I have had to write to Flanders and I await the response, which only redoubles my ennui. I am taking a little trip of four days to go to Metz. It is not so much, my handsome man, for my amusement as for my curiosity, to see the machines that the magistrates ordered from Paris. I know they are not worth much, for in spite of this expense the city also bought mine, but if there is something good about them, and that I don't know, I swear to you I will always take it. That's the purpose that drives me there.

Just imagine, Monsieur, that I am not yet paid by Besançon, isn't that shameful? Anxiety is beginning to overtake me. It is awkward to have my rest time now, and yet because of delays of this kind, to find myself in embarrassed circumstances. Again, if you were in charge all would be well.

The machine for Ste. Menehould will be delivered by the coach to the address of the magistrates. The surgeons and these men seem to want it, for they write me of their impatience to receive it. As for the two others, they will go to you. About the one for Rocroy, if I were to believe M. Lamarre, it would be destined for him. He claims to have gotten news that M. d'Orfeuil would intercede for him. This matter will be decided. But in truth, I fear he confuses his dreams for reality, for I have no more faith in all he tells me than in my slipper. But this machine will do very well in the hands of one M. Girardin, surgeon at Rauvay near Rocroy, who seemed to us a real man of honor. He would have an additional advantage, for he has his son with him . . . [and] one or the other can go to Rocroy to give the lessons. By the way, the woman from Montfaucon came to find me. This poor woman has already done nine deliveries with the greatest possible success, but she has not yet received her book. And I told her I would ask you for it right away. I embrace you with all my heart, as well as dear Miss Frinon. Fanfan does too. The rest of my suite present their respects to you. I don't know if I will take with me the dragées [sugar-coated almonds] I am amassing. I am fed up with Theuveui. He is incapable of profiting from all the good I could teach him. This profession is not made for him with his extreme negligence. Goodbye, hello. Love me always. You owe it to the sentiments of friendship and gratitude with which I am, Monsieur, your very humble and obedient servant.

du Coudray[1]

Neither springtime nor the loveliness of this windy city on the river Meuse can cheer up du Coudray's household, not even the aniseed preserves so reputed in this region.[2] Everyone is exhausted, sick, and as always, short of funds.

The intendant Calonne has put his quite competent first secretary M. Cantat in charge, and the lessons have drawn a huge crowd and lasted four months.[3] But the midwife is uncomfortable. She does not trust Calonne. He has, after all, allowed the nearby city of Metz to purchase some machines from another source, and he endorses an unknown surgeon there rather than one of her disciples.[4] She thinks he is faithless and a poor planner. All this she confides to St. Etienne, and the letter writing *does* seem to cheer her. The act of composing these missives is somehow cleansing. That they are often dictated through a servant/secretary in no way diminishes their spontaneity or candor; du Coudray has no secrets from her staff. She sorely misses the efficiency of St. Etienne, and even more his caring and sympathetic ear. Is "dear Miss Frinon" perhaps a housekeeper, a maiden aunt, a younger relative of his who has befriended the midwife's niece (now referred to affectionately by her nickname, Fanfan)? The friendliness of the families and the openness with which du Coudray teases—"my handsome man," "love me always," "I embrace you"—suggests there was nothing illicit about their relationship. Rather, it comforts her to be reminded of past good times.

And she has many more complaints to unload! She is
with one of her surgeon trainees and may leave him behind.
slacker, it seems, and it is an impossible burden to have in her house
hold someone who does not pull his weight. Furthermore, the future hangs in the balance, for she does not know where to go next.
They are all stuck here, marking time, so she busies herself by delivering lots of babies and gathering lots of dragées, the traditional
compensation for such work.

She has been misled by Calonne into thinking that all was worked
out for her to move on. Now, instead, she has to organize everything herself. She will soon, while waiting for things to be decided,
write to Amiens, attempting to coax the intendant Dupleix, who
she mistakenly believes to be stationed there:

> The good that I do for humanity . . . is perhaps known to you,
> but in case you haven't heard, I do not doubt, (knowing your
> reputation), that you will seize with enthusiasm the offer I
> make to you. . . . The brevet with which I am honored autho-
> rizes me and makes me safe from the cabal that surgeons often
> instigate; anyway, the most zealous intendants don't even con-
> sult them. You will see, Monsieur, that I cost nothing. The King,
> who desires that this establishment be set up everywhere in
> his realm, has taken care of my honoraria. . . . I hasten to do
> this good [*faire ce bien*] only as long as all cooperate with me
> and when those in power understand its full price, knowing
> how to animate *the master and the disciples*. (emphasis mine)[5]

This terse, self-congratulatory sales pitch reveals her impatience at
having been victimized by administrative indifference before. She
is, as she puts it, "the master." "I cost nothing" is of course not quite
true, but she wants it believed that His Majesty keeps her in cash.
What an enormous effort to explain her mission over and over again
to these intendants! She must labor constantly to keep herself prominent in their thoughts.

That she has competition for her machines now is just the latest,
newest problem, another major setback. Mlle Bihéron has of course
been making anatomical models in Paris since the 1750s, but these
are of wax. Now there is a Mme Lenfant on rue des Mathurins, who
has begun to advertise in the Paris papers models made of cloth,
"appropriate for surgeons, *accoucheurs*, and midwives to give them
practice in the maneuvers of delivery. The natural proportions both

₂ fetus are exactly observed."[6] Du Coudray
∕ that she is curious to observe these manne-
ateliers in the capital, to learn some tips, per-
ts. Her interest is predatory, for this item, of
he main producer if not the sole inventor, now
ɔf becoming easily and more cheaply available.
al textbook, now a rival machine. Not only Bous-
z, but surgeons in southern areas where she had
have started using these, buying them from man-
ufactu⌐⌐ s and automata in Paris who readily adapt to filling special orders.[7] Things are beginning to slip out of du Coudray's
grasp. What has become of her exclusive rights? Feeling beleaguered,
she obsesses in her letter about a copy of her book for one of her
students in Montfaucon, a reminder of her authority, her authorial
voice.

The psychological importance of her letter writing cannot be over-
estimated. What ultimately puts the midwife back on track again
and again is her own inner sense of meaning, reanimated in the
act of writing. It provides her steadying ballast. Here, for example,
du Coudray works herself into a stronger managerial mode when
she speaks of the distribution of her own machines. By weighing
and judging the relative merits of the men she has trained and their
suitability to become keepers of the mannequin, the midwife boosts
herself in her own eyes. A large number of people constitute her
network, and she is the final arbiter of their worth. This kind of
affirmative reminder works as a tonic, regenerating her sense of
purpose. The increasing momentum, the racing of her pulse, is almost palpable in the letter to St. Etienne, as she proceeds from a recitation of her problems to a renewed activist focus on her raison
d'être and on what needs to be done. Her correspondence is her best
medicine.

If only the men of Besançon will finally pay her, and if only the
men who determine her next moves will organize themselves, she
can get going again.[8] Instead they are negligent, forever getting their
signals crossed. A full seven months ago Controller General Terray,
in an apparent act of support for du Coudray, had authorized the
purchase of eight or ten machines for the cities around Besançon,
volunteering that his tax receivers would pay if the municipal officers refused to.[9] The midwife produced the machines in good faith,

but neither one group nor the other has come forth with the funds. Typical. She, on the other hand, gets things done, sticks to her obligations. In some sense she sees herself as more manly than the males with whom she deals. Her classes are methodical, her students amenable, obedient. One letter recommending someone for her course assures her that the pupil "will be a woman submissive to your orders, with whom you will be pleased."[10] Le Nain's *Mémoire* was careful to speak of the "mistress" and her disciples, but du Coudray transforms the phrase and calls herself the "master" (*maître*). She is on a par with male authorities any day. Indeed, she functions a good deal better than many of them do. Why must she dissipate so much of her energy hounding debtors and incompetents?

38. She "Partakes of the Prodigious"

Neufchâteau, Fall 1773

Things have worked out after all for the Lorraine. Traveling past firetrap houses, wood-roofed with no chimneys, from which smoke escapes, if at all, through ceiling holes or window slits, the midwife has also seen, in the Vosges area, huts sunk into the earth, damp comfortless dwellings with the inevitable dung heap by the door. Many of her students, she knows, will come from such homes. Neufchâteau itself is a small cloudy town where, despite their love for *baba au rhum* and *madeleine* cakes, the people are reputed to be cold and taciturn.[1]

For a while du Coudray had not known where she would end up. Mistakenly thinking the intendant Dupleix is in Amiens, she wrote to him from Verdun attempting to arrange a visit. He, however, turns out to be in charge of Brittany now and received her forwarded letter in Rennes, much farther away. Dupleix fervently wants her to come there, and makes a note to himself: "We must send a courteous letter to this woman that I know by her great reputation. This establishment would be very desirable, but the means are not easy. Promise her that I am looking into it."[2] Meanwhile her original plan nearer by materialized and she wrote again to Dupleix: "The intendant of Nancy, having had I think a letter from the Controller General, finally *does* want me, and I leave to go to Neufchâteau, which is the center of French Lorraine. The minister must write also to the intendant of Strasbourg, who set his mind against [my teaching there] last September. As for you, Monsieur, I will write that you don't need it [right now]. I will be honored to let you know what happens, and although I have pledged myself to travel only step by step, as much for my health as for the considerable costs of my voyages, I will spare neither one nor the other to fulfill your wishes as promptly as possible."[3] Thus the midwife lines up a potential future engagement. With Dupleix duly informed by this little geography lesson, blandished by the sacrifice she is willing to make, and satisfied to stay on hold for a while, du Coudray has now come to Neufchâteau, traveling through the town of Domrémy-la-Pucelle, where Joan of Arc was born. Does she ever fancy that her own heroic mission to save France bears some resemblance to the efforts of that maiden?

Contrary to the midwife's advice, local lords and parish priests have sought volunteers among the ranks of matrons already practicing. Du Coudray knows this is stupid. One, for example, who has delivered hundreds of babies, protests that she is too old for the aggravation of having to take lessons and "would rather stop practicing midwifery than go." A second is so preoccupied with her duties at home that she could not concentrate, would have to rush back to preside at births of village women in her care. One curé after another, running into obstinacy on the matrons' part, reports that the recruiting efforts have been "to no purpose," "a pure waste of time," "not a single one wanted to follow [our invitation]."[4] Du Coudray had predicted this in a letter they initially ignored, and when they finally turn to her advice, ninety-two untrained but willing girls are brought in from surrounding towns and many more from Neufchâteau itself.[5]

They seem to stick together a lot even when not in class. Some stay with aunts and sisters, some at inns—two at the Poule Qui Boit, eight at La Croix d'Or—others in private rooming houses run by merchants and widows. They cook for themselves to economize and to keep each other company at mealtime, when they might feel especially homesick. A few are grouped together in a hospice run by the sisters of charity.[6] The surgeons who arrive next for their class are a varied bunch without the same cohesiveness.[7]

One of the midwife's male students here is none other than the surgeon-major M. Saint Paul, who has been a devotee of hers since her stop in Poitou nearly a decade ago. He pours out to a friend a cascade of heartfelt praise. One must really see the superb du Coudray in action to believe the miracles she can work! Her lessons "surprised and enchanted me . . . realistic demonstrations . . . as well as happy and unfortunate positions that the practice of delivery presents. . . . All this chaos, hidden to the eye and often to the touch, is intelligibly disentangled by her, so much does her vast knowledge partake of the prodigious. Also the intendant of the Lorraine, who is gifted in general understanding of all the sciences, evinced surprised admiration at the demonstrations he came to see her do. He heaped upon her, in my presence, the most flattering eulogies, in my view most deserved."[8]

On the last day of the course, du Coudray is honored by the singing of a musical mass for all her successes with her 150 female and male students.[9] She amasses the familiar stack of thank-yous from adoring trainees pledging to be "eternally her student," and now M. Coutanceau is also gathering a following.[10] The midwife has enjoyed here a sense of settlement, an agreeable calm. There is much socializing. The intendant, La Galazière, has outdone himself to enhance du Coudray's comfort. And the subdelegate of Neufchâteau, M. Rouyer, is a friendly man with a gracious wife who opens their home to the midwife and her team, makes her welcome, and introduces her to his friends. She will remember his kindness and hospitality for a long time and will still be merrily reporting back to him about her odyssey many years later.

39. ROMANCE IN THE ENTOURAGE

Nancy, 27 February 1774

The niece and Coutanceau have fallen in love! Any responsible guardian must organize her young ward's dowry. It is her protection. It is what she brings to the marriage, though it remains hers and can be reclaimed. So Du Coudray has hastened to Paris, leaving her provost in charge here in Nancy, a city proud of its history as the capital of the dukes of Lorraine, and recently made elegant by the erstwhile king of Poland, Stanislas Leszczynski, father-in-law of Louis XV. It is a thriving metropolis compared to tranquil Neufchâteau, but even here life is rather low key.[1]

Before leaving for Paris, du Coudray has of course seen to it that all is in perfect order. As the accommodations found for her were only meagerly furnished, she has discovered a source of secondhand goods that she can resell when she leaves. She booked lodgings for six months, but the turnout is so small that the stay will probably be much shorter. Neither the residence nor the classroom is in good shape. A locksmith-handyman has presented bills for replacing hinges, pins, eyebolts, cane, bells, wires, bolts, and hooks, and has also supplied or repaired binding, hoops, and spindles needed for making the machines.[2]

The students here are eager to buy their own copies of du Coudray's book, and a helpful surgeon named Didelot, who had earlier written a small midwifery manual of his own, is graciously assisting with the distribution of the recent third edition of the *Abrégé*.[3] What a comfort that he, unlike other male authors on obstetrics, makes no attempt to steal the midwife's luster. Far from it: he appreciates her contribution and has written passionately himself about the essential "multiplication of the human species," even providing a rudimentary statistical analysis of depopulation.[4] Literacy in this northern part of France, above the St. Malo–Geneva line, is considerably more widespread than elsewhere. But pupils also want the midwife's book for its illustrations, and for its value as status symbol and souvenir. They clamor for it, making elaborate arrangements for its transport and delivery.[5] Nine machines are being ordered by surgeons to take back to surrounding towns, and two more expensive silk models for the Hôtel de Ville.[6] In general, though, the numbers of students are low, the pace slow, and there is not very much to keep the teaching team busy. At least as far as teaching goes.

Today Coutanceau answers a letter they have received from their friend Rouyer, who evidently accompanied them briefly to Nancy but then returned to Neufchâteau. Rouyer, who addresses the surgeon with an honorific title and clearly admires him, has requested more books and one of their old machines for his demonstrator. Coutanceau says he is having the women refurbish one of their used "phantoms" for him and that it will soon be on its way.

We still have twenty bound copies of [du Coudray's] treatise on *Accouchements*. Tell me the quantity you need and I shall send them. Be good enough to decide pretty quickly about this last matter because I will have more of them bound if I'm short of them for the dozen students to whom I am giving my course.

We have received since your departure two letters from Frère Côme who tells us of our next trip, to Douai, a city in French Flanders, or to Lille, capital of that province. I presume our stay in Nancy will not last long and I am delighted. I am bored with living in idleness. I am developing a distaste for pleasures. The theater, for which I longed, is becoming insipid to me. I taste real satisfaction only by being near the amiable Mlle de Varennes, who asks me to assure you that she loves you dearly. She doesn't at all mind exciting in me some sign of jealousy, and I of course promise that I will obey her. So you are my declared rival! I will do all I can do to supplant you. On your side, try as you will to make me yield my place if you want to steal from me my coquette.[7]

So here is a rare glimpse of Coutanceau himself. Though clearly captivated by feminine charms, he plans to write to du Coudray next week about business matters. He has been saving up many things to tell her and is eager to learn what is going on in the capital and what the final decision might be on their next destination. This is a restless man. Even in his lovesick state he cannot enjoy cultural distractions or entertainment for long. His feelings for du Coudray's niece appear to be inextricably bound to his duties in their great joint mission. Proudly shouldering the responsibility of partner and agent in this enterprise, he takes over not only the instruction but also the business of books and machines in du Coudray's absence. And he is unfailingly correct, still maintaining the "de Varennes" masquerade even with Rouyer, not letting any secrets slip.

But the couple must be wondering how things are working out in Paris, where the midwife has gone to stake out the "family" claim.

40. Brevet No. 3: The Succession

Versailles, 1 March 1774

Brevet authorizing Mlle Du Coudray mistress midwife to hold conjointly with and to inherit from Dame Du Coudray her aunt, courses of public instruction.

Today . . . the King being at Versailles, His Majesty being informed of the talents and experience that Mlle Marguerite Guillaumanche du Coudray has acquired in the art of delivery under the direction of Dame Du Coudray her aunt that His Majesty chose by his brevet of 18 August 1767 to give public courses on the art of delivery in all the provinces of his realm, on the basis of reports made to His Majesty on the good that results from these instructions, and of the efforts and infinite cares that said Dame Du Coudray has taken to attain this, His Majesty thought he could not accord her a greater recompense than naming said Mlle Marguerite Guillaumanche du Coudray to conjointly, and as her heir, continue said courses. By this His Majesty wills that she be able to teach in the whole extent of the realm, jointly with or in the absence of her aunt, the art of delivery, and to hold public and private courses on all related subjects without her being troubled under any pretext whatever. . . . [1]

Seeing the seriousness of the romance, the midwife goes straight to the monarch and secures her "niece" officially as her conjoint and heir. She may even have initiated some formal adoption procedure, because His Majesty refers to the young woman by her aunt's surname. In any case du Coudray wasted no time, traveling in such a rush that, although she went right through Châlons, she did not stop even to visit St. Etienne. And it is a good thing that she hurried, for Louis XV is about to contract a fatal case of smallpox. This is the third brevet he has granted her over the last fifteen years, each one more favorable than its predecessor. Despite all the ministerial upheavals, Louis XV himself has not wavered in his support. This brevet is, as it turns out, one of his last royal acts. Had the midwife put off her business a mere two months longer, she would have needed to deal with a new king.

41. "A Reward So Justly Deserved"

Amiens, 15 April 1774

Du Coudray will soon be sixty. Ever since the scandal with her niece's unscrupulous suitor in Auch she has been determined to clarify and secure the young woman's future. Now she and Coutanceau are engaged and have posted their marriage bans here. Thanks to the midwife's tireless maneuverings the state has officially recognized that her niece is eminently qualified, with all her years as trainee and assistant demonstrator, to inherit the royal pension and mission in her own right. This gives the niece security. To du Coudray it gives a feeling of immortality. Extremely pleased with this guarantee from Controller General Terray and the king, she is focusing on it now, drawing strength from it to fortify her against new difficulties.

Today she writes letters to two special friends, Rouyer in Neufchâteau and St. Etienne in Châlons, sure that these loyal supporters will want to be kept abreast of her doings. It is more clear than ever how this process serves her. She writes with the spontaneous excitement of on-the-spot reporting, even though the cherished brevet has already been in her hands for six weeks. This knack has helped du Coudray adapt to her jolting lifestyle. She can wait for good moments and write in a state of composure. Her rhythms are erratic, months of routine punctuated by enormous upheavals and changes of scene. She is sometimes surrounded by people, other times very alone, always readjusting. But she is uniquely able to set aside time to replay things in her mind whenever she wishes, giving them fresh life, enjoying them again, often rewriting them in ways more to her liking than the reality. Her epistolary activity gives her the perfect respite from her solitude and her worries. And she can choose her moment, like this one, when she is actually rather demoralized, to inhabit instead a better world. Right now, feeling isolated and uncertain, the correspondence allows her to connect with old and distant friends, to bridge time and space. It is conversation, it is company. She turns to it instead of brooding.

Getting settled in this city, the capital of Picardy, has kept her busy. Its people, according to the accepted wisdom, are excessively hotheaded; one is even advised to stay away from them unless looking for a fight. Yet the landscape belies this reputation with its serenity, its scattered windmills and misty horizons. Amiens itself has the largest Gothic cathedral anywhere in France, and an inordinate number of beggars; one report suggests that a third of the inhabitants of Amiens consists of the loitering poor in the streets. No one seems much to care.[1]

Du Coudray's experience confirms the province's apathy toward the public's well-being. Her course has been advertised only perfunctorily.[2] "Why can't you be here?" she writes to Rouyer. "I knew I wouldn't find you everywhere. What a difference! Believe me, everything happens here with a negligence that is not pardonable. I saw the intendant in Paris, and Mme de la Galazière. She asked me if I had been pleased with you. Guess what I said to her. They told me that this didn't surprise them, that they expected it and that they had placed me with you on purpose." She turns now to news of her achievement at Versailles, which, it develops, was a major coup financially for her as well. "I could not have been more satisfied with having made my voyage. I was Queen of the ministers! They couldn't have been more obliging. And I have the sweet expectation that for my own retirement compensation my 8,000 livres will keep coming for the rest of my life, instead of restricting me to a thousand ecus [3,000 livres]. I got the inheritance for my niece, so our future is provided for. . . . Embrace for me Mme Rouyer, M. and Mme Roussel. Tell me news of her health because I want you to write to me and keep me informed of everything that regards you. I am interested for my whole life."[3]

In contrast to this largely informative letter, she writes to St. Etienne a more affectionate but also more demanding one, bossy and revealing. Theirs was a closer, more complex relationship. She drops her defenses, intermittently. Things are good, but things are also bad.

> Never was a voyage more successful. The six matters that took me [to Paris] were settled beyond my wildest dreams. I am promised that I will not be limited to a thousand ecus when I

retire, but that the 8,000 [livres] will stay with me by virtue of a reward so justly deserved. And I got the inheritance for Fanfan. I had not dared hope they would be so disposed in my favor. I also found ways to settle Fanfan's business . . . [since] the lieutenant general of Clermont just happened to be in Paris then. Everything worked out beautifully. I am in Amiens, but you are not here. They could not care less. I cannot tell you what a different attitude [there is] toward the general good. Everything goes limping along [*cahin-caha*] and I have still never received a visit or any interest from the person who has your job here.

I don't know if the agricultural gazettes of other provinces reach you. I would like you to read the one from Soisson of the ninth of this month. There is an article about Soisson which concerns the establishment that intendance is setting up for the instruction of midwives. Lucky for me to be rid of them. I don't know whether you recall the repugnance I felt to be forced to go there. But in this article there is one thing that shocks me. That is that they proclaim [the teaching] more lasting [there] than elsewhere. You alone would be in a position to prove that M. d'Orfeuil as well as other intendants always had the intention to make this institution durable, since M. d'Orfeuil just had a number of women instructed by twenty-three demonstrators in each city where the machines were left. You do this whatever way you wish, and I think it is very necessary that it be put in the Gazette de France. Besides, it's only just to do this for M. d'Orfeuil, who stopped at nothing to produce such a great good and to make it more permanent than elsewhere.

Just think how those other courses are run. A demonstrator need only keep these women eighteen days! I have one of my disciples in Soisson, and I shall be informed of all that goes on there.

A thousand embraces from me to Mlle Frinon and from Fanfan, respects from M. Coutanceau. From me a thousand tender fondnesses.[4]

Feeling that she reigned royally over the ministers, du Coudray surely has something to celebrate. Her readjusted pension, 8,000 livres even in retirement, is that of a decorated military general; there is only one category higher.[5] So, given this new measure of her importance, certain things must immediately be set straight for the record. She will not have her mission upstaged or the trail of triumphs she leaves in her wake overshadowed by press coverage of other midwifery projects. Her work should now be broadcast in the national newspaper, the *Gazette de France*. That she feels defensive is understandable. The journals of the capital, including the medical papers, have basically ignored her mission. The *Journal de médecine* has said nothing. The *Gazette de santé* devotes many articles to the appalling state of rural midwifery, but avoids all mention of du Coudray herself, discussing only male *accoucheurs* and their efforts to educate in this area. Her protest that she merely wants to vindicate the honor of the intendant d'Orfeuil is patently transparent: her own proper recognition is at stake here. Her mission is no mere fleeting episode; from the start, with her training of a network of teachers and demonstrators, the goal has been to perpetuate its impact, make it take root and endure forever.

Soisson is a particular sore spot for du Coudray. She may say good riddance, but the fact is that she was roundly rejected back in 1760 when there was talk of her going there from Clermont or Moulins. Hurt, she wrote it off as a hopelessly backward place. The subdelegate of the town of Ribemont near Soisson claimed to be entirely content with the state of things, even though in some villages the most experienced person around, in matters of birthing, was the shepherd.[6] The issue of her teaching there had arisen again in 1773 while du Coudray was in Châlons. By that time, however, a doctor from nearby Laon, Augier du Fot, had begun to discredit her. An aggressive man, he had made it his business to court such influential members of the scientific community as the great chemist Macquer, wooing him with fulsome letters, Latin epigrams, and rare cheeses.[7] He had ingratiated himself with the intendant in Soisson, Le Peletier, by persuading him that midwives, including du Coudray, are more dangerous with their hooks and fingernails than are cannons and swords, and that it is foolish to put "the life of men, the hope of future generations . . . in their hands."[8]

Recently du Fot has even won some support in Versailles, and he is publishing a ninety-page obstetrical manual endorsed by the Royal Academy of Sciences and Paris Medical Faculty. This echoes disturbingly the incident with Raulin's rival book several years ago, but in fact it is worse. Du Fot is using the "phantoms" or machines made by Mme Lenfant in the capital.[9] His whole pedagogical program for Laon and Soisson is modeled on du Coudray's, but he acts as if she does not exist, exclaiming in his booklet: "May [my] establishment, the first of its kind, be imitated throughout France."[10]

A more complete annihilation of the midwife's mission, leaving no vestige or trace, cannot be imagined. Now, as if this were not bad enough, newspapers carry on about du Fot's teaching as a wonderful novelty. Du Coudray finds this almost unbearable, as her second letter reveals. Just when she leaves the subject behind in that letter, giving St. Etienne his orders, she again brings up Soisson, obsessively reiterating, almost as if even this special, loyal friend needs convincing that the superficial lessons being given there are altogether inferior to her own. That she has an informant in that town is small comfort; the reports only alarm her. She will not stand back and relinquish her priority as a pioneering figure. She will not be blotted out. Local newspapers can say what they wish, but the *Gazette de France* must carry news of her deeds throughout the entire kingdom.

Well, at least things are settled for her "niece," Marguerite Guillaumanche, "Fanfan," alias Mlle de Varennes, now, in the king's brevet, Mlle du Coudray, soon to be Mme Coutanceau. This eighteen-year-old woman, with her many names and public and private identities, whose real relation to du Coudray, if any, remains a mystery, is the closest thing the midwife has to a daughter. She has been quite passive in this story so far, her husband-to-be the far more significant player. But du Coudray has molded her in her own image and plans to pass on the mantle to her. At this point will the midwife begin to take her ward more seriously as an adult?

It is worth noting that now, with this new approval of a retirement pension equal to her salary, du Coudray could stop working any time and still get handsome compensation. She could turn things entirely over to the younger generation and take it easy. Instead, propelled by her promise to her king and to herself, she aggressively maintains her pace for another eight years, working ever harder in the face of increasing adversity.

First, however, this "Queen of the ministers" does treat herself to an extracurricular trip across the frontier.

42. Overtures Beyond the Border

Lille, 24 December 1774

To His Royal Highness Prince Charles . . . Governor of Austrian Flanders.

The infinite miseries that result from the incapacity of persons practicing childbirth determined His very Christian Majesty to authorize and commission Dame du Coudray to demonstrate throughout France this so necessary art and to give to his subjects lessons furthering their preservation, a most salutary step, whose great value and necessity Your Royal Highness can surely sense, since religion, humanity, and patriotism unite in it. We see far too often children perish without baptism, others buried alive, mothers dying, and those not killed by ignorance falling prey to infirmities even worse than death. Thus the state finds itself deprived of a multitude of subjects who, multiplying in their turn, would have made the population most abundant.

Dame du Coudray, being presently in Lille ready to finish her course, invites Your Royal Highness to form the same establishment in the Low Countries: to send her *prévot* [M. Coutanceau], who for the past five years has demonstrated for her this aspect of surgery, and to serve as his interpreter the person who has the honor of presenting this letter to you, who knows the Flemish tongue well and who has even translated into that language the treatise on childbirth written by Dame du Coudray. This person already took her course in Dunkerque and is following it again most exactly at Lille, which will put him in a position to offer his services to Your Royal Highness should he decide to do for the happiness of the Flemish what Louis XV did for that of the French. Her *prévot* would come to Brussels on 8 January next; Your Royal Highness would make use of this interval to dispatch orders so that fifty communities each send one woman, every one of whom will be provided with 20 livres' living expenses per month for as long as this course of instruction lasts, which would be six weeks or two months. Your Royal Highness would also give orders so that a surgeon from each principal city of the Low Countries come for the last month of the course to learn the mechanism of the machine used by demonstrators, so that once back home he can instruct in his turn other fellow citizens on the same machine. Which each city would purchase, as Furnes and Nieuport already have, whose magistrates, knowing full well all the advantages of this instruction, sent a surgeon who, upon returning, started his own course. The magistrates ordered all surgeons and midwives in their jurisdiction to attend these lessons, threatening to train new subjects if they refused to profit from the enlightenment one must have to practice this art. The course being given now at Furnes is composed of thirty-five subjects. The price paid by the magistrates of this city for the machines was approved by [the appropriate official]. The expense once made, all that is required is maintenance. The demonstrators become very excellent *accoucheurs* by the daily practice of this art.

What assures me of success, in offering to Your Royal Highness this benefit, is the number of people that I found in the Queen's country who came with alacrity to learn and who sacrificed, in doing this, their time and a part of their resources.

Dame du Coudray can offer Your Royal Highness only these two months. She will not consider going anywhere until she receives the honor of a response. She has no doubts that she will be accepted, considering the good this establishment does for humanity. She has as guarantee the sentiment of love that enflames the heart of Your Royal Highness for the happiness of the people he governs.[1]

So this is how the midwife writes when approaching royalty directly! France now has a new king, Louis XVI, and du Coudray is negotiating with a relative of his Austrian mother-in-law, the empress Maria Theresa, who has enticed her to consider this cross-border excursion. How has this international contact between the midwife and the dowager monarch come about?

In the fall du Coudray had left Amiens for Dunkerque, an ocean port town, named for its church on the dunes, with an altogether Flemish flavor, well-paved streets, and high brick houses.[2] While teaching there she attracted the attention of the comte de Néry, trusted friend and scout of the Austrian empress. He reported about du Coudray: "All the doctors and surgeons agreed unanimously that she was of a rare ability and that she joined to her theoretical and practical knowledge of the art of delivery the talent to communicate them with an admirable clarity, and that these advantages were enhanced still further by the patience and gentleness with which she gave her lessons, never getting discouraged by the low aptitude she found sometimes in her students." He added that her royal brevet is "shining testimony of the high opinion in which her talents are held."[3]

Since the 1750s the Austrian Netherlands has been concerned about the lack of well-trained midwives. Now that the empress's daughter Marie Antoinette has just become queen of France, Maria Theresa has taken a special interest in du Coudray's mission and insists that courses be set up in her domain while the famous midwife is so close by. She has dispatched many students to study with her in France, and has already ordered machines for several of her towns. The medical faculty of the University of Louvain, however, has claimed to have no confidence in du Coudray. Jealously guarding their turf for academically trained insiders, they refuse to admit that a woman can know enough about this art, which requires "a person very enlightened in anatomy and the other parts of medicine" to treat it in sufficient depth. Furthermore, her much-touted "machine . . . is no secret," and they already know all about it. Néry's glowing report has forced a reconsideration, however, and when du Coudray moves still closer, from Dunkerque to Lille, and word of the swooning adoration of her surgeon conquests in this city comes flowing across the border, the authorities in the Austrian Netherlands feel they must have her come. It is urgent, for when she finishes here at Lille the midwife will have only two months free before her next commitment, in Normandy.[4]

Lille is the richest, most populous city in French Flanders. Its fortifications and citadels still stand, built by Vauban as part of a "belt of iron" guarding the vulnerable northeast frontier of France.[5] Dog-drawn carts scurry about under somber, foggy skies. Constant crop rotation throughout the year enlivens the soil of the surrounding flatlands, and windmills are always busy, many pressing poppy-seeds for oil to light the city's lamps.[6] The practitioners here idolize du Coudray and fuel her ambitions.

The letter she writes today, on Christmas Eve, is actually addressed to Prince Charles of Lorraine, governor of the Low Countries, but there seems to be some conflating, some slippage in du Coudray's mind as she pictures the recipient. She is writing to the prince exactly as she would write to the empress herself. Her only nod to the elevated status of the addressee is her assumption of the third person, but even this breaks down in the penultimate paragraph. Otherwise, she is entirely undaunted, unleashing the same enthusiastic tumble of words, giving orders about the preliminary steps for setting up the course, using the conditional mode but all the while presuming that the thing will certainly come to pass. The only new wrinkle is that she volunteers M. Coutanceau to teach in her stead. Perhaps she is afraid of appearing disloyal to her own country, which might consider her trip to be some self-indulgent junket. The upshot, however, is that Maria Theresa insists on du Coudray herself; as a result, although she shuttles back often to nearby Lille, she goes in person to conduct the class. She has attracted the attention and high regard of yet another monarch. That the empress will settle for nothing less than her own presence must gratify her vanity. And the break, the novelty, will do her a world of good.

43. A Wedding Across the Flemish Frontier

Ypres, 28 February 1775

This lacemaking town in Austrian Flanders has welcomed du Coudray and her crew ecstatically. She has been teaching since 16 January—assisted throughout by a translator, Van Daele, who is also an able doctor—and her lessons are packed with 130 students. Male practitioners from Bruges and Courtrai are here too. The *Abrégé* has been adapted into a Flemish version, printed in catechism form with questions and answers but based entirely on du Coudray's pedagogical strategy.[1] There has been such a commotion about her visit, such wild demand for her book, that pirate printers are circulating counterfeit editions which undercut her profit. Soon Maria Theresa will need to crack down and grant the approved publisher, one Jacques-François Moerman, an exclusive six-year privilege on the official Flemish edition (fig. 9).[2]

The surrounding towns have pooled 2,200 livres for du Coudray, and in addition some give her extravagant bonuses of up to 4 louis, or 1,000 livres. They know she has taken precious time for this, and

ONDERWYS

VOOR

DE LEERLINGEN

In de Vroed-Kunde ofte Konst der
Kinder-Bedden,

By Vraegen ende Antwoorden getrokken uyt
de Leffen der vermaerde Vroed-vrauw DU
COUDRAY, door F. D. VANDAELE,
Vrymeefter in de Genées-konft, verciert met
Kópere Printen, en d'Uytlegging van iedere
Verbéeldinge,

Met een Byvoegfel aengaende de Geeftelyke
Sorge, die de Vroe-vrauwen moeten draegen,
foo voor de fwangere ende baerende Vrauwen,
als voor hunne Vrucht.

> . . . . *Omnem, qua nunc obducta tuenti*
> *Mortales hebetat vifus tibi, & humida circùm*
> *Caligat, nubem eripiam . . . . .*
>
> Virg. Æneid. L. II.

Tot YPER, by J. F. MOERMAN.

Met Goedkeuringe ende Privilegie Excluffic

Figure 9. Mme du Coudray's lessons in Flemish, translated by a Dr. Van Daele. Courtesy of Wellcome Institute Library, London.

they want to make it worth her while.[3] This has been a clever move for the midwife, lifting her out of the somber melancholy of Amiens, fattening her purse, healing her pride. Perhaps she is destined to change not only France, but the whole of Europe?

Today, however, a much more personal event is taking place: the wedding of her niece to M. Coutanceau.[4] She is nineteen, he thirty-seven. It is exactly one year since the two had confided their mutual affection in a letter to Rouyer. During the interim the couple posted marriage bans in many cities, publicly making known their intention to marry in Ypres, Dunkerque, Amiens, Bordeaux—Coutanceau's hometown—and most recently in the parish of St. Catherine in Lille. Nobody voiced any objections. Just yesterday the curé in Lille "deputized and gave commission" to the curé in Ypres "to join in his name these two people" in the sacrament of marriage.[5] Coutanceau's students have dressed up in cockades and finery, escorting the happy couple festooned with garlands of flowers to St. Nicolas Church, and they have followed the ceremony with a splendid marriage feast.[6]

Du Coudray is curiously quiet about these festivities. How does she feel about it all? Her chatty letters of recent months have made absolutely no mention of the formal betrothal. Is it possible that in some odd way she does not approve of it but knows it must be? There is no question that she thinks highly of M. Coutanceau; unofficially he has been a member of her traveling "family" for years, reliable and trustworthy. But she has gone to considerable trouble to arrange that her niece will inherit her mantle precisely to avoid all confusion, lest anyone imagine Coutanceau himself the more obvious choice to succeed her. On the one hand she knows it is her duty in society's eyes to marry the young woman off; she was already preoccupied by that five years ago in Bordeaux. On the other hand she herself has thrived without any such ties to a spouse, enjoying freedom's great sweetness. Had she perhaps envisioned for her niece a similar independent course? In any case, something is very odd about her attitude and her silence.

The couple may even sense her ambivalence. It seems peculiar that they choose to marry during their one brief spell outside of France's borders, feted by students who are not even their countrymen and countrywomen. Do they wed in a foreign land because, caught up in the general euphoria of this change, they find the surroundings exotic? Or does the calendar constrain them? February is the favorite wedding month for the French by a great margin. In their case, they couldn't have married earlier because the six-week course just ended yesterday, and the Catholic period of Lent proscribes weddings in March.[7] They are evidently too impatient to put things off until April. The moment may matter more than the location. Incredible as it sounds, du Coudray, who during this time kept shuttling the few miles back and forth across the frontier, may not even have attended the ceremony, for the note from the pastor in Lille says permission was given in that town by the niece's *tuteur* (guardian) for the underaged, unemancipated woman (women are considered "minors" until age twenty-five) to be wed elsewhere.[8]

One thing is clear. The great midwife is not dewy-eyed or sentimental about marriage. There's no point in romanticizing it. But she has come to depend on both of these people for the smooth functioning of her enterprise and must respect their wishes. Ignoring their mutual desire could imperil the whole mission. At the very least this union seems a reasonable business arrangement among professional colleagues. You can be resigned to the inevitability of a thing without seeing it as cause for particular rejoicing. As men go, Coutanceau is a good man. May he never complicate their lives.

Anyway, du Coudray already has her mind on her next stop, Normandy, though her supporters here wish she would not rush off so soon. M. Chastenet, a surgeon at the military hospital, reports that she is

a woman of the greatest worth, not only in her profession, in which she excels, but in her way of thinking, in her character, and in her conduct. I have never seen anything like it, and certainly this woman is a phenomenon. I am sorry that she was so briefly among us, but the little she was here produced the greatest good for the country. If only she had been able to stay longer she would have derived a great benefit for herself . . . [and] could have reaped an abundant harvest. She had already negotiated with Ypres, Courtrai, and Ghent; Brabant, the vicomté of Alost, Malines, Antwerp, Bruges, Louvain, etc. would have followed the same plan. Holland, without a doubt, would have wanted to have her, and it was a windfall for her. Her fortune would be made if, less attached to her duty and to the engagement she had agreed to with the intendant of Caen, she would have been willing to spend eighteen months in a country where they had already acknowledged her science and her talents. I sincerely regretted it very much. Mme du Coudray is not rich; she is of a certain age; her health will surely deteriorate from the fatigue of her voyages. Here everything was smooth for her easy transport from one city to another and she would have earned in a short time what she will pursue futilely passing in France from one province to another, where she will [only] suffer affronts.[9]

M. Chastenet reads things correctly. Du Coudray is heading into some very rough waters.

Meanwhile, within a month of their marriage, the newlywed Coutanceaus conceive a child.

44. MINISTERIAL MUTINY?

Caen, 2 July 1775

Du Coudray has been in this city, once the favorite of William the Conqueror, since spring.[1] She and her retinue, now at its largest with eight people, are elegantly housed. The intendant, Fontette, knows that she has sacrificed a lucrative stay in the Netherlands to honor her promise to his province, but she assures him that "you can count on me, and on all my solicitude."[2] The students are, as one curé says, eager to learn and "not idiots either." One woman has come with no money at all; du Coudray, as always, intervenes in her behalf and demands to know why she has not been properly funded. It develops that she was not the one chosen by her parish, and has simply struck out on her own without authorization to get herself trained by the famous midwife! Many surgeons have come also, from Bayeux, Cherbourg, St. Lo. Enthusiasm is high.[3]

But trouble is brewing, precipitated by Ormesson, the right-hand man of the new controller general, Turgot. He has begun to send around, at government expense, free copies of other midwifery manuals. Besançon, shortly after du Coudray's stay there, had received Raulin's textbook. Now Ormesson is distributing the one by Augier du Fot, du Coudray's bitter rival from the Laon/Soisson school. Luckily, when Fontette receives instructions to give out ninety of these catechisms on *accouchement*, he bothers to peruse them and sees that they are not at all equivalent to the midwife's *Abrégé*. Fontette is very protective of his honored guest du Coudray, and quite confused by this flagrant breach of faith in the capital. He writes to Ormesson for clarification, asking if the du Fot book "accords" with du Coudray's teaching, suggesting that "it would perhaps be troublesome if [it] did not." He and the subdelegate of Caen, Malafait, decide that du Fot's book is under no circumstances to be distributed to her students, that they should receive her *Abrégé* only, the illustrated edition.[4] Such insubordination on the part of the king's own men in the provinces, their determination to defend du Coudray's interests against conflicting ministerial orders, must be heartening, but the rival books are elsewhere making serious inroads into du Coudray's potential market.[5] Versailles's betrayal is profoundly upsetting. Ormesson might only be doing Turgot's bidding, yet Turgot had once, back in Limousin, thought highly of her—or so she imagined.

She manages temporarily to put it out of her mind, for at least Fontette's support here is unfailing. He personally attends her course as often as he can in its huge room overflowing with chairs and benches, watching her demonstrate at her large table. He marvels at the harmonious atmosphere that prevails in her bursting classroom, and comments that du Coudray's female students would themselves be capable of teaching groups of others.[6] It is "a pleasure to see the unity and the satisfaction that reign between these women."[7]

The curés believe the midwife to be heaven sent:

> Providence . . . delivers now and then one of those extraordinary subjects, useful to society in both the spiritual and temporal. . . . You confirm it, Madame, our century must thank [Providence] for destining to us a so necessary person as you . . . teaching the art of saving subjects for the Kingdom. This great well of religion that animates you at the expense of your tranquillity . . . [your] heroic unselfishness with your students . . . [because of this] you deserve in the end the reward of the faithful servant. . . . Who can, in fact, not recognize this, seeing coarse women from the depths of the backcountry, without principles or other education but that of knowing, connecting, and sometimes scrawling the letters of the alphabet, coming back [from you] filled as if by infusion with a science no less delicate than useful in its operations.

Du Coudray is a miracle worker. The surgeons of this town see her as a *libératrice*.[8]

Today, amidst the anxieties and the accolades, a more intimate matter distracts du Coudray. Trying to organize her next trip, she is writing to both Rouen and Rennes, seeking a place relatively nearby where they can keep busy a good long while; she wants to settle in for a full six months. "I have married [off] my niece. She finds herself pregnant. She will give birth around Christmas." This information is so flatly divulged, so economically and unemotionally stated. Of course, du Coudray is writing ahead to officials she does not know, to total strangers, and might be purposely avoiding mawkishness. But this blunt, bald statement of the facts also probably reflects her true view of the matter. She does not want her niece to travel at the end of her term, and in exchange for being able to stay a half year, her team is willing to do extra teaching.[9]

How does the midwife handle the prospect of a baby in the household? Babies are her business, yet ironically this is the first time a particular baby will have a pronounced impact on her life. One private pregnancy will complicate her public work delivering for the state. It will be both an amusement and an encumbrance, and the pragmatic du Coudray is already preparing for every eventuality. A wet nurse may be needed; her niece may be out of commission for a spell. The main thing is to get one of these intendants to commit. "Absolutely no old women nor any who already practice this profession," she tells officials in Rennes who inquire about her criteria for selecting students. She plays on the traditional antipathy between the province she is currently in and the one to which she would go, cajoling the next into still better behavior than its rival. "I hope that the Bretons will be as grateful for the boon you will procure them as are the Normans. I will leave this province well satisfied to have brought a blessing they so knew how to appreciate."[10] Meanwhile, to the intendant in Rouen, where it seems there is some trouble finding her adequate housing, she explains that she is willing to live very simply. Even a section of a building will do. "A thought has occurred to me, Monsieur, that would not be costly." If he is away she can use *his* house—only the rooms he designates, of course— "and your antechamber can be my classroom. I have been lodged this way several times. I do not demand magnificence, and I know how to adjust to anything to avoid too much expense." The intendant, however, claims to be living himself in a borrowed home. All renting agents are very busy and not even a small place is available. In spite of their eagerness to receive her, they fear that she might need to be put up somewhere other than Rouen.[11]

So nothing has been resolved, and time is running out. It is causing the niece undue anxiety, a bad thing when a woman is expecting, and the midwife's lease is up, forcing her to move to an *auberge* and pay out of her own pocket. She increases the pressure on

Rennes, now the more likely prospect, insisting that she needs to travel soon. In summer there can be more than fifteen hours of daylight, in winter as few as eight. "I want to take advantage of the length of the days," she will explain in September, by which time she is so desperate for a go-ahead that she instructs the carrier of the letter to wait for or even force a reply.[12] The hovering pays off, and the party with a very pregnant Mme Coutanceau will make its way in late autumn to Rennes.

45. A Newborn and a Wet Nurse

Rennes, 8 January 1776

Hello and Happy New Year. Accept, dear friend, all the sincerest wishes that my affection and esteem form for you. M. and Mme Coutanceau join me, as does even the little newborn. My niece delivered most happily on the Day of the Innocents [28 December], but she did have the sorrow of not being able to breast-feed, so here I am in the difficult situation I had pretty much foreseen of dragging along with us a wet nurse. Please give the news to M. and Mme Roussel whom you will be good enough to assure of all the good wishes we send to them. I owe him six livres and I am posting them under your name.

Send us your news and Mme Rouyer's. You will oblige us by keeping a tender memory of us for life. . . .

A postscript adds "Many kisses to Mme Rouyer and Mme Roussel and make sure you acquit yourself well of this duty, please."[1]

Nostalgic and effusive today, cast as she is for the first time in a grandmotherly role, the midwife is reaching out to whole families, reiterating her greetings particularly to the ladies, as if sensing an unusual connectedness to them just now. Business has yielded for a moment to tenderness, even gushiness. The exuberance of the new year and her excitement in spite of herself over the new arrival bubble through this short note.

The little boy is eleven days old, born and baptized on 28 December 1775 at St. Sauveur Church. Du Coudray is the godmother, one Godefroy Brossay de St. Marc is godfather, and the child has been christened Godefroy Barthélémy Ange, the middle name af-

ter Coutanceau's father.[2] With great accuracy the midwife had predicted less than three months into her niece's pregnancy that the
baby would be born "near Christmas," and he arrived right on
schedule. The timing is perfect; thanks to du Coudray's planning,
the 15 October class has just ended and the next one has not yet
started up. The group is being treated well here, in a nice apartment
with separate attic accommodations for the servants. As in a fairy
tale, they have been told "everything that you will need will be provided."[3] All in all, a comfortable place for this important event to
have transpired.

Ensconced here in Rennes it is easy to forget the strangeness of
the surrounding lands. The Palais de Justice was the scene just a
few years ago of the stormy rebellion of the Breton *parlement* against
the crown. Guidebooks describe the inhabitants of this province as
headstrong but sociable, big drinkers who hold their liquor well and
who love anyone who speaks ill of Normans.[4] Du Coudray and her
company are housed in an area of old mansions that miraculously
escaped the devastating fire of 1720, a giant blaze that reddened the
sky for days.[5] The city itself has nothing Celtic or regional about
it. Yet they have entered Brittany, one of the least French parts of
France, isolated for centuries by its remoteness; full of mystery, nocturnal festivals, healing saints, medieval pardons; full of heath, furze,
broom, and bog; full of its own legends, loyalties, and pride, its own
very special tongue.

Here for the first time the language barrier is a potential problem
in the midwife's teaching.[6] Officials in this region have not been easily convinced that French instruction will be of any use. Twice before, in 1765 and in 1773, du Coudray was to have come, but curés
had responded that many of the volunteers from their parishes
spoke only Breton and that therefore an expensive interpreter would
be necessary. Quimper already had a quite competent Breton teacher
and *accoucheur,*[7] and French-speaking women seemed to disdain this
profession, "which, by a crazy and singular quirk, is associated in
certain parishes with unfavorable prejudices."[8] One curé had lamented "the blindness and scorn into which the profession of midwife has fallen since it became the province of a multitude of miserable old women addicted to debauchery and to a thousand ridiculous
superstitions that make them the laughingstock of the populace."
This attitude "has given an aversion and a kind of horror to all those

who pride themselves on their sensitivity."[9] One woman explains that her advanced French training has caused her problems and she is now prosecuting an old crone in her town.[10] Her eloquence and sophistication regarding legal redress against her enemy shows the class differences often masked by the linguistic issue. "I have the pain, after having sold what I had to advance myself in the art I practice and to pay for my reception, to see myself deprived of a very large portion of my income. The trial has been under way for some time." Pregnant women in the villages still prefer the locals who speak the dialect, even though she has saved many "women who without me would have indubitably perished."[11] Despite these problems, a new intendant, Caze de la Bove, has managed to gather seventy-two French-speaking students for du Coudray's first course, and will attract sixty for the second. But these are modest numbers compared to some recent groups.[12]

Obliged and determined now to attract consumers to *her* products and away from competing books and mannequins, du Coudray has begun making vehement entrepreneurial pronouncements; surgeons may work with her only if they pledge to be loyal, if they use only "*my* method of instruction" and demonstrate only on "the machine that *I* invented."[13] Not everyone cooperates; one town sees no point in buying a machine only to watch it "rot with worms and fall apart from decay."[14] But in the end about twenty are ordered. And du Coudray stipulates that the biggest city in the region *must* also purchase the expensive silk model and keep it in the Hôtel de Ville, making this a requirement for her teaching. "This machine stays in the archives . . . and it serves as a *monument to humanity for the centuries to come*" (emphasis mine). Demonstrators from all around can come study these pristine machines and repair their used ones accordingly, thus making the instruction durable. Citing her favorite example of Champagne, she points out that each of the twenty-three demonstrators there taught twelve students, so in the first year alone 276 women were trained according to her method.[15] The ripple effect, if things work properly, can be impressively lasting. Targeting posterity, du Coudray is going over the heads of those currently present. She is putting her stamp on the future.

But when she stops to think about it, her position is no longer secure. The nationwide *Gazette de France* finally has taken notice of her, publishing a short piece on the success of her teaching in Caen, where she turned out 150 young women "perfectly educated."[16] It has not, however, discussed the wider impact of her mission, its pattern of broader significance for the nation. She had so looked forward to this exposure, yet finds the coverage meager and anticlimactic. The *Gazette de santé* continues to ignore her, describing instead courses given by men, though they are far less successful. A M. Le Grand who began teaching in Amiens after her departure has modeled his teaching on hers, but few students come, and even fewer stay. The paper makes excuses for the attrition because his lessons take place from 9 A.M. to 12 P.M. and 2 to 5 P.M.: "There are no chests that can inhale lessons so long and so frequent. . . . It is mentally impossible that a student retain such intense instruction, more capable of frightening the understanding and overwhelming the memory of those who receive it than of truly enlightening them on the manner of delivery, however good it might be from the mouth of M. Le Grand."[17] Nonsense! The midwife has always given much longer lessons than those and has rarely lost a student. But about her the medical press says not a word.

And the ministers are far less steady in their support these days. Turgot, controller general since Louis XVI's accession in 1774, did approve prizes for her best students, 300 livres for a first prize, 200 and 100 livres respectively for second and third place;[18] but he has his mind on other medical reform projects now. As of a few months ago he was busy forming the new Royal Society of Medicine in Paris, approaching the matter of public health on a much grander, more modern scale, using surveys and statistics. Perhaps what du Coudray is trying to do singlehandedly seems quaint to him now, artisanal, old-fashioned, or even wasteful. Also, it is not clear he even believes any longer that France has a population crisis, because there is much debate among physiocrats and demographers on the issue.[19] His assistant Ormesson, who has never liked the midwife, scribbles on a note he receives from Brittany requesting additional funds for more of du Coudray's machines that "the minister is not fully persuaded of the utility of this woman's lessons."[20] In any event, it seems Turgot has been beguiled by her rival Augier du Fot. At the latter's recent, untimely death the government paid 2,400 livres for five thousand copies of his book, which are being sent all about in lieu of du Coudray's more expensive manual. Turgot is even providing du Fot's widow with a modest pension.[21]

Dangerous times, these. If du Coudray has not lost ministerial support entirely, she is at least sharing it with many questionable players, many rivals and foes. She tries now to deflect the money allotted for prizes so that it will be used for the purchase of her *Abrégé* instead, arguing that the competition for awards set up among her students is divisive and benefits only three members of the group, whereas distributing a copy of her book to each of them makes them all feel equally important and proud, enhances their solidarity.[22] Du Fot's book is not the only competition. Raulin's *Instructions succinctes* has actually been translated into Breton and printed in a practical, split-page edition with text in both languages.[23] Anxiety is making her ill, and a case of gout now plagues her. Her leg bothers her so much at times that she sends little notes to officials right here in town rather than heave herself up and go see them, as is her custom. She is "tormented with mail" and asks for help with the voluminous correspondence. She fights to stay busy, yet the work overwhelms her.[24]

On top of everything else, a wet nurse has had to join the entourage—the ultimate irony. Du Coudray devotes an entire chapter of the *Abrégé* to "the qualities required of a good *nourrice*," should one be needed,[25] but at least as many pages throughout the text to why one should be avoided at all costs. It is noteworthy that her dim view of wet nurses has only gotten worse with time. In her second edition, that of 1769, published ten years after the first, she added eight new pages on the problems they create. In fact, she explains, they are a major cause of depopulation, for most women who suckle for money are compelled to do so by their poverty and suffer from poor nutrition and still poorer sanitation. Some accept children knowing full well they have no milk. Others, more irresponsible than malicious, take the child into bed with them, then roll over and crush or suffocate them. "What number of children [are] dead or maimed by the negligence of their wet nurse? It is indeed shameful that the state loses so many subjects."[26] Du Coudray deplores hired "mercenary" help who might swaddle the baby in its own excrement, leaving it to cry itself to death.

But now, right in the midwife's very own household, Mme Coutanceau's milk has failed, and they have no choice but to hire a wet nurse. Honey in sugar water can work briefly, but is not an adequate long-term nutrient substitute.[27] Given her strong feelings on this matter, du Coudray has almost surely selected a woman to fit the specifications she spells out in the *Abrégé*. This person, after all, will be responsible for piloting her grandnephew safely through his hazardous first years. She must be healthy, not the child of parents with transmittable maladies like gout, scrofula, or epilepsy. Her breast must be of "sufficient volume, not too large, not too small . . . not sagging, not too firm . . . but pear-shaped . . . the size and form of the nipple must correspond to those of a hazelnut. It must be pierced by several little holes enabling milk to easily escape so that the nursling has less trouble sucking. When the child leaves the breast, the milk, neither too thin nor too serous, should come out in several spokes, like water from a sprinkler. . . . Milk that is too watery does not nourish enough . . . that which is too thick, besides it being hard to get out, is difficult to digest . . . it must be white, smooth, and a little sweet."[28]

Wet nurses must not be too young or too old; youth is too hot, age too abundant in humors. The best age is from twenty-five to thirty-five. "They should have black or brown hair, not blonde or red or rusty," for these last have a disagreeable odor. If the skin is not white, at least it should not be livid, which announces a bilious temperament. One must examine the neck and under the chin "to check for scrofula. In checking the arms, one can tell by the number of bloodletting scars whether she has been sickly." She should not have her menses while nursing, for that diminishes the milk. "And she should not be cross-eyed, or have rotten teeth, which can cause bad breath capable of upsetting the child."

Never take a wet nurse right after she gives birth, because during that time her milk is good only for her own child and would be contrary to another nursling different in temperament. If her own child has died, one must determine whether this was from a contagious malady such as scarlet fever, venereal ulcerations, or scabies. If her child is alive, one can judge her on the basis of it. If its tone is bright red, if its skin is brittle, and if, examining it all naked, one find abrasions between the thighs, this will show the unsavoriness of the wet nurse, who will surely be still more remiss with a child she takes only out of greed. Particular attention must be given to her lifestyle, as the character of the woman who suckles will greatly influence the child. Is she prone to drinking, stealing, or some other moral weakness? Is she violent or unpredictable? Does either she or her husband have the falling sickness? Does the couple get along? There must be no chance that "as they quarrel, or strike each other, the blows might fall on the child." In short, "one must neglect nothing to learn about all these circumstances, and one must never be swayed either by friends or by the hope of receiving gifts from the one chosen. Although [such bribery] does not seem a crime, it is one, and the child is often the victim of it, either in dying early or in living long in infirmity." In small towns where there is much gossip and little privacy one can easily find out about people's peculiarities.

Once the wet nurse is chosen, du Coudray gives elaborate instructions on nursing properly and safely. Until the age of one the woman must not take the baby into her bed, or lean over the cradle to nurse, or give nocturnal feedings when she might nod off and crush the infant. Instead, at the same time each evening, while she is wide awake, the wet nurse should feed the baby and wean him or her of the hazardous habit of waking and demanding to be fed during the night. Babies, she says repeatedly, must be seen by the wet nurses as "precious treasures" entrusted to their care.[29]

If du Coudray speaks thus of newborns in general, we can imagine her feelings toward the "priceless" infant in her own family. He is a baby among babies. Whether she exercised such rigorous scrutiny in choosing a woman to nourish and nurture him we cannot know with certainty, but it is a safe bet.

46. "Attend, Monsieur, to My Little Interests"

Nantes, Summer and Fall 1776

Spaniards bring their wines, fine woolens, iron, liver, oils, oranges, and lemons to this busy Atlantic port; they leave with linen and other fabric, costume jewels, and wheat. The Dutch send their salt fish and spices in exchange for wines and eau-de-vie. The Swedes trade copper, the British lead, pewter, coal. They mix their business with amusements, visiting the nearby Pierre Nantoise, a rock on which, though it is steeply slanted and smooth, small boys dance gracefully for small change, defying the laws of gravity.[1]

But who has time for such diversions? Coutanceau is doing most of the teaching, and it is double the usual trouble. Du Coudray tells the intendant: "I hope, Monsieur, that you will be good enough not to forget my nephew and his bonus. It is a matter I cannot let go by, because it would become prejudicial to me in the other provinces I still need to do and it is in truth very justly deserved because of the low comprehension of Breton women, especially those of Nantes. . . . My nephew has to repeat his demonstrations twice each week, something that has never happened to us before. And it is only by the strength of his efforts that we hope to train a few good subjects. So please attend, Monsieur, to my little interests and I will be much obliged to you."[2] Coutanceau has also been approached by officials in Vannes, who offer 300 livres to do a brief course.[3] Such teaching side trips bring in some much-needed extra money for the household, and in any case they are, as usual, all killing time waiting around to be paid for the machines.[4]

Many reminders are necessary before Coutanceau eventually gets his gratification.[5] Du Coudray has urged him to pursue on his own what is rightfully his, but his style is too obsequious. He, after all, is not pensioned by the king, and he cannot presume to deserve his aunt's treatment. "M. Coutanceau, nephew of the Dame Du Coudray, represents to your greatness that he has always been honored with a bonus given by the intendants with the approval of the minister. If, Monseigneur, you ask M. Caze de la Bove, he will not hesitate to assure you of the care he has taken for the instruction of students that he trained in four courses. . . . This bonus is ordinarily 25 louis [600 livres] for three courses, and the fourth will be at your pleasure. This gift does him too much honor for him not to urgently beseech your greatness to accord it to him." Only in the spring of next year will this money finally come through, and Coutanceau will get just the minimum 600 rather than any additional payment for the fourth course.[6] His third-person voice is too deferential; he is not making enough noise to be promptly and fully obliged.

Du Coudray's style is far bolder, and that is fitting. In her letters she is always the dominant "I"—present, in charge, commanding. In spite of the fact that Coutanceau presides over this set of classes, she is still widely recognized as the leader of the enterprise. It is *she* who receives the 400-livre gift of a gold box engraved with the arms of the city of Nantes.[7] And it is *she* who gets the rave review from the city officials; they commend the uprightness of her conduct, her talent, wisdom, and fairness, her courtesy with everyone involved.[8] This is still *her* mission. The subtle shift, the gradual pass-ing of authority from one generation to the next, will be tricky. Her junior partners, she realizes, need coaching, will have to learn to act with greater confidence, with the rhetorical energy of the "good of humanity" behind them.

Geographically, it would be far more convenient for du Coudray to head from here to the Tours area next, but she has promised to return to Normandy and teach in the inland, eastern part of that province. She will go now to Evreux, because Rouen does not want her. The claim of having failed to find housing is a feeble excuse masking the real reasons du Coudray is not welcome there. Rouen was the headquarters of Claude-Nicolas Le Cat, Frère Côme's arch-enemy, and his doctor disciples keep alive the hostility.[9] Moreover, professional controversy and scandal, rife in that town, have bared raw emotions.

Since 1772 Rouen has been split apart by an ugly feud between the corporation of surgeons and the midwives. On 23 July of that year one Blanchard, a veteran with twenty-six years of practice, had been called to assist a woman in labor, two of whose children she had successfully delivered before. She was maneuvering a very deli-cate breech birth when a surgeon entered, had a tantrum that he had not been summoned, pushed her aside, and with the help of his male assistant began to mangle things. "Regardless of your in-sults to me," the midwife had said, "I believe I am obliged to tell you that the child has its mouth turned against the pubic bone on the side of the mother's right hip. Pay attention to that, or it might die during your intervention." The two men disregarded her re-port, severed the already delivered trunk from the head that was still inside the mother, went in after the head with forceps, left without a word to the woman whose child they had killed, and eight days later had the Rouen corporation of surgeons bring Blanchard to trial for incompetence and insubordination.[10]

Blanchard, speaking for all midwives, defended herself eloquently and even amusingly, imploring the tribunal to "put a brake on the caprice, irresponsibility, and fury of a man who allows himself any-thing to make me accountable" for his crime. She claimed in just the space of those few days to have lost her credit and reputation with her clientele because of his defamation. In front of everyone in the *parlement* courtroom she reminded the surgeon that she had once been his trusted friend, had given him many lessons at his request, had delivered his wife when he was so distressed by her cries that he ran from the room, crashing into two skeletons and sustaining such severe head contusions as he fell down that she didn't know whether to tend to him or to his laboring spouse. Now he was "hiding behind the curtain" and provoking his corporation to bring charges against her and to try to discredit all women in her profession. After outlining why, historically and morally, midwives had stronger claims to birthing expertise, she accused the surgeons of "jealous despotism." A doctor from Montpellier had even come to the defense of midwives at this very public and very talked-about trial, arguing that women could handle this branch of medicine at least as well as men and accusing surgeons of "oppression," even going so far as to suggest that midwives should instruct themselves and each other in an exclusively female network. Another doctor brought up the way *accoucheurs* deprive midwives of their pay. Rouen surgeons had been successfully squeezing women out of the birthing room; the gratuities offered to the midwife by parents and godparents—each would give anywhere from 24 sous to 6 livres—were routinely usurped by the surgeon who had attended the birth. Such extortion, concluded this doctor, one might expect to see in the deserts of Arabia, but not in civilized France.

This case had dragged on for years, flaring up again in 1774 and 1775 when the same patient gave birth again, triggering heated fights on these larger issues of professional and gender rivalry. It is now on everyone's lips once more. Only in 1779 will it finally be resolved, with an *arrêt* of the Rouen *parlement* ordering the surgeons to pay 1,000 livres in damages to the exonerated Blanchard, to expurgate from their writings anything hurtful or calumnious, and to post fifty copies of this decree around the city at their own expense. But even from the beginning the winds of popular opinion have been blowing in favor of the midwives, as they are now, and the surgeons refuse to have the spectacular du Coudray appearing in their midst to display her virtuosity. Frère Côme is in touch with the intendant of Rouen about this whole trial. He, who knows well how ruthless surgeons can be, is suggesting that a way be found to get midwives out from under their jurisdiction entirely.[11] Rouen, then, is far too explosive at the moment to tolerate the presence of the national midwife, so Evreux it will be instead.

The route back up north actually takes the midwife through Angers and Le Mans, places she will need to return to. Sometimes the whole runaround so far afield must strike her as crazy. As it turns out, she will even overshoot Evreux and head to Paris first. She has had a lot on her mind. A trip to the capital feels necessary, for she now clearly senses things shaping up against her.

DETRACTORS, DEFENSES, DAZZLING DISPLAYS

47. The Attack

Paris, 5 March 1777

Monsieur,

You did me the honor of saying to me when I had that of seeing you, that the courses in Moulins did not have much success. I have just found a memoir by the late M. Le Nain which
will give you a very great proof of the contrary and you will
easily sense that the greatest good does not always find advocates. If you wish to procure it in your province, decide quite
soon so that I can make the arrangements accordingly. I have
the honor to be with respect, Monsieur, your very humble and
very obedient servant

du Coudray[1]

This snippy note, shot off from Paris to the intendant of Tours, reveals the midwife's displeasure at his attempt to deprive her of credit
for a past accomplishment. She has had reason to go through her
papers just now, and has unearthed Le Nain's early memoir, part of
her arsenal of weapons against such indifference. She encloses it
with her letter.

Several things have brought her here, first to check on the health
of her dear Frère Côme, who was at death's door for a spell. The illness of this celebrated healer has alarmed the city; at one point the
Journal de Paris mistakenly reported his passing. But he is recover-
ing. She has come also for reassurance from old supporters like Bertin, for votes of confidence from new ministers—there has been a
dizzying series of controller generals since the disgrace of Turgot a
year ago—and for talks with the publisher Debure, who is to bring
out yet another edition of the *Abrégé*. Most important of all, she en-
trusts to her friends here copies of the many letters and recommendations she has accumulated on her travels. These validating testimonials are her most precious possessions, far more meaningful to

her than the cumbersome gifts she receives, and she has been collecting them for seventeen years on Bertin's advice. Frère Côme has
used this technique himself, depositing his saved letters of praise
with his notary when one of his rivals attempted to defame his character.[2] Du Coudray's documents, powerful and eloquent affirmations of her past triumphs, could prove useful in an emergency. Her
advocates here in the capital can deploy this evidence to defend her,
if necessary, while she journeys on.

Such machinations are called for now because the midwife fears
that a crisis is imminent. It has been building. At first it took the
form of a conspiracy of silence. Du Fot's book was dangerous in its
gross distortion of the facts, its flagrant denial of her accomplishments. He raves about the mannequins made by Mme Riel and
Mlle l'Enfant, "whose intelligence and dexterity have perfected these
models. . . . Useful people deserve the esteem and gratitude of the
public when their talents . . . profit society. . . . Let's give each his
due." There follows a list of twenty-six writers on obstetrics, from
which she, of course, is missing.[3] Du Fot's friend J. J. Gardanne,
royal censor of his midwifery manual but also editor of the *Gazette
de santé*, has discussed male midwives as "generous citizens" and
great "patriots" but has never acknowledged du Coudray's existence
in his paper.[4] Nor has another health journal, the *Gazette salutaire*,
which raves about books on midwifery by men and about heroic
feats performed with forceps by male surgeons like Levret.[5] This
paper rails against the "murderous ignorance of village matrons,"[6]
and admires a school for midwives set up in Altenburg by the duke
of Saxe-Gotha, concluding, "it is to be hoped for the good of humanity that this example be followed in other countries."[7] Du Coudray feels she has been the victim of systematic effacement.

Then there has been the belittling of her and her field. *L'Anarchie
médecinale*, a popular exposé by a Montpellier doctor named Gilibert, has a merciless attack on lower-class "femmelettes" who try
to meddle in medical matters but have no more chance of being
right than an astrologer. Even educated women with pretensions as
healers are hazards, Gilibert asserts, more so than poisons, swords,
and daggers; they cause a degenerate race.[8] Tissot's wildly successful *Avis au peuple sur la santé* damns with faint praise, saying that, at
best, one might come across a midwife who is "a little less misinformed."[9] Buchan's *Domestic Medicine*, translated now into French

and warmly received, criticizes female healers for "knowing everything, doing everything, except their duty. To hear them tell it, they
are doctors, surgeons, apothecaries, they do not need anyone."[10] The
Affiches . . . du Dauphiné advertises a course by a man in Grenoble.
It does mention the earlier visit of du Coudray—"we remember
still with what affluence people initiated in these mysteries flocked
to [her]"—but the very language suggests something secretive
and witchlike about her attraction, and the impact of her lessons
is dismissed as "fleeting." Any real progress has been due to the
male "*gens de l'art* who succeeded her, having more intelligence and
aptitude."[11]

Lately the conflict has escalated, and a group is forming specifically against her. They will no longer tolerate her threat to their entrenched birthright of power, and mean to undo the king's mistake
of having vested so much authority in this woman in the first place,
allowing her to appropriate privileges and prerogatives hitherto associated exclusively with men, to act as a recognized celebrity of
enormous consequence. She has something of the indestructible; difficulties appear to energize rather than thwart her. And the longevity of her reign—nearly two decades now—defies all odds. Worst of
all, her widespread teaching activities have reinforced professional
possibilities for large numbers of other women too. Although she
has always been scrupulously careful not to mention this indirect
result of her work, several intendants have recently noted it. Fontette in Caen and Caze de la Bove in Rennes just now, for example,
both comment that her capable female students could easily train
other students themselves with no help from surgeons, indeed, that
"great union and satisfaction reigns among them."[12] This female
bonding, observed admiringly by the two intendants, is seen by male
medical practitioners as a disaster.

So her foes have been growing in number and she is attacked now
frontally in print. A Doctor Nicolas of Grenoble has published a *Cri
de la nature en faveur des enfants nouveau-nés*, denouncing women who
think they are omniscient after a few lessons, targeting especially
the famous midwife's students. "We are scarcely better off today
than before *la dame* Du Coudray traveled through the provinces. . . .
These women brought back from their voyages to the capitals only a
lot of effrontery and an insolent but dangerous confidence."[13] Nicolas had written much of this as a knee-jerk reflex when du Coudray

was in Grenoble in 1772 but has held off publishing his book until recently when, inspired by Du Fot and Gardanne, to whom he refers constantly, he can jump on the bandwagon of du Coudray detractors. Her opponents are really gaining momentum; his is no longer a lone voice of protest.

Alphonse Le Roy is the newest and worst of this network of hostile doctors. He has published a *Pratique des accouchements*, dedicated to the king's first physician, in which he claims that women do not understand what they are doing and should be forbidden to write. Elizabeth Nihell's six-hundred-page book "contains absolutely nothing on the Art." This absurdly cavalier dismissal of the serious issues she raises is an emotional reaction against Nihell's vehement feminism, the kind of anti-male language that du Coudray has gone to such effort to avoid. But Le Roy makes no distinction between these two women: in his eyes they are equally out of control. He next sinks his teeth into the *Abrégé*. "This work does not substantiate the kind of reputation that this midwife has acquired. This new preacher who goes from city to city teaching and practicing with fanfare the art of delivery, this woman who they say has even gone so far as to obtain orders forcing surgeons to attend her courses, seems, in this work, to know absolutely nothing of the mechanism of childbirth. Even as she says she will reveal the art, she only designs the accessories and clings to the marvelous. Her ideas are often neither felicitous nor true." After listing her "vulgar errors that could only arise from blind routine," with liberal doses of sarcasm—"Mme du Coudray, to distinguish herself, now announces an even more marvelous discovery"—he sums up: "That is enough dwelling on the mistakes, as humiliating for reason as they are distressing for humanity, which is the victim."[14] Le Roy promises to bring about a "revolution" in the teaching and practice of childbirth. "Oh weeping women, do not fear any longer the instant that establishes your maternity. The art . . . can be perfected to the point of always assuring your days and most often those of your children." And *he* will be the savior![15]

Le Roy objects to du Coudray on a number of counts. As a man he finds something perverted, a kind of saturnalian misrule, in the notion of surgeons being taught by a midwife. A regent of the Paris Medical Faculty, an academic doctor trained in scholarly theory and Latin book learning, he is totally unsympathetic to a woman argu-

ing for the superiority or even equal worth of practice and experience. He does not respect the traditions of crafts and trades. He is
Parisian and disapproves of the peregrinations of science throughout the countryside. The proper hierarchical arrangement calls for
students to make the reverent pilgrimage to the center, the capital,
the sanctuary of medicine, and to hear whatever the great masters
there deign to divulge in their displays of erudition. No teacher of
any worth or with any sense of dignity would willingly step down
off such a pedestal and wander shamelessly about. The crux, though,
is that Le Roy has a deep distrust of women, a notion he will continue to develop in all his writings. He considers them flawed by
nature, useful only for understanding "human disorders. . . . The
degeneration of the species always starts in nature with the females;
studying the ills of women is to go back to the source of those of the
whole human race. Woman is a feeble being whom pain besieges
in the spring of her age, in the midst of her life, in the decline of
her days."[16] So women as objects of study are pathetically weak; as
agents of healing they are positively deadly.

Now Le Roy prints up a diatribe against the famous midwife and
circulates this pamphlet far and wide. His broadside is the first outright attempt to slander her.[17] It is being distributed free with his
book in the shop of his *libraire*, Le Clerc, on the quai des Augustins.
In response, du Coudray selects for her Paris headquarters a new *libraire*, Debure, on the same street. Debure is putting out a new edition of her *Abrégé* and is well positioned to soon play an even bigger
role in her defense. The new edition of her book is the beginning of
her mobilization, reproclaiming her authenticity and special status.
Unlike any previous edition, this one has her two brevets from the
king published right with the text. It also states for the first time on
the title page directly under her name that she is "pensioned and
sent by the King . . ."—all this to show that she and only she is the
genuine article (fig. 10). Let them try to question her legitimacy now.

So it is open war. This certainly helps explain the curt tone of
du Coudray's letter to Tours. Permanent damage to her reputation
must be prevented at all costs, and there is no time to lose. She needs
to proceed with business as usual, continuing to travel at her characteristic clip, but she must now face two harsh facts. First, free and
broadly circulated pamphlets can make or break a person, targeting
as they do an increasingly sophisticated readership eager to involve

ABRÉGÉ
DE L'ART
DES ACCOUCHEMENTS,

DANS lequel on donne les préceptes néceffaires pour le mettre heureufement en pratique, & auquel on a joint plufieurs Obfervations intérestantes fur des cas finguliers.

OUVRAGE très-utile aux jeunes Sages-femmes, & généralement à tous les Eleves en cet Art, qui defirent de s'y rendre habiles.

NOUVELLE ÉDITION.

Volume in-8°. avec Figures gravées en taille-douce & imprimées en couleurs.

PAR ·Madame LE BOURSIER DU COUDRAY, Maîtreffe Sage-femme de Paris, penfionnée & envoyée par le Roi pour enfeigner à pratiquer l'Art des Accouchemens dans tout le Royaume.

Le Prix eft de fept livres quatre fols, relié.

A PARIS,

Chez DEBURE, Pere, Libraire, Quai des Auguftins, au coin de la rue Gît-le-Cœur, Maifon du Notaire.

M. DCC. LXXVII.
Avec Approbation & Privilege du Roi.

Figure 10. Title page of the 1777 edition of the textbook, where Mme du Coudray, under fire now from powerful detractors, spells out her royal credentials directly under her name for all to see. She also includes in this edition printed copies of her brevets from the king, again to underscore her legitimacy for any who would call her a charlatan. Courtesy of the UCLA Biomedical Library, Rare Books Collection.

itself in judging all matters. As fissures develop in the Old Regime hierarchies, public opinion is appealed to more and more by those fighting for causes, and her detractors have turned to that new influential tribunal.[18] Second, doctors spurred on by the professionalizing tendencies of the Royal Society of Medicine are leveling accusations of charlatanism right and left. They are insiders, she is an outsider. They seem especially bent on shoring up their own prestige by negating the idea that a woman can be knowledgeable and skillful. Competence has become gendered in their rhetoric, and it is male.[19]

The midwife will have to deal with these new realities.

48. Counterattack: "It Is the King Who Pays Me"

Evreux, 27 October 1777

"The great production of machines is finally done, and I plan to send them by way of Rouen next week according to your orders."[1] Du Coudray is immensely relieved today that this tedious work is over, for "it is very disagreeable to make one after another,"[2] and she is under so much strain lately. They have made many hundreds of these machines by now, and it gets no easier, building up the models with stuffing, yards of material, durable sutures, leather straps, bindings and sponges, all the organs made exactly to lifelike proportions. Usually the machines are constructed with an inner structure of wood or cane, but now the midwife uses real skeletons, and the traffic in corpses cannot be pleasant. A complaint came recently from the surgeon Barotte in Chaumont: "The pubic bones of the machine entrusted to me broke during my last course, which makes me presume that the pelvis Mme du Coudray used . . . was fairly corrupted, or that it was taken from a cemetery, because a fresh pelvis would not have done this."[3] She seems to be cutting corners.

Du Coudray and her party—her niece, nephew, a "boy for the machines," chambermaid, lackey, and a cook (perhaps brought just now from Paris as a special indulgence in her hour of need?)—are living in the marshalsea of this town,[4] joined by a guard who sleeps in the foyer of the great mansion because the front door fails to close securely.[5] The baby and his wet nurse seem to have been shed along the way; they have probably returned to the woman's native village. On the surface all looks normal, for the midwife is going through all the motions of her established routine.[6]

But the pamphlet war begun in Paris has followed her here. Despite the immense popularity of the class, on 24 May the subdelegate reported to the intendant that a letter allegedly from Frère Côme was circulating, full of attacks on du Coudray, her teaching team, her method, and that it had "produced the most violent effect." The midwife had been frantic, so shaken by the formation of the claque in Paris that she easily doubted Frère Côme's loyalty too. "She was beside herself," unable to understand any possible motives for such a public betrayal.[7]

The subdelegate, who thinks very highly of the midwife, from the beginning suspected the letter to be a forgery and was dismayed by the pain it caused her. He tried desperately to reassure and calm down du Coudray so that the malicious writing would not wreak havoc on her entire operation. In mid-June the subdelegate went to the course himself to see if there was any substance to the noise about bad teaching or discontent.[8] On the contrary, the students reported "in a unanimous voice that they had nothing but a lively sense of gratitude to M. the intendant, who was good enough to obtain for them these advantages, and to Mme du Coudray, who has seconded those views with all her might." Seventy-one students signed a statement to this effect; presumably the others could not write.[9]

Another mean rumor also had to be squelched. Because the course had not occupied the students all day (perhaps the teacher is shortening the length of the lessons to conserve her strength), some had taken jobs and made some extra money through outside work.[10] They used some of that money to give du Coudray and her niece gifts, including a gold watch. It soon got around that the midwife had wrested the funds for these gifts from her students, had tyrannized and scared them, depriving the girls of hard-earned money they needed for food and lodging. The subdelegate, eager to vindicate her, has tracked down the person who put about the story of extortion, and he has also managed to learn the identity of the letter forger. The "nasty intrigue" is now over, and a punishment to fit the crime has been meted out.[11] The record says no more about the identities of the perpetrators, but they were almost surely inspired by the groups working against the midwife in Paris and Rouen.

Du Coudray has remained occupied, negotiating with Debure

about special discounts for students on the new edition of her *Abrégé*.[12] But these accusations of thieving vanity are ghastly. Do many, or any, believe them? For in fact, the exact opposite is true. These particular students have been very poorly provided for and borrow sums from her frequently. They have only nine sous a day: three for one and a half pounds of bread, three for a small piece of meat, one for salt and vegetables, two for a *pot* of cider.[13] Some have been forced to find extra work spinning cotton and wool, or sewing and knitting (a few even try to sneak their handiwork into the classroom).[14] It cannot please du Coudray to see them distracted in this way by tasks other than her lessons, and the last thing she would do is add to their financial hardship. The mere suspicion of rapacity is crushing.

The surgeons' antipathy to the midwife here is such that the intendant has had to bribe them with four louis each to attend the course.[15] One, coming from far away, gets this welcome home from a colleague: "You, sir, a student of the Hôtel Dieu of Rouen, a lieutenant of the first surgeon, and made to give lessons to a woman, you, going to receive them from Mme du Coudray! Are you not ashamed?"[16] Such cabals add fuel to Le Roy's accusation that surgeons study with du Coudray only under duress. The subdelegate reports that the midwife does none of the manual demonstrations anymore, that she is just not up to it these days. Coutanceau, whom this official finds a rather hard person, presides over all of them, and the tedium of performing these maneuvers again and again for such a large number of students has done nothing to loosen up the nephew.[17]

Somehow, though, du Coudray sees to it that the actual lectures, still given by her, are as spectacular as ever. She raised a few eyebrows by insisting on converting prize money into funds for purchasing her book, and by increasing the price of machines to 300 livres for the regular linen model and 500 for the silk one in the Hôtel de Ville.[18] But having observed her teaching closely, the subdelegate is now utterly convinced of her virtues, and he tells the officials of Le Mans, where du Coudray will go next: "You will find her a very amiable woman who in no way gives the lie to what her fame proclaims. Her truly estimable talents are supported by a lively and penetrating intelligence as fair as it is agreeable, adorned with useful knowledge and enhanced by the best society manners. With these qualities she cannot help but add to the consideration which she has won by the services she has rendered to the state and to humanity and that she continues to render."[19] The intendant, de Crosne, has also been completely won over, reporting to Frère Côme that he is impressed with her "beyond all expression."[20] She will leave behind many conquests, 120 well-trained students, a slightly disgruntled used-goods merchant upset about a few damaged plates, and a green taffeta umbrella. The subdelegate, who had gotten to know her well during the gold watch scandal, will feel at her departure a keen sense of loss.[21]

How has du Coudray managed to bounce back from hurt and pain? Always happiest when taking action, she has notified her Paris contacts that the moment is finally ripe for a counteroffensive. They rapidly compose a written defense of her and her work to undercut the impact of Le Roy's libelous malignings and of the Evreux watch scandal. Their signal to print came from her soon after the forged letter episode of 24 May, and a censor approved their pamphlet on 11 June. The result is a twenty-two-page "Letter from a Citizen, Lover of the Public Good . . . in defense of the mission of Mme du Coudray who trains midwives throughout the realm for the King, attacked in a public writing." It is distributed free in large numbers by her bookseller, Debure, on the busy corner of the quai des Augustins and the rue Gît-le-Cœur on the Left Bank of the Seine, next door to Le Roy's publisher. This brochure contains a sampling of letters collected over the years by du Coudray from ministers of state, city officials, doctors and surgeons, regional administrators, curés, and of course her two brevets from His Majesty, testifying to the scope and longevity of her impact. The letters span the time from her earliest stop at Moulins to her most recent stay in Nantes. This is the kind of attention she had wanted but never gotten in the press. It is so satisfying, finally, to have her story made known to the public.

The letters themselves are preceded by four pages in which the anonymous editor-apologist gives the history of du Coudray's mission for the "political government . . . to preserve and even augment its state forces in all respects."[22] Du Coudray's success salvaging babies in Auvergne marked the beginning of her special work. "The noise of this marvel spread," and the national program was inaugurated. Next come some gory descriptions of rural delivery practices encountered by du Coudray before she introduced reforms; her method eliminates all these abominations once and for all. More than four thousand students have been trained so far in the course of this "laborious mission," whose toilsome circumstances "triple the work toward the principle goal." It requires amazing zeal to surmount disgusts "against thousands and thousands of unpleasantnesses much more repulsive than we can imagine. To undertake and persevere in such a career, a person would have to be unique in every way, combining all qualities joined and sustained by religion, honor, and humanity, a prodigy the likes of which the provinces in this Kingdom have probably never seen before, and will not see again, unless this unique personage leaves several heirs and heiresses of her zeal and her way of instructing . . . whose reproduction will perpetuate such a precious memory."

The substantiating material presented proves definitively that du Coudray is beyond suspicion of charlatanism. Fourteen examples follow, the two royal brevets first, then some choice letters. Finally, the editor adds a short conclusion. It is now manifestly clear that Alphonse Le Roy accused her wrongly of coercing people to take her course. The national midwife would "never think of committing such violence. She is, on the contrary, very flattered when doctors and surgeons honor her with their presence in her lessons and elsewhere."

So, with the help of the *Lettre d'un citoyen*, du Coudray rises like the phoenix from near destruction. Her mission has been lauded before in long books—Roussel's *Système physique et morale de la femme* and the *Etat de médecine*, for example. The surgeon Pierre Süe's two-volume *Essais historiques sur l'art des accouchements*, being written around this time, keenly supports her and disparages Alphonse Le Roy, who has the presumption to think that "nobody before him understood a thing about childbirth." So familiar does Süe seem with the conflict between them that he might actually be the compiler/author of the *Lettre*.[23] But this pamphlet serves a new and different purpose from these endorsements in long books. Short, readable, accessible, it is her most effective vindication, a dramatic polemical reminder of du Coudray's service to the country and an admonition against national amnesia and ingratitude. And it works, softening some of her former adversaries. The *Gazette de santé*, probably as a result of this brochure, now mentions her work for the first time. Under its new editor, J. J. Paulet, a friend of Frère Côme's, it publishes a review of the latest edition of the *Abrégé*. Though critical

of some of the illustrations, the editor praises du Coudray's knowledge and her strength in surmounting obstacles, borrowing almost
word for word from the *Lettre*, and concludes that the country should
be grateful to her.[24]

This development reanimates du Coudray. It is in that renewed
spirit that she reminds the dawdling intendant of Tours of her elevated status, ending with the flourish "it is the King who pays
me." This is her second letter today.[25] To Rouen she writes about
completed machines, about finished business. To Tours she writes
briskly about arranging the future. Tidying up behind and laying
ghosts to rest, then forging bravely ahead—this is the rhythm that
keeps her going. Things may close in on her, but she stands her
ground. Ten years ago lesser problems nearly led her to quit. Now,
when she could easily retire at full pay, she deploys a fresh set of
tricks to preserve her life's work. She will play the enemies' game,
adapt her responses, roll with the punches. If blocked, she will go a
different way.

49. COURTING THE NECKERS

Paris, 31 December 1777

Back in Paris yet again, her second time this year, du Coudray needs
to stay close to the pulse of the crisis. But she has just received an
emergency summons from her nephew in Le Mans, where he has
gone on ahead to start teaching. He is overwhelmed, and she must
rush to his aid immediately, drop her personal business matters,
cut everything short.

At least while in the capital she and Frère Côme have had time to
discuss strategy, especially the deployment of the *Lettre*, which the
monk distributes liberally as a "sample of what this unique woman
is worth."[1] And she has managed to meet the new minister of finance, Necker, reputed to be a wizard with money. Bertin, somehow always present in the background, has put in a good word for
her. "The advantages she can procure through the students she trains
in her art, and the special good that I wish for her, will always lead
me to eagerly approve whatever tends toward that goal."[2] Necker,
well liked and powerful, was installed shortly after the midwife's
March trip to Paris, and she has been eager ever since to get back
here to meet with him. His job is nothing less than to save the coun-

try from bankruptcy. As a self-made millionaire with great success in banking, Necker is looked to as the treasury's savior.

He has announced that he plans to deal with the deficit by eliminating unnecessary offices, and du Coudray feared the man might not have been properly briefed, or briefed at all, about her mission. She cannot afford to remain silent and risk being swept off the books. Necker has a stated goal of reducing royal pensions. At least on this trip there has been occasion to persuade him not to reduce hers, and to alert him to her work.

She would, however, have liked more time to get to know his very influential wife as well, for Mme Necker is an avid supporter of hospitals and public health projects, and du Coudray will soon be requiring her assistance.[3] But Coutanceau is in a panic, and she must run to the rescue.

50. Pandemonium

Le Mans, 11 January 1778

A near riot that had to be subdued by a police squad! What a scene du Coudray has come upon. But listen to how she processes it.

> Monsieur,
> The number of students that my nephew received is so considerable that I abandoned all my business in Paris to get here as quickly as possible, but we have turned away a still greater number who now are counting on a second course. M. de la Boussinière, who is charming and who could not support you better, has explained to you the condition of those we sent back. . . .
> This establishment must be forever. The good you wished to do would be only momentary, or else too expensive. Everywhere I have gone I have been able merely to get things started, and I made it perpetual in the following way: the intendants engage the municipal officers of each town within ten to twelve leagues of the chief city to purchase the machines I use for my operations, which cost 300 livres complete. Then the city corps chooses from the membership of the corps of surgeons the most zealous, to send him to me at the time allotted by you, Monsieur, to learn from me how to make use of this machine. Then

the surgeon becomes a demonstrator and instructs himself, if he does not already know it, in the art of delivery; he becomes an excellent *accoucheur*. [More] students, on the recommendation of the first ones trained by me, when they live near the demonstrator, come without great expense . . . or resistance . . . as long as you promise them something. The principal city must also buy a model machine, and the demonstrator of that city is in correspondence with the others [regarding] the maintenance of the machines. . . . All these ways together . . . make this establishment lasting.

The late M. Le Nain thought to inspire competition among the women by giving three prizes. This continued in several provinces, but these three prizes crown only three in approximately ninety-seven and caused so much trouble that I have changed the way this sum is distributed. I have had printed a book for my students which contains all necessary information about the positions of the woman, and twenty-six colored illustrations which remind them of the demonstrations they had, making this book essential for them. The sum for the prizes given previously is now used to give each of my students a copy of this book so that they all get the same honor, and when it is given to them by you, Monsieur, we add the King's arms, resulting in a cost of 6 livres 6 sous per copy.

M. de Crosne had funds to spend on the book and the machines because the women were financed by their parishes, or local seigneurs, or paid their own way, and consequently they cost him nothing. But you, Monsieur, who out of goodness have undertaken to feed and house these women—such expenditures might jeopardize the rest of my establishment. It would be better, if you approve, that my students in Anjou and Touraine be paid for by their communities. We will perhaps have fewer of them, but the surgeons entrusted to continue my demonstrations will fulfill your wishes for all the parishes of your generality. M. Rouillé d'Orfeuil did it this way in Champagne. There were twenty-two demonstrators and each one took about twelve students at a time, and little by little all parishes were served. I will await your decision so my publisher in Paris can send copies. This is how the establishment works, and it is worthy of you.

I have the honor to be, with respect, your very humble and very obedient servant,

du Coudray[1]

Perceived to be unruly, a huge convening of women had been forcibly put down, but the midwife has succeeded in getting things back on track, dedramatizing the situation. The intendant of Tours, a strange bird named du Cluzel, is responsible for the extraordinary mess. For months he dragged his feet, failing to respond to a veritable bombardment of correspondence about the midwife's visit. (Evidence suggests that he is somewhat scattered; on the top of one of Frère Côme's letters he scribbled that he no longer remembered if he had done anything about this matter or not.)[2] Finally from Evreux the midwife had said bluntly that she was winding up her "operations" and that his delay in replying was depriving other areas of her services. "So please make up your mind, Monsieur, because I must make an accounting of anything that causes me to remain in inaction."[3] This threat to report him to Versailles for wasting her time, combined with the aggressive letters from Frère Côme and especially the reading of *Lettre d'un citoyen*, had finally shaken du Cluzel into awareness and galvanized him into action. But then, careening from utter indifference to the extreme of generosity, he announced that all women attending the course *would receive twelve livres each month from him!* No other intendant has promised a supplemental stipend, much less one so extravagant.

The response was a wild stampede of 240 women. Pandemonium reigned, for Le Mans was not equipped to deal with such an influx. The mounted police, conservators of the public peace usually occupied with patrolling the outskirts of the city, had to be brought in to restore order. Ironically, this was the first time the midwife herself had not been present to open the course, and Coutanceau was clearly in over his head. So the midwife has come swooping down and trimmed the group to 135 students, with nearly as many waiting in the wings for the next course. The triage took two full days and caused many hard feelings. She sent home the old, the clumsy, the squeamish, the frail, who were obliged to retrace a long voyage, with cries of protest and dismay, especially from the husbands who accompanied them for nothing and missed many days of farm work and earnings as a result.[4]

The conscientious subdelegate here, Prudhomme de la Boussi-nière, is frustrated by the vagueness of his intendant and has writ-ten imploring him to be more precise about his rash offer. How was it to be implemented? "You see, Monseigneur, that we are groping in the dark, for want of knowing your intentions on the lodging and feeding of students."[5] In the end he had to take matters into his own hands and improvise, finding free room and board for the stu-dents in the homes of the bourgeois of the town. The city's drapers guild offered its assembly hall, near the great cathedral, for the les-sons.[6] But even the well-meaning Boussinière has not done his home-work thoroughly enough. Unfamiliar with du Coudray's training program for surgeon-demonstrators, he has made a frightening cal-culation. It will take many years and 47,200 livres, according to his reckoning, for the midwife herself to train one student from each parish in his region.

Du Coudray must be very annoyed that these officials have paid no attention to explanations of how her system works; neverthe-less, the letter she writes today shows great restraint and patience, reassuring the intendant that they need not fear any such expendi-ture. She does insist, however, that she cannot again teach a class of such grotesque proportions, which creates unreasonable amounts of work for her and her nephew. It is too late to remedy the situation here, but she must check this dangerous precedent; at her next two stops she takes care to ensure that the money be used for things that can benefit her directly, like the purchase of her own products.

Her letter is, for the officials, a welcome revelation and a relief. Du Cluzel's first secretary, who hates to throw money away and thinks these country women are "often imbeciles and without apti-tude," mourns the funds already lost on the first group,[7] but imme-diately prepares a printed announcement explaining that the sec-ond course will be handled differently. "If the intendant has decided to retract the 12 livres for students, it is only to be able to assure the success of the teaching. He will replace this good turn with the pur-chase of a work by Madame Du Coudray, of which he will give a copy to each student, in which engraved and colored illustrations can recall even for those who cannot read the maneuvers appro-priate for each circumstance. You will learn soon the precautions he is taking to transmit to future generations the utility of this first establishment."[8]

Meanwhile du Coudray is working even more than her usual magic with the students. Boussinière reports that "she is worshipped among them to a point that it is difficult to describe." New motivating tactics are introduced to keep the enormous group riveted. She offers them little ribbon rosettes to decorate their hair, for example, as incentive for doing difficult maneuvers well. On the day he observes the class, many won these small tokens of encouragement, but the losers "felt so much sorrow that the session became a scene of tears and wailing that could not be calmed. It is by a number of similar methods that she reanimates their activity." Du Coudray, radiant being that she is, has managed to persuade all involved that her *Abrégé* is a prize infinitely more valuable than money.[9]

51. The Niece's Rest Cure

Forges-les-Eaux, Spring 1778

Overwrought, the midwife's niece has traveled to this peaceful resort spa with a chambermaid and a domestic, to take the waters. She has suffered some sort of breakdown and plans to stay until July.[1] Twenty-three years old, Mme Coutanceau is of a frailer constitution than her crusading aunt. True, she has endured the pains of childbirth, but supervised and delivered as she was by the nation's expert midwife this should not have been for her an event fraught with fear or peril. A weakness of some kind, however, had prevented her from providing the milk necessary to nurse her baby. Du Coudray had foreseen this, which suggests a history of fragile health. The niece's own baptism had taken place many days after her birth, indicating that even as a newborn she might have been too sickly to be taken to church immediately. Perhaps the sorrow of having to send her son away to a wet nurse, combined with the wear and tear of extremely demanding teaching since his birth, especially just now in Le Mans, has contributed to her present collapse.

Surely letters, now lost, were exchanged during this separation, concerning the young woman's recuperation, news of the new baby, how the course was going in her absence. Was du Coudray aggravated about the inconvenience, worried, magnanimous, businesslike? Was the niece apologetic, self-indulgent, defensive? All we know is that this rest cure at the mineral springs must be desperately needed, or Mme Coutanceau would not have left at such an inopportune time. She must realize what her departure costs the teaching team, in both money and morale, and has not deserted them lightly. The infirm and the healthy bathe together here at the source through the lengthening evenings, and some come to this special spot as tourists just to admire nature and socialize. But du Coudray's niece must really be unwell to exact such a sacrifice from her aunt.

The trip from Le Mans has been long, through dense woods and across many streams that need to be forded, their swift waters rushing in under the carriage doors. Once here, however, the days are soothing, though quite structured. A century ago the routine at Forges was dominated by religious observances. One rose at six, went to the fountain and drank the invigorating waters until eight, walked in the gardens, attended the mass run by the Capuchin friars. Then one did one's toilette for the main dinner meal, served at noon. Some days at three in the afternoon actors from Rouen would give a performance. After a light supper at six in the evening one went to do litanies with the monks, liturgical prayers with invocations and supplications and alternative responses between clergy and congregation. Then one walked leisurely about until nine and retired to sleep. Not much has changed since then, except that the mass and sacred litanies are less a part of the ritual for most of the visitors, and the place has become more fashionable.[2]

Mme Coutanceau herself has undergone great transformations since the time of her birth to an obscure, illiterate peasant couple. She is now part of a celebrated team, traveling in state from place to place, holding as of four years ago a joint brevet with her aunt from the king. She had assumed for a spell the aristocratic pseudonym Mlle de Varennes and has rather learned to play the part. She even has some of the physical *delicatesses* and emotional susceptibilities of the noble lady. And right now those need to be indulged.

She has left the road show at the worst possible moment. Naturally du Coudray has had to finance her niece's unanticipated voyage, and it is a major hardship for her. The subdelegate of Le Mans who advanced her 1,000 livres explains that the high cost of this side trip has made her position "difficult and straitened"; she is in debt to a number of merchants, for she has no reserves at all. Short of help, du Coudray and her nephew work exceedingly long hours juggling more students than ever before, teaching from eight in the morning until eight in the evening with only one break for the mid-day meal.[3] They are also feverishly busy making machines so that she can reimburse the subdelegate.[4] Le Mans gives her as a token of its appreciation a gift worth over 120 livres, a purse of crimson velour, embroidered with the arms of the city, containing silver pieces.[5]

The very rough beginning in Le Mans and the overwork notwithstanding, du Coudray reports brightly to the intendant: "Our course is going wonderfully, thanks to the intelligence and enthusiasm of our women."[6] More have excelled than have simply passed the examinations, thirty even getting a grade of "very capable."[7] And with the surgeons things are going unusually well: they seem reluctant to disperse even after all-day sessions.[8] Might this be the result of du Coudray's new tact in handling them, her psychological skill in finessing delicate relations? She is particularly mindful of the need for such sensitivity ever since Le Roy's accusation. She wants it clear that men attend her classes of their own volition. "In the letter of invitation to the surgeons," she instructed the intendant, "make sure that the word *lesson* is never included. This will revolt the pride of some, and maybe all of them at once. Say simply that you invite them to come learn with Mme du Coudray the mechanism of the machine she uses for her operations."[9] Learning *with*, rather than learning *from*, as she used to put it, suggests parity and cooperation.

So the younger generation has caved in under pressure, and du Coudray continues to be the sturdiest of them all. Her nephew could not launch the course alone; her niece could not withstand the stress. The resilient old midwife is made of sterner stuff. She won't allow what she has gone through to rule her life. It will take more than this to bring her down.

52. Class/Mass/Vacation

Angers, 1 July 1778

Monsieur,

After having carefully examined with M. de la Marsaulaye the plan for this establishment, we came to an agreement on the changes I have put in the margin, as the surest for perpetuating the good, and the most promptly. M. Rouillé d'Orfeuil, intendant of Champagne, has assigned twelve students to each demonstrator. You could learn from him, Monsieur, what sort of recompense he gave them.

M. de la Marsaulaye is sending you no doubt the list of our women. Because of the high number we were not able to accept all the surgery students who applied and admitted only four, who are about ready to go back home. I promised them that I would ask you, Monsieur, to allow them to draw between them for a prize that, given by you, will honor them infinitely. It costs very little, a matter of 36 livres, and consists of a sharkskin box lined in silver containing six lancets, and at each end of the box is a silver plaque engraved with your arms, and the other those of the King, or of the city. I would like to have them hope that you will not refuse this because everything that is good is worthy of you.

I have the honor to be with respect, Monsieur, your very humble and very obedient servant,

du Coudray[1]

The subdelegate of this town, La Marsaulaye, has drawn up an elaborate plan for refresher courses and written it on the righthand half of the page, leaving the left column for du Coudray's corrections. These she has not hesitated to make, for she believes the plan puts her women in an unfavorable light, and she is bent on defending them. Her businesslike marginal notes—written in the third person so there will be no confusion about the identity of the "I"—insist on the importance of protecting her students from the cabals of surgeons that they may encounter, from their discouraging tactics and downright sabotage. Although du Coudray's own relations with surgeons have been good of late, time has shown that they usually treat her trainees badly, and sometimes send them back to repeat lessons. "It is easy to see that these women will not hold up under so many vexations, and it is to be feared that they will give up entirely. The mind of the peasant cannot be governed with such facility. Du Coudray knows this from her long experience." Surgeons who are genuinely *eager* to learn midwifery, on the other hand, "are as precious to instruct as midwives, because [otherwise] when they finish their apprenticeship they find jobs in towns and cities, and having had only the feeblest notion of this art they often do a great deal of harm, whereas if trained they do the greatest good possible."[2] The central issue, then, is competence, not gender, and she wants the officials of Angers to recognize this. Men who interest themselves especially in her mission should be rewarded. Hence the proposed set of lancets. Not a bad system, to bestow gifts and get the government to pay!

Angers, a city of blue-black roofs and red chimneys on the river Maine, is the scene of many festivals and fairs, such merrymaking, in fact, that nobody wants to leave town, so housing du Coudray's students has been a problem.[3] The subdelegate had wondered at first if lodging them could be imposed, forced on the townspeople like the obligatory billeting of soldiers, and had argued for it. Du Coudray's mission, he pointed out, is as much "in the King's interest" as the quartering of troops, so why not? She herself has requested accommodations for eight, anticipating her niece's return and perhaps a visit from the baby and his nurse.[4]

The mayor has meanwhile donated the Hôtel de Ville for the lessons. High on a hill at the top of a magnificent double staircase that ascends from the main town square across a garden, this city hall is a wondrous sight. But the midwife, whose accommodations are fairly distant from the Hôtel de Ville, cannot teach so far from her lodgings. She is putting on weight and getting no younger; she could never manage the climb. Even being shuttled back and forth in a carried chair, bumping about over so many narrow, winding, rutted streets and up and down that great hill is simply unacceptable.[5] The subdelegate reports to his superior that he considers this objection well founded, "once I saw her age and her size," so a classroom closer by is quickly arranged.

She has rarely taught men and women in the same class because it can cause problems. In Châteauroux recently a surgeon disciple of hers reported extreme bawdiness when he tried to instruct a mixed group: "the subject treated lending itself to off-color jokes, words became too free, even indecent."[6] Such scenes of hilarity seem unthinkable under the midwife's watchful eye; it is difficult to picture the oft-reported decorum slipping at all. Evidently, however, she does teach a mixed class here, including five surgeons from Angers's own Hôtel Dieu,[7] and some rowdiness does result, causing 100 livres' worth of damage to du Coudray's classroom by the end.[8] Keeping control of this group seems to have exhausted her.

She badly needs a break. Sales of the book and machine here

have totaled more than 3,500 livres; some time off is warranted. She has an acquaintance (*une connaissance*) outside Tours to whom she has promised a visit, the only known instance of time strictly for socializing taken out of her rigorous schedule. About this friend-ship we as usual can learn nothing more, except that the midwife is tempted to stay there longer and revises her original plan of starting her Tours class on 1 October. The middle of November now sounds much better, she says, after the vintaging and vacations.[9] To observ-ers she is looking old and heavy, ready for a rest. A concerned curé sends the midwife on her way with a thanksgiving mass and wishes for peace and health, blessing this "sincere friend of humanity" at the baptismal font.[10]

4

Delivering the Goods

Alfort 1780–1781
ÎLE-DE -FRANCE

53. Protecting du Coudray's Method

Marly, 7 May 1779

The King being informed that in the courses of demonstration on the art of delivery held in the generality of Tours by Mme du Coudray, the number of women trained there does not approach the number needed in the parishes of said countryside, His Majesty judging it a propos not only to have all provinces benefit from this same advantage, but also to perpetuate the method and teaching of Mme du Coudray, as the best for the complete instruction of peasant women who want to learn, . . . the King . . . ordains that . . . the intendant . . . will establish in those cities and places he would like to choose, demonstrators trained in said methods and informations. . . . These commissions can only be given to people having the right and credentials to practice medicine and surgery. [The King] forbids the Colleges of surgery and all others to prevent or otherwise trouble said demonstrators in the exercise of their functions . . . enjoins all intendants . . . to put their hand to the execution of this *Arrêt*.[1]

Thus has a new king, Louis XVI, recognized that the royal protection originally afforded the midwife must now be extended to those male demonstrators whom she trains. The female ingredient in the pedagogy is being squeezed out entirely, but the du Coudray *method* is being sanctified. Louis XV had issued three royal edicts regarding du Coudray, and they all concerned the woman herself; this is the first proclaimed by his successor, and it is much more impersonal. But it is necessary. Anyone can see that du Coudray will not be able to continue her rounds indefinitely. In most regions the courses that were to have continued in perpetuity have dwindled and died. Just now in Tours the surgeon Chevreul was appointed "inspector general" in charge of ensuring that refresher courses continue, but Necker is very concerned. To make good on the investment in the midwife's now twenty-year-old mission, the monarch must authorize what was before only an informal arrangement. Besides, His Majesty has something new and special up his sleeve for the midwife, a different kind of job for her to do.

54. WOMEN AND COWS

Alfort near Charenton, October 1780

Animal doctors! The midwife is to teach animal doctors! The Royal Veterinary School here, a complex of grand buildings and grounds at the end of the Charenton bridge on the left bank of the Marne, is a bustling place, more so now than usual, because the king has decided that those trained to care for the beasts of the field should also be taught human delivery.[1] Despite the efforts to perpetuate du Coudray's methods, despite the king's recent *arrêt* protecting her demonstrators, attendance has often been poor at follow-up classes in the provinces taught by these men. They lack the great lady's knack, her charisma. For du Coudray audiences are still abundant. Excited about the spectacle surrounding the famous midwife, caught up in the momentum of her historic visits, happily suspended from their routine, country women everywhere have flocked to become her disciples. But small rewards, if any at all, await these trainees, who leave the city starry-eyed, the proud possessors of a treasured book most of them cannot read and a certificate to practice whose promised alchemy frequently fails to transmute jealousy into welcome. Of course, in many regions the whole system works very successfully, and du Coudray's legacy is perpetuated. But this cannot be counted on. So something new is now being tried.

Underlying the government's pronatalist policy there has gradually developed a view of women as national property, breeders for the state, to be managed, administered, husbanded with the same sort of care that a farmer gives his land and chattels (read: cattle). Officials implementing the royal will often claim they need to upgrade the view of wives so that they *will* be taken as seriously as livestock. To the country poor their pigs, cows, sheep, hens—if they are fortunate enough to have them—are precious sources of protein, milk, butter, cheese, fleece, and of the manure that ensures the soil's fertility. Also the young can be sold at market. It is the elite perception that peasants do not value the mothers of their children, or their children, nearly as much as they prize their owned things. Rural animals appear to be getting better medical attention than rural people.

The subdelegate of Ribemont, near Soisson, implied this link between wives and beasts when he reported to his superior in 1760 that in his region, when it came to birthing of any kind, "shepherds are the most experienced, and often in difficult [human] deliveries it is to them that one has recourse."[2] From Champagne has come the lament that parishioners "care more about their cows when they want to drop their calves, than about their wives when they have to give birth."[3] Augier du Fot's manual on midwifery had stated baldly the woeful ignorance of country fathers, their intense loyalty to their herds at the expense of their families.[4] And from Tours just now, where Chevreul's master plan for training midwives is supposedly in full swing, this inspector has complained of the peasants to the intendant: "You know better than I their character. If it were to train a veterinarian, the hope of having a man who could forestall or prevent mortality in their cattle would bring them to donate all that was asked without repugnance. But to save their wives, it's another matter entirely. One lost, another found."[5]

So it has been decided by monarch and ministers that veterinarians should be taught human obstetrics, on the facile assumption that this can be accomplished merely by adding another twist or two to the mechanical birthing skills they have already acquired. The king in his goodness, it is now proclaimed, wants to make this innovation at the Royal School of Alfort, because veterinarians trained there return to serve in remote areas where midwives are unavailable. The king has studied the situation and is convinced that animal doctors "really are in a fit state to render the service hoped of them."[6] So a course has been set up to be taught by a royal appointee, with none other than du Coudray herself occupying the coveted chair. She is sixty-five years old, and the mechanics of birthing is, after all, her specialty.

The midwife appears to acquiesce to this blurring of human and animal without any detectable sense of outrage or even reluctance. She functions as usual, her faith in the mission undented, her teaching and letter-writing activity unabated and, if anything, more intense than ever, for she is now trying to organize separate routes for herself and for the Coutanceaus. Have women become for her, as for the administration, just beasts to be manipulated? It is time to examine again her view of "mes femmes." How does she reconcile her humanitarian sentiments with her complicity here, her willingness to make childbirth part of the province of veterinarians, to liken human mothers to so many cows?

Du Coudray has always had deep feeling for her female "flock," has worked unstintingly with and for them. These women are worthy of her attention, her instruction, her help, her inspiration, her very life. She never talks of them as idle, morally depraved, unruly, or threatening. She even respects many of the customs and collective rituals of their traditional, oral subculture, what most male medical authors disdainfully call their "superstitions," allowing them to recite chants or cling to relics, for example, if it comforts them during birthing. Women are her concern, always. Peasant husbands are conspicuous in du Coudray's book and letters only for their absence. She has absolutely no interest in them. It is the women she cares about, the laboring women in the fields, around whose vital farmwork at harvest time she carefully tries to schedule her courses. Communicating with them is her mission, and she does it in many ways. The book is for those who can read, the illustrations for those who cannot. The months of lessons, recitations, and demonstrations on the machine are for all of them. She agrees that the inept, slovenly, unreliable women being blamed for France's depopulation must be squeezed out and does not hesitate to condemn such untrained matrons, but she will redeem her profession, distinguishing her fresh new trainees from the old ones with their variety of failings. Her students over two decades have been young, unspoiled by prejudice, guided through the newest techniques, shaped and molded entirely by her. Proud of this cadre of skilled women, she involves herself getting them supplies and gifts and bonuses, pleading at their trials, lending them small sums and sometimes even large ones. Deep attachments and feelings of intense loyalty have frequently developed between them.

But there is another side to this. The very scope of her ambition necessarily and increasingly privileges efficiency over personal attention. Whatever du Coudray's links with her students and however sympathetic her book, the obstetrical mannequin itself encourages a rote approach to women in labor and to delivery. This objectified pelvis contributes to a reductive view of the female in childbirth as a puzzle of parts to be dexterously realigned. The body as an object inevitably becomes the focus; the person as individual can and does get lost. Years of traveling and teaching the mechanism of midwifery on the "machine" has made it almost numbingly automatic. Not such a big step, really, from this view of mothers to sheep and cows, to goods, to things. Du Coudray brings the *bien* but also the *biens* wherever she goes. On some level, all along, her job has been to do good *and* to deliver the goods.

The illustrations for the *Abrégé*, which du Coudray commissioned specially over ten years ago, reinforce the idea of babies as national product; there is nothing innocent or accidental about her intention. Her pictures deviate markedly from most of the obstetrical representations in midwifery texts by men, which are sexual and feature the mother quite centrally.[7] Du Coudray's have a different ideological message, a different metaphoric vibration. They are pragmatic, images in the service of a patriarchal establishment, of an omnivorous state that needs more subjects. With their outstretched waiting hands, inspired perhaps by the disembodied hands always busy in the workshop plates of the *Encyclopédie*, these pictures very much emphasize the midwife's claim on the new child, rather than any attachment to or interest in the mother, who is merely a site (fig. 11). By the same token, the *Abrégé* images are far more decorous than those in male texts, which either show the mother in sensual poses, gratuitously featuring breasts and external genitalia, or display her cut up and flayed like so much dead meat (fig. 12). Du Coudray rejects such impolite, relentless pictures and substitutes something radically different, more along the lines of antiseptic abstractions.[8] Her illustrations barely allude to the mother at all, rendering her invisible in a kind of denial of the womb, a latter-day X-ray. The fetus is primary, center stage, almost autonomous; only the pelvic bone reminds us of the mother, who is otherwise absent. One can forget that these babies depend for their lives not on empty space but on a nurturing childbearer. Looking inside the mother, making her body invisible in order to view the baby, supports the system of medical and political patriarchy. And the fetus in these very technical images— male, of course—is developed, a person already, all pink and alive and willing to be born and to serve. Du Coudray's pictures, in short, although they do help her students remember maneuvers, are also politically laden. In balance, they show the midwife to be more of a patriot than a feminist.[9]

To some it seems that this turn of events at Alfort ominously reinforces that tendency. Mme Necker, for one, is appalled at du Coudray's willingness to accept the appointment to teach animal doctors, and even before that to train so many male demonstrators. The

Cette Planche répresente encore une fauße manœuvre en préférant de tirer l'enfant la face en devant plutôt que de lui avoir tourné par derri-
ère, ce qui donne lieu au menton de l'enfant de s'accrocher sur les os Pu-
bis et en continuant de le tirer dans cette position la tête se renversant
en arrière la machoire peut se luxer, d'ailleurs l'occiput par ce renverse-
ment appuyant sur l'os Sacrum, il est impoßible de faire paßer la tête
dans le détroit du petit baßin, il faut donc en repoußant l'enfant un
peu en haut lui retourner la face en arrière.

Peint par P. Chapparre.   Gravé en Couleur par J. Robert.

Figures 11 and 12. Compare Mme du Coudray's textbook picture (*above*),
almost an X-ray, which zeros in entirely on the baby, to the picture by
Gauthier d'Agoty (*opposite*), which concentrates in both morbid and
sensual ways on the mother.

midwife has had trouble worming her way into the controller general's pompous Swiss heart and rightly figured out that his ambitious wife, the former Suzanne Cuchod, rumored to be the real architect of his political career, might be a better contact. She had written asking for her support, and last March, when the midwife was teaching not far from the capital in Meaux,[10] Mme Necker had sent a friendly response praising du Coudray's dedication, calling her "the woman to whom humanity has such great obligations and to whom I delight in having an occasion to show my deep esteem." Meeting her in person, thanking her "by mouth" for all she has done, will be possible soon, she hopes, but now "the distribution of my time and the weakness of my health prevent me from granting private rendezvous. As soon as my chest is better, I will hasten to find a way to speak to you, or more accurately to hear you, as I have been for a long time an admirer of your talents and of the respectable use you make of them."[11] More letters have been exchanged, and perhaps in the meantime the two women have even met. The midwife no longer hesitates to ask for help from her new ally. In response to a request from du Coudray for payment of some funds still owed her from her last stop, Mme Necker has explained that she passed the matter on to her husband. "He wrote in my presence to the intendant, and if the answer is not satisfying, I will ask that the Royal Treasury pay you what is so legitimately your due. You must not doubt that M. Necker will do with pleasure what is agreeable to you and that he shares with me the esteem inspired by your virtues and by your zeal, as active as it is enlightened."[12]

The friendly tone has changed, however, since du Coudray settled into her new post at the veterinary school a few months ago and, temporarily at least, ceased teaching women altogether. She has recently asked her new patroness for help in finding Coutanceau a job. But now Mme Necker recoils. There is a new distance, a stiffness in the letter; the midwife must be admonished. Du Coudray, having committed the sin of training only men for the post of demonstrator, and now of seeking employment for her nephew rather than for her niece, receives this answer:

> Whatever pleasure I take in obliging you, Madame, I cannot do what you ask. . . . But you are so generally esteemed that you should not need other support than yourself. Or else you can write to M. Necker asking for the letter that I dare not give

you myself. You know, moreover, that I have some repugnance to see the practice of your art passing into the hands of men, which has always seemed to me to be of a veritable indecency. The lively interest that I take in you, founded first on your humanity and on your talents, is based also on your sex, which should be the only one destined for the branch of surgery you profess with such success.[13]

How does du Coudray react to this scolding? She probably makes note of it, but it is to have a much more profound effect upon young Mme Coutanceau. Mme Necker is at this moment raising and educating her daughter, the future Mme de Staël. She believes deeply in female dignity and intelligence, feels the need for no male tutor, and takes great pride in her womanhood. Du Coudray's niece picks up on this attitude eagerly. Both Mme Coutanceau and Mme Necker, unlike the midwife, have actually had babies. They believe that birthing should be and should remain strictly women's work. Du Coudray, they would concur, has been entirely too ready to compromise on this matter.

Perhaps they do not realize the pressures she is under, or that, had she not from the start yielded on points such as this, her mission would never have materialized in the first place. Du Coudray has been able to establish her vast control over childbirthing only by working within the patriarchal system, only by obliging the paternalistic medical hierarchy already in place. And even despite her total cooperation on this score, certain ministers and men like Le Roy feel she is excessively grasping. The recent campaign against her only confirms that she is not sufficiently compliant for their tastes.

Now yet another surgeon calls her an ignoramus and an impostor. Jean Le Bas, who is also a royal censor, has taught delivery in a Paris clinic near the Observatory.[14] He uses his new *Précis de doctrine sur l'art d'accoucher* to decry the proliferation of worthless books on his subject. "Some are disguised behind terrible illustrations grotesquely colored, which contribute only to bringing out more ridiculously the errors they betray. I would advise the greatest suspicion of this rash of writings." He has it from a curé

that he was forced to extol . . . a mannequin presented to him, but that after reading the certificate delivered by the author of this machine attesting to its perfection, . . . he soon recognized it as no more than a fable, a phantom, a simulacrum, a shadow of reality, capable of giving false ideas to beginners who, once their heads are thus filled, will not be able to avoid practicing bad work on live subjects. . . . But a mannequin, they reply, is an ingenious expedient. I would answer, and just as adroit for training *accoucheurs* and midwives as is the theater or the opera for training soldiers and sailors, that a midwife, leaving the mannequin on which she has practiced, will remedy a hemorrhage, convulsions, an infinity of abnormal positions, just as skillfully as a *petit maître*, to whom the sea and weapons are unknown, would know how to fight a tempest, avoid a shipwreck, do military maneuvers, or command a battle at the end of a play.

Du Coudray's pictures and machines, in other words, "will end by killing the greater part of humanity."[15] They will also encourage midwives' temerity and presumption. Women, to put it bluntly, must be put in their place and kept there.[16]

Du Coudray has two choices. She can back off, intimidated by these attacks, or she can fight to stay relevant. Teaching at Alfort is her way of remaining at the forefront of her field right now. To her it seems a sensible decision, the best way to protect her livelihood. Significantly, Le Bas is about to succeed her teaching midwifery at Alfort. Le Bas has a nightmare of his own to put behind him. Recently released from eighteen months in prison for carelessly approving, in his capacity as royal censor, the publication of Delisle de Sales's controversial *Philosophie de la nature,* he badly needs to exonerate himself and so has his own reasons for demonstrating his loyalty to his kingdom. Reminding his readers that before his incarceration he had been trusted by lieutenant general of police Sartine to deliver babies throughout the city of Paris, and especially in his own clinic, he refers to the latter as a "maison patriotique."[17] Now that he is free once again, he wants nothing more than to reingratiate himself with "superior magistrates." As it was for du Coudray, so it will now be for him: a display of pure patriotism to teach *accouchement* at the Royal Veterinary School.

5

Turning over the Keys

55. "My Age and My Infirmities"

Bourges, 25 December 1781

Monsieur,

I have put off writing to you so as to render a more exact account. I spent fifteen days waiting for a sufficient number of students, and this interval has gotten me twenty-eight. I cannot receive more now, whatever my desire to second your benevolence toward humanity. I will even be obliged to keep these women eight or ten days longer than the two months I ordinarily do. I am very happy with their intelligence.

I have already received, Monsieur, the visit from the surgeon whom you gave me the honor to tell me about. M. Gerlet seems very happy with the honor you were good enough to give him in charging him to give courses. He is to come take private lessons, which I will give him with great pleasure. I think you will be pleased with him.

I must see, Monsieur, the men of the administration. M. ____, municipal magistrate, does not want to furnish me with wood, my landlord will not give me an advance, and if M. de la Brugièrre, secretary of Monsieur to whom I was referred, also refuses both my wood and my light, in truth, Monsieur, I will have no other choice to make but that of resting and sleeping as much as I can, because I don't want to be the dupe either. I am afraid if I pay I will not be paid back. And good God, what grandiloquent nonsense! Well, if I had nothing to ask I would be very satisfied. I will tell this whole story to M. Daly, with whom I can speak my thoughts out loud. . . .

I have the honor to be, Monsieur, your very humble and very obedient servant

du Coudray[1]

Christmas Day. The sixty-six-year old midwife should be enjoying a feast, but instead she huddles, chilled and humiliated, writing this letter before it gets dark. Bourges has done it again! She is paying a second visit to this town where she suffered such indignities in 1768. What has possessed the midwife to come here once more?

Frère Côme cannot help her this time. He expired in the arms of his devoted friend Süe this past summer, and mobs of mourners forced the doors of the monastery's cloister again and again, throwing themselves weeping onto his coffin.[2] Of course, her official letters make no mention of her grief, but this loss is surely a turning point for her. It probably signals, if only in the privacy of her mind, the beginning of the end of her teaching.

And now she is facing yet another great change in her life, a parting of the ways, the breakup of her faithful ménage. Much of her time in Alfort was spent writing around to find a stable position for the Coutanceaus. This couple, whose son is now six, would like to settle somewhere rather than continue to roam about. The midwife had written an exceptionally diffident letter to Caen, addressing the intendant Esmangart with an uncharacteristic "Monseigneur," trying to interest him in her nephew. She had not felt strong that day; her sadness can be detected in the letter's unusually large hand and the recurring themes of advancing age, sickness, and mortality.

> Lower Normandy is lacking in a sufficient number of midwives. A portion of those I trained are dead, those still living cannot get around everywhere. The generality gets only small benefit from an institution started under M. de Fontette and which it is up to you to perfect and give stability and duration. The government has approved my method of teaching to be the most accessible to the limited intelligence of country women. No one knows this method better than M. Coutanceau, to whom I have married my niece, who by the services she has rendered has won from the King the right to succeed me. . . . The eulogy of M. Coutanceau by me might seem suspect. I assure you though, Monseigneur, that nobody better deserves your confidence. More than ten years ago I put him in charge of the largest part of the instruction. My age and my infirmities have forced me to turn it over to him almost entirely.[3]

But there had been a swift rebuff, and the chances were dashed. By return mail the intendant replied that thanks to the thoroughness of du Coudray's work the first time around, the region's surgeons were adequately trained to do all that was necessary. "The presence of M. Coutanceau in my generality would be of no utility."[4]

So she set her sights instead on Bordeaux, her nephew's native city, pitching for a permanent place for the couple there. Letters indicate that her old friend Duchesne is still employed in the intendant's office there. Though no correspondence exchanged between them exists for this period, he may have been helping, as he did years before, with her desired arrangements. She knows the present intendant there, Dupré de St. Maur, from when he occupied the same post in Berry, and had announced herself with brio.

"The good of humanity, which is so dear to you, will easily recall me to your mind." Now that his intendancy has been augmented by a part of Gascony, "which I did not do [before], I offer to repair the wrongs of a subdelegate general who, when I was in Auch, refused that Bayonne and the other cities receive the succor that they hoped for with my arrival." In addition, she argued, Bordeaux itself needs a good permanent teacher of childbirth. She had offered her nephew's services for both purposes. "It is for the general good of humanity, but it is [also] for me the greatest service one could render to secure the future of a little family that is dear to me, and this kindness will mitigate the infirmities of my old age. It is you who will decide their happiness and mine. You are made to make people happy, and you will not refuse to make us so by your actions. I will await with confidence the honor of your reply." It had come immediately. Put that way, what choice did Dupré de St. Maur really have? He assured her he would welcome Coutanceau, and he encouraged her to do whatever was necessary at Versailles to get the appointment approved.[5]

So far, clearly, the midwife promotes her nephew more vigorously than her niece, who comes along as part of a package deal with her important husband, not as an independent talent in her own right. Fondness has not yet ripened into respect or identification. But perhaps Mme Necker's urgings give du Coudray pause now. When things bog down again in the negotiations with Bordeaux she tries, at least fleetingly, a new tack, suggesting that a post should be worked out for both her nephew *and* niece, because many girls would refuse such intimate instruction from a man. It is not an argument she has ever used before, and she then slips back into referring to them as "M. Coutanceau and his wife." Nonetheless, she does say that as a couple they could satisfy all demands, spell each other if one became ill, and that they both speak the regional dialect (*le langage vulgaire du Bordelais*). Assuming that her favor would be granted, she had thanked the ministers in advance for this "most precious recompense for all [my] services."[6]

Necker had then been dismissed for bringing confidential and embarrassing details of the Royal Treasury dramatically before the public, and her request sank from sight on some desk and went unanswered. She had had to keep after everybody all through the next winter, spring, and summer for "slowing down the good of humanity." If the two Coutanceaus would be leaving, she needed to know definitely so she could find other permanent assistants. "Let us finish this affair," she pleaded at one point. "I am concerned for the fate of my children." Were they or were they not assigned to Bordeaux? "Let me know their destiny and my own."[7]

Vergennes, the foreign secretary, part of whose job it was to supervise border and coastal provinces, had been vaguely interested in the Coutanceaus for a while, though he took no action. Only with the advent of a new controller general, Joly de Fleury, were final arrangements made. Frère Côme, in the months before his death, had disposed Joly de Fleury, on whom he had successfully operated for stone seven years ago, in du Coudray's favor. The new minister has therefore approved a Bordeaux position and a 600-livre salary for the couple, to start in 1782. A new brevet is even negotiated giving M. Coutanceau an official title. It has taken a full year and at least forty letters back and forth to solidify the post and its meager salary for the midwife's adoptive heirs.[8] But it is, finally, one big weight off her mind.

At the same time, du Coudray has been trying to set up a travel plan for herself. She wants to cover new ground, especially Toulouse, Montpellier, and other southern cities that she has not "done," but the powerful archbishop of Narbonne seems dead set against her instruction. Mme Necker had earlier written to officials in Vivarais, the area north of Avignon, and to the archbishop of Aix on du Coudray's behalf,[9] but it had come to nothing. Restless during a big gap between veterinary courses, the indefatigable midwife complained: "I spend time costing money and producing no fruit, founding my hopes on my *Grand Voyage*." The former intendant St. Priest had led her to believe a full decade ago that she would be invited to the Midi; she therefore sees this as unfinished business. "If the cabalists of Languedoc have triumphed, be good enough to work on the *états* of Provence, where there will perhaps be fewer difficulties." Refusing to take no for an answer, she has decided to travel elsewhere in order to keep busy while awaiting the big invitation. "That way I will always be making use of my time."[10]

For a while it had seemed as if du Coudray might return to the area near La Rochelle, where a demonstrator in St. Jean d'Angély had reawakened the intendant's interest in the midwife.[11] But she feels that that area never really mustered the appropriate veneration. "In 1766 I did your generality. I had the unpleasant experience of not producing there as much good as the government has always wished me to do. I did not find any zealous surgeons to continue the good I brought, which was very momentary, in order to make it durable. The machines I leave with surgeons must be used each year to renew the lessons for the country women, and the lessons must be given at times that these women are not occupied with cultivating the earth." It must depress her to realize that the impact of her glorious mission—through no fault of her own, of course—has not been as lasting as all had hoped.[12]

But the intendant of La Rochelle, still hoping to persuade her to come, visited her in Alfort, reporting back to his surgeons whose delicate vanity he must not ruffle. "I saw all her machines. I talked a lot with her and she is, truly, not an ordinary woman. I do not claim that she is an able surgeon. She does not pretend to be, though clever and full of spirit. She is of the greatest modesty, but her taste for humanity engaged her with science to make herself accessible to country women, and her greatest lesson is to recommend prudence to them, to instruct them to mistrust their own strength, to call capable surgeons early to help them out, to save the subject and turn her over in good shape to the surgeon without waiting." He implores his surgeons back home to read her book, to "put pride aside, and, sure as you should be that you are a far more skilled surgeon than Mme du Coudray is, you ought to have no problem consulting her on objects that long habit and experience with her machine make her more familiar with than you are." Taking particular care to help the surgeons save face and spare them open correspondence with her, the intendant has said they should write "under cover" to him and he will forward letters of inquiry to her.[13] One surgeon, though, has already confirmed the touchiness of this group, sending back a four-page book review of the *Abrégé* that points out "confusions," "errors," and "paradoxes" in the text. He has had to have the last word.[14]

In the end, du Coudray sticks by her decision not to go where male egos must be so ridiculously coddled, and comes here to the Bourges region instead. Though the chief city itself is ungracious and mean, failing to provide her with her usual desiderata, the towns in the area are thrilled to have her back, overjoyed to learn that the great midwife "still exists!"[15] And here she will have the pleasure of being reunited with Mme Jouhannet, her prize pupil of thirteen years ago from nearby Châteauroux, who has matured into a great teacher in her own right, sufficiently esteemed to have delivered the intendant's own child.[16] Jouhannet will come next February to help with a refresher course.[17]

Knowing that the new controller general Joly de Fleury is very much behind her because she brings "to people, and especially to the unfortunate, the greatest service possible," satisfying "religion, humanity, and the state by saving its subjects," the midwife would have Bourges believe she is doing the city an enormous favor by returning, claiming to have refused numerous other engagements to make herself available.[18] Consider the contrasting style of a male *accoucheur* trying to win the same intendant's favor with a fawning, flowery letter full of promises. "I will not neglect a single occasion to merit the honor of your benevolence, Monseigneur. . . . I beseech your greatness to accord me your protection and I will daily make new efforts to render myself deserving."[19] Far be it from the ever proud du Coudray to grovel so. It is for the intendants to deserve *her* by demonstrating their patriotic appreciation. An official copying over her letters here actually censors such self-important passages.[20] Either this particular clerk disapproves of her brash tone or fears his superiors will react badly to it.

Actually, the beginning of the midwife's stint here went rather well.[21] But now the city has abruptly cut off its support. Their excuse is that they overextended themselves buying gifts earlier this fall for the much-celebrated birth of the dauphin on 22 October, and have run out of funds to pay her.[22] The appearance of this royal son, born to Louis XVI and Marie Antoinette after eleven years of barren marriage, is indeed a great event for France. But how ironic that the birth of a baby should oblige the nation's most famous midwife to sit freezing in the dark in Bourges, threatening (as she had thirteen years ago in this same town) that she might need to shut down and hibernate if they refuse to provide the vital necessities.

We can only guess how du Coudray must be feeling. Frère Côme is gone. She has developed around herself a matrix of ties and loyalties, but with the imminent departure of the Coutanceaus she will lose that also. Perhaps Jouhannet is a temporary substitute, but even so it would be easy to feel deserted. It would be easy, especially now, to turn in, to quit. She would earn as much resting as working. On the face of it there is no reason to continue.

Except there is. Du Coudray has a job to finish. As the letters show, she sees her "time" as still immensely valuable. She would not "spend" it fruitlessly, but instead means to "make use of it." She basically still has her health and stamina, and genuinely wants to make that *Grand Voyage*. It is, quite simply, a matter of honor. She cannot let the kingdom down. She cannot disappoint herself.

56. FAMILY SEPARATION

Belley, 30 December 1782

Du Coudray had thought she might go back to Limoges next,[1] but she has come east instead. Bourges finally paid her and kept her busy until May, when she had set out for Auxerre in Burgundy. The trip took ten days for some reason;[2] perhaps the team gave themselves extra time knowing this would be their last spell together for a while. The teaching had lasted through summer and fall, and after her class graduated the midwife made plans to come through again and do another course next year.[3] The parting of the ways has finally taken place, so on her own now the midwife has traveled south to this town in Bresse. Here she has attracted a contingent of students from Chambéry in Savoy, and especially a surgeon named Rey who is much enamored of her methods. They have awarded du Coudray a silver coffee pot in gratitude for her fine teaching.[4] Still in the hope that a visit to Viverais, Languedoc, or Provence will work out, she is making her way farther south, strategically positioning herself to move fast if she gets the call.

It is looking increasingly unlikely, though.[5] Many southern areas are distributing copies of yet another rival obstetrics text, Jean-François

Icart's *Leçons pratiques*.[6] Icart himself, a respected doctor and surgeon, is teaching in the areas of Castres, Toulouse, and Carcassonne, fully supported by the powerful prelates of the dioceses of Haut-Languedoc. He may even be the author of the anonymous *Petition of Protest . . . from the Unborn Babies Against So-called Midwives*, presented to the *états* of Languedoc, in which an embryo, representing a hitherto unheard-from constituency, refuses to leave the womb unless delivered by his students. Signed "Fetus," this little pamphlet states that however much subjects are needed to defend the *patrie*, cultivate the soil, or advance arts and crafts, the very act of being born is simply too brutal, disgusting, and painful as presently practiced. Only courses approved by the "episcopal cities" will set things right.[7] Under this new humorous facade lies the same deep hostility to the midwife's mission that she encountered in this very region during her year of wandering more than a decade ago. Du Coudray's hoped-for *Grand Voyage* is looking less and less promising under the circumstances, so she is making plans to head slightly north again to Bourg-en-Bresse in the *pays de cocagne*—the land of milk and honey.[8] She will still be close enough if the Midi has a change of heart and invites her.

The Coutanceaus, meanwhile, are far away and have been setting up their own independent operations in Bordeaux. With such a small number of students in Bourges, du Coudray's nephew had felt free to leave the two women there, and journeyed south in January of this year. He registered his wife's royal brevet at the city hall of Bordeaux, collected the 600 livres salary as an advance so he could put things in place for their teaching, and even began to lobby for the couple's dream project, a permanent maternity hospice. This idea of a clinic is the way of the future and something to which the two of them have obviously given a lot of thought, now that they will be settling down. While both appreciate the value of teaching on the mannequin, and especially the advantage of that method when they are on the road so much, they believe there is no substitute for practicing on live women. "Experience," says Coutanceau, "shows that the cries of a woman in labor excite so powerfully the sensitivity of young midwives that they are deprived of the ability to apply their knowledge and to function at critical moments. . . . It is certain that students practicing under the eyes of their teacher and putting into use their lessons on live subjects will necessarily lose their timidity or that excessive sensitivity which is always harmful in the operation of the art."[9] By June Coutanceau had successfully trained one group of students on the machines, and had invited the intendant Dupré de St. Maur to be present at the final examination. The point was, he would be able to do still better with live mothers in a clinic.[10]

Du Coudray's niece stayed with her aunt through the teaching in Auxerre, but by October she had joined her husband in Bordeaux. For the first time she could operate beyond the great midwife's shadow. Upon arrival she had seen instantly that the 600 livres were inadequate for setting up shop and declared to the intendant that a second course should be given in the fall to bring in an additional 600, without which they would find themselves in extremely "disagreeable circumstances." She phrased things as though she and her husband had been "summoned"; answering a call to duty, they had already won the public's confidence.[11] Just today, thanks to her refusal to be put off, Mme Coutanceau has finally been granted the doubled salary of 1,200 livres for their two courses.[12]

This is a surprisingly strong start. Now this woman of twenty-seven can begin to come into her own. As it turns out, she is bold and altogether ready to complain in an explicit, frontal way when things are bad. Du Coudray prefers, as much as possible, to end letters on an optimistic note, to leave a positive last word. Frequently she hints that she is sparing the recipient unpleasant details. Her niece, frank and assertive, has no such scruples. She is developing her own style. Today she has won a round.

And what of du Coudray? The departure of the "little family" she forged for herself closes a chapter of her life, perhaps the fullest and most challenging of all. This last decade she has done her widest and hardest traveling, her heaviest teaching, her most vigorous fighting to protect her career, and she has accomplished all this even as her emotional involvements multiplied and grew complicated. From 1760 to 1770 she built her reputation, keeping resolutely free of entanglements, holding herself apart. Since 1770 she has mustered enormous energy to maintain and enhance that reputation, all the while becoming more intensely intertwined with her new relationships, letting in friends, taking on, indeed seeking out and creating, family. A complete development of her being on all fronts at once has been unfolding. These ties, demanding but sustaining, have enriched her, strengthened her, filled her out in ways she pretended not to need or want at first. Self and profession have flourished together.

Now that the younger generation is gone, how will she divide her loyalties between them and herself?

57. Cunning and Calonne

Paris, 12 July 1785

Du Coudray has returned to the capital yet again, staying at the Hôtel de Berri on a street by the same name in the Marais. Since a brief follow-up course in Auxerre in 1783 she has done no public teaching, resigning herself finally to the fact that her *Grand Voyage* is not going to happen. Less than one year after the Coutanceaus left the team, her peregrinations had come to an end.

Since then she has spent some of her time in Bordeaux, where things have been extremely stormy for the younger generation. After a number of successful courses in Bordeaux itself the couple began the itinerant part of their mission. Mme Coutanceau traveled to Dax, a city of hot springs, thermal mists, and healing mud formerly under the intendance of Pau. She spent nearly five months there but ran into serious problems. One Durozier, a surgeon, conspired to undermine her efforts, even influencing the king's first surgeon in Versailles, Andouillé, to turn against the couple. Morale was low and Mme Coutanceau had only twenty students, yet despite all this the magistrates of Dax reported that she conducted herself proudly and most definitely "merited the public's esteem."[1]

She knew there was a showdown coming. Once back in Bordeaux Mme Coutanceau bluntly told all to the intendant. "[Durozier's] jealousy and his interest manifested themselves publicly the day of the examination," and ever since "he refuses to give licenses to practice to the midwives I have taught, under the pretext that they are not filled up with the formalities prescribed by the statutes of surgery." Making no bones about her distaste for useless theory and bureaucracy, she demanded that the matter be straightened out.[2] In particular, official diplomas were needed from Versailles, where Andouillé was holding things up. So Mme du Coudray had been dispatched to Paris to use her connections to secure them. She had worked tirelessly through the spring of last year to get those certificates for her niece's students printed and validated.[3]

Mme Coutanceau has also done something to help herself, figuring out, as had her aunt nearly thirty years ago, that a printed book would enhance her status in the eyes of male practitioners. After Dax she wrote up a short manuscript of her lessons, asking that her textbook be published with the approval of the Academy of Bordeaux to further bolster her position. She also insisted that it be distributed, at the intendant's expense, to her past, present, and future students.[4]

Mme Coutanceau's *Eléments de l'art d'accoucher* (1784) opens with high praise for du Coudray, being based on the "principles of an aunt whose celebrity I do not need to boast about, but whose goodness toward me I cannot proclaim enough. Raised by her, depository of all her knowledge both theoretical and practical which won for her the government's confidence, I owe that same favor entirely to this respectable aunt; I owe to her all that I am. Can I be blamed for paying her here this just tribute of my gratitude?"[5] The niece explains that du Coudray's machines, or "phantoms," are still in use throughout the kingdom, especially in Picardy, Dauphiné, Touraine, Anjou, Champagne, Flanders, Normandy, Brittany, and Lorraine, so her pedagogical impact has been both personal and national.

Once having paid these respects, however, Mme Coutanceau presents her own issue. She makes a strong case for keeping the profession of midwifery exclusively female, refusing to let it fall irretrievably into male hands as Mme Necker had feared it might. "In training students with this in mind, the art of delivery will one day be practiced only by truly educated women." If the ranks of competent midwives increase in number all the time, "men will no longer be obliged to get involved with a function that was never their province in antiquity, and women, unfortunate enough for the pain they suffer in labor, will no longer need to blush at being surrendered to hands that offend the natural modesty of our sex." Society must learn to value and praise this profession, to validate young women who choose to help in "the most painful action of life."[6] They fulfill "divine law" by soothing suffering mothers who cannot curse, who can only use the "language of lamentation." We get a hint here that Mme Coutanceau has tapped into a level of repressed female anger that her aunt did not acknowledge and that might explain her more proprietary, feminist view of her profession.[7] Or perhaps she simply reasons that this is another pragmatic coping strategy. Just as her aunt made the adjustment to teach veterinarians to secure her livelihood, the younger woman must adapt in her own way to safeguard her position. It is a different response to the medical "experts'" attack. By stressing female modesty, Mme Coutanceau has found an argument against which doctors and surgeons cannot prevail. Birthing is women's work, and that is that.

Is du Coudray proud of her niece for joining the ranks of published authors? Her behavior suggests some mixed feelings. While in Paris she has just now brought out a sixth edition of the *Abrégé*, a thing of rare beauty, a gem of its kind. Mme Coutanceau's *Eléments* is a much simpler, more modest and economical little volume with no illustrations, criticized in fact on aesthetic grounds by one reviewer for its small format and narrow margins, which make it less "agreeable" than it might otherwise have been.[8] Du Coudray's sudden publication of a new edition at this moment is puzzling. She seems to have produced it in haste, not even bothering to secure the new privilege she needed. (The one granted in 1777 had expired.) Is this an aging woman's refusal to surrender just yet? Is her action meant to upstage her niece? Or does du Coudray intend, more nobly, to try to make from its sale some additional money for the Coutanceau *ménage*? If so, does even this gesture betray a touch of vanity, of patronizing superiority?

For the last year du Coudray has been busy involving Boutin on the side of her niece and nephew, the self-same Boutin who had nixed the midwife's visit to Bordeaux twenty years ago and had hurt her so deeply. He is now once again a sort of interim intendant, and he feels an unusual sense of obligation to the whole du Coudray company, perhaps a desire to right the wrongs of the past. But Andouillé has turned the minister Vergennes against midwives in general. He now speaks of them as pernicious, for they know too little and then presume to teach others, making the danger contagious.[9] Boutin is trying to help the couple open their hospice, but he worries that his efforts may be futile, and he becomes more pessimistic with every passing day.

Mme Coutanceau has had her moments of panic. Printed memoirs against her are circulating in Bordeaux, as they had against her aunt in Paris a decade ago, and though she fights back valiantly, she fears her reputation is irreparably damaged: "I will certainly lose public confidence."[10] Boutin had needed to tell the couple candidly that the royal ministers now have a mind to put all instruction of midwives in Bordeaux into the hands of surgeons at the city hospital. "Your [future] projects will be totally overthrown and you may perhaps even lose the [present] position you enjoy in Bordeaux." He strongly recommended that Mme Coutanceau come as soon as possible to Paris in person, "to put into effect your protestations and those of Mme du Coudray."[11]

She made this trip in winter, and the voyage exhausted her.[12] For all the trouble, her personal appearance accomplished little; she returned to Bordeaux dispirited and sick with a fever that now, months later, has still not subsided.[13] Ever since this failed trip Boutin has been struggling to keep the Coutanceau cause alive, pressing for their ten- to twelve-bed hospice in the Collège de la Magdeleine and driving home to Vergennes that it is in the ways of country women to always prefer midwives over the village surgeon.

None of this has helped, however, until du Coudray herself undertakes the long trek to Paris to try her own hand. Throughout the spring she has met repeatedly with Boutin, coaching him on what to say to the ministers, urging him to make sure that justice is served.[14] Unfortunately, the new controller general is none other than Calonne, who had badly scrambled du Coudray's plans while intendant of Flanders. Many see this beguiling courtier as brilliant and charming, but her instincts tell her otherwise. Right now he is trying to salvage the royal treasury, so badly depleted by French support of the American War for Independence. He would far prefer to give money to his supporters at court and to men of letters who flatter the crown than to the unglamorous cause of midwives. Du Coudray's retirement pension, which in 1774 had been hiked from 3,000 to 8,000 livres, strikes Calonne as unduly generous. He is angling to reclaim some of it, and is definitely not going to shell out more for the Coutanceaus. Thinking fast, du Coudray contrives to have part of her pension officially rerouted to her niece and nephew. It is a cunning maneuver, because she intercepts the cut that would otherwise have been made in her own payments, and diverts the money to exactly where she wants it.

Today, in Paris, du Coudray receives Calonne's letter from Versailles:

> I have, Madame, reported to the king your request that one-quarter of your salary of 8,000 livres accorded to you for midwifery courses you give in the provinces pass and be promised to Mme Coutanceau your niece, as a pension revertible to M. Coutanceau her husband who serves as your assistant, and that one Bouchard, your student, receive a pension of 500 livres taken also from your personal salary, which will henceforth be reduced to 5,500 livres. It is my pleasure to announce to you that His Majesty has willingly accorded you this grace, but on the express condition that the Coutanceaus commit themselves to continuing your courses on delivery in the provinces.[15]

Look what the shrewd midwife has accomplished! Calonne is even pleased, explaining smugly to an official that the 2,000 livres now promised the couple, up considerably from their earlier 1,200, should placate Mme Coutanceau who complains unceasingly that "the excessive cost of life in Bordeaux will not permit her to survive there on such a paltry sum." This new arrangement should at last silence the woman. And it is no skin off his back. As he sees things, only du Coudray has lost out.[16] But the midwife sees it as *her* victory. The important thing is that a royal act now guarantees a salary for her family. The immediate menace to the Coutanceau establishment is over. Fixing her sights on the long-range goal of securing power and rank for her heirs in the future, she has put things very much in order.

And she may even have gotten through to Calonne on a deeper level. He has initiated a study of medical practice in the countryside, and only eight months from now, on 22 March 1786, he will send an elaborate questionnaire throughout the kingdom in cooperation with the Royal Society of Medicine. Originally this form gathered information only about doctors, surgeons, and epidemics, but, quite possibly sensitized by his encounters with du Coudray, Calonne approves an addition to the survey devoted to midwives—their location, name, age, training, and skill in exercising their profession. Many of the replies have since been lost, but of the nearly six thousand midwives whose answers survive, fully two-thirds of them had trained with du Coudray or one of her surgeon-demonstrators.[17] The figure is staggering. And she is the only teacher whose person and pedagogy are referred to *by name* on the otherwise impersonal printed form.

Even without benefit of such tabulations, du Coudray must know that she has pioneered popular obstetrics on a grand scale, engaged the nation in this task, inspired countless imitators. She can now graciously turn over the keys to the Coutanceaus. She has already achieved a kind of immortality.

58. Rumblings and Discontent

Sarlat, March 1787

Mme Coutanceau, arriving at this ochre-toned town in "Black Périgord," is terribly distressed that city officials have set up her lessons in the Hôtel de Ville. It is out of the question, absolutely indecent. Her earthier aunt has many times taught without any hesitation in such public places, but it offends the younger woman's sensibilities. She must in the past have cringed and suffered in silence at each of du Coudray's sessions in such surroundings. Now that Mme Coutanceau is in charge she insists on a classroom entirely "closed to men," not an open public building. Her instruction should be heard, her "phantoms" seen, only by her female students. The distractions and interruptions of the city hall would be "very prejudicial" to her pupils; her machines might not be treated with the proper respect. These models of intimate parts are only for those initiated in the art—"for their eyes only." "Any citizen can walk into the Hôtel de Ville. The pieces that are essential to my teaching could be stolen or ruined." She has just persuaded the men in charge of her visit to find her a better, more private location.[1] There is nothing more to be said.

Mme Coutanceau, ever since acquiring the 2,000-livre brevet on her aunt's pension about two years ago, has been traveling alone and teaching throughout Guyenne and Gascogne, radiating out from Bordeaux to Libourne, north to Lesparre-Médoc, southwest as far as Bayonne (where she had needed a Basque interpreter), southeast to Nérac, and now due east to Sarlat. Her husband stays behind in Bordeaux giving courses there, and their son, age twelve, is probably occupied these days with a preceptor or tutor, getting occasional coaching from his elderly great-aunt when she visits. He is already studying medicine. Mme Coutanceau finds the traveling arduous, emotionally draining, and complained to the authorities at one point that she was on the road for nine out of the previous fifteen months. Her contract obligates her to make such trips, but she feels it is excessive. As a wife and mother she is psychologically far less free to roam than had been her aunt. She is rooted, anchored, and feels always that she is "away." Du Coudray, unattached to spouse, children, or home, had seemed to relish the nomadic life; each place had equal claim on her attention. Even now, at her advanced age, she has not really settled anywhere, staying sometimes with the Coutanceaus, sometimes in Paris. She still talks of the elusive "big trip" to Toulouse or Montpellier, claiming that she would go there in a flash if summoned.

Toulouse is something of a mystery in this story. Completely closed to du Coudray, it had turned her away during 1771, her year of wandering, and has rejected her repeatedly since. Yet for some reason Mme Coutanceau feels the need to cultivate a connection with that city. Her area of itinerant instruction, according to the royal agreement, included all of Gascogne and Guyenne, so Toulouse and Castres were just across the border, at the very edge of her jurisdiction. She quoted the powerful archbishop of Toulouse, Loménie de Brienne, at length in her *Eléments de l'art d'accoucher*, perhaps recognizing his political aspirations, for he is soon to become controller general. She consulted with the marquis of Castres about anatomical models when he was planning to send one with a demonstrator to Martinique.[2] At some point she even bought property in Toulouse, and will still be listed as a landholder there at her death.[3] Mme Coutanceau has her own methods for smoothing troubled waters and, despite sincere expressions of appreciation for her aunt, wants to be dealt with independently.

Her strength shows more and more. She has spent a lot of money on her machines but has also invested in a newer "complete anatomy," a figure of the entire female body "necessary to have the students learn the position of all the viscera." Mme Coutanceau's letters stress, these days, that she is in the vanguard of obstetrical pedagogy, taking her teaching in innovative directions and therefore, naturally, deserving of increased support. "I cannot keep silent," she tells the new Bordeaux intendant Le Camus de Neville, "on the desire I have to obtain from you a certain sign that you are satisfied with the zeal I have always put into instructing my students."[4] And he, using the old, time-honored model, requests charity from local seigneurs and priests to finance the women.[5]

But that won't work anymore. The political climate is changing, and the idea of these courses is no longer so graciously received, especially by the curés and the churchgoers. When a priest during his sermon reluctantly announces the latest call for midwifery students, a *sabot* maker tries to incite others to mock the whole idea, creating a ruckus. His, though perhaps the noisiest, is not the only protest against the assumption that ecclesiastics should have anything to do with the business of "regulating the temporal interests of their parishioners."[6] It seems an "insurrection" has allied the parish priests increasingly with the Third Estate, and there is widespread suspicion of royal policy. Animosity is directed not toward the monarch himself but toward his insensitive ministers and administrators. Many curés find the intendant's request for support from the villages for midwifery students patently absurd; these stricken peasants can barely eke out a living from the soil, and the pastors being asked to underwrite the training are almost as impoverished themselves.

One priest, for example, spells out his frustration in these terms: He earns a mere few hundred livres a year. He has hardly any food, a crumbly old church overrun by spiders, mice, and worms. How can he possibly sponsor an indigent peasant woman for a midwifery course? Besides, he questions the validity of the entire enterprise, which can only have been cooked up by irresponsible elites. "With the government interested in saving the lives of children about to be born, it is surprising that it is not [interested] in those who are born already. Experience has taught me that because of the ignorance of women who pass themselves off as midwives, children and mothers have died, but experience also teaches me that many, many subjects of the King who are very useful to the state, both men and women, boys and girls of all ages, die for lack of aid and the necessities of life, and that the number of these infinitely surpasses the others." Peasants live in misery, often even without bread and water. He, the curé, unable to afford either horse or mule, is obliged to travel on foot and often does not reach his parishioners in time to perform the sacraments; when he finally does arrive, he is powerless to do anything but cry and mourn with them. Meanwhile, it is considered indecent to disturb the "grand designers"—the abbots, priors, canons, monks, marquis—who remain deaf to the cries of the dying. After describing graphically these inequities and the extreme poverty of the French countryside, he closes: "If the King were informed of all these calamities his paternal goodness would provide for his subjects the necessary help they need, and many more would escape the arms of death by this means than by all the art of ten thousand Mme Coutanceaus."[7]

The winds of rebellion seem already to be blowing in this diatribe. It is a time of revolt by curés all over France, involving not only resentment between lower and upper clergy, but also intense politicization in the priests' struggle for their "rights."[8] The du Coudray/Coutanceau venture is a royal initiative and therefore suspect. Support from the curés, upon which both midwives have always relied, is therefore rapidly falling away.

Du Coudray, all this while, is still shuttling back and forth between Bordeaux and the capital. She still makes machines.[9] A Paris guidebook for this year lists a woman named du Coudray living on the rue Ste. Barbe near the Louvre and selling medicinal ointments.[10] Perhaps this is how the great midwife stays in touch with the world of healing. Perhaps it is during this time that she befriends the apothecary Noel Seguin on the nearby rue St. Honoré, who will be entrusted with power of attorney to handle her business affairs during the Revolution. It may seem a demeaning occupation for the famous midwife, but there is no way she can participate, assuming she even wished to, in the formal teaching of obstetrics in the capital. Since her departure from Paris in 1751 courses have sprung up all over the city and are very much in vogue, but that lively public instruction is dominated entirely by male professors, some of whom are her declared foes. The same Paris guidebook provides a list of them. The surgeon Sigault, friend of Alphonse Le Roy and inventor of the controversial *section de la symphise* operation, offers lessons on the rue du Renard. A. M. Deleurye, author of yet another rival textbook, gives classes on the Île St. Louis, and a M. Desormeaux teaches on the rue des Mathurins. The great Baudelocque, who may have studied with du Coudray in Angers but who has now married the daughter of Mme Lenfant, manufacturer of rival mannequins, advertises his course in the quartier St. Germain. And Alphonse Le Roy—whose celebrity is such these days that Jacques-Louis David has recently painted his portrait—himself holds forth near the quai des Augustins on the rue Pavée St. André.[11] Together, these men pretty much have the city covered. Pedagogy, du Coudray's specialty, is more clearly than ever a patriarchal monopoly.

Under the circumstances, selling remedies may seem like a safe alternative, discretion the better part of valor. The king's midwife is, after all, in retirement from her great mission, and nothing would be served by stirring up old antagonisms, reminding insecure men of her past power. Although she never valued peace and tranquillity before, her "age and infirmities" make the lower profile advisable. Very soon, however, she will be busy trying to cover up another liability: the taint of her long and close association with royalty.

6

Citoyenne Midwives
and the Revolution

59. As the Bastille Falls

Castillonès, 14 July 1789

Today, while Paris mobs storm the Bastille, Mme Coutanceau is preparing to give a course in this *bastide*, one of many fortified walled towns constructed throughout southwest Aquitaine during the Franco-English wars. She has just come from a course up north in Pauillac, center of the wine trade of Médoc. There she had nearly frozen, and her wood provider had made a special petition imploring the town authorities to furnish her with additional logs so she would not take sick.[1] The carriage to come to Castillonnès, privately hired this time, was expensive, but she must conserve her health.[2] Her class is to start tomorrow morning, and of course the payments from Versailles haven't come. Dismally familiar, all of this.[3] Yet she, like her aunt, has always counted on this system of funding, however imperfectly it sometimes functions.

Now, however, the monarchy is much closer to bankruptcy than ever before. Calonne was unable to resolve this fiscal crisis, and he was exiled to his lands in Lorraine, whence he fled to England. His short-lived successor, none other than Loménie de Brienne, whom Mme Coutanceau had been cultivating, was equally unsuccessful in persuading the privileged orders of nobles and clergy to relieve the tax burden that fell almost exclusively on the poor, and last summer in Paris he was burned in effigy as angry crowds cheered. Fresh acts of disobedience have been erupting all over France ever since. Intendants throughout the provinces have been warning that popular agitation will soon turn into full-scale civil war. A decision was made to summon the Estates General, an elected representative assembly that had not been convened since 1614, in the hopes that it could resolve the nation's problems, and the popular Necker was reappointed.

The estates in each area have been invited to draw up lists of grievances and suggestions for reform called *cahiers de doléances*. These, drafted in a spirit of great hope, are full of requests for more equity and liberty, for standardization of laws, for an end to government wastefulness. In April the deputies traveled to Versailles to meet. The Third Estate broke away, declaring itself the National Assembly, and many members of the First and Second Estates, clergy and nobles respectively, have since joined them. Louis XVI turned in alarm to the army, sending troops to surround Versailles and Paris. Then, just three days ago, he fired Necker, who seemed to be championing the cause of the commoners; this dismissal added to the already great distress in Paris, where garrisons of mercenaries have been converging in a menacing buildup. There is widespread fear that the price of bread, which has risen sharply in recent weeks, will shoot still higher in Necker's absence. Results of the disastrous harvest of 1788 are being felt now, and there is rumored to be a plot to starve the people for the benefit of grain speculators.

Suddenly Paris has exploded. Attempting to arm and defend themselves, mobs have attacked the Bastille, the ancient fortress, symbol of an increasingly unresponsive, intolerable regime. Misunderstandings, mounting rage, mutilations, and slaughter are rampant. Bleeding heads are being paraded around on pikes, to wild applause in the streets. Some voices in the celebrating crowds are urging a march on Versailles to demand the recall of Necker. The tocsin rings constantly. Everywhere in the capital barricades are being built as mistrustful people wait to see what the king will do next.

How much news of this ferment, mounting over these last weeks and escalating these last days, has filtered south to Castillonnès? Mme Coutanceau's region has seen its share of flaring political tempers. In Pau, near Dax where the midwife recently taught, violent popular disturbances erupted last summer, when bands of mountaineers were incited to invade the town on the belief that the king, in a "pacte de famine," was planning to tax them still more harshly. Riots broke out in Bordeaux and Toulouse as well. Mme Coutanceau is thus aware of the problems, but probably not of their severity, and certainly not of the extreme form they have taken in the capital. As she prepares for this next teaching stint, she can have no inkling that the revolt of Paris will lead to the collapse of the royal administration, that crowds of artisans and journeymen from the faubourg St. Antoine have, this very day, dealt the regime she knows and the purse she relies on a mortal blow.

60. THE LAFAYETTE CONNECTION

Paris, Fall 1790

The scene is the National Assembly. Mme Coutanceau has hastened here to appeal to the deputies because her whole enterprise in Bordeaux is in jeopardy. The money has dried up. Wherever she turns officials now tell her "circumstances are not favorable" for her teaching.[1] With the administrative reorganization of France, old provincial boundaries have given way to new *départements*, resulting in great bureaucratic confusion. The Assembly has issued treasury notes called *assignats* based on the value of nationalized church property, but no one seems to know whether to trust this new, already depreciating currency. Events occur with such alarming speed that it is never clear who is really in charge of France.

A rapid succession of ephemeral leaders and lawmakers in the capital have almost surely lost track of her mission, for in the political turmoil following 1789 midwifery is clearly not a top priority. She has heard the Friends of the Constitution, meeting in Bordeaux's Jacobin monastery, debate with passion many political issues. Women stand in line waiting as long as three hours to be admitted to the public galleries, thirsty for political education, full of zest for reform. But even in her own town's clubs and popular societies, midwives are scarcely mentioned. The current authorities in Paris probably do not even know who she is. She had best remind them; but how should she present herself? Since the women's march on Versailles in October 1789 the king has been in a strange position, a virtual prisoner in the Tuileries yet still the head of the country. Sovereignty has been transferred to the people, but Louis XVI continues to claim the throne. For the time being, although she must recognize the new realities, Mme Coutanceau can still speak proudly of her mission's royal origins. The rhapsodic apologia she now delivers for her famous aunt is designed to do just that.

Her *Mémoire* has been presented to the National Assembly's Committee for the Extinction of Mendicity, whose purpose is to replace voluntary charities for poor relief and put all public health services on a national footing. In this *Mémoire* she explains first the accomplishments of du Coudray, who among other claims to fame saved the life of the infant Lafayette, hero of the American expedition, popular idol, presently general of the National Guard of Paris, and one of the most powerful men in France. By mentioning this early on, she no doubt hopes to have Lafayette use his influence to protect her enterprise, but he is far too busy suppressing mutinies in the army at Nancy and trying to maintain his loyalties to both the Assembly and the king. Also, his feud with Mirabeau is already beginning to undermine his standing. If Mme Coutanceau knew that

Lafayette would soon be denounced by the Revolution as a traitor, flee the country, and spend the next many years in an Austrian jail, she might not be so quick to credit du Coudray with his very survival.

After reviewing the history of the traveling midwifery mission, the king's endorsements, the superb teaching record, and the invention of the "phantom" with its stamp of approval from the Academy of Surgery, she introduces her favorite theme: the paramount importance of the female teacher. "The sensitivity of women, their relations among themselves, their smaller and more delicate hands making them preferable, a great number will find in the vocation and exercise of midwifery an honorable and useful profession." Perhaps she is trying to counter here the new Comité de Salubrité just formed by the Royal Society of Medicine's Vicq d'Azyr, which intends to replace midwives with male professors. In any case, she makes much of the female aspect of birthing, stressing not only the role of the midwife but also the importance of motherhood. Du Coudray had never explicitly credited mothers as civilizing forces, educators in the household, moral backbones of society; to her, women were more childbearers than childrearers. But Mme Coutanceau is better attuned to the Revolution's arguments about civic, republican motherhood as a national obligation and sober responsibility. She is a mother herself, after all. In a nod to the newly fashionable language of classes, groups, constituencies, she ends by assuring the Assembly that she is totally devoted to "procuring assistance for the class of mothers, [which is] of such interest to the state."[2]

Unbeknownst to her, this valiant plea has been challenged by another urgent report to the Assembly, this one from none other than du Coudray's nemesis Alphonse Le Roy, casting aspersions on midwives and on most of what they have written about the subject of delivery, and zeroing in especially on Mme Coutanceau's aunt, who he says has led the nation astray with her books and mannequins. "As for midwives, they know neither the art nor the science [of obstetrics] . . . if their ignorance is enterprising, they themselves create dangers. The old government . . . set up a spinster [*demoiselle*] as the evangelist of delivery . . . but a figure of a doll was her whole instruction."[3] Le Roy, who ignores the matter of educating midwives throughout France and fails to grasp the sheer magnitude of that task, wants to have doctors and surgeons in Paris take over all instruction, setting up at the Salpetrière hospital a clinic for delivering poor women while others watch and learn.[4] He is trying to appeal to the new order, but his report oozes with elitist disdain for the masses. Professionals in Paris are his only real concern. He appears, characteristically, to care not at all about what, if anything, the rest of the nation learns on the subject of obstetrics.

Whom will the Assembly favor? Mme Coutanceau's *Mémoire* stresses links with the past, whereas Le Roy mocks the teaching of *accouchement* in the ancien régime. And the deputies might take exception to her claims for women. In fact, however, much more aggressive and angry feminist complaints have already been presented to the Assembly, one by a midwife in Clermont who feels rebuffed and wronged as a woman because she lacks "a brain crowned by a doctoral bonnet, which is the only thing to confer the prerogative of assassinating the human race with impunity. . . . I am not a person of letters: I have not grown white sitting on benches like the majority of *messieurs* the academicians." She concludes by arguing that her vast experience is as "worthy" as all *their* "oratorical discourses." This midwife's railing against intellectual and professional "despotism" that "casts its general oppression over all human faculties" is aimed, of course, at men, but also at their elite theoretical schooling.[5] Maybe she is inspired by the current discourse on women's rights and the need to protest disenfranchisement. Compared to this, the request from Mme Coutanceau must sound measured and reasonable.

Temporarily at least, she is given approval and told somewhat vaguely to continue her teaching with the endorsement of the new government.[6] That she will actually be paid is unlikely, but at least she has put the need for provincial midwifery instruction once again before the Assembly. The *cahiers de doléances* of 1789 were full of complaints about childbirth practices and pleas for better training. Forty grievances classified under public health and twenty-two under education—all but ten from towns and areas where du Coudray had never taught—explicitly bemoaned the fact that provincial women are not taught the rudiments of this art.[7] The Assembly should have been paying close attention to the *cahiers* on this subject, but it was not. At least not until Mme Coutanceau's *Mémoire*.

As her aunt had done a few years ago, she now raises awareness of the problem; she may even catalyze yet another survey of *accouchement* in the countryside, for shortly after her departure from Paris Vicq d'Azyr's new committee initiates its own extensive examination (*enquête*) of rural medical practice. Six questions are specifically aimed at *sages-femmes*. Here, as in the Royal Society of Medicine's study of 1786, Mme du Coudray's teaching team and method are the only ones designated by name, and once again the astonishing impact of both aunt and niece is measured in depth and breadth. Responses pour in from all the *départements* in the hope that their voices, ignored in the *cahiers*, will this time really be heeded and will contribute to decision making and policy reform.[8]

A few replies to this new *enquête* are negative or critical. Narbonne, Toulouse, and Castres boast that they never needed du Coudray—but of course, this is the area that consistently refused to let her come, stubbornly insisting that whatever teaching took place be done by men.[9] The surgeons of Belley complain that because du Coudray's original students received their own certificates and thus bypassed the usual examination by the surgical community, the precedent was set for later widespread indulgence of irregular practitioners and for general laxness of standards.[10] Angoulême, Agen, and Rochefort report that the follow-through on du Coudray's teaching has been inadequate, that interest in the subject could not be sustained after her departure.

The vast majority of regions, however, either realize their deprivation if the famous midwife has never passed their way, lament that her stay was too short, or glory in the triumphant success of her mission in their midst. Crest explains how doctors fought to be chosen to learn from her.[11] Mont-de-Marsan in the Landes area mourns the fact that it never benefited from her teaching, as does Villeneuve-de-Berg north of Nîmes, where the local health officials blame the former intendants for being deaf to du Coudray's talent and usefulness. As a result, now "there is an infinity of women who pretend to be midwives and who, without the slightest knowledge of this important art, benefit with impunity from the public credulity and blindness." The author of this report is single-handedly battling the frightening trend, in the process making himself "a mob of enemies."[12] Once again, this southern area of Vivarais was one where du Coudray tried and failed repeatedly to penetrate. Laon, another region that spurned the fabled midwife, favoring instead the doctor Augier du Fot, now regrets that du Fot's teaching was purely theoretical, not based on experience or tactile training and consequently entirely useless to unschooled country women. Only du Coudray understood how to reach these women, and, sorry that she herself can no longer come, Laon is now hoping at least to secure some of her machines and some surgeon-demonstrators trained in her method. Better late than never.[13] What sweet revenge it would be for her to know that she is admired and missed even in enemy territory.

All the other replies to the questionnaire sing the praises of the great midwife and her team. Her influence is still marked in Châtel, St. Dizier, St. Dié, Ste. Menehould, Lyon-la-Forêt, Nérac, Dur-le-Roi, Nuits, Ussel, Tartas, Vouvans—towns where she never taught but to which her trainees radiated out and instructed others in her method. And of course many cities where the courses actually took place—Montauban, Poitiers, Moulins, Bourges, Tours, Issoudin—bear du Coudray's imprint still more strongly and express real nostalgia for her.

It is a proud legacy, though in all probability the two women never learn of this questionnaire. Surely they get no thanks in the form of remuneration. And as the pace of the Revolution escalates, the responses to this *enquête*, like the *cahiers* before them, are forgotten. No attempt is made on the national level to redress midwife shortages in needy areas, to strengthen and encourage regions where things are going well, to institute overall rigor and standardized examinations, to show gratitude to the impassioned pioneers. On the contrary, during the whole revolutionary decade all legal distinctions between professional and charlatan, all entry qualifications for practice, will be swept away, and a medical free-for-all will ensue with everyone, licensed or not, claiming to be an *officier de santé*.[14] Du Coudray's high standards become, in most areas of France, a thing of the past, to be revived only in the next century.

And Lafayette, the hoped-for ally, could not care less.

61. WHAT TREASURY WILL PAY?

Bordeaux, 1 July 1791

Du Coudray, who has been living in this port city with her niece's family at the Collège de la Magdeleine for several years, is no doubt alarmed by news of the king's flight and ignominious capture at Varennes just now. For the third time in two years, Louis has been brought back to Paris as a prisoner. The Assembly has suspended the king's authority until further notice, and people sense that this is a major turning point in the Revolution. Before the king has even signed the constitution, the constitutional monarchy appears to be ending; his apparent betrayal fans the flames of suspicion about internal conspiracies and the fear of external invasions by armies of émigrés. Republicanism is in the air, "Ça Ira" on everyone's lips, male and female alike. The *Gazette universelle* reports on the activities of Bordeaux's revolutionary women, about four thousand of whom are assembling to parade. France is in a swirl of passions.

This afternoon the old midwife, calling herself Demoiselle Angélique Marguerite Le Boursier du Coudray, summons her notary, Trimoulet, to her home to draw up a document. The king's new powerlessness means that her retirement pension is more seriously imperiled than ever. But then, all around her she sees that the Revolution has plunged many others into poverty as well.

Since her first visit to Bordeaux in 1770 the city had prospered and enjoyed a building boom. Its population doubled, and until recently it was all abustle with merchant shipping, factories, sugar refineries, tidal corn mills, ropeworks, and of course the wine trade. Firms from Germany, Ireland, and Holland had offices here in beautiful new structures. Du Coudray had seen Bordeaux become a thriving, diverse metropolis.[1]

The scene is dramatically different now; some noble families are in ruins, many priests are in jail, merchants are in shock, common people are starving. Activities in the once-vigorous seaport and commercial center have virtually ground to a halt. Bad harvests several years running have yielded little wine for trade. Foreign goods are not coming in, there is no sugar, coffee, tobacco, or indigo from the colonies, grain is terribly short. Artisans and day workers cannot find jobs. Meat has gone up four times in price; bread, once 4 sous a pound, today costs 1 livre 5 sous.

Du Coudray and her family are badly in need of funds, yet the payment of pensions has been disrupted already by all the upheavals. Now, with the king's botched escape, things will only get worse. Far from the capital as they are, they cannot continually journey there to argue their cause in person. So du Coudray designates her acquaintance, the well-known master-apothecary Noel Seguin, as her proxy in Paris, authorizing him to "claim and receive, from all treasuries, accountants, and other bookkeepers, previously for his majesty and now for the nation, the payment of arrears due or coming due, of annuities, pensions, bonuses, and other graces which have been bestowed upon her, or which might be granted to her in future by whatever title or denomination it might be, earmarked from the former royal treasury or others, and for all that is received to furnish receipts and letters of discharge to all involved, and generally to succeed in getting paid in full, as said *demoiselle constituente* would herself do in person."[2] In other words, he is to collect her overdue back pay and what is currently accruing as well. Wishful thinking!

The language of this notarized act reflects the confusion of du Coudray's household in dealing with the changing revolutionary governments, but also their desire to understand and change with the times. Is the Treasury His Majesty's? Is it the nation's? Is it royal or "others'"? Authority is so ephemeral, so dislocated. Traditions offer more risk than security; the country seems thrown into a kind of amnesia where old names mean nothing any longer and new ones never last long enough to ring true. Seguin's notary will register this document in Paris nearly two months later,[3] and shortly after Seguin will try to obtain the money. The Constituent Assembly is then in the process of dissolving, to be replaced by the Legislative Assembly, and is perplexed regarding the actual status of this legendary midwife who now is old and useless. Why honor her retirement salary? Embarrassed, they refer her request for payment to the Committee on Pensions, where it is shelved indefinitely. Approval *is* given though, at least in principle, for Mme Coutanceau to be paid, because she is still active.[4] It is not clear if the whole 8,000 is now promised to Mme Coutanceau, or only the 2,000 originally designated to her. But it makes no difference because the funds, whatever the amount, do not arrive. On 22 December the niece follows suit and empowers Seguin to fight also for her money,[5] but his efforts in her behalf are equally fruitless.

Mme Coutanceau will declare on 6 April 1793 to her notary in Bordeaux that, despite all assurances and her highest expectations of good faith, she has been paid absolutely nothing by the state for her labors during the three and a half years since her appearance before the Assembly in 1790. She seeks at that point someone else to represent her interests more successfully in Paris.[6] But clearly, her advocate is not the problem. By then France is at war; Lafayette and Dumouriez have deserted; the king has fallen, been imprisoned in the Temple, been renamed Citizen Capet, and lost his head; the Girondins who have dominated the National Convention, many of them from Bordeaux, are slipping from power; and the new republic is putting all of its energies into militarily "exporting" liberty, equality, fraternity to other oppressed peoples of Europe. There is great scarcity throughout the land, famine and food riots everywhere.

Paris cannot be bothered right now. That salary from the capital is never to be seen.

62. Mme Coutanceau's Clinic

Bordeaux, 30 August 1793

Much has happened these last two months to enmesh the midwife's family in the revolutionary fray. The Coutanceaus have somehow finally gotten their maternity hospice, assigned to them on the very day that Charlotte Corday stabbed Marat in his bathtub. France's situation in the international war has meanwhile been deteriorating. Valenciennes has fallen in the north, and Toulon in the south. Now, on top of the threat of foreign invasion, Marat's murder has initiated a purge of internal traitors and anybody else suspected of moderate views. Everyone must show total devotion to the *patrie*. The National Convention, exactly one week ago, called for general conscription, a *levée en masse* requiring all young men between the ages of eighteen and twenty-five to "report without delay to the chief town in their district where they shall train in the use of arms each day while they await the order to depart."[1]

The Coutanceaus' son, Godefroy Barthélémy Ange, a medical student and only seventeen, has studied with his mother and has dedicated himself to "the art of healing" since 1790. He has been working as a *chirurgien externe* at Bordeaux's Hôtel Dieu since 1792. This call to "rise up against tyranny" changes his life. He will respond to it even though he is underage and must lie about his years, stating on an official form that he is twenty-one when he enlists as a surgeon in the Army of the Western Pyrenees.[2] Does he do this out of a genuine sense of commitment? Or is it perhaps a gesture to prove the family's patriotism? Mme Coutanceau will later say that she meant her son to become part of her teaching and birthing operation at the new hospital, but starting now he takes a very different course.[3]

Meanwhile, the senior Coutanceaus have continued to work feverishly. Somehow, almost miraculously, despite the lack of funds from the central government, they proceed to teach and train midwives year in and year out. The balance of power in the household is shifting in interesting ways. The annual Bordeaux almanac always advertises the courses, dominated now very much by Mme Coutanceau (fig. 13) rather than her husband.[4] The municipality has put her in charge of an extra pavilion in the Collège de la Magdeleine to use as a maternity ward. The General Council of the commune of Bordeaux officially established on 13 July 1793 a new "hospital for women where they may deliver and to which will be admitted without discrimination unwed mothers and the poor." The clinic, on the street renamed Fossés de la Commune, has twelve beds, and the city council "names the *citoyenne* Coutanceau director of this hospice and . . . her husband *accoucheur*." The couple must apply their talent and patriotic zeal to the task of delivering babies, but also to keeping them healthy and strong "by supplementing mother's milk with another food." Despite the lamentable fiscal state of the municipality, a promise is made—3,000 livres for her, 1,000 for her husband—and Bordeaux will continue to provide them with free lodging, wood for heat, and candles for light.[5] Although the city cannot keep its word on the money, it continues to give the clinic its moral support.

A midwife established as founder and director of a permanent clinic is a historic first in France. Mme Coutanceau has far surpassed her husband in importance, fame, and administrative responsibility. Once he had written in his hand the letters she dictated, and she had been quite dependent on him.[6] Now this accomplished woman is the boss, and he her underling. Although he continues to work alongside her for some time longer, he will branch off into other businesses, taking over some émigré property for example, to earn extra money. Meanwhile, du Coudray's niece is well on her way to becoming another great, famous midwife. Her aunt's taste for success and recognition, inexorably transmitted to her over years of training but latent until now, has really kicked in. She is almost forty, as was her aunt when she left Paris, striking out on her own, deciding to be separate and strong.

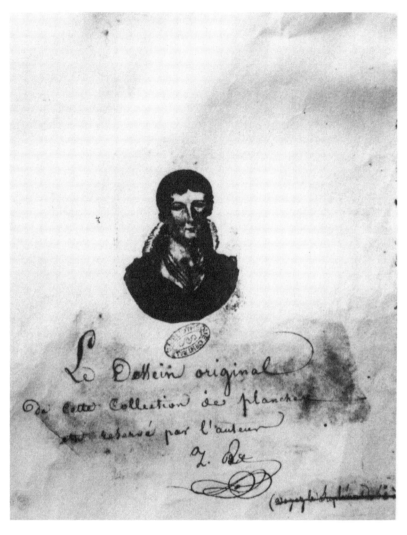

Figure 13. This drawing of Mme Coutanceau is the only one of Mme du Coudray's "niece" I have been able to locate. It is in an unpublished book of illustrations by the Bordeaux artist Bouthenot in the Val-de-Grâce Hospital in Paris. The printed volume, with planned engravings based on these drawings, never appeared. Photograph courtesy of the Val-de-Grâce Hospital Library, Paris; may not be reproduced elsewhere.

It is not clear what role du Coudray plays in all this. Perhaps she is still healthy and dexterous enough to assist a bit with the teaching, or even to deliver babies privately for some extra money. Almost certainly she has been providing financial support for the household and clinic operations. Probably she has paid for everything. How else could they have stayed afloat? There were no other sources of philanthropy. The niece, as we saw, claims not to have been paid a single sou from Paris in the last three years, and Bordeaux, gallant intentions notwithstanding, cannot make good on its obligations. But the grand old lady has kept the valuable gifts she collected during three missionary decades, and has probably been melting them down and selling them off for several years already. Although there is no direct evidence of this, what else explains how, in the absence of all promised pensions from either state or city, the Coutanceau enterprise continues to thrive?

63. Du Coudray, Casualty of the Terror

Bordeaux, 28 Germinal An II (17 April 1794)

The *citoyenne* du Coudray is dead. Not guillotined, but a casualty of the Terror nonetheless. Today two men from the Bureau of Tax Collection report to the authorities that she expired during the night, at 11:30.[1] Why are these total strangers, rather than her relatives, the bearers of this news? (This is not the pattern for other entries in the same register, where either friends, neighbors, or kin report the deaths.) And what have the midwife's last months, last days, last moments of life been like? How, before finally succumbing, has she felt the impact of Robespierre's regime? Though spared execution, she has certainly not been allowed to pass peacefully away.

Bordeaux has always had a history of disobedience and insubordination. Its particularist character can be traced back to medieval times, and during the Fronde it had negotiated with Cromwell and nearly broken from France to form a republic. Early in the Revolution this region, now called the department of the Gironde, had lent its name to a federalist revolt against the Jacobin dictatorship in Paris. When the Girondins were expelled from the National Convention for their too-moderate views, a provincial armed force had drilled and prepared to march on the capital in protest against the tyranny of the radicals. The revolutionary authorities decided to starve Bordeaux, as punishment for its defiance, by means of a grain embargo. More recently Robespierre has threatened to invade it. The feeling has been that this city, with its record of glaring disloyalty in the history of France's statebuilding, will need to be subdued, even purged. Why, the local officials might *themselves* be mutinous traitors!

On 23 October 1793, the beginning of the revolutionary month of Brumaire, with the erection of a guillotine on the Place Nationale, the Terror came to Bordeaux. Before it is over many will flee or go into hiding, several thousand will be tried or incarcerated, and more than three hundred will be beheaded by the "national razor," the "blade of the law." A military commission and surveillance group has already instituted severely repressive measures even against the Third Estate, jailing actors who utter any word with a taint of royalism in a performance, arresting businessmen to "bleed" their purses and "purify" them. M. A. Jullien, the "eye" of Robespierre, a Jacobin fanatic only nineteen years old, was sent to Bordeaux to tighten the vise still more on this hotbed of "incivisme." He made his first inspection just twenty-five days ago, leaving a terrible fear in his wake. On his orders alone, 217 inhabitants of this city will be guillotined within a few short months in the name of "public safety."[2]

But Bordeaux had become nightmarish even before Jullien's arrival. A winter more bitter and brutal than any in memory had left city and countryside on the brink of famine, and, although it is now spring, breadlines and riots are still common. Ice made the river unnavigable for a while, boats were lost, people stole benches, cut down trees from public promenades, and in desperation pillaged the wood frame of an old church to burn so they could cook soup and thaw their half-frozen bodies. Fields and shipyards were totally deserted. In the words of a visitor, it was a scene everywhere of "men and women dead from starvation, others, of a more robust temperament, all bloated, still others expiring in the middle of the streets and roads; there is reason to believe that without the pains, the care, the solicitude of the representatives sent to Bordeaux, half of the people would have perished."[3]

The "representatives" referred to, erroneously credited in this Jacobin account with ameliorating the terrible situation, have been dispatched from Paris by the Committee of Public Safety to impose, incongruous as it may seem, yet another new tax on the already devastated city. Into the midst of confusion and agitation caused by internal economic and health problems have come a group of officials to oversee the city's political "regeneration" or re-Jacobinization. This "forced loan of the Year II"—one more attempt on the part of the revolutionary government to raise money for its war against Europe and the Vendée—is designed to support the "fatherland in danger" against both external and internal foes.

Incivisme, the absence of patriotic devotion, is a new category of offense invented by the Terror and punishable by death.[4] It means indifference to "virtue," and consequently enmity to the *patrie*. Simple denunciation by one person of another can warrant execution, so now everyone is in danger—bourgeois, peasants, and workers as much as nobles. One way of being a "good citizen" and escaping accusations of apathy is by making a monetary donation to the state. The call for contributions had originally been issued on a voluntary basis, and all were encouraged to keep receipts enumerating their presents as evidence of their loyalty to the republic. But the pressure to feed the coffers increased daily. Soon bureaus were set up throughout Bordeaux, and the names of all citizens who failed to contribute were posted for everyone to see. Shame and guilt are very public matters, suddenly. Newspapers and church sermons have been urging everyone to comply and donate. "Gifts" have now become essentially obligatory, and households are searched by special commissioners checking to see if the declarations made by each inhabitant of his or her worth, on the basis of which the tax is calculated, are true and accurate. Artisans, doctors, clerks, merchants, and lawyers can no longer evade the impost.[5] Nor can bachelors or widows with more than 1,000 livres of revenues. Payments were to have been made between December 1793 and February 1794 to any of a growing number of tax collectors, inspectors, assistants, and "verifiers."[6] Now, though, the hunt for more goods has been extended.

For du Coudray and Mme Coutanceau all this has been harrowingly tense. Over the last half year, since all citizens feel it is their duty to denounce suspects, the threat of decapitation has filled everyone with uncertainty and dread. In theory, according to the books, the two women are the recipients of government pensions far in excess of 1,000 livres. Yet it is not clear who, if anyone, has paid them these salaries during this period of national turmoil and bankruptcy. How do they explain this discrepancy? Just a few months ago, on 1 Pluviôse An II (20 January 1794), note was made of the "deliverance of certificates of *civisme* to the *citoyennes* Coutanceau and du Coudray."[7] At that point, anyway, they had either satisfied the collectors of the forced loan by making some contribution, or persuaded them that they honestly had no means to make one, had nothing left to donate. Chances are that the gifts du Coudray had amassed during her travels—trays, plaques, boxes, coffeepots, gold and silver pieces bearing the coats of arms of two kings and the royal intendants—have been cashed in over the last few years to provide for the Coutanceau hospice. But are they exhausted? Trafficking in goods so redolent of the Old Regime has become increasingly risky in an atmosphere that abhors anything smacking of royalism. Just as early in the Revolution it had been prudent to dispose of them, perhaps even conspicuously, the way women in Paris donated their jewels to the National Assembly, it would be still more prudent now to hide them. That is, if there are any left.

Is that what the tax men are thinking? Do they suspect the old midwife is holding out on them? Why are they back bothering du Coudray on the night she dies? Why do they give her no peace or privacy? This is surely not an innocent, friendly visit. The Law of Suspects virtually assumes the guilt of all former employees of the nobility. She is something far worse, a once-trusted agent of the dethroned, beheaded, and vilified king. The midwife, seventy-nine years old, is for some reason alone. Have the tax men deliberately taken advantage of her solitude to hound her, to confront her with suspicions that, despite the prevailing austerity, she is still harboring some treasures? The obsession with frugality is such that even wearing clean linen can be cause for denunciation. Is it the strain caused by their interrogation that finally breaks her spirit? That kills her? And where are her people? If her niece and nephew had been with her, they, and not two complete strangers, would have been the witnesses to report her death. That they have left her that evening suggests she is not particularly ill or feeble. Either they are momentarily away with no thought that their aunt is in danger, or they have been forcibly separated from her while she endures the examination. They themselves do not appear to be suspects. Indeed, just before the Terror the Coutanceaus were commended for their service to the "French Republic one and indivisible."[8] They have, after all, contributed their precious boy to the revolutionary cause, and he is presently defending his country and healing soldiers on the Spanish frontier.[9] Huge posters advertise their midwifery courses, to begin next month on 15 Floréal.[10] The couple would seem to be in good standing. It is evidently du Coudray the authorities are after. But why? Questions abound.

Perhaps it is fitting that the end finds her by herself, that she exits, as she entered, alone and mysterious. Her grave, like her birthplace, will remain unknown and unvisited. She has left, apparently, no testament or succession; at least the notaries of Bordeaux have no record of such. It is true that notarial offices are extremely disrupted during the Terror. It is also true that death inventories have gone out of style; they are in bad taste, and politically dangerous. It is not public-spirited to make official lists of one's possessions at a time of such deprivation and want, at a time when the private self is all but obliterated. Most plausibly, however, du Coudray simply has nothing material left to pass on. The tax officials have almost surely wrested from her whatever last valuables she may have tried to salvage for her niece and nephew. Her legacy to the Coutanceaus will instead be of an intangible kind. In fact, she has given it already, bit by bit, over the last decades, bequeathing to them her knowledge and technique, her sense of purpose, her wholehearted belief in the *bien de l'humanité*.

Epilogue
Paris and Los Angeles, 1994–1996

Today we know, although France feared it was shrinking, that its population rose during the eighteenth century from 20 million to 27 million, and demographers have pinpointed 1750 as the beginning of this transformation, when a marked increase in life expectancy among infants set in. Historians do not credit or even mention Mme du Coudray's mission in this connection, but they should.[1] Of course many other factors contributed to the upswing, such as the abating of plague, improved agricultural production, progress in some areas of public health. But without being worshipful, we can argue that the training by du Coudray and her disciples of an estimated ten thousand women, during her lifetime alone, in the art of childbirth must have had considerable impact. The silence on this count has been deafening.

And what of the follow-through? The great midwife surely had help, so we should say a few words about the others, since she made them her relatives, considered them extensions of herself, and expected them to carry on the work.

The men in the family, as it turns out, did little to keep the momentum of the mission going; indeed, they seemed to disconnect from it. After du Coudray's death in 1794, M. Coutanceau was the next to go. When he died in 1805 he was nearly seventy.[2] Although still listed in various documents as an *officier de santé*, he had by then receded into the medical background and was busy managing property instead.[3] In 1797 he appears to have separated briefly from his wife, though they did reconcile. He freed her to function legally as a *feme sole* even when he was still alive.[4] At his death he left some revenues which enabled her to give gifts to those in need.[5]

The Coutanceaus' son, exhausted after a rude winter campaign in the Alps in 1800, took a break from the army, studied at the Val-de-Grâce military hospital, and received a medical degree from the

Paris Faculty of Medicine. In 1808 he married, becoming the brother-in-law of Napoleon's great and favorite surgeon, Baron Dominique Larrey. Larrey wrote passionate letters home from the front to his wife, seemingly unthrilled about her sister's choice of a spouse, but he put in a good word anyway, and in 1813 Coutanceau received the Cross of the Legion of Honor.[6] He had written a curious "Notice on Pernicious Fevers" describing an epidemic in Bordeaux in 1805 during which three thousand died in the space of five months. He too was there then, fell ill himself, and gives a detailed, almost gossipy narrative of the dramatic events and of his own symptoms, mentioning numerous local health officials. This is hardly a cold, clinical article, but there are some glaring omissions. Although he was staying on the rue des Incurables, he never says this was his parents' home and maternity hospice, stressing instead that he was there merely "in passing." And he never relates that his own father was among the dead.[7] It is unclear why he held himself apart from the family and the midwifery mission; none of his published papers deal with the subject of *accouchement*. His wife died, then his mother died, he married a second time and had two children, but left them all impoverished at his untimely death in 1831.

His widow had more desire to connect with his lineage. In seeking financial support from the government, she believed the recitation of the whole family's patriotic contributions going back generations might buttress her plea.[8] It was almost surely she, the only survivor, who conveyed the packet of du Coudray's private papers to Delacoux in 1834, for he then wrote of the young widow's deceased husband, his father and mother, and his great-aunt du Coudray as members of a brilliant but unsung medical dynasty.[9]

And what of the "niece"? She lived until 1825 and, like her aunt, came into the fullest manifestation of her being in later life after weathering many crises. The anonymous portrait I found of her shows a thin woman in a green dress (symbolizing fertility?) with a delicate, serious, long face—quite a contrast to the robust du Coudray.[10] Mme Coutanceau attracted adoring students from far and wide who referred to her as "at once our professor and our mother,"[11] and who commissioned as a gift for her a (now lost) painting in which she leans over the mannequin, describing it to a peasant girl standing beside her.[12] She had somehow gone on teaching through the Terror,[13] and published a second textbook in the late 1790s, her

Instructions théoriques et pratiques, "free of all erudition and all *systèmes* . . . simple like [my students]."[14] She tells of how hard it was moving from their first hospital, the Collège de la Magdeleine, "an agreeable asylum," to the new one "where we had no salary and were missing everything—twenty shabby bedsteads, nine pairs of sheets, six towels, a bucket, and a lamp composed the entire list of furnishings. We needed to supplement it. Food was soon lacking, and I made all the sacrifices that these trying circumstances necessitated to satisfy the needs of the unfortunate pregnant women entrusted to my care." She was (partially) reimbursed only with the rise of Napoleon.[15]

"I had begun, I dare say it, to reap the fruits of my labors when death took my husband from me." Having taught her son the art of midwifery, then sending him to study "with the greatest masters" in Paris for nearly ten years at enormous expense, she hoped he would succeed his father as her assistant (although it was not obvious the son wanted to). But he was passed over for a protégé of the prefect's. "I thus lost, in the space of eight days, my husband, my place, and the legitimate hope for my son's post." For all her hard work in her Bordeaux clinic, renamed the Royal School of Midwifery ever since the Bourbon Restoration of 1815, she requested, "on the basis of justice," a payment for her son so that "after me he can enjoy a part of the benevolence of the government without which, at my death, he will have only the memory of my affection and of my works." This was the thanks she asked for her long career of service, hoping to perpetuate her mission and pension within the family just as her aunt had. But the son had not followed in her professional footsteps, had not assisted her in Bordeaux, and her request was not granted.

When she finally retired in 1822 at sixty-seven—exactly the same age at which du Coudray gave up her traveling mission—she asked that a transcript of her last class be kept in the archives as a lasting "precious monument" and a "powerful motive of emulation." She also announced plans to publish a new book, *Cours élémentaires . . . d'accouchement,* more ambitious than any so far, a beautiful, path-breaking volume with 120 colored pictures. She had already commissioned the Bordeaux artist Bouthenot, who drew 96 sketches, but she still needed to get them engraved: "It is only in Paris that I can have this work executed, by the great draftsmen of anatomy."[16]

The sketches give an idea of Mme Coutanceau's intentions. We can see that du Coudray was a powerful role model still, almost thirty years after her death, for many of the anatomical designs and their whole style bear a marked resemblance to the original pictures in the *Abrégé*. But the niece had of course moved beyond these to cover new ground, reflecting progress in the field. She illustrated the importance of gloves, the danger of puerperal fever, the use of forceps, the technique of vaccination with cowpox pus—complete with a charming illustration of a Welch cow—surgical removal of uterine polyps, special kinds of lithotomy, the cesarean operation, and more.[17] Although the textbook with its finished pictures never materiaized, Mme Coutanceau's last two decades of life, widowed and working alone, were her strongest and most productive. As director of her own hospital and a woman with vision, she did her aunt proud in the end.

The lives of these two remarkable women have broad implications for current historiographical debates about feminism and the medical profession in both the old and new regimes. Both of them exercised keen tactical instincts and well-learned habits for advancing their careers by making constant adjustments—to changing political imperatives, to increasing hostility between learned and popular medicine, to the creation of a hierarchy of medical expertise based on schooling and male appropriation of knowledge, to heated challenges from fashionable quarters about the place of women in the birthing arena, to a proliferating press and pamphlet literature informing and swaying an alert, involved, ever-broadening audience. What is surprising is not the problems they faced but the originality of the strategies they designed to overcome those obstacles, the way they scrambled cultural expectations regarding gender, class, and age with their special rhetoric of patriotic service to destabilize their antagonists and secure a privileged professional niche for themselves. The two needed to find different solutions, the aunt navigating through the crumbling bureaucracy of the old regime's twilight, the niece unstymied by the limitations supposedly placed on feminist ambitions by the Revolution.[18] Both defied the marginalization of women common in their day. Their example helps explain why midwifery was not eclipsed in the nineteenth century. Napoleon created the first chair in obstetrics—the first chair ever in a medical specialty—for the *accoucheur* Baudelocque, and wanted to squeeze women out entirely, but in spite of his wishes female midwives continued as a potent force in France up into the twentieth century.[19]

Mme du Coudray had indomitable faith in her mission and in the right of her women to practice this art, but knew she would accomplish nothing in a frontal assault and instead artfully constructed the image of her students as obedient, deferential midwives in order to advance herself and them without causing a furor. On the face of it she might appear an unquestioning, willing official, a government henchwoman subscribing uncritically to what Mary Daly calls the patriarchal agenda of "proliferation, propagation, procreation." But it seems to me she was practicing something more like "boundary living," working from within the existing system but communicating contagious courage, "volcanic virtues," to countless other women in ways not immediately measurable.[20]

Now, what of my search for the mysterious Mme du Coudray, for the woman behind the mask? It is often said that biographical subjects are victims of our prying who cannot fight back.[21] Yet Mme du Coudray was merrily defiant from the start; and not only did she fight, but she won, in the sense that her desire for concealment prevailed. The packet of private papers remains at large—and after all these years of hoping to find it, I am actually glad to be left with questions to probe, with the lively awareness that parts are always missing, that stories remain unfinished, that the past is never over. I would no longer choose to flatten and smooth out my subject, explain away seeming contradictions and wrap things up, for du Coudray inspires tentative rather than triumphant conclusions. She herself, unable to complete her *Grand Voyage*, felt she left her own life work undone. No womb-to-tomb closure here.

In my search for the interior life du Coudray strove so hard to suppress, I think I came to understand why she did as she did. There is abundant evidence of an extremely passionate nature, one kept under control by a strong will forever forcing itself to stay on track. Imagine the emotional highs and lows that would buffet her about and throw her off course if she allowed them to. The currency she dealt in was nothing less than human life. I do not think it anachronistic to suppose that she was awed by the resourceful and vigorous tiny bodies making clear that they wanted to be born, that she was moved by their tender folds, their strange tufts of hair, their ardor to nurse. Of course she was performing a delivery, but each time, also, a child was being born. That she experienced again and again the wonder of it I feel certain, but it had no place in the official biography she meant to manufacture. Nor did she share her fears—over breech presentations, for example—so determined was she to pass on her "can-do" attitude. Stillbirths probably haunted her, the terrible surprise and silence of them. And malformations. Besides the common clubfeet and hip luxations she saw, there must occasionally have been a true monstrosity—a gaping hole where a face should have been, a child so ghastly that the mother was too revolted to nurse it, so misshapen that it could not nurse anyway and so died of starvation. Others she heroically reanimated, weaklings brought back from apparent lifelessness; but with ones like that, so ill equipped for the world and so hideous, she no doubt wished for them to die mercifully and fast.

There is of course the common argument that because morbidity and mortality were so omnipresent in the preindustrial world, people did not grieve in the way we do today. Certainly it is true that mothers were very much in the habit of seeing their babies die. But du Coudray devoted her life to fighting with all her might against such resignation. This was not just a technical, but an emotional affirmation. Babies *could* be saved. She was very positive, very steady, and she allowed herself neither elation nor grief. She simply could not afford to. Too much was at stake.

But along with this tremendous self-control we see du Coudray's sense of fun. She surprised those she dealt with, surprised me, surprised even herself as she discovered within her, in middle age, strengths and strategies to leave behind the sameness and tameness of her former job, to attempt brave and untried things. Her journey violated the conventional domestic enclosure of women, created for her a special kind of freedom and excitement. Her road show had all of France for its stage, and she was a ham, a stunning performer, giving a more sustained and spectacular solo display than almost any other female, save royalty, in early modern Europe. She might have remained a successful Paris midwife, which would surely have been an easier way to make a living. But hers was a bid for glory, for transcendence. Actors, it is said, throw themselves convincingly into a part but often cannot face their true selves. Du Coudray was a consummate shaper of reality into forms that served her better; a bold, restless, mischievous teller of truths and lies; a manipulator of her own self-presentation; a maker of her own myth. It was a perilous game, to survive and even excel out in the great world by her will and skill and unflagging inventiveness. But she was a player. One need only look at her portrait to see it.

Some have suggested that a biographer must give her subject what that subject wants, must treat her as she treated others.[22] Du Coudray took chances; she was impressed with her king and her responsibilities but not intimidated. Balancing safety and risk, she assessed situations and people, then tried to bend them to suit her. I have attempted here to do something of the same—to not be too energetically her champion, to respect her ways but assert my needs also. She took herself and her work very seriously, but we see always her sustaining wit. I fancy she would have wanted my account of her great mission to be somewhat adventurous and embrace her joie de vivre—getting things basically straight, of course, but taking some gambles too.

Abbreviations

AD Archives Départementales
A   Ain (Bourg-en-Bresse)
AIS   Aisne (Laon)
AR   Ardèche (Privas)
AU   Aube (Troyes)
BP   Basses-Pyrenées (Pau)
C   Cher (Bourges)
CA   Cantal (Aurillac)
CAL   Calvados (Caen)
CM   Charente-Maritime (La Rochelle)
CO   Côte d'Or (Dijon)
D   Doubs (Bescançon)
DOR   Dordogne (Périgueux)
DR   Drôme (Valence)
G   Gironde (Bordeaux)
HG   Haute-Garonne (Toulouse)
HM   Haute-Marne (Chaumont)
I   Isère (Grenoble)
IL   Indre-et-Loire (Tours)
IV   Ille-et-Vilaine (Rennes)
L   Loiret (Orléans)
LO   Lot (Cahors)
M   Marne (Châlons-sur-Marne)
ME   Meuse (Bar-le-Duc)
MM   Meurthe-et-Moselle (Nancy)
MO   Moselle (Metz)
N   Nord (Lille)
O   Orne (Alençon)
PD   Puy-de-Dôme (Clermont-Ferrand)
R   Rhône (Lyon)
S   Somme (Amiens)

SEM   Seine-et-Marne (Melun)
SM   Seine-Maritime (Rouen)
TG   Tarn-et-Garonne (Montauban)
V   Vienne (Poitiers)
VE   Vendée (La Roche-sur-Yon)
VO   Vosges (Epinal)
AM   Académie Nationale de Médecine, Paris
AN   Archives Nationales, Paris
MC   Minutier Central (notarial records)
BN   Bibliothèque Nationale, manuscrits français, Paris
BR   Bibliothèque Royale, Brussels
EM   Ecole de Médecine

Notes

1. THE PORTRAIT: *PARIS, SUMMER 1985*

1. For interesting thoughts on portraiture, see Michael Fried, *Absorption and Theatricality: Painting and Beholder in the Age of Diderot* (Berkeley: University of California Press, 1980); Patricia Simons, "Women in Frames: The Gaze, the Eye, the Profile in Renaissance Portraiture," *History Workshop*, no. 25 (spring 1988): 4–31; and Harry Berger, "Fictions of the Pose: Facing the Gaze in Early Modern Portraiture," *Representations* 46 (spring 1994): 87–120.

2. Shelby T. McCloy, *Government Assistance in Eighteenth-Century France* (Durham, N.C.: Duke University Press, 1946), p. 173 (including n. 80).

3. See, for example, Jacques Gélis, "La Formation des accoucheurs et des sages-femmes aux 17e et 18e siècles: évolution d'un matériel et d'une pédagogie," *Archives de démographie historique*, 1977, pp. 154–180.

4. Bernard This, *La Requête des enfants à naître* (Paris: Seuil, 1982), p. 94.

5. In 1988, three years after I embarked on my project, Jacques Gélis's *La Sage-femme ou le médecin. Une nouvelle conception de la vie* (Paris: Fayard, 1988) appeared, in which there is a rather good chapter on Mme du Coudray and a fairly accurate map of the sort I put together myself. Gélis, too, it seems, had corresponded with some provincial archives. Had this work been available sooner it might have saved me some time, but then there was a certain thrill in charting it all out myself and watching the picture of the great midwife's route emerge.

2. BIOGRAPHY AS HISTORY AND MYSTERY: *LOS ANGELES AND FRANCE, 1986–1996*

1. A. Delacoux, *Biographie des sages-femmes célèbres anciennes, modernes et contemporaines* (Paris: Trinquart, 1834), p. 30.

2. See Joyce Appleby, Lynn Hunt, and Margaret Jacob, *Telling the Truth About History* (New York: W. W. Norton, 1994).

3. Hayden White, *Tropics of Discourse: Essays in Cultural Criticism* (Baltimore: Johns Hopkins University Press, 1978), p. 98. One might look also at discussions about and experiments with the history/fiction borderline in the works of Natalie Davis, Susan Sontag, Simon Schama, Susan Daitch, Eunice Lipton, Robert Rosenstone, Barbara Chase Riboud, and Phyllis Rose.

4. Keith Jenkins, *Rethinking History* (London: Routledge, 1991), p. 69.

5. See Marilyn Yalom, *Blood Sisters: The French Revolution in Women's Memory* (New York: Basic Books, 1993).

6. See Eric Homberger and John Charmley, eds., *The Troubled Face of Biography* (London: Macmillan, 1988), p. 54.

7. See Liz Stanley, *The Auto/Biographical I: The Theory and Practice of Feminist Autobiography* (Manchester: Manchester University Press, 1992); and Phyllis Rose, "Fact and Fiction in Biography," in her *Writing of Women: Essays in a Renaissance* (Middletown: Wesleyan University Press, 1985), esp. p. 68.

8. Norman Denzin, *Interpretive Biography* (Newbury Park, Calif.: Sage, 1989), pp. 70ff.

9. Mary Daly, *Websters' First New Intergalactic Wickedary of the English Language* (Boston: Beacon Press, 1987), pp. 77, 116, 126, 138.

10. Susan Groag Bell and Marilyn Yalom, eds., *Revealing Lives: Autobiography, Biography, and Gender* (Albany: State University of New York Press, 1990), p. 6.

11. For the difficulty of finding interior space in biographical subjects, see Leon Edel, *Writing Lives: Principia Biographica* (New York: W. W. Norton, 1984), pp. 16–19.

12. Carolyn G. Heilbrun, *Writing a Woman's Life* (New York: W. W. Norton, 1988), pp. 121, 81, 23. See also Sydonie Smith, *A Poetics of Women's Autobiography: Marginality and the Fictions of Self-Representation* (Bloomington: Indiana University Press, 1987), pp. 123–150.

13. See Mary Poovey, *Uneven Developments: The Ideological Work of Gender in Mid-Victorian England* (Chicago: University of Chicago Press, 1988); and Lois A. Monteiro, "On Separate Roads: Florence Nightingale and Elizabeth Blackwell," *Signs* 9 (spring 1984): 520–533.

14. Mary Catherine Bateson, *Composing a Life* (New York: Penguin/ Plume, 1990).

15. See Gloria G. Fromm, ed., *Essaying Biography: A Celebration for Leon Edel* (Honolulu: University of Hawaii Press, for the Biographical Research Center, 1986), pp. 59ff.; and Gail Parker Mandell, *Life into Art: Conversations with Seven Contemporary Biographers* (Fayetteville: University of Arkansas Press, 1991), pp. 115, 177–178.

16. Natalie Zemon Davis, *Fiction in the Archives: Pardon Tales and Their Tellers in Sixteenth-Century France* (Stanford: Stanford University Press, 1987), p. 3.

17. Quoted by Paul Delaunay, *L'Obstétrique dans la Maine aux 18e et 19e siècles* (Le Mans, 1911), pp. 20–21.

18. Adrienne Rich, *Of Woman Born: Motherhood as Experience and Institution* (New York: Bantam Books, 1977), pp. 252–257.

3. THE NATIONAL MIDWIFE'S MISSION STATEMENT:
CLERMONT, 1 AUGUST 1760

1. AD C C319, fol. 24.

2. AD PD C1401, fol. 4. See my "Books and the Birthing Business: The Midwife Manuals of Madame du Coudray," in *Going Public: Women and*

Publishing in Early Modern Europe, ed. Elizabeth Goldsmith and Dena Goodman (Ithaca: Cornell University Press, 1995), pp. 79–96.

3. See Gélis, "Formation des accoucheurs."

4. Janet Gurkin Altman, *Epistolarity: Approaches to a Form* (Columbus: Ohio State University Press, 1982).

5. See Carla Hesse, "Reading Signatures: Female Authorship and Revolutionary Law in France, 1750–1850," *Eighteenth-Century Studies* 22, no. 3 (spring 1989): 469–487.

6. Bateson, *Composing a Life*, pp. 28 (Mead quotation); and Monteiro, "On Separate Roads," pp. 530.

7. On Louise Bourgeois, see Wendy Perkins, "Midwives Versus Doctors: The Case of Louise Bourgeois," *Seventeenth Century* 3 (1988): 135–157; and idem, "The Relationship Between Midwife and Client in the Works of Louise Bourgeois," *Seventeenth-Century French Studies* 11 (1989): 28–45. See also Achille Chereau, *Esquisse historique sur Louise Bourgeois dite Boursier, sage-femme de la reine Marie de Médici* (Paris, 1852).

8. Camille Bloch, *L'Assistance et l'état en France à la veille de la Révolution* (Paris: A. Picard, 1908), p. 234; and James Boswell, *The Kindness of Strangers: The Abandonment of Children in Western Europe from Late Antiquity to the Renaissance* (New York: Pantheon Books, 1988), pp. 15–26.

9. See Angélique Marguerite Le Boursier du Coudray, *Abrégé de l'art des accouchements* (Châlons-sur-Marne: Bouchard, 1773), pp. 3–4.

10. Piarron de Chamousset, *Mémoire politique sur les enfans* (Paris: Lambert, 1757), pp. 5, 32–35.

11. On pseudonymity and role-playing, see Joan DeJean, "Lafayette's Ellipses: The Privileges of Anonymity," *PMLA* 99, no. 5 (Oct. 1984): 884–902.

4. HANGING HER SHINGLE: PARIS, 22 FEBRUARY 1740

1. AN Y10556, Régistre matricule des officiers . . . etc., 1731–1767, p. 76v.

2. Nicholas Toussaint Le Moyne Des Essarts, *Dictionnaire universel de police*, 7 vols. (Paris: chez Moutard, 1786–1790), 2:627–630. See also Alfred L. Franklin, *La Vie privée d'autrefois*, ser. I, vol. 14: *Variétés chirurgicales* (Paris: Plon, 1894), pp. 74–78.

3. AN Y10555, Dossiers de réceptions . . . , 1731–1790. Le Boursier's supplication is not among those preserved, but the format is constant.

4. *Encyclopédie, ou Dictionnaire raisonné des sciences, des arts et des métiers, par une société des gens de lettres. Mis en ordre et publié par M. Diderot: et quant à la partie mathématique, par M. D'Alembert*, 17 vols. (Paris: Briasson, David l'aîné, Le Breton & Durand, 1750–1780), 14:495–496: "Sage-femme."

5. See the many inscriptions of midwives in AN Y10556. A few, including Le Boursier's, are abbreviated, but that appears to be haste on the scribe's part rather than special exemption.

6. See Gustave Pessard, *Nouveau Dictionnaire historique de Paris* (Paris:

Eugène Rey, 1904), p. 501; and Jacques Hillairet, *Dictionnaire historique des rues de Paris* (Paris: Editions de Minuit, 1979), 1:459.

7. Delacoux, *Biographie des sages-femmes célèbres*, p. 30: "Bairsin."

8. Louis Sébastien Mercier, *Tableau de Paris*, 12 vols. (Amsterdam, 1782–1788), 5:32–35: "Sage-femme."

9. Ibid., 9:96–97: "Tavaïolle."

10. Ibid., 5:32–35.

11. Le Boursier du Coudray, *Abrégé*, p. 20.

12. Ibid., 30–32. See also Alan Williams, *The Police of Paris, 1718–1789* (Baton Rouge: Louisiana State University Press, 1979), p. 229.

13. Le Boursier du Coudray, *Abrégé*, pp. 28–29.

14. See the number of times midwives are consulted in Des Essarts's *Causes célèbres, curieuses et intéressantes de toutes les cours souveraines du royaume*, 98 vols. (Paris: P. G. Simon, 1773–1789).

15. Jean Verdier, *La Jurisprudence particulière de la chirurgie en France*, 2 vols. (Paris, 1764), 2:449.

16. Paul-Emile Le Maguet, *Le Monde médical parisien sous le Grand Roi, suivi du porte-feuille de Vallant, Médecin de S.A.R. Madame de Guise et de Madame la Marquise de Sablé* (Paris, 1899; repr. Geneva: Slatkine, 1971), pp. 304–305; and Gustave J. Witkowski, *Accoucheurs et sages- femmes célèbres* (Paris: G. Steinheil, 1891), p. 38.

17. BN ms. Joly de Fleury 220, fols. 2–8.

18. Albert Isnard and S. Honoré, *B.N. Catalogue général—Actes Royaux* (Paris, 1938), 3:354.

19. BN ms. fr. 21737, fols. 255, 275, 277, 287, 292–295.

20. Des Essarts, *Dictionnaire*, 1:39–45: "Accouchements."

5. A BIRTH: *PARIS, JANUARY 1744*

1. The birth described in this chapter is based entirely on principles from Mme du Coudray's *Abrégé*, a composite of different cases she discusses. I have used here, and throughout my book unless otherwise noted, the 1773 edition of her text. For prenatal treatment, see Jacques Gélis's *History of Childbirth: Fertility, Pregnancy, and Birth in Early Modern Europe*, trans. Rosemary Morris. (Boston: Northeastern University Press, 1991), pp. 70, 79ff.

2. Le Boursier du Coudray, *Abrégé* (1773), 102.

3. Ibid., p. 37.

4. Ibid., pp. 47–48.

5. Ibid., pp. 34–35, 41–42.

6. Ibid., p. 36.

7. Ibid., p. 56.

8. Ibid., p. 36.

9. Ibid., pp. 55–56, 81.

10. Ibid., p. 64.

11. Ibid., p. 51.

12. Ibid., pp. 55–58.

13. Ibid., p. 59.
14. Ibid., pp. 109–110.
15. Ibid., pp. 105–106.
16. Ibid., pp. 65–72.
17. Ibid., pp. 44–46.
18. Ibid., p. 76.
19. Ibid., pp. 134–136.
20. Isabelle Vissière, *Procès de femmes au temps des philosophes* (Paris: Des Femmes, 1985), p. 392n.104.
21. Le Boursier du Coudray, *Abrégé*, pp. 76–77.
22. Ibid., chaps. 1 and 38.
23. Ibid., pp. 80–84.
24. Ibid., pp. 85–87.
25. Ibid., pp. 131–134.
26. Ibid., pp. 137–138.

6. THE PETITION: *PARIS, 17 MAY 1745*

1. This description of the capital's rhythms is based on Louis Sébastien Mercier, *Tableau de Paris*, ed. Gustave Desnoiresterres (Paris: Pagnerre, 1853), pp. 206–213 ("Les Heures du jour"). See also Pierre Gaxotte, *Paris au 18e siècle* (Paris: Arthaud, 1982), pp. 77–104; Patrick Süskind, *Perfume* (New York: Washington Square Press, 1991); and David Garrioch, *Neighborhood and Community in Paris, 1740–1790* (Cambridge: Cambridge University Press, 1986).
2. AN MC XV 640 (29 June 1745); for the petition's full text and context, see EM, Commentaires de la Faculté XX, pp. 953–974. All quotations in this chapter are from these pages. See also Jacques Hazon, *Eloge historique de la Faculté de médecine de Paris* (Paris, 1773).
3. See AN Y10556, showing her formal reception to the office of midwife on 22 February 1740. Her apprenticeship began in 1736, according to Delacoux.
4. *Encyclopédie* 14:495–496: "Sage-femme"; also 1:81–85: "Accouchement."
5. Verdier, *Jurisprudence particulière de la chirurgie*, 2:484.
6. Franklin, *La Vie privée*, ser. 1, vol. 14, *Variétés chirurgicales*, pp. 57–121.
7. This is the approximate figure given in most contemporary sources.
8. For more on Verdier and Morand, see Toby Gelfand, *Professionalizing Modern Medicine: Paris Surgeons and Medical Science and Institutions in the Eighteenth Century* (Westport, Conn.: Greenwood Press, 1980), pp. 47–48, 63.
9. EM, Commentaires, pp. 953–974. See also Hillairet, *Dictionnaire historique*, 1:556–559.
10. See Gelfand, *Professionalizing Modern Medicine*, passim.
11. Edmond Jean François Barbier, *Journal historique et anecdotique du règne de Louis XV*, ed. A. de la Villegille, 4 vols. (Paris, 1847–1856), 2:365–366 (May 1743).
12. On the Hôtel Dieu, see Marcel Fosseyeux, *L'Hôtel Dieu de Paris aux*

17e et 18e siècles (Paris: Berger-Levrault, 1912); and Paul Delaunay, *La Maternité de Paris* (Paris: J. Rousset, 1909).

13. EM, Commentaires, pp. 960–965.

14. I am indebted for some of these insights to Mary Lindemann and Monica Green.

15. *Etat de médecine, chirurgie et pharmacie en Europe pour l'année 1776* (Paris: Didot, 1776), p. 127.

7. APPRENTICES AND ASSOCIATES:
PARIS, 22 JANUARY 1751

1. See *Etat de médecine, chururgie et pharmacie en Europe pour l'année 1777* (Paris: Thiboust, 1777), p. 172, which lists midwives by dates of reception and shows the many-year gap from April 1743 to June 1749.

2. AN MC LXXV 617 (22 January 1751); the original contract with Heuzé is LXXV 615 (30 September 1750). It was not uncommon for apprentices to switch teachers midstream; see, for example, LXXVII 235 (30 January 1751), LXV 311 (8 May 1751), and XI 576 (2 November 1751). Most of the comparative data for this chapter has been drawn from apprenticeship contracts filed during the same year, 1751.

3. AN MC LXXV 617 (28 January 1751). Heuzé's new apprentice is one Barbe Mangin. Could she have been related to Le Boursier's teacher, Anne Bairsin, *dame* Philibert Mangin? If so, why didn't she sign up with du Coudray?

4. AN MC X 497 (10 September 1751).

5. AN MC XXXV 668 (4 October 1751).

6. AN MC LXV 311 (8 May 1751). Others, like XCIII 24 (1 December 1751), say "conforme aux bonnes mœurs."

7. AN MC CI 446 (4 May 1751).

8. AN MC LXXVII 237 (27 July 1751).

9. AN MC LXXXV 529 (1 September 1751).

10. More will be said below regarding the special eagerness of the intendant of Châlons to make progress in this area.

11. AN MC CXII 705A (20 July 1751).

12. AN MC CXVII 785 (7 June 1751).

13. AN MC LXXXIX 537 (13 November 1751).

14. AN MC LXV 311 (24 May 1751).

15. AN MC LXVI 488 (19 July 1751). See also XXXVIII 391 (15 October 1751).

16. Des Essarts, *Causes célèbres n. LXXVII*, discussed in Vissière, *Procès de femmes*, pp. 93–104.

17. AN MC LXI 450 (22 May 1751).

18. See, for example, AN MC XLIV 397 (30 June 1751), XCIII 24 (1 December 1751), LX 301 (18 February 1751), X 497 (10 September 1751), LXII 425 (30 August 1751), LIII 332 (27 May 1751), LXXVI 332 (10 October 1751), and LXV 311 (8 May 1751).

19. AN MC XCIII 23 (15 September 1751).

20. See Jacques-Louis Ménétra, *Journal of My Life*, with an introduction and commentary by Daniel Roche, foreword by Robert Darnton, trans. Arthur Goldhammer (New York: Columbia University Press, 1986), pp. 174–177 and passim, for examples of women running the financial affairs of the household.

21. AN MC XIII 293 (18 November 1751).

22. AN MC LXII 426 (17 November 1751).

23. AN MC LIV 848 (20 January 1751).

24. AN MC XLVI 329 (11 October 1751).

25. AN MC LXXVI 332 (20 December 1751). On death inventories, see Annik Pardailhé- Galabrun, *La Naissance de l'intime. 3000 foyers parisiens aux 17e et 18e siècles* (Paris: PUF, 1988), chap. 1. For those of surgeons in particular, see Marie-Andrée Thomachot, "Chirurgie et chirurgiens parisiens au 18e siècle" (*thèse du 3e cycle*, University of Paris IV [Sorbonne], 1982), pp. 159–163, 171.

26. *Etat de médecine . . . 1776*, pp. 126–138, provides a list of midwives, only two of whom are in the St. Avoie quarter. See also Jaillot, *Liste des rues*, "Tableau des XX quartiers" (Paris: Lottin, 1775); and Hurtaut and Magny, *Dictionnaire historique de la ville de Paris*, 4 vols. (Paris, 1779), esp. 4:193.

27. See Jacques Hillairet, *Evocation du vieux Paris* (Paris: Editions de Minuit, 1954), 1:121–126.

28. For more on Bihéron, see P. Dorveaux, "Les Femmes médecins— Notes sur Madamoiselle Bihéron," *La Médecine anecdotique*, fasc. IV (1901): 165–171; fasc. V (1902); and the notice in T. F. La Croix, *Dictionnaire portatif des femmes célèbres* (Paris, 1788), vol. 1, suppl., pp. 763–765.

29. On Frère Côme, see A. Chevreau, *Un grand chirurgien au 18e siècle, Frère Côme* (Mesnil-sur-l'Estrée, 1912); BN ms. fr. 22141, fols. 74–82; and AM MS 86 (58), fol. 103. On his letter-writing network, see AN MC III 954 (19 March 1753).

30. Frère Côme's early support for the midwife is documented repeatedly. See, for example, Le Nain's *Mémoire sur les cours publics d'accouchements faits à Moulins, par Mme Du Coudray* (n.p., n.d.), p. 3; and the minister Ormesson's letter of 22 March 1768 (AD CAL C981) in which he says it is "Frère Côme who made the talents of la dame du Coudray known to the Controller General and the other ministers, who obtained for her through his solicitations the *brevet* . . . and who directs her travels."

31. BN ms. Joly de Fleury 1215, fols. 27–33, 75–112.

32. Ibid., fols. 56–63, 237–247.

33. Fosseyeux, *L'Hôtel Dieu*, pp. 286–295. See also his "Sages-femmes et nourrices à Paris au 18e siècle," *Revue de Paris*, 1921.

34. Le Maguet, *Monde médical*, p. 297.

35. Des Essarts, *Dictionnaire*, 2:627–630; and Franklin, *La Vie privée*, ser. 1, vol. 14, *Variétés chirurgicales*, pp. 74–78.

36. BN ms. Joly de Fleury 1215, fols. 65–67, 69–71.

37. See *Lettre d'un citoyen amateur du bien public, à M***, pour servir de*

défense à la mission de la dame du Coudray, qui forme des sages-femmes par tout le royaume, de la part du roi, attaquée dans un écrit public, etc. (Paris: Debure, 1777), pp. 1–2, for more on the recruitment of Le Boursier to Thiers-en-Auvergne.

8. BREAK TO THE PROVINCES:
THIERS-EN-AUVERGNE, 1 OCTOBER 1751

1. AD PD C1399, fol. 6.
2. Claude Marin Saugrain, *Nouveau Voyage en France, géographique, historique et curieux* (Paris: Morin, 1778), pp. 279–282. See also Louis Dutens, *Itinéraire des routes les plus fréquentées, ou Journal d'un voyage* (Paris: Pissot, 1777); and Henri Cavaillès, *La Route française—son histoire, sa fonction* (Paris: Armand Colin, 1946).
3. AN MC LXXV 617 (22 January 1751), addendum, pp. 2–3.
4. *État de médicine . . . 1777*, p. 176, shows Fourcy-Amy "reçue 22 décembre 1753."
5. Theodore Besterman, ed., *Voltaire's Correspondence*, 135 vols. (Geneva: Institute et Musée Voltaire, 1953–1977), letters D7420 and D7516.
6. AD PD C1398, fols. 3–25, 27–36; C1399, fol. 1.
7. AD PD C1399, fols. 6–9.
8. Ibid., fol. 7. For more on this region, see Brigitte Degiorgis-Fayet, "L'Art des accouchements en Auvergne, de Du Coudray à Nivet aux 18e et 19e siècles" (*thèse de médecine*, nº 138, Clermont-Ferrand, 1984); and V. Nivet, *Note historique sur Mme du Coudray, maitresse sage-femme à Clermont Ferrand en 1756* (Clermont-Ferrand: Thibaud, 1879).
9. *Encyclopédie* 1:85.
10. Delacoux, *Biographie des sages-femmes*, p. 70.

9. "THE STORIES THEY TOLD ME":
CLERMONT, 9 MAY 1755

1. AD PD 3E113 dep Fonds 1.78, *Registre de baptêmes.*
2. See Olwen Hufton, *The Poor of Eighteenth-Century France* (Oxford: Oxford University Press, 1974); idem, "Women and the Family Economy in Eighteenth-Century France," *French Historical Studies* 9, no. 1 (spring 1975): 1–22; and idem, "Women, Work, and Marriage in Eighteenth-Century France," in *Marriage and Society: Studies in the Social History of Marriage*, ed. R. B. Outhwaite (New York: St. Martin's Press, 1981), pp. 186–203.
3. Le Boursier du Coudray, *Abrégé*, "Avant-propos."
4. On such twice-told medical narratives, see Johanna Geyer-Kordesch, "Whose Enlightenment? Medicine, Witchcraft, Melancholia, and Pathology," *Clio Medica* 29 (1995): 113–127.

10. THE "MACHINE": PARIS, 13 MAY 1756

1. Le Boursier du Coudray, *Abrégé*, "Avant propos," pp. v–viii.
2. *Lettre d'un citoyen*, p. 2.

3. See, for example, the explication of machine numbers in La Rochelle, AD CM liasse D 10, fol. 45, p. 3.

4. *Lettre d'un citoyen*, p. 2.

5. Jacques Gélis, Mireille Laget, and Marie-France Morel, eds., *Entrer dans la vie. Naissance et enfance dans la France traditionelle* (Paris: Gallimard, 1978), pp. 213–214.

6. Le Boursier du Coudray, *Abrégé*, "Extrait des registres de l'Academie de chirurgie du 13 mai 1756."

7. See, for example, AD PD C1400, fols. 2 (2 June 1756) and 3 (12 August 1756).

8. Le Boursier du Coudray, *Abrégé*, "A Monseigneur Bernard de Ballainvillier."

9. See, for example, the *Encyclopédie* article "Pitié" (12:662–663) for a contemporary discussion of this concept.

10. See Otto Mayr, *Authority, Liberty, and Automatic Machinery in Early Modern Europe* (Baltimore: Johns Hopkins University Press, 1986).

11. EARLY LESSONS: *CLERMONT, JULY 1757*

1. The *Abrégé*, which first gets approved for publication in July 1757, is a collection of the lessons du Coudray has been giving since arriving in Auvergne, assembled in order. There are thirty-eight chapters, each presumably corresponding to a day-long class session. See "Avant-propos," p. vi, for her description of the subdelegate's assessment.

2. Le Boursier du Coudray, *Abrégé*, p. 1.

3. Ibid., p. 2.

4. Ibid., p. 3.

5. Ibid., p. 4.

6. Ibid.

7. Ibid., p. 5.

8. Ibid., p. 18.

9. Ibid., p. 22.

10. Ibid., p. 23.

11. Ibid., p. 29

12. Ibid., pp. 60–61.

13. See Jacques Gélis, *History of Childbirth*, pp. 284–288. The respected authors of the last few centuries—Riolan, Guy Patin, Mauriceau, Mauquette de la Motte, Deleurye, Baudelocque—all endorsed bleeding. Interestingly, Louise Bourgeois did not.

14. Le Boursier du Coudray, *Abrégé*, pp. 37–38.

15. Ibid., p. 51.

16. Ibid., p. 48.

17. Ibid., pp. 62–72.

18. Ibid., p. 58.

19. Ibid., pp. 117–121.

20. Ibid., pp. 121–130.

21. Ibid., pp. 91–92.

22. Ibid., p. 136.

23. Ibid., p. 144.

24. Ibid., "Avant-propos," p. viii. Twice on this page du Coudray says she gave out these lessons to be read. Tim Pyatt, former rare books curator at the University of Maryland with whom I discussed the earliest (1759) edition of the *Abrégé*, believes from its strange collation formula and gatherings that du Coudray was trying to utilize portions of earlier pressings, perhaps the installments she had distributed separately.

12. A FUTURE HERO:
CHAVANIAC, 7 SEPTEMBER 1757

1. Parish Register of S. Roch de Chavagnac, quoted in G. Dansaertle, *Le Vrai Visage de Lafayette* (Brussels: L'Avenir, n.d.), p. 19.

2. AN F^{16} 939, "Mémoire de la dame Coutanceau, sage-femme" (undated).

13. TEXTBOOK AS PATRIOTISM:
CLERMONT, JANUARY 1759

1. Ménétra, *Journal*, p. 361n.20, states that as late as 1785 only 7 percent of peasants rounded up by police in Paris could sign, so the figures for earlier in the century would have been still lower.

2. For the political background in this period, see John Lough, *Introduction to Eighteenth-Century France* (London: Longmans, 1961), pp. 159–231.

3. AD PD C1400, fol. 4 (26 July 1757).

4. Ibid., fols. 5 and 6 (27 August and 3 September 1757).

5. Both approbations can be found bound in the back of the *Abrégé*.

6. AD PD C1400, fols. 12, 15, 17.

7. AD C C319, fol. 24. See my "Books and the Birthing Business."

8. AD PD C1401, fols. 4 and 6 (4 and 26 June 1760).

9. Le Boursier du Coudray, *Abrégé*, "A Monseigneur Bernard de Ballainvilliers." Here as elsewhere my page numbers are to the 1773 octavo edition of the *Abrégé*. Many of the pages in this edition were added after that of 1759 (12°), and those of course play no part in this discussion, coming up later only as chronologically appropriate.

10. Ibid., "Avant-propos," p. viii.

11. Ibid., p. v. The *Encyclopédie* article "Compassion" (3:760–761) explains the special eighteenth-century meaning of the word: "a feeling one experiences at the sight, recitation, or memory of the misfortune of someone. It is a sentiment one yields oneself up to with a kind of pleasure. . . . The pleasure one gets from it comes as well from the witnessing of one's own humanity. . . . Not only does one never run from this sentiment, one even seeks out situations that excite it."

12. Le Boursier du Coudray, *Abrégé*, p. 79.

13. Ibid., p. v.

14. Ibid., p. viii.

15. Ibid., pp. ix, x.

16. Ibid., pp. 3, 144. Du Coudray, raised and educated in the capital, seems to betray disdain for such "little places."

17. Disparaging remarks about incompetent village matrons abound. See, for example, pp. 5, 86, 126, 139. Here and there a country surgeon is criticized too, as on pp. vi, 91–92.

18. She confesses to near mistakes on pp. 49 and 79 and praises men on pp. 65–72.

19. Ibid., p. 46.

20. Ibid., p. viii.

21. Ibid., pp. 89–90.

22. See Gélis, *Sage-femme*, pp. 157–160; and Mireille Laget, *Naissances*. *L'Accouchement avant l'âge de la clinique* (Paris: Editions du Seuil, 1982), pp. 213–219.

23. *Année Littéraire*, 1759, I, pp. 351–355.

24. *Mercure de France*, April 1759, p. 144.

25. Friedrich Melchior Grimm, et al., *Correspondance littéraire, philosophique et critique*, ed. Maurice Tourneux, 16 vols. (Paris, 1877–1882), vol. 4, April 1759, p. 99.

26. *Censeur hebdomadaire*, 1760, II, pp. 121–124.

27. *Annales typographiques*, 1761, I, pp. 516–518.

28. Le Boursier du Coudray, *Abrégé*, p. 63.

14. PROTEST FROM A VILLAGE MATRON: *PLAUZAT, 12 JUNE 1759*

1. AD PD C1400, fol. 17 (12 June 1759).

2. Ibid., fol. 12 (3 May 1759).

3. Ibid., fol. 18 (9 June 1759).

4. Ibid.

5. Ibid.

6. Mireille Laget, "Childbirth in Seventeenth- and Eighteenth-Century France: Obstetrical Practice and Collective Attitudes," in *Medicine and Society in France*, Selections from the *Annales* 6. ed. Robert Forster and Orest Ranum (Baltimore: Johns Hopkins University Press, 1980), pp. 137–176; and Edouard Brissaud, *Histoire des expressions populaires relatives à l'anatomie, à la physiologie et à la médecine* (Paris: G. Masson, 1892), pp. 313–324.

7. See Gélis, *History of Childbirth*, pp. 47, 48, 53, 70. Much of this chapter is based on Gélis's discussion of provincial ways of birthing, and on Laget, *Naissances*. It also draws on "country" practices du Coudray condemns in her *Abrégé*.

8. Gélis, *History of Childbirth*, pp. 90, 100, 145.

9. Ibid., p. 120.

10. Ibid., pp. 126–133.

11. Ibid., passim to p. 172.

12. See Marie-France Morel, "City and Country in Eighteenth-Century

Medical Discussions About Early Childhood," in Forster and Ranum, eds., *Medicine and Society*, pp. 48–65.

13. Gélis, *History of Childbirth*, p. 134.

14. See Brigitte Jordan, "Knowing by Doing: Lessons Traditional Midwives Taught Me" (Department of Anthropology, Michigan State University, Working Paper No. 169, April 1988).

15. AD PD C1400, fol. 15 (12 June 1759).

16. Ibid., fol. 17 (12 June 1759).

15. ROYAL BREVET: "SENT BY THE KING": *VERSAILLES, 19 OCTOBER 1759*

1. See, for example, the article in the *Encyclopédie* on "Population" (13: 88–103).

2. On France's populationist politics, see Michel Foucault, *The History of Sexuality*, vol. 1: *An Introduction*, trans. Robert Hurley (New York: Pantheon Books, 1978); and Frances May Feinerman, "Population and Prosperity: Messance and Expilly Challenge the Physiocrats, 1757–1770" (Ph.D. diss., University of Illinois, Chicago Circle, 1981).

3. The full text of the brevet is in *Lettre d'un citoyen*, pp. 5–6.

4. Approbation of 2 July 1757.

5. Approbation of 20 December 1758.

6. AD PD C1400, fols. 6–8.

7. Ibid., fol. 11.

8. Ibid., fol. 7.

9. Ibid., fols. 2, 3. See also various letters from and about surgeons in AD PD C1401.

10. AD PD, assorted letters on follow-up courses in C1402, 1403, 1404. See also AD CA, Archives communales de la ville d'Aurillac BB23.

16. TRAVELING FOR HIS MAJESTY: *MOULINS, NOVEMBER 1761*

1. Saugrain, *Nouveau Voyage*, pp. 114–116. See also Cavaillès, *La Route française*, p. 108.

2. AD PD C1405, fols. 3 and 4.

3. *Lettre d'un citoyen*, p. 13.

4. The following quotations are from [Le Nain], *Mémoire*, pp. 1–6.

5. *Journal Encyclopédique* 1760, II, iii, 34–48.

6. I have used the French translation of this work. See Elizabeth Nihell, *La Cause de l'humanité référée au tribunal du bon sens et de la raison, ou Traité sur les accouchements par les femmes* (Paris: Antoine Boudet, 1771), p. 148.

7. Quoted in Jean Towler and Joan Bramall, *Midwives in History and Society* (London: Croom Helm, 1986), p. 104.

8. Nihell, *Cause*, p. 7.

9. Ibid., pp. 43, 118.

10. Nihell, as quoted in Adrienne Rich, *Of Woman Born*, pp. 140–142.

11. AD IV C1326, fol. 2.

17. BOASTS, REBUFFS, AND BOUTIN:
CHALON-SUR-SAÔNE, 19 MARCH 1763

1. AD G C3302, fol. 4.
2. AD A Arch. bibl. D342; AD PD C1405, fol. 2.
3. Saugrain, *Nouveau Voyage*, p. 143.
4. AD CO C363.
5. AD CO E3383. See Dr. P. Baron, *Sages-femmes et maternité à Dijon* (Dijon, 1933).
6. AD G C3302, fol. 4. This note from the intendant is written directly on the letter in which Mme du Coudray invites herself.
7. AD G C3302, fol. 13.

18. TURGOT: *TULLE, 29 DECEMBER 1763*

1. John Lough, *France on the Eve of Revolution: British Travelers' Observations, 1763–1788* (Chicago: Dorsey Press, 1987), pp. 38, 46, 55, 66–67, 112.
2. Saugrain, *Nouveau Voyage*, pp. 272–273.
3. Gustave Schelle, ed., *Oeuvres de Turgot et documents le concernant avec biographie et notes*, 5 vols. (Paris: F. Alcan, 1913–1923), 2:322–324.
4. AD G C3302, fols. 5, 7.
5. Saugrain, *Nouveau Voyage*, pp. 274–275.
6. AD G C3302, fol. 9.
7. Ibid., fol. 8.
8. AD PD C1405, fol. 9.

19. "HER UNENDURABLE ARROGANCE":
ANGOULÊME, 30 JULY 1764

1. Quotations in this section are from AD G C3302, fol. 6.

20. THE THRIFTY LAVERDY:
FONTAINEBLEAU, 16 OCTOBER 1764

1. AD O C301. Most departmental archives have a copy of this letter/circular, which was distributed to every region.
2. AD IV C1326, fols. 3, 4.
3. On Laverdy's reforms for municipalities and the obstacles they encountered, see Maurice Bordes, *L'Administration provinciale et municipale en France au 18e siècle* (Paris: SEDES, 1972), pp. 254–345.
4. AD IV C1326, fol. 2.

21. SOUNDING HER MOOD:
BOURDEILLES, 12 DECEMBER 1764

1. See AD G C3302, fol. 6, where this strategy is mapped out for him by his Angoulême colleague.
2. Ibid., fol. 10.
3. *Lettre d'un citoyen*, p. 18.

22. DELIVERING "LIKE A COBBLER MAKES SHOES": *POITIERS, FEBRUARY 1765*

1. AD IV C1326, fol. 3.
2. M. Dutens, *Itinéraire des routes les plus frequentées, ou Journal d'un voyage* (Paris: Pissot, 1777), p. 23.
3. AD V C62.
4. Gélis, *Sage-femme*, pp. 162–163.
5. AD IV C1326, fol. 6.
6. *Affiches de Poitou*, n° 33, 1779, and n° 4, 1783. See also Pascal Herault, "La Formation des sages-femmes du haut Poitou à la fin du 18e siècle," in *Entrer dans la vie en Poitou* (Poitiers: Department of History, Université Inter-Ages, 1986), pp. 23–43.
7. AD V C622, "Auchier, Project sur les accouchements."
8. See *Lettre d'un citoyen*, p. 3.
9. AN F^{17} 2276, dossier 2, pièce 293.

23. SURGEONS OF THE KING'S NAVY: *ROCHEFORT-SUR-MER, 30 APRIL 1766*

1. Saugrain, *Nouveau Voyage*, 311.
2. Quotations of M. Saint Paul are from *Lettre d'un citoyen*, 11–14.
3. Dutens, *Itinéraire*, p. 25.
4. AD VE, Private communication with photocopy of Registre des délibations des Sables d'Olonne, 20 June and 24 October 1765; originals are not extant.
5. Saugrain, *Nouveau Voyage*, p. 314.
6. See John Rothney, ed. *The Brittany Affair and The Crisis of the Ancien Régime* (New York: Oxford University Press, 1969), esp. pp. 175–178.
7. Archives Communales de Rochefort, cartons 20(1), 679(1), 680(31), 710, and 732.
8. AD D liasse 1C598.
9. AD CM D10, fol. 87.
10. I am indebted to Bert Hansen for thoughtful comments on this subject.
11. Saugrain, *Nouveau Voyage*, pp. 314–316.
12. AN F^{17} 2276, dossier 2, pièce 350.
13. *Lettre d'un citoyen*, pp. 18–19.
14. AN F^{17} 2276, dossier 2, pièce 286.
15. AD CM D10, fols. 25, 38, 48.

24. BREVET NO. 2: THE ROYAL TREASURY: *COMPIÈGNE, 18 AUGUST 1767*

1. AN O1 111, fol. 226. Another copy of this is in AD G 5M552, and it is reprinted in *Lettre d'un citoyen*, pp. 6–7, and in the 1777 and 1785 editions of the *Abrégé*.
2. See, for example, AD IV C1326, fol. 7.

25. THE *BIEN(S) DE L'HUMANITÉ*:
MONTARGIS, 30 SEPTEMBER 1767

1. AD PD C1405, fols. 7 and 8.
2. AD L C871. This series was destroyed, but a thorough inventory remains that cites this reference.
3. *Annonces orléanais*, 1766, p. 173, and 1767, p. 14. See also AD C C319, fols. 18, 31.
4. AD C C319, fol. 26.
5. The following quotations are from AD C C319, fol. 27.
6. See my article "Delivering the Goods: Patriotism, Property, and the Midwife Mission of Mme du Coudray," in *Early Modern Conceptions of Property*, ed. John Brewer and Susan Staves (London: Routledge, 1995), pp. 467–480.

26. THE STUDENTS—"MES FEMMES":
BOURGES, ALL SAINTS' DAY 1767

1. The following outline of peasant life comes in large part from Bonnie S. Anderson and Judith P. Zinsser, *A History of Their Own: Women in Europe from Prehistory to the Present* (New York: Harper & Row, 1988), 1:87–181, "Women of the Fields." There are also repeated references to the farm duties and work obligations of her students throughout du Coudray's letters.
2. AD C C319, fol. 26.

27. "A FURIOUS DISGUST":
BOURGES, 9 FEBRUARY 1768

1. AD C C319, fols. 28, 29.
2. Ibid., fol. 43, and unnumbered letter from Laverdy at Versailles dated 16 December 1767.
3. This and the following discussion draw on Cissie Fairchilds, *Domestic Enemies: Servants and Their Masters in Old Regime France* (Baltimore: Johns Hopkins University Press, 1984); and Sarah C. Maza, *Servants and Masters in Eighteenth-Century France: The Uses of Loyalty* (Princeton: Princeton University Press, 1983).
4. E. P. Thompson, "Patrician Society, Plebeian Culture," *Journal of Social History* 7, no. 4 (summer 1974): 382–405.
5. See Smith, *Poetics of Women's Biography*, p. 148.
6. Maza, *Servants and Masters*, p. 56.
7. See section 32 below.
8. AD C C319, fol. 58.
9. Ibid., fol. 60.
10. AD CAL C981, letter dated 20 March 1768.
11. Ibid.
12. A copy of this is in the *estampes* department of the Bibliotheque Nationale. It reads:

> Savante Du Coudray tu te couvres de gloire
> Ton âme et ton génie t'ouvrent les plus beaux champs
> Le héros destructeur, prodigue de son sang
> Vient à travers les morts au temple de Mémoire
> Ton art conservateur t'y place au premier rang.

13. For Robert's letter, see *Mercure de France*, April 1756, I, pp. 209–213. Robert was professor at the Ecole de Dessin de Reims from 1752 to 1762 (Archives municipales de Reims—private communication from E. T. Lemaire). Le Blon's priority disputes can be found in BN ms. fr. 22136, fols. 3–64. His death inventory tells still more about his associates; see AN MC LIII 298 (31 May 1741). For general discussions of color engraving, see Emmanuel Benezit, *Dictionnaire . . . des peintres, sculpteurs, dessinateurs et graveurs*, 8 vols. (Paris: Gründ, 1948–1955); Antoine Gautier de Montdorge, *L'Art d'imprimer les tableaux traité d'après les écrits, les opérations et les instructions verbales de J. C. Le Blon* (Paris, 1756); André Hahn et al., *Histoire de la médecine et du livre médical* (Paris: Oliver Perrin, 1962); Peter Krivatsky, "Le Blon's Anatomical Color Engravings," *Journal of the History of Medicine and Allied Sciences* 23, no. 2 (1968): 153–158; and George Wildenstein, "Jakob Christoffel Le Blon, ou Le Secret de peindre en gravant," *Gazette des beaux arts* 56 (1960): 91–100.

14. AD CAL C981, letter dated 20 March 1768.

15. Le Boursier du Coudray, *Abrégé*, "Avant-propos," p. ix.

16. AD C C319, fol. 188.

17. Ibid., fols. 96, 97, and 160.

28. PRIZE PUPIL: *ISSOUDUN, 2 AUGUST 1768*

1. See, for example, AD G C3302, fol. 27.

2. AD C C319, fol. 299.

3. Ibid.

4. AD CAL C981, letter from Frère Côme dated 20 March 1768.

5. The new privilege, an extension of the one for the original edition, was issued 1 June 1768. The full text can be found in the back of the 1769 edition of the *Abrégé*.

6. AD C C319, fols. 288, 137.

7. For an interesting discussion of attention and lack of attention to hygiene, see George Vigarello, *Le Propre et le sale. L'Hygiène du corps depuis le Moyen Age* (Paris: Seuil, 1985).

8. AD C C319, fol. 292.

9. AD G C3302, fol. 27.

10. AD C C319, fol. 137.

29. NEW EDITION, STRONG WORDS: *PÉRIGUEUX, 4 SEPTEMBER 1769*

1. AD G C3302, fols. 20, 29, 30, 34.

2. AD DOR, Archives Communales de Périgueux, BB38.

3. AD G C3302, fol. 36.
4. See, for example, Le Boursier du Coudray, *Abrégé*, pp. 97, 124 and 125. The corresponding section in the edition of 1759 is quite different.
5. Ibid., p. 11.
6. Ibid., p. 12.
7. Ibid., p. 5.
8. Ibid., p. 6.
9. Ibid., p. 7
10. Ibid., p. 9.
11. Ibid., pp. 10–12.
12. Ibid., p. 13.
13. Ibid., pp. 9, 12, 13.

30. THE KINDNESS OF STRANGERS:
AGEN, 30 NOVEMBER 1769

1. Albert Babeau, *Les Voyageurs en France depuis la Renaissance jusqu'à la Révolution* (Geneva: Slatkine, 1970), p. 326.
2. AD G C529, fol. 3.
3. Ibid., fol. 8.
4. Ibid., fol. 11.
5. Ibid., fol. 2.
6. AD G C3302, fols. 32, 33.
7. *Lettre d'un citoyen*, pp. 8–9.
8. See section 32 below, note 6.
9. AD G C529, fol. 8.
10. Ibid., fols. 85, 86.

31. FRIENDSHIP AND FORTIFICATION:
BORDEAUX, SPRING 1770

1. Saugrain, *Nouveau Voyage*, pp. 220–224.
2. AD G C282, fol. 26.
3. On this student, Mlle Devaux, see Archives Municipales de Bordeaux, GG 1204. Ironically, she later gets displaced by du Coudray's niece and nephew.
4. See Ménétra, *Journal*, for stories of the *tour de France* of *campagnonage*.
5. Pierre Rousseau, *Histoire des transports* (Paris: Fayard, 1961), pp. 145–272; and Elison Hawks, *The Romance of Transport* (New York: Thomas Y. Crowell, 1931).
6. On the omnipresent poor, see Hufton, *The Poor of Eighteenth-Century France*, "Women and the Family Economy," and "Women, Work, and Marriage"; and Lough, *France on the Eve of Revolution*, p. 121.
7. *Gazette de France*, 1776, p. 466 (23 December).
8. See Smith, *Poetics of Women's Biography*, pp. 123–150.

32. THE SUITOR AND OTHER CALAMITIES:
AUCH, 19 DECEMBER 1770

1. AD G C3302, fols. 39–40.
2. M.-L. Bompeix, "Mission de Mme du Coudray, sage-femme royale en 1770: école d'accouchement d'Auch," *Bulletin de la Société archéologique du Gers* 13, no. 3 (1912): 262–271. See also AD G C3302, fol. 37.
3. AD G C3302, fol. 41, dated 18 July 1770.
4. Ibid., fols. 37, 38.
5. By 1775, when Guillaumanche married M. Coutanceau, both her parents were already deceased, but they might have died years earlier. In a later document, the baptismal record of Mme Coutanceau's son, du Coudray is referred to as a "maternal cousin" of the baby. It is difficult to know what to make of this.
6. J. Raulin, *Instructions succinctes sur les accouchements en faveur des sages-femmes des provinces, faites par ordre du ministre* (Paris: Vincent, 1770). Missa, the censor of the second edition, says on 2 June 1770 that the first edition sold out in four months: "It is none too soon to reprint this work for the good and the conservation of humanity." So the approval for the first edition was given while Mayon d'Invau was in power.
7. Raulin, *Instructions*, "Avertissement," p. vi.
8. *Dictionnaire raisonné universel des arts et métiers, contenant l'histoire, la description, la police des fabriques et manufacturers de France et des pays étrangers . . . par M. l'abbé Jaubert*, 5 vols. (Lyon, 1801), 4:34 ("Sages-femmes").
9. Raulin, *Instructions*, pp. vi, 16–33.

33. COUTANCEAU, "PROVOST" AND PARTNER:
MONTAUBAN, WINTER 1771

1. Saugrain, *Nouveau Voyage*, p. 267.
2. AD G C3302, fol. 37.
3. Ibid., fol. 46.
4. AD TG, Archives Communales de Montauban, 27GG1, letters of 21 December 1770 and 6 January 1771. Le sieur Barthélémy Coutanceau, his father, was surgeon of the prisoners in the Bordeaux Hôtel de Ville. See *Archives Communales de la Jurade*, 8 vols., 3:306–307.
5. Saugrain, *Nouveau Voyage*, pp. 269–271.
6. AD IV C1326, fol. 33.

34. "HAPPY AS A QUEEN":
GRENOBLE, 16 JUNE 1772

1. AD G C3302, fol. 49.
2. *Lettre d'un citoyen*, pp. 19–20.
3. For a full, though sometimes careless, discussion of midwifery in this region, see Jean-Serge Carles, "Initiation populaire à l'obstétrique à la fin du 18e siècle en France et surtout en Languedoc" (*thèse*, University of Toulouse, 1973).

4. AN H 1092, fols. 122, 123, 143, 147, 148. For good discussions of the difference between *pays d'états* and *pays d'élection*, see Alexis de Toqueville, *The Old Regime and the French Revolution* (New York: Doubleday/Anchor Books, 1955), pp. 212–221.

5. Saugrain, *Nouveau Voyage*, pp. 129–136.

6. Archives Municipales de Grenoble, GG carton 239. See also AD DR C1/34, printed "Avis de Grenoble."

7. See, for example, Archives Municipales de Crest, GG17, letter of 6 April 1772.

8. One of her students, Louise Dechaux, *veuve* Marrel, will still be practicing during the Revolution. See AD I L532.

9. AD G C3302, fol. 48. See also C. Courcy and A. Pecker, "Aperçus sur l'enseignement de l'obstétrique en France au 18e siècle: Angélique du Coudray à Grenoble," in *Verhandlungen des XX Internationalen Kongresses für Geschichte der Medizin, Berlin, 22–27 Aug. 1966* (Hildesheim, 1968), pp. 671–678.

10. Coutanceau will brandish this letter later when he needs to impress the officials of Le Mans, and then Bordeaux, with his credentials. See, for example, AD IL C355, letter dated 18 December 1777.

35. NETWORKS, NEWSPAPERS, AND NAME GAMES:
BESANÇON, 16 NOVEMBER 1772

1. Saugrain, *Nouveau Voyage*, pp. 206–211, 214–215.

2. AD D 1C598, letter dated Grenoble, 24 July 1772.

3. Ibid., letter dated Grenoble, 18 May 1772.

4. AD R 1C21.

5. AD D 1C598, letter dated 20 June 1772.

6. Ibid., letter dated 24 July 1772.

7. AD D 1C599, fol. 3.

8. AD D 1C598, letter dated 20 December 1772.

9. See assorted letters in AD D 1C599, and Archives Communales de Baumes-les-Dames, BB35 and CC31.

10. AD D 1C598, letter dated 24 October 1772.

11. AD D 1C599, letter dated 28 August 1772.

12. Ibid., letter dated 21 September 1772.

13. *Lettre d'un citoyen*, p. 3.

14. *Affiches de Franche-Comté*, 23 October 1772. There is also a handwritten copy of this article in AD M C355, fol. 148.

15. *Affiches de Franche-Comté*, 27 October 1772.

16. *Lettre d'un citoyen*, p. 17.

17. For some general discussion of midwifery in this region, see Philippe Clère, "Obstetrix et Medicus. Mésaventures, ombres et lumières d'un enseignement en Franche-Comté à la fin du 18e siècle" (*thèse*, University of Bescançon, 1983).

18. AD M C355, fol. 144.

36. FLIRTATION IN CHAMPAGNE:
CHÂLONS-SUR-MARNE, MARCH 1773

1. Saugrain, *Nouveau Voyage*, pp. 198–200.
2. AD M C355, fols. 138, 150.
3. Ibid., fol. 139.
4. Ibid., fol. 57.
5. Lough, *France on the Eve of Revolution*, p. 66.
6. AD M C356, unnumbered folio, in which du Coudray styles herself "sage-femme à Paris," perhaps for extra clout or to counter the tendency to mistake her for a local person.
7. AD M C355, fol. 143.
8. AD AU C1167. I thank the archivist in Troyes, Benoit Van Reeth, for his assistance in reconstructing this episode.
9. These *Affiches* articles are reprinted in AD M C356, fol. 1.
10. *Lettre d'un citoyen*, p. 14.
11. See especially AD M C355, fol. 140; C356, fols. 23–25, 77; C357 (all); and C358 (all).
12. *Lettre d'un citoyen*, p. 13.
13. See Pierre Morel and J.-M. Alasseur, "Mme le Boursier du Coudray et les prémices d'une éducation obstétricale populaire dans la généralité de Caen," in *La Femme en Normandie* (Caen: Archives départementales du Calvados, 1986), pp. 239–251.
14. See Amédée Lhote, *Histoire de l'imprimerie à Châlons-sur-Marne* (Nieuwkoop: B. De Graaf, 1969), pp. 96–97.
15. See Gélis, *Sage-femme*, pp. 157–159.

37. "I COST NOTHING":
VERDUN, 17 JUNE 1773

1. AD M C355, fol. 142.
2. Saugrain, *Nouveau Voyage*, pp. 196–198.
3. AD ME, Archives Communales de Verdun, BB35.
4. AD MO C858.
5. AD IV C1326, fol. 17.
6. These mannequins are being advertised widely in the press at this time. See, for example, *Avant Coureur*, 1773, no. 13, p. 197 (29 March). See also *Etat de médecine . . . 1776*, pp. 229–231. Mme Lenfant's daughter would later marry the renowned Paris obstetrician Baudelocque and fabricate all the mannequins for the Maternité.
7. Gélis, *Sage-femme*, p. 161.
8. Le Coré in Bescançon sympathizes with her and has been trying to get his refractory province to pay up so she can be on her way. See, for example, AD D 1C598, letter dated 19 February 1773.
9. See AD D 1C598, Terray's letter of 25 November 1772.
10. AD D 1C599, letter dated 28 August 1772.

38. SHE "PARTAKES OF THE PRODIGIOUS": *NEUFCHÂTEAU, FALL 1773*

1. Lough, *France on the Eve of Revolution*, pp. 64, 67.
2. AD IV C1326, fol. 17.
3. Ibid., fol. 20, letter of 18 July 1773 from Verdun.
4. AD MM C314, fols. 44–48.
5. AD VO 1C43, fol. 27.
6. AD VO 1C65.
7. AD MM C314, fol. 77.
8. *Lettre d'un citoyen*, pp. 13–14.
9. *Affiches, annonces et avis divers pour les trois évêchés et la Lorraine, ou Affiches de Metz*, 1773, p. 204 (11 December).
10. AD VO 1C43, fols. 56, 102.

39. ROMANCE IN THE ENTOURAGE: *NANCY, 27 FEBRUARY 1774*

1. Saugrain, *Nouveau Voyage*, p. 192, and author's observations.
2. AD VO 1C43, fols. 33, 34, 38.
3. Ibid., fols. 55.
4. See Charles Gabriel Didelot's *Instructions pour les sages-femmes, dédié à M. de la Galaisière, intendant de Lorraine et Barrois* (Nancy, [1770]), pp. xxix–xxxv.
5. AD VO 1C43, fols. 57, 60.
6. Ibid., fol. 41. For more background on this region, see François Hacquin, *L'Histoire de l'art des accouchements en Lorraine des temps anciens au 20e siècle* (n.p., n.d.); and P. Pillement, "L'Enseignement de l'obstétrique en Lorraine au 18e siècle," *Revue médicale de l'est*, 1902, pp. 1–9.
7. AD VO 1C43, fol. 58.

40. BREVET NO. 3: THE SUCCESSION: *VERSAILLES, 1 MARCH 1774*

1. AN O1 121, fol. 23. Another copy of this new brevet is in AD G 5M552.

41. "A REWARD SO JUSTLY DESERVED": *AMIENS, 15 APRIL 1774*

1. Saugrain, *Nouveau Voyage*, pp. 424–426; and Lough, *France on the Eve of Revolution*, p. 121.
2. AD S C2823, printed avis. See also AD SM C95, fol. 7.
3. AD VO 1C43, fol. 63.
4. AD M C355, fol. 145.
5. I would like to thank David Bien for pointing this out. See also *Archives Parlementaires 1787–1860*, ser 1, 13:303, "Avertissement."

6. Georges Meynier, "Un cours provincial d'accouchement au 18e siècle (generalité de Soissons)" (*thèse de médecine*, University of Paris, 1899), pp. 14–15.

7. BN ms. fr. 12305, letter from du Fot to Macquer dated Laon, 10 March 1773.

8. Meynier, "Cours provincial d'accouchement," pp. 30–31.

9. AD AIS C629, C630.

10. Augier du Fot, *Catéchisme sur l'art des accouchements pour les sages-femmes de la campagne fait par ordre et au dépens du gouvernement* (Soissons and Paris: Didot & Ruault, 1775), pp. vi, ix, xvi.

42. OVERTURES BEYOND THE BORDER: *LILLE, 24 DECEMBER 1774*

1. BR, Conseil Privé, Période Autrichienne, dossier 1224A.

2. Saugrain, *Nouveau Voyage*, pp. 415–419.

3. Vanhamme, "Documents concernant l'enseignement de l'obstétrique et le problème de la maternité aux Pays Bas autrichiens," *Bulletin de la Commission royale d'histoire* 108 (1943): 41–59. Documents have been reclassified, however, since this article appeared. See unnumbered documents in BR, dossier 1224A, dated from December 1774 to May 1775.

4. BR, dossier 1224A, with cover letter dated 27 December 1774. See also letters in dossier 1227.

5. Saugrain, *Nouveau Voyage*, pp. 395–398.

6. Lough, *France on the Eve of Revolution*, pp. 33–34.

43. A WEDDING ACROSS THE FLEMISH FRONTIER: *YPRES, 28 FEBRUARY 1775*

1. *Onderwys voor de leerlingen in de vroed-kunde ofte konst der kinder-bed-den, by vraegen ende antwoorden getrokken uyt de lessen der vermaerde vroed-vrauw Du Coudray, door F. D. Vandaele, vrymeester in de genées-konst* (Ypres: J.-F. Moerman, 1774). There is a copy of this rare text at the Wellcome Institute in London.

2. The privilege, in French, can be found printed in the back of the London copy.

3. AD N, C Flandre Wallone 1451*, 1457*, 1402*, and C Flandre Maritime 60* and 58*.

4. The Ypres archives were bombed by the Germans on 22 November 1914, so it is not possible to document the teaching stint here. The parish archives (Fonds Merghelynck, MS 43, vol. 7, p. 252) show the Guillauman-che/Coutanceau marriage on 28 February 1775 (personal communication).

5. AD N, Commune de Lille, Paroisse Ste. Catherine, *Mariage, 27* February 1775.

6. Jules Cordonnier-Van der Mursel, *Ephémérides yproises, ou Relation des événements qui se sont passés dans Ypres depuis les temps les plus reculés jusqu'à nos jours* (1833–1889), p. 431, "Ecole de Sages-Femmes" (personal commu-

nication). See also R.-A. Blondeau, "Vroedkundig onderwijs te Ieper in de 18e eeuw," in *Wevend aan het verleden Liber Americorum O. Mus.* (Veurne, 1992), pp. 39–50.

7. On marriage patterns and preferences, see Pierre Guillaume and Jean-Pierre Poussou, *Démographie historique* (Paris: Armand Colin, 1970), pp. 135–196, esp. 183–184.

8. AD N, Commune de Lille, Paroisse Ste. Catherine, *Mariage*, 27 February 1775.

9. *Lettre d'un citoyen*, pp. 14–15.

44. MINISTERIAL MUTINY? *CAEN, 2 JULY 1775*

1. Lough, *France on the Eve of Revolution*, pp. 41, 67; and Saugrain, *Nouveau Voyage*, pp. 371–373.

2. AD CAL C981, letter dated 31 January 1775, from Lille.

3. See the unnumbered folios of AD CAL C981. One of the students is a grandson of the great seventeenth-century surgeon Mauquest de la Motte, whom Mme du Coudray quotes liberally and admiringly in her *Abrégé*.

4. AD CAL C981.

5. AD CAL C983–990. Several surgeons, perhaps inspired by du Fot's success, deviate from du Coudray's method and write manuals of their own for their students. See especially C984 and C988.

6. AD CAL C981, letter of 8 September 1775; and C982. See also P. Morel and Alasseur, "Mme le Boursier du Coudray."

7. AD IV C1326, fol. 13.

8. *Lettre d'un citoyen*, pp. 15–16.

9. AD SM C95, fol. 37.

10. AD IV C1326, fol. 21. See Saugrain, *Nouveau Voyage*, pp. 350–351.

11. AD SM C95, fols. 1–4, 7, 8.

12. AD IV C1326, fol. 24. For more on midwifery in this region, see Jean-Marc Alasseur, "De la commère à la sage-femme, ou l'essor de l'enseignement obstétrical au 18e siècle en basse Normandie" (*thèse*, University of Caen, 1980).

45. A NEWBORN AND A WET NURSE: *RENNES, 8 JANUARY 1776*

1. AD VO 1C43, unnumbered folio near end of folder.

2. Archives municipales, Rennes, Paroisse St. Sauveur, *Naissances*.

3. AD IV C1326, fol. 22.

4. Saugrain, *Nouveau Voyage*, pp. 350–351.

5. Ibid, pp. 350–354.

6. AD IV C1326, fols. 1–3, 7.

7. Ibid., fols. 58, 59, 119.

8. AD IV C1327, p. 19.

9. AD IV 7J8 (Fonds Hardouin), p. 54.

10. AD IV C1327, fol. 47.

11. Ibid., fol. 92.

12. AD IV C1326, fols. 15, 14, 11, 29. See also A. Dupuy "Les Epidémies en Bretagne au 18e siècle," chap. 4: "Les Sages-femmes," *Annales de Bretagne* 3 (1887): 179–204, esp. pp. 198–200.

13. AD IV C1328, fol. 83.

14. AD IV 7J8 (Fonds Hardouin), pp. 58–66.

15. AD IV C1326, fol. 18.

16. *Gazette de France*, 1775, p. 346.

17. *Gazette de santé*, 1775, pp. 66–67.

18. AD IV C1326, fol. 27.

19. See Feinerman, "Population and Prosperity."

20. AN H613, "Cours d'accouchement—Bretagne."

21. Meynier, "Cours provincial d'accouchement," pp. 37, 81; and AD AIS C630, letter of 4 October 1775. See, for example, AD D 1C598, memo dated 8 July 1775, in which Ormesson explains to Besançon officials that Turgot is sending multiple copies of du Fot's book.

22. AN H613.

23. Henri Stofft, "Utilisation de la langue bretonne pour la formation professionelle des sages-femmes au 18e siècle," in *DALC HOMP SONJ! Revue historique bretonne*, no. 9 (1984): 11–17.

24. See, for example, C1326, fol. 28.

25. Le Boursier du Coudray, *Abrégé*, pp. 139–144.

26. Ibid., pp. 9–14, esp. 12. This is no exaggeration. Ménétra, in *Journal of My Life*, tells how careless wet nurses killed two children and blinded another.

27. Fairchilds, *Domestic Enemies*, pp. 193–200. See also Nancy Senior, "Aspects of Infant Feeding in Eighteenth-Century France," *Eighteenth-Century Studies* 16, no. 4 (summer 1983): 367–388.

28. This and the following quotations are from Le Boursier du Coudray, *Abrégé*, pp. 139–144.

29. Ibid., pp. 9–12.

46. "ATTEND, MONSIEUR, TO MY LITTLE INTERESTS": NANTES, SUMMER AND FALL 1776

1. Lough, *France on the Eve of Revolution*, pp. 96–97; and Saugrain, *Nouveau Voyage*, pp. 326–329.

2. AD IV C1326, fol. 30.

3. Archives municipales de Vannes, BB24, fol. 5r.

4. AD IV C1326, fol. 31. See also AN H613, "Cours d'accouchement—Bretagne."

5. AD IV C1326, fols. 31, 33.

6. Ibid., fols. 36 and 37; see also fol. 38 on the diminished payment.

7. Archives municipales de Nantes, BB104, fol. 115v, and GG 666. See also Dupuy, "Epidémies en Bretagne," p. 194.

8. AD IV C1326, fol. 34; and *Lettre d'un citoyen*, pp. 9–10, 20–21.

9. See Pierre Huard, *Biographies médicales et scientifiques, XVIIIe siècle* (Paris: Dacosta, 1972), p. 87*n*.7; and N.L.M. Des Essarts, *Les Siècles littéraires de la France*, 7 vols. (Paris, 1800), 2:154–155.

10. This case is No. CLXXV in Des Essarts's *Causes célèbres*, and is written up in Isabelle Vissière's *Procès de femmes*, pp. 287–304.

11. See, for example, Abbé A. Chevreau, "Un grand chirurgien au 18e siècle, Frère Côme," *France médicale*, 1912, p. 105.

47. THE ATTACK: *PARIS, 5 MARCH 1777*

1. AD IL C355, letter dated 5 March 1777, from Paris.

2. When Le Cat first attacked him, for example, he deposited his fan mail with a notary; see AN MC III 954 (19 March 1753).

3. Augier du Fot, *Catéchisme*, pp. vi–viii, ix, xiii, xvi, xx.

4. For examples of their mutual admiration, see *Gazette de santé*, 1775, pp. 2, 21, 99, 117, 128, 144, 147, 166. Gardanne also praises the clinics set up by Alphonse Le Roy and Jean Le Bas, two other du Coudray rivals; see ibid., pp. 19, 30, 76–77, 98, 123.

5. *Gazette salutaire*, no. 21 (1770): 4; and no. 29 (1770): 4.

6. Ibid., no. 3 (1774): 3; and no. 37 (1774).

7. Ibid., no. 18 (1770): 4.

8. Jean-Emmanuel Gilibert, *L'Anarchie médicale, ou La Médecine considerée comme nuisible à la société*, 3 vols. (Neufchâtel, 1772), pp. 242–252.

9. S.A.D. Tissot, *Avis au peuple*, 7th ed. (Lausanne, 1777), pp. 49–52.

10. William Buchan, *Médecine domestique, ou Traité complet des moyens de se conserver en santé* (Paris: Desprez, 1775), 1:97.

11. *Affiches, annonces et avis divers du Dauphiné*, 20 May 1774, p. 16.

12. AD IV C1326, fols. 13, 15.

13. M. Nicolas, *Le Cri de la nature en faveur des enfants nouveau-nés* (Grenoble, 1775), p. 40 and note, p. 28*n*.

14. Alphonse Le Roy, *Pratique des accouchements* (Paris: Le Clerc, 1776), pp. 173–174.

15. Ibid., pp. 211–212.

16. Alphonse Le Roy, *Essai sur l'histoire naturelle de la grossesse et de l'accouchement* (1787), p. viii. For interesting views on Le Roy, see This, *Requête*, pp. 86–87.

17. Madeleine Coulon-Arpin, *La Maternité et les sages-femmes de la préhistoire au XXe siècle*, 2 vols. (Paris: Dacosta, 1981), p. 148.

18. For the critical atmoshphere of this period and the increasingly radical use of *mémoires*, see my "Frondeur Journalism in the 1770s," *Eighteenth-Century Studies* 17, no. 4 (summer 1984): 493–514; and chapter 6 of my *Feminine and Opposition Journalism in Old Regime France: "Le Journal des Dames," 1759–1778* (Berkeley: University of California Press, 1987). See also Sarah Maza, *Private Lives and Public Affairs* (Berkeley: University of California Press, 1993).

19. See L.W.B. Brockliss, "Medical Reform, the Enlightenment, and Physician Power in Late-Eighteenth Century-France," *Clio Medica* 29 (1995): 64–112, esp. p. 72.

48. COUNTERATTACK: "IT IS THE KING WHO PAYS ME": *EVREUX, 27 OCTOBER 1777*

1. AD SM C98, fol. 106.The one remaining extant model is now in the Musée Flaubert, a museum of the history of medicine, in Rouen.

2. AD SM C95, fol. 116; see also C95, fol. 91, and C98, fol. 83. For a detailed description of a machine, see Gélis, "Formation des accoucheurs."

3. AD HM C33, p. 84.

4. AD SM C95, fol. 90.

5. AD SM C98, fol. 84.

6. AD SM C98, fol. 86. See also AD IL C355, letter of 9 November 1777.

7. AD SM C95, fol. 68.

8. Ibid., fol. 74.

9. AD SM C97, fol. 102.

10. AD SM C95, fols. 80, 81.

11. AD SM C97, fol. 100.

12. AD SM C95, fols. 61, 114.

13. AD SM C96.

14. AD SM C95.

15. AD SM C97, fol. 77.

16. AD SM C98, fol. 43. See also AD CAL C982, letter of 1 October 1777; and Archives municipales d'Evreux, BB11, fols. 36v (10 July 1777) and 46v (4 December 1777).

17. AD SM C95, fol. 104.

18. AD SM C98, fol. 83. Actually, 300 had been the original price, later reduced to 200 when large numbers began to be ordered.

19. AD IL C355, letter of 9 November 1777.

20. Ibid., letters of 13 August and 15 September 1777.

21. AD SM C95, fol. 95, letter of 5 December 1777, "Elle nous a quitté. . . ."

22. *Lettre d'un citoyen.* For full title, see above, section 15, note 3. All the following quotations are taken from this brochure.

23. See Pierre Roussel, *Système physique et morale de la femme, suivi du système morale et physique de l'homme*, 5th ed. (1775; repr. Paris: Caille & Ravier, 1809), pp. 193–194n.1; St. Ildefont, *Etat de médecine, 1776* (Paris: Didot, 1776), p. 127; Pierre Süe, *Essais historiques, littéraires et critiques sur l'art des accouchements*, 2 vols. (Paris, 1779), 2:419, 506–514. Süe (1:131, 2:493) attacks Le Roy for being absurdly boastful and ruthless in his treatment of others. See especially his discussion of du Coudray's counterattack: "Here once again is M. Alphonse Leroy who, having meddled in something he knew nothing about, is given the lie in a public writing. May it be, please God, the last, and may he henceforth have to blush only from his past faults without

incurring more and more the justifiable indignation that his multiple and renewed errors always bring down upon him" (2:514).

24. *Gazette de santé*, July 1777, pp. 117–122.

25. AD IL C355, letter of 27 October 1777, from Evreux.

49. COURTING THE NECKERS: PARIS, 31 DECEMBER 1777

1. See, for example, AD IL C355, letters of 13 August and 15 September 1777, where he uses it to sway the intendant of Tours.

2. Ibid., letter of 24 June 1777, from Versailles.

3. See the letters from Mme Necker to du Coudray in AD G 5M552. These will be discussed in section 54 below.

50. PANDEMONIUM: LE MANS, 11 JANUARY 1778

1. AD IL C355, letter of 11 January 1778.

2. Ibid., note on top of letter of 13 August 1777.

3. Ibid., letter of 27 October 1777.

4. Ibid., letters of 18 and 25 December 1777.

5. Ibid., letter of 23 November 1777.

6. Saugrain, *Nouveau Voyage*, pp. 341–342.

7. AD IL C355, letter of 14 October 1777.

8. Ibid., printed circular of 14 February 1778.

9. Ibid., letter of 5 February 1778.

51. THE NIECE'S REST CURE: FORGES-LES-EAUX, SPRING 1778

1. AD IL C355, letter of 25 April 1778; and C356, letter of 10 June 1778.

2. Babeau, *Voyageurs en France*, pp. 127–128.

3. AD IL C355, letters of 23 April and 7 May 1778; see also du Coudray's letter of 8 February 1778.

4. Ibid., letter of 8 February 1778; and C356, unnumbered folio.

5. Delaunay, *L'Obstétrique dans la Maine*, p. 33.

6. AD IL C355, letter of 8 February 1778.

7. Ibid., letter of 15 February 1778.

8. Ibid., letter of 7 March 1778.

9. Ibid., letter of 8 February 1778.

52. CLASS/MASS/VACATION: ANGERS, 1 JULY 1778

1. AD IL C356, letter of 1 July 1778.

2. Ibid., *mémoire* and letter of 1 July 1778.

3. Saugrain, *Nouveau Voyage*, pp. 329–333.

4. Delaunay, *L'Obstétrique dans la Maine*, p. 35.
5. AD IL C356, letters of 4 April and 10 June 1778.
6. AD C C320, fol. 53.
7. AD IL C356, letters of 19 and 27 June 1778.
8. Delaunay, *L'Obstétrique dans la Maine*, p. 35.
9. AD IL C356, letter of 7 July 1778.
10. AD IL C357, fol. 142. For more on this region, see Dr. Louis Dubreuil-Chambardel, *L'Enseignement des sages-femmes en Touraine* (Paris, 1911).

53. PROTECTING DU COUDRAY'S METHOD:
MARLY, 7 MAY 1779

1. AD G 5M552.

54. WOMEN AND COWS:
ALFORT NEAR CHARENTON, OCTOBER 1780

1. See A. Railliet and L. Moulé, *Histoire de l'Ecole d'Alfort* (Paris, 1908), pp. 280–281 and p. 58*n*.5.
2. Meynier, "Cours provincial d'accouchement," pp. 14–15.
3. Bloch, *Assistance et l'état*, p. 246.
4. Du Fot, *Catéchisme*, "Discours préliminaire," p. xv. See Hufton, *Poor of Eighteenth-Century France*, pp. 52–54.
5. Jocelyne Leymarie-Couturier, "Histoire de la fondation de l'école de sages-femmes à Bordeaux" (*thèse de médecine*, University of Bordeaux, 1987), p. 57.
6. *Almanac vétérinaire pour 1782–1790*, new ed. (Paris, 1792), pp. 32–33.
7. See my "Delivering the Goods."
8. Roland Barthes, in his discussion of the "poetics" of representations ("The Plates of the *Encyclopédie*," in *A Barthes Reader*, ed. Susan Sontag [New York: Hill & Wang, 1982], pp. 218–236, esp. 230–231), talks of how pictures reverberate far beyond their physical essence, how visual information is never innocent. As beholders we must be aware of the "sphere of infinite vibrations of meaning at the center of which is the visual object." (And of course, these resonances of a picture are all the more influential for a largely illiterate audience because the impact is not tempered by the written text.) See also Ludmilla Jordanova, "Gender, Generation, and Science: William Hunter's Obstetrical Atlas," in *William Hunter and the Eighteenth-Century Medical World*, ed. W. F. Bynum and Roy Porter (Cambridge: Cambridge University Press, 1985), pp. 385–412.
9. For provocative discussions of some of these themes, see John Berger, *Ways of Seeing* (New York: Penguin Books, 1972); Michelle Fine and Adrienne Asch, "Who Owns the Womb?" *Women's Review of Books* 2 (May 1985): 8–10; E. Ann Kaplan, "Is the Gaze Male?" in *Powers of Desire: The Politics of Sexuality*, ed. Ann Snitow et al. (New York: Monthly Review Press, 1983), pp. 309–327; E. F. Keller and C. R. Grontkowski, "The Mind's Eye," in *Discovering Reality: Feminist Perspectives on Epistemology, Metaphysics, Methodology, and Philosophy of Science*, ed. Sandra Harding and Merrill B. Hintikka

(Dordrecht: D. Reidel, 1983), pp. 207–224; and Rosalind Pollack Petchesky, "Fetal Images: The Power of Visual Culture in the Politics of Reproduction," in *Reproductive Technologies: Gender, Motherhood, and Medicine*, ed. Michelle Stanworth (Minneapolis: University of Minnesota Press,1987), pp. 57–80.

10. AD SEM, Registre de délibération de 1778–1780 de la municipalité de Meaux, 54EdtBB9, shows that du Coudray rented a house in that city.

11. AD G 5M552, letter of 18 March 1779.

12. Ibid., letter of 31 July 1780.

13. Ibid., letter of 3 October 1780.

14. Le Bas is discussed in the *Etat de médecine . . . 1776*, p. 269.

15. Jean Le Bas, *Précis de doctrine sur l'art d'accoucher* (1779), pp. x–xiii.

16. Ibid., pp. 165, 183. For his repeated insistence that *men* be called on for anything difficult or complicated, see pp. 44, 47, 52, 53, 129, 131, 136, 148, 151, 152, 181, 212, 220, 233–234.

17. See BN ms. fr. 22121, fol. 40.

55. "MY AGE AND MY INFIRMITIES": *BOURGES, 25 DECEMBER 1781*

1. AD C C320, fol. 189.

2. Des Essarts, *Siècles littéraires*, 2:154–155.

3. AD CAL C982, letter of 13 August 1780.

4. Ibid., letter of 18 August 1780.

5. Both letters are in *Archives historiques de la Gironde* 25 (1887): 438–439. They were written in September 1780, hers on the ninth, his with an unreadable date but clearly several days later in the same month. For mention of Duchesne, see AD G C3303, fol. 17.

6. AD G C3303, fol. 2.

7. Ibid., fol. 10.

8. Ibid., fols. 9, 10, 13, 15–18; and C2519, fol. 35. The official brevet referred to in these letters, which now included M. Coutanceau and is dated October 1781, is last.

9. AD G 5M552, letter of 3 October 1780.

10. AN H1092, fols. 122–133, 140–152.

11. AD CM D10, fols. 10, 27, 51, 55.

12. Ibid., fols. 25, 28, 57.

13. Ibid., fol. 58.

14. Ibid., fol. 29.

15. AD C C320, fol. 51.

16. Ibid., fol. 53.

17. Archives municipales de Châteauroux, BB5 (Délibérations), fol. 127, and BB6 (Délibérations), fol. 40. See also GG43, p. 493.

18. AD C C320, fols. 31, 14.

19. Ibid., fol. 34.

20. Ibid., fols. 14, 23.

21. Ibid., fols. 17, 104, 191.

22. Ibid., fol. 106.

56. FAMILY SEPARATION:
BELLEY, 30 DECEMBER 1782

1. AD C C320, fol. 196.
2. Archives municipales d'Auxerre, BB36 (Déliberations), 17 May 1782.
3. AD CO C363.
4. Jean-René Nicolas, *La Vie quotidienne en Savoie* (Paris: Hachette, 1979), p. 108.
5. AD AR C12, p. 145.
6. Icart, *Leçons pratiques sur l'article des accouchements destinées à l'instruction des sages-femmes de Languedoc* (Castre, 1784). There is more on this in AD LO C1272–1285. The infamous *Requête en plainte présentée à nosseigneurs des états de Languedoc par les enfants à naître contre les prétendues sages-femmes* (1783) has been (perhaps wrongly) attributed to Icart. For more, see This, *Requête*.
7. See Icart, *Requête en plainte*, in This, *Requête*, pp. 56–59, and discussion of Icart on pp. 64ff.
8. Saugrain, *Nouveau Voyage*, p. 142.
9. Archives municipales de Bordeaux, GG 1204. See also AD G C3304, fols. 2, 18, and Coutanceau's "Projet d'hospice pour les accouchements gratuits" (1782), AD G C3504, p. 21.
10. AD G C3304, fol. 16.
11. Ibid., fol. 24.
12. Ibid, fol. 20; and C3303, fols. 19, 20.

57. CUNNING AND CALONNE:
PARIS, 12 JULY 1785

1. AD G C3303, fol. 27.
2. Ibid., fol. 26.
3. Ibid., fols. 37, 52, 21, 22.
4. Ibid., fols. 28, 23–25; and C3304, fol. 39. See Marguerite Gillaumanche Coutanceau, *Eléments de l'art d'accoucher en faveur des sages-femmes de la généralité de Guienne par Mme Coutanceau, brevetée du roi en survivance pour enseigner l'art des accouchements dans tout le royaume* (Bordeaux: Michel Racle, 1784).
5. This and the following quotations are from Coutanceau, *Eléments*, "Avertissement."
6. This and the following quotations are from ibid., pp. 334–356, "Qualités nécessaires aux sages-femmes."
7. For interesting insights into female anger, see Heilbrun, *Writing a Woman's Life*; and Davis, *Fiction in the Archives*.
8. AD G C3303, fols. 28, 23, 24.
9. Ibid., fols. 30, 34, 35, 29.
10. Ibid., fol. 32.
11. Ibid., fol. 31.
12. Saugrain, *Nouveau Voyage*, pp. 242–243.

13. AD G 5M552, letter of 10 April 1785.

14. See, for example, ibid., letter of 30 April 1785.

15. Ibid., letter of 10 July 1785. Bouchard's identity is never clarified, nor is she ever mentioned elsewhere.

16. AD G C3303, fol. 92.

17. See Jacques Gélis, "L'Enquête de 1786 sur les sages-femmes du royaume," *Annales de démographie historique,* 1980, pp. 299–343.

58. RUMBLINGS AND DISCONTENT:
SARLAT, MARCH 1787

1. AD G C3303, fol. 101; and C2519, fol. 37.

2. AD G C3303, fol. 12.

3. See Archives de la Seine, DQ8 968.

4. AD G C3303, fol. 12; and C3304, fol. 75.

5. See, for example, AD G C3303, fol. 85.

6. Ibid., fol. 70.

7. Ibid., fol. 66.

8. See Timothy Tackett, *Priest and Parish in Eighteenth-Century France* (Princeton: Princeton University Press, 1977), pp. 225–268.

9. AD BP C1517.

10. Watin *fils, Le Provincial à Paris, ou Etat actuel de Paris—ouvrage indispensable à ceux qui veulent connaitre et parcourir Paris sans faire aucune question* (1787), vol. "Quartier du Louvre," p. 11.

11. Ibid., p. 99 and pt. 2, pp. 121–122.; vol. "Quartier Notre Dame," pp. 46, 51; vol. "Quartier St. Germain," pp. 22, 45. David scholars have taken his painting of Le Roy to indicate that he probably delivered David's own son in 1783 and was considered quite brilliant, if somewhat charlatanesque, by Parisian society. Le Roy was ruthless, however, and after this period of fame and prosperity he would spiral down into madness and in the end be assassinated by his domestic.

59. AS THE BASTILLE FALLS:
CASTILLONÈS, 14 JULY 1789

1. AD G C3304, fols. 63, 71.

2. AD G C2519, fol. 38.

3. See, for example, AD G C3302, fol. 52.

60. THE LAFAYETTE CONNECTION:
PARIS, FALL 1790

1. See, for example, AD G C4671, p. 34.

2. AN F^{16} 936, "Mémoire de la dame Coutenceau, sage-femme" (undated). All the following quotations are from this brochure.

3. AN F^{15} 1861, "Mémoire d'Alphonse Le Roy: Motifs et plans d'établissement dans l'hôpital de la Salpétrière d'un séminaire de médecine pour

l'enseignement des maladies des femmes, des accouchements, et de la conservation des enfants" (undated), pp. 4–6.

4. Ibid., p. 14.

5. See BN 8° Te101–8. My thanks to Suzanne Desan for bringing this to my attention.

6. Mme Coutanceau explains this in a later work, *Instructions théoriques et pratiques à l'usage des élèves de Mme Coutanceau, imprimé par l'ordre de l'Administration central du département de la Gironde d'après l'autorisation du ministre de l'Intérieur* (Bordeaux: A. Levieux, An VIII [1800]), "Avertissement," p. 1*n.*

7. I would like to thank Steven M. Beaudoin at Carneigie Mellon University for this analysis of the *cahiers.*

8. See Toby Gelfand, "Medical Professionals and Charlatans: The Comité de Salubrité *Enquête* of 1790–1791," *Histoire sociale/Social History* 11, no. 21 (May 1978): 62–97.

9. AN F^{17} 2276, dossier 2, pièces 274, 302.

10. Ibid., pièce 309.

11. Ibid., pièce 326.

12. Ibid., pièce 357, 301.

13. Ibid., pièce 314.

14. Gelfand, "Medical Professionals," p. 92. See also Matthew Ramsey, *Professional and Popular Medicine in France, 1770–1830: The Social World of Medical Practice* (Cambridge: Cambridge University Press, 1988), pp. 74ff. A law of 2 May 1791 established the liberty of professions, and a decree of 18 August 1792 suppressed all degree-granting faculties, colleges, and scholarly societies. See Gélis, *Sage-femme,* pp. 219ff.

61. WHAT TREASURY WILL PAY?
BORDEAUX, 1 JULY 1791

1. See Richard Munthe Brace, *Bordeaux and the Gironde, 1789–1794* (Ithaca: Cornell University Press, 1947); and Alan Forrest, *Society and Politics in Revolutionary Bordeaux* (Oxford: Oxford University Press, 1975).

2. AD G 3E13.275 (1 July 1791), "Procuration."

3. AN MC II 754 (23 August 1791).

4. *Procès verbaux et rapports du comité de mendicité de la constituente 1790–1791* (Paris: Imprimerie Nationale, 1911), p. 128 ("Séance du 4 septembre 1791, matin").

5. AN MC II 757 (10 February 1792).

6. AD G 3E13.277 (6 April 1793), "Révocation de procuration."

62. MME COUTANCEAU'S CLINIC:
BORDEAUX, 30 AUGUST 1793

1. See Gordon Wright, ed., *The French Revolution: Introductory Documents* (St. Lucia: University of Queensland Press, 1988), p. 182.

2. Maurice Cren, *Le Médecin de la Garde Coutanceau de l'Académiè de méde-*

cine (privately published), document no. 2. He enlists on 11 Brumaire An II (1 November 1793).

3. AD G 5M552, letter of 3 June 1818.

4. See, for example, *Almanac de commerce, d'arts et metiers pour la ville de Bordeaux pour l'année 1791*, pt. 2, pp. 62–63.

5. Archives Municipales de Bordeaux, Q10, "Extrait des registres des déliberations du Conseil général de la commune de Bordeaux du 13 juillet 1793, l'an 2 de la République une et indivisible." The Q series is called "Assistance." See D139 (Registre 1791) for how these lessons are referred to as the "Ecole de Mme Coutanceau." See D146 (9 Ventôse An III) for the way other cities ask the couple for advice. For a summary of these and more, see Ariste Ducaunnès-Duval, *Inventaire sommaire des Archives municipales de Bordeaux: période révolutionnaire 1789–An VIII*, 4 vols. (Bordeaux, 1896), 1:294, 322, 378, 401; 2:63, 259, 268, 319; 4:499, 504.

6. See, for example, AD G C3303, fols. 98 and 101, in his hand. Cf. C3302, fol. 52, in hers.

63. DU COUDRAY, CASUALTY OF THE TERROR: *BORDEAUX, 28 GERMINAL AN II (17 APRIL 1794)*

1. AD G 4E785. This is also listed in 4E768, the table for 1794, "Sud, décès."

2. François-George Pariset, *Bordeaux au 18e siècle* (Bordeaux: Fédération historique du Sud-Ouest, 1968), pp. 402–433.

3. Tustet, *Tableau des événements qui ont eu lieu à Bordeaux depuis la Révolution de 89 jusqu'à ce jour* (Prairial An II), p. 38; quoted in Roger Brouillard, *Des impositions extraordinaires sur le revenu pendant la Révolution (contributions patriotiques, emprunts forcés) et de leur application dans la commune de Bordeaux* (Bordeaux: Y. Cadoret, 1910), pp. 96–97.

4. For new and changing definitions of "incivisme," see the speeches made by deputies to the National Convention during this period.

5. Brouillard, *Des impositions extraordinaires*, p. 45.

6. Ibid., pp. 74–91.

7. Ducaunnès-Duval, *Inventaire*, 2:63.

8. Ibid., 4:499, 504.

9. Maurice Cren, "Coutanceau, le beau-frère de Dominique Larrey," *Médecine et armées* 15 (1987): 701–702.

10. See AD G 6 Fi 1830 for one such poster.

EPILOGUE: *PARIS AND LOS ANGELES, 1994–1996*

1. See, for example, Fernand Braudel, *The Identity of France*, vol. 2: *People and Production*, trans. Siân Reynolds (New York: Harper & Row, 1990), pp. 176–179, esp. 179.

2. Leymarie-Couturier, "Histoire de la fondation de l'école de sages-femmes de Bordeaux," p. 116.

3. See AD G 3E13.280 (21 July 1796) and 3E13.281 (26 July 1797). Also

see AN MC XVI 971 (20 February 1808). This is the wedding contract of Coutanceau's son, which refers to this family property.

4. See, for example, AD G 3E13.282 (13 Thermidor An VI).

5. AN MC XVI 971 (3 February 1808).

6. Cren, *Médecin de la Garde Coutanceau.* The letters from Larrey to his wife (years 1808–1809) are at the Val-de-Grâce Museum, carton 1302, dossier 2.

7. G.B.A. Coutanceau, *Notice sur les fièvres pernicieuses* (Paris: Crochard, 1809).

8. Cren, *Médecin de la Garde Coutanceau,* document no. 15.

9. A. Delacoux, *Biographie des sages-femmes,* p. 62 ("Coutanceau").

10. Bouthenot, "96 Planches sur les accouchements pour la nouvelle édition de l'ouvrage de Mme Coutanceau, 1821, Bordeaux." This manuscript is in the library of the Val-de-Grâce hospital, L1526.

11. AD G 5M550 and 5M552, "Procès Verbal," 5 August 1822.

12. Gabriel Pery, *Recherches historiques sur l'école d'accouchement, l'hospice de la maternité et la clinique d'accouchement de l'hôpital St. André de Bordeaux* (n.p., n.d.), pp. 19–20.

13. See, for example, AD G 6Fi 1830, poster.

14. Coutanceau, *Instructions théoriques et pratiques,* pp. 1–3.

15. The quotations here and in the next paragraph are from AD G 5M552, letter of 3 June 1818.

16. Ibid., "Procès Verbal."

17. Bouthenot, "96 Planches." These illustrations also include a scene of Mme Coutanceau handing out diplomas to her students.

18. In a debate on this subject, Lynn Hunt and Mona Ozouf have argued, in opposition to Carol Pateman, Dorinda Outram, and Joan Landes, that the Revolution *did* advance the cause of women.

19. See Yvonne Knibiehler and Catherine Fouquet, *Histoire des mères du Moyen Age à nos jours* (Paris: Montalba, 1977), pp. 154, 164.

20. Daly, *Websters' . . . Wickedary,* pp. 67, 87–88.

21. See, for example, Jonathan Spence's remarks in Mandell, *Life into Art,* pp. 149–150.

22. See the remarks of Elisabeth Young-Buel on Hannah Arendt in ibid., p. 195.

Bibliography

PRIMARY SOURCES

Manuscripts

Detailed citations of material in the archives listed below, upon which this book is largely based, can be found in the notes.

AD Archives Départementales: Ain (Bourg-en-Bresse); Aisne (Laon); Ardèche (Privas); Aube (Troyes); Basses-Pyrenées (Pau); Cantal (Aurillac); Calvados (Caen); Charente-Maritime (La Rochelle); Cher (Bourges); Côte d'Or (Dijon); Dordogne (Périgueux); Doubs (Besançon); Drôme (Valence); Gironde (Bordeaux); Haute-Garonne (Toulouse); Haute-Marne (Chaumont); Ille-et-Vilaine (Rennes); Indre-et-Loire (Tours); Isère (Grenoble); Loiret (Orléans); Lot (Cahors); Marne (Châlons-sur-Marne); Meurthe-et-Moselle (Nancy); Meuse (Bar-le-Duc); Moselle (Metz); Nord (Lille); Orne (Alençon); Puy-de-Dôme (Clermont-Ferrand); Rhône (Lyon); Seine-et-Marne (Melun); Seine-Maritime (Rouen); Somme (Amiens); Tarn-et-Garonne (Montauban); Vendée (La Roche-sur-Yon); Vienne (Poitiers); Vosges (Epinal)
AM Académie Nationale de Médecine, Paris
AN Archives Nationales, Paris
  MC Minutier Central, Paris (notarial records)
BN Bibliothèque Nationale, Paris
BR Bibliothèque Royale, Brussels
EM Ecole de Médecine, Paris

Printed Works

Periodicals

Almanach royal
Gazette de France
Gazette de santé
Gazette salutaire
Journal de médecine, chirurgie et pharmacie

Other Printed Works

Almanac de commerce d'arts et métiers pour la ville de Bordeaux pour l'année 1791.

Almanac vétérinaire pour 1782–1790. Third ed. Paris, 1792.

Archives parlementaires. 1st ser., 1787–1799. Edited by J. Mavidal and E. Laurent. Paris, 1862–1969.

Arthur Young's Travels in France During the Years 1787, 1788, and 1789. London, 1892.

Barbier, Edmond Jean François. *Journal historique et anecdotique du règne de Louis XV.* Edited by A. de la Villegille. 4 vols. Paris, 1847–1856.

Briquet, Marguerite U.F.B. *Dictionnaire historique, littéraire et bibliographique des Françaises et des étrangères naturalisées en France.* Paris: Gille, 1804.

Buchan, William. *Médecine domestique, ou Traité complet des moyens de se conserver en santé.* Paris: Desprez, 1775.

Chamousset, Piarron de. *Mémoire politique sur les enfants.* Paris: Lambert, 1757.

Côme, Frère Jean. *Recueil des pièces importantes sur l'operation de la taille faites par le lithotomé caché.* 1751.

Coutanceau, Marguerite Guillaumanche. *Eléments de l'art d'accoucher en faveur des sages-femmes de la généralité de Guienne par Mme Coutanceau, brevetée du roi en survivance pour enseigner l'art des accouchements dans tout le royaume.* Bordeaux: Michel Racle, 1784.

————. *Instructions théoriques et pratiques à l'usage des élèves de Mme Coutanceau, imprimé par l'ordre de l'Administration central du département de la Gironde, d'après l'autorisation du ministre de l'Intérieur.* Bordeaux: Alexis Levieux, An VIII (1800).

De la Porte, Joseph. *Histoire littéraire des femmes françaises.* 5 vols. Paris: LaCombe, 1769.

Des Essarts, Nicholas Toussaint Le Moyne. *Causes célèbres, curieuses et intéressantes de toutes les cours souveraines du royaume.* 98 vols. Paris: P. G. Simon, 1773–1789.

————. *Dictionnaire universel de police.* 7 vols. Paris: chez Moutard, 1786–1790.

————. *Les Siècles littéraires de la France.* 7 vols. Paris, 1800.

Deventer, Hendrik van. *Observations importantes sur le manuel des accouchemens.* Paris, 1734.

Dictionnaire raisonné universel des arts et métiers, contenant l'histoire, la description, la police des fabriques et manufactures de France et des pays étrangers . . . par M. l'abbé Jaubert. 5 vols. Lyon, 1801.

Didelot, Charles Gabriel. *Instructions pour les sages-femmes, dédié à M. de la Galaisière, intendant de Lorraine et Barrois.* Nancy, [1770].

du Fot, Augier. *Catéchisme sur l'art des accouchements pour les sages-femmes de la campagne fait par ordre et au dépens du gouvernement.* Soissons and Paris: Didot & Ruault, 1775.

Dutens, Louis. *Itinéraire des routes les plus fréquentées, ou Journal d'un voyage.* Paris: Pissot, 1777.

Eloy, N.F.J. *Dictionnaire historique de la médecine ancienne et moderne.* 4 vols. 1778.

Encyclopédie, ou Dictionnaire raisonée des sciences, des arts et des métiers, par une société de gens de lettres. Mis en ordre et publié par M. Diderot: et quant à la partie mathématique par M. D'Alembert. 17 vols. Paris: Briasson, David l'ainé, Le Breton & Durand, 1750–1780.

Etat de médecine, chirurgie et pharmacie en Europe pour l'année 1776. Paris: Didot, 1776.

Etat de médecine, chirurgie et pharmacie en Europe pour l'année 1777. Paris: Thiboust, 1777.

Gauthier d'Agoty, J. *Anatomie des parties de la génération.* Paris, 1773.

Gautier de Montdorge, Antoine. *L'Art d'imprimer les tableaux traité d'après les écrits, les opérations et les instructions verbales de J.C. Le Blon.* Paris, 1756.

Gilibert, Jean-Emmanuel. *L'Anarchie médecinale, ou La Médecine considerée comme nuisible à la société.* 3 vols. Neufchâtel, 1772.

Hazon, Jacques Albert. *Eloge historique de la Faculté de médecine de Paris.* Paris, 1773.

Hurtaut and Magny. *Dictionnaire historique de la ville de Paris.* 4 vols. Paris, 1779.

Icart. *Leçons pratiques sur l'article des accouchements destinées à l'instruction des sages-femmes de Languedoc.* Castre, 1784.

———. *Requête en plainte présentée à nosseigneurs des états de Languedoc par les enfants à naître contre les prétendues sages-femmes.* 1783.

Le Bas, Jean. *Précis de doctrine sur l'art d'accoucher.* 1779.

Le Boursier du Coudray, Angélique Marguerite. *Abrégé de l'art des accouchements.* Paris, 1759; Saintes, 1769; Châlons-sur-Marne, 1773; Ypres (Flanders), 1774; Paris, 1777; Paris, 1785.

La Croix, T. F. *Dictionnaire portatif des femmes célèbres.* Paris, 1788.

[Le Nain]. *Mémoire sur les cours publics d'accouchements faits à Moulins, par Mme du Coudray.* N.p., n.d.

Le Roy, Alphonse. *Essai sur l'histoire naturelle de la grossesse et de l'accouchement.* 1787.

———. *Mémoire d'Alphonse Le Roy . . . pour l'enseignement des maladies des femmes, des accouchements et de la conservation des enfants, à l'Assemblée Nationale.* 1791.

———. *Pratique des accouchements.* Paris: Le Clerc, 1776.

Lettre d'un citoyen amateur du bien public, à M***, pour servir de défense à la mission de la dame du Coudray, qui forme des sages-femmes par tout le royaume, de la part du roi, attaquée dans un écrit public, etc. Paris: Debure, 1777.

Mercier, Louis Sébastien. *Tableau de Paris.* 12 vols. Amsterdam, 1782–1788.

———. *Tableau de Paris.* Edited by Gustave Desnoiresterres. Paris: Pagnerre, 1853.

Nicolas, M. *Le Cri de la nature en faveur des enfants nouveau-nés.* Grenoble, 1775.

Nihell, Elizabeth. *La Cause de l'humanité référée au tribunal du bon sens et de la raison.* Paris, 1771.

————. *Treatise on the Art of Midwifery*. London, 1760.

Onderwys voor de leerlingen in de vroed-kunde ofte konst der kinder-bedden, by vraegen ende antwoorden getrokken uyt de lessen der vermaerde vroed-vrauw Du Coudray, door F.-D. Vandaele, vrymeester in de genées-konst. Ypres: J.-F Moerman, 1774.

Raulin, J. *Instructions succinctes sur les accouchements en faveur des sages-femmes des provinces, faites par ordre du ministre*. Paris: Vincent, 1770.

Roussel, Pierre. *Système physique et morale de la femme suivi du système physique et morale de l'homme*. 5th ed. Paris: Caille & Ravier, 1809.

Saugrain, Claude Marin. *Nouveau Voyage en France, géographique, historique et curieux*. Paris: Morin, 1778.

Süe, Pierre. *Essai historique, littéraire et critique sur l'art des accouchements*. 2 vols. Paris, 1779.

Thomas, Antoine-Léonard. *Essai sur le caractère, les moeurs et l'esprit des femmes*. Paris, 1772; repr. Geneva, 1987.

Tissot, S.A.D. *Avis au peuple*. 7th ed. Lausanne, 1777.

Tustet. *Tableau des événements qui ont eu lieu à Bordeaux depuis la Révolution de 89 jusqu'à ce jour*. Prairial An II.

Verdier, Jean. *Essai sur la jurisprudence de la médecine en France*. Alençon, 1763.

————. *La Jurisprudence particulière de la chirurgie en France*. 2 vols. Paris, 1764.

Watin *fils*. *Provincial à Paris, ou Etat actuel de Paris—ouvrage indispensable à ceux qui veulent connaître et parcourir Paris sans faire aucune question*. 1787.

SECONDARY SOURCES

Alasseur, Jean-Marc. "De la commère à la sage-femme, ou l'essor de l'enseignement obstétrical au 18e siècle en basse Normandie." *Thèse*, University of Caen, 1980.

Altman, Janet Gurkin. *Epistolarity: Approaches to a Form*. Columbus: Ohio State University Press, 1982.

Anderson, Bonnie, and Judith Zinsser. *A History of Their Own*. 2 vols. New York: Harper & Row, 1988.

Appleby, Joyce, Lynn Hunt, and Margaret Jacob. *Telling the Truth About History*. New York: W. W. Norton, 1994.

Archives historiques de la Gironde. Vol. 25. Bordeaux, 1887.

Arney, William Ray. *Power and the Profession of Obstetrics*. Chicago: University of Chicago Press, 1982.

Ascher, Carol, et al., eds. *Between Women: Biographers, Novelists, Critics, Teachers, and Artists Write About Their Work on Women*. Boston: Beacon Press, 1984.

Babeau, Albert. *Les Voyageurs en France depuis la Renaissance jusqu'à la Révolution*. Geneva: Slatkine, 1970.

Badinter, Elisabeth. *L'Amour en plus*. Paris: Flammarion, 1980.

Balard, Paul. "Le Contrôle de la profession de sage-femme sous l'Ancien

Régime." *Gazette hebdomadaire des sciences médicales de Bordeaux* 45 (1924): 6–7.

Baron, Dr. P. *Sages-femmes et maternité à Dijon.* Dijon: Librairie Rebourseau, 1933.

Barthes, Roland. "The Plates of the *Encyclopédie.*" In *A Barthes Reader,* edited by Susan Sontag, pp. 218–236. New York: Hill & Wang, 1982.

Bateson, Mary Catherine. *Composing a Life.* New York: Penguin, Plume, 1990.

Bell, Susan Groag, and Marilyn Yalom, eds. *Revealing Lives: Autobiography, Biography, and Gender.* Albany: State University of New York Press, 1990.

Benezit, Emmanuel. *Dictionnaire . . . des paintres, sculpteurs, dessinateurs et graveurs.* 8 vols. Paris: Gründ, 1948–1955.

Berger, Harry Jr. "Fictions of the Pose: Facing the Gaze in Early Modern Portraiture." *Representations* 46 (spring 1994): 87–120.

Berger, John. *Ways of Seeing.* New York: Penguin Books, 1972.

Bloch, Camille. *L'Assistance et l'état en France à la veille de la Révolution.* Paris: A. Picard, 1908.

Blondeau, R.-A. "Vroedkundig onderwijs te Ieper in de 18e eeuw." In *Wevend aan het verleden Liber Amicorum O. Mus.,* pp. 39–50. Veurne, 1992.

Bompeix, M.-L. "Mission de Mme du Coudray . . . sage-femme royale en 1770: école d'accouchement d'Auch." *Bulletin de la Societé archéologique du Gers* 13, no. 3 (1912): 262–271.

Bordes, Maurice. *L'Administration provinciale et municipale en France au 18e siècle.* Paris: SEDES, 1972.

Boswell, James. *The Kindess of Strangers: The Abandonment of Children in Western Europe from Late Antiquity to the Renaissance.* New York: Pantheon Books, 1988.

Bouteiller, Marcelle. *Médecine populaire d'hier et aujourd'hui.* Paris: Maisonneuve & Larose, 1966.

Brace, Richard Munthe. *Bordeaux and the Gironde, 1789–94.* Ithaca: Cornell University Press, 1947.

Braudel, Fernand. *The Identity of France.* Vol. 2: *People and Production.* Trans. Sîan Reynolds. New York: Harper & Row, 1990.

Brissaud, Edouard. *Histoire des expressions populaires relatives à l'anatomie, à la physiologie et à la médecine.* Paris: G. Masson, 1892.

Brockliss, L. W. B. "Medical Reform, the Enlightenment, and Physician Power in Late-Eighteenth-Century France." *Clio Medica* 29 (1995): 64–112.

Brouillard, Roger. *Des impositions extraordinaires sur le revenu pendant la Révolution (contributions patriotiques, emprunts forcés) et de leur application dans la commune de Bordeaux.* Bordeaux: Y. Cadoret, 1910.

Carles, Jean-Serge. "Initiation populaire à l'obstétrique à la fin du 18e siècle en France et surtout en Languedoc." *Thèse,* University of Toulouse, 1973.

Cavaillès, Henri. *La Route française—son histoire, sa fonction.* Paris: Armand Colin, 1946.

Chambon, Dominique. "Madame Angélique Du Coudray." *Thèse de médecine,* n° 113, Paris/Broussais, 1979.

Chartier, Roger. *The Cultural Uses of Print in Early Modern France.* Trans. Lydia G. Cochrane. Princeton: Princeton University Press, 1987.

Chereau, Achille. *Esquisse historique sur Louise Bourgeois dite Boursier, sage-femme de la reine Marie de Médici.* Paris, 1852.

Chevreau, Abbé A. "Un grand chirurgien au 18e siècle, Frère Côme." *France médicale,* 1912, pp. 102–105.

———. *Un grand chirurgien au 18e siècle, Frère Côme.* Mesnil-sur-l'Estrée, 1912.

Citerne, Guy. "Madame du Coudray, maitresse en accouchement: un enseignement 'moderne' de l'obstétrique au 18e siècle." *GAVROCHE: revue d'histoire populaire,* no. 19 (Jan.–Feb. 1985): 1–7.

Clère, Philippe. "Obstetrix et Medicus. Mésaventures, nombres et lumières d'un enseignement en Franche-Comté à la fin du 18e siècle." *Thèse,* University of Besançon, 1983.

Cobbett, James Paul. *A Ride of Eight Hundred Miles in France.* London, 1824.

Cordonnier-Van der Mursel, Jules. *Ephémérides yproise, ou Relation des événements qui se sont passés dans Ypres depuis les temps les plus reculés jusqu'à nos jours.* 1883–1889.

Coulon-Arpin, Madeleine. *La Maternité et les sages-femmes de la préhistoire au XXe siècle.* 2 vols. Paris: Dacosta, 1981.

Coury, C., and A. Pecker. "Aperçus sur l'enseignement de l'obstétrique en France au 18e siècle: Angélique du Coudray à Grenoble." In *Verhandlungen des XX Internationalen Kongresses für Geschichte der Medizin, Berlin, 22–27 Aug. 1966,* pp. 671–678. Hildesheim, 1968.

Cren, Maurice. "Coutanceau, le beau-frère de Dominique Larrey." *Médecine et armées* 15 (1987): 701–702.

———. *Le Médecin de la Garde Coutanceau, de l'Académie de médecine.* Privately published.

Daly, Mary. *Gyn/Ecology: The Metaethics of Radical Feminism.* Boston: Beacon Press, 1978.

———. *Websters' First New Intergalactic Wickedary of the English Language.* Boston: Beacon Press, 1987.

Davis, Natalie Zemon. *Fiction in the Archives: Pardon Tales and Their Tellers in Sixteenth-Century France.* Stanford: Stanford University Press, 1987.

———. *Society and Culture in Early Modern France.* Stanford: Stanford University Press, 1975.

Dechambre, A. *Dictionnaire encyclopédique des sciences médicales.* 100 vols. Paris, 1864–1889.

Degiorgis-Fayet, Brigitte. "L'Art des accouchements en Auvergne, de Du Coudray à Nivet aux 18e et 19e siècles." *Thèse de médecine,* nº 138, Clermont-Ferrand 1984.

DeJean, Joan. "Lafayette's Ellipses: The Privileges of Anonymity." *PMLA* 99, no. 5 (Oct. 1984): 884–902.

Delacoux, A. *Biographie des sages-femmes célèbres anciennes, modernes et contemporaines.* Paris: Trinquart, 1834.

Delaunay, Paul. *La Maternité de Paris.* Paris: J. Rousset, 1909.

———. *Monde médical parisien au 18e siècle.* 2d ed. Paris: J. Rousset, 1906.

————. *L'Obstétrique dans la Maine aux 18e et 19e siècles.* Le Mans, 1911.

————. *La Vie médicale aux 16e, 17e et 18e siècles.* Paris: Editions Hippocrate, 1935.

Denzin, Norman K. *Interpretive Biography.* Newbury Park, Calif.: Sage, 1989.

Dictionnaire des sciences médicales. 7 vols. Paris, 1820–1825.

Dock, Terry Smiley. *Woman in the Encyclopédie: A Compendium.* Madrid: J. Porrua Turanzas, 1983.

Donnison, Jean. *Midwives and Medical Men: A History of Inter-Professional Rivalries and Women's Rights.* London: Heinemann Educational, 1977.

Dubreuil-Chambardel, Louis. *L'Enseignement des sages-femmes en Touraine.* Paris, 1911.

Ducaunnès-Duval, Ariste. *Inventaire sommaire des Archives municipales de Bordeaux: période révolutionnaire 1789–An VIII.* 4 vols. Bordeaux, 1896.

Dupuy, A. "Les Epidémies en Bretagne au 18e siècle." Chap. 4: "Les Sages-femmes." *Annales de Bretagne* 3 (1887): 179–204.

Edel, Leon. *Writing Lives: Principia Biographica.* New York: W. W. Norton, 1984.

Ehrenreich, Barbara, and Dierdre English. *Witches, Midwives, and Nurses: A History of Women Healers.* Old Westbury, N.Y.: Feminist Press, 1973.

Entrer dans la vie en Poitou du XVIe siècle à nos jours. Paris: Musée Sainte Croix, 1988.

Fairchilds, Cissie. *Domestic Enemies: Servants and their Masters in Old Regime France.* Baltimore: Johns Hopkins University Press, 1984.

Farge, Arlette. *Vivre dans la rue à Paris au 18e siècle.* Paris: Gallimard/Julliard, 1979.

Feinerman, Frances May. "Population and Prosperity: Messance and Expilly Challenge the Physiocrats, 1757–1770." Ph.D. diss., University of Illinois, Chicago Circle, 1981.

Fine, Michelle, and Adrienne Asch. "Who Owns the Womb?" *Women's Review of Books* 2 (May 1985): 8–10.

Forrest, Alan. *Society and Politics in Revolutionary Bordeaux.* Oxford: Oxford University Press, 1975.

Fosseyeux, Marcel. *L'Hôtel Dieu de Paris aux 17e et 18e siècles.* Paris: Berger-Levrault, 1912.

————. "Sages-femmes et nourrices à Paris au 18e siècle." *Revue de Paris,* 1921, pp. 535–555.

Foucault, Michel. *The History of Sexuality.* Vol. 1: *An Introduction.* Trans. Robert Hurley. New York: Pantheon Books, 1978.

————. *Naissance de la clinique. Une archéologie du regard médical.* Paris: PUF, 1963.

Franklin, Alfred L. *La Vie privée d'autre fois.* Ser. 1, vol. 14: *Variétés chirurgicales.* Paris: Plon, 1894.

Fried, Michael. *Absorption and Theatricality: Painting and Beholder in the Age of Diderot.* Berkeley: University of California Press, 1980.

Fromm, Gloria E., ed. *Essaying Biography: A Celebration for Leon Edel.* Honolulu: University of Hawaii Press, for the Biographical Research Center, 1986.

Gamman, Lorraine, and Margaret Marshment, eds. *The Female Gaze.* Seattle: Real Comet Press, 1988.

Garrioch, David. *Neighborhood and Community in Paris, 1740–1790.* Cambridge: Cambridge University Press, 1986.

Gaxotte, Pierre. *Paris au 18e siècle.* Paris: Arthaud, 1982.

Geertz, Clifford. *The Interpretation of Cultures.* New York: Basic Books, 1973.

Gelbart, Nina Rattner. "Books and the Birthing Business: The Midwife Manuals of Madame du Coudray." In *Going Public: Women and Publishing in Early Modern France*, edited by Elizabeth Goldsmith and Dena Goodman, pp. 79–96. Ithaca: Cornell University Press, 1995.

———. "Delivering the Goods: Patriotism, Property, and the Midwife Mission of Mme du Coudray." In *Early Modern Conceptions of Property*, edited by John Brewer and Susan Staves, pp. 467–480. London: Routledge, 1995.

———. *Feminine and Opposition Journalism in Old Regime France: "Le Journal des Dames," 1759–1778.* Berkeley: University of California Press, 1987.

———. "Frondeur Journalism in the 1770s." *Eighteenth-Century Studies* 17, no. 4 (summer 1984): 493–514.

———. "Mme du Coudray's Manual for Midwives: The Politics of Enlightenment Obstetrics." *Proceedings of the Western Society for French History* 16 (1989): 389–396.

———. "Midwife to a Nation: Mme du Coudray Serves France." In *The Art of Midwifery: Early Modern Midwives in Europe*, edited by Hilary Marland, pp. 131–152. London: Routledge, 1993.

———. "The Monarchy's Midwife Who Left No Memoirs." *French Historical Studies* 19, no. 4 (fall 1996): 997–1023.

Gelfand, Toby. "Medical Professionals and Charlatans: The Comité de Salubrité *Enquête* of 1790–91." *Histoire sociale/Social History* 11, no. 21 (May 1978): 62–97.

———. *Professionalizing Modern Medicine: Paris Surgeons and Medical Science and Institutions in the Eighteenth Century.* Westport, Conn.: Greenwood Press, 1980.

Gélis, Jacques. "L'Accouchement au 18e siècle, pratiques traditionelles et contrôle médicale." *Ethnologie française* 6, nos. 3–4 (1976): 325–340.

———. *L'Arbre et le fruit. La Naissance dans l'occident moderne, XVIe–XIXe siècles.* Paris: Fayard, 1984.

———. "L'Enquête de 1786 sur les sages-femmes du royaume." *Annales de démographie historique*, 1980, pp. 299–343.

———. "La Formation des accoucheurs et des sages-femmes aux 17e et 18e siècles: évolution d'un matériel et d'une pédagogie." *Archives de démographie historique*, 1977, pp. 154–180.

———. *History of Childbirth: Fertility, Pregnancy, and Birth in Early Modern Europe.* Trans. Rosemary Morris. Boston: Northeastern University Press, 1991.

———. *La Sage-femme ou le médecin. Une nouvelle conception de la vie.* Paris: Fayard, 1988.

———. "Sages-femmes et accoucheurs: l'obstétrique populaire aux 17e et 18e siècles." *Annales économies, sociétés, civilisations* 32, no. 5 (Sept.–Oct. 1977): 927–957.

Gélis, Jacques, Mireille Laget, and Marie-France Morel. *Entrer dans la vie. Naissance et enfance dans la France traditionelle.* Paris: Gallimard, 1978.

Geyer-Kordesch, Johanna. "Whose Enlightenment? Medicine, Witchcraft, Melancholia, and Pathology."*Clio Medica* 29 (1995): 113–127.

Goldsmith, Elizabeth. *Writing the Female Voice.* Boston: Northeastern University Press, 1989.

Goubert, Jean-Pierre. *Malades et médecins en Bretagne, 1770–1790.* Paris: C. Klincksieck, 1974.

Guillaume, Pierre, and Jean-Pierre Poussou. *Démographie historique.* Paris: Armand Colin, 1970.

Hacquin, François. *L'Histoire de l'art des accouchements en Lorraine des temps anciens au 20e siècle.* N.p., n.d.

Hahn, André, et al. *Histoire de la médecine et du livre médical.* Paris: Olivier Perrin, 1962.

Hall, Jacquelyn Dowd. "Second Thoughts on Writing a Feminist Biography." *Feminist Studies* 13, no. 1 (spring 1987): 19–37.

Heilbrun, Carolyn G. *Writing a Woman's Life.* New York: W. W. Norton, 1988.

Herault, Pascal. "La Formation des sages-femmes du haut Poitou à la fin du 18e siècle." In *Entrer dans la vie en Poitou,* pp. 23–43. Poitiers: Department of History, Université Inter-Ages, 1986.

Hesse, Carla. "Reading Signatures: Female Authorship and Revolutionary Law in France, 1750–1850." *Eighteenth-Century Studies* 22, no. 3 (spring 1989): 469–487.

Hillairet, Jacques. *Dictionnaire historique des rues de Paris.* Paris: Editions de Minuit, 1979.

———. *Evocation du vieux Paris.* Paris: Editions de Minuit, 1954.

Homberger, Eric, and John Charmley, eds. *The Troubled Face of Biography.* London: Macmillan, 1988.

Hufton, Olwen. *The Poor of Eighteenth-Century France.* Oxford: Oxford University Press, 1974.

———. "Women and the Family Economy in Eighteenth-Century France." *French Historical Studies* 9, no. 1 (spring 1975): 1–22.

———. "Women, Work, and Marriage in Eighteenth-Century France." In *Marriage and Society: Studies in the Social History of Marriage,* edited by R. B. Outhwaite, pp. 186–203. New York: St. Martin's Press, 1981.

Hunt, Lynn, ed. *Eroticism and the Body Politic.* Baltimore: Johns Hopkins University Press, 1991.

Hurd-Mead, K. C. *A History of Women in Medicine.* Haddam, Conn.: Haddam Press, 1938.

Isambert, A., et al., eds. *Recueil général des anciennes lois françaises.* 29 vols. Paris, 1821–1833.

Isnard, Albert, and S. Honoré. *B. N. Catalogue générale—Actes Royaux.* Paris: Imprimerie nationale, 1938.

James, Henry. *A Little Tour in France*. Oxford: Oxford University Press, 1984.

Jenkins, Keith. *Rethinking History*. London: Routledge, 1991.

Jonas, S. *Cent portraits de médecins illustres*. Ghent: Academia, 1960.

Jones, Colin. "The Great Chain of Buying." *American Historical Review* 101, no. 1 (Feb. 1996): 13–40.

Jordan, Brigitte. "Knowing by Doing: Lessons Traditional Midwives Taught Me." Department of Anthropology, Michigan State University, Working Paper No. 169, April 1988.

Jordanova, Ludmilla. "Gender, Generation, and Science: William Hunter's Obstetrical Atlas." In *William Hunter and the Eighteenth-Century Medical World*, edited by W. F. Bynum and Roy Porter, pp. 385–412. Cambridge: Cambridge University Press, 1985.

Kaplan, E. Ann. "Is the Gaze Male?" In *Powers of Desire: The Politics of Sexuality*, edited by Ann Snitow et al., pp. 309–327. New York: Monthly Review Press, 1983.

Keller, E. F., and C. R. Grontkowski. "The Mind's Eye." In *Discovering Reality: Feminist Perspectives on Epistemology, Metaphysics, Methodology, and Philosophy of Science*, edited by Sandra Harding and Merrill B. Hintikka, pp. 207–224. Dordrecht: D. Reidel, 1983.

Knibiehler, Yvonne, and Catherine Fouquet. *La Femme et les médecins. Analyse historique*. Paris: Hachette, 1983.

———. *Histoire des mères du Moyen Age à nos jours*. Paris: Montalba, 1980.

Krivatsky, Peter. "Le Blon's Anatomical Color Engravings." *Journal of the History of Medicine and Allied Sciences* 23, no. 2 (1968): 153–158.

Laget, Mireille. "Childbirth in Seventeenth- and Eighteenth-Century France: Obstetrical Practice and Collective Attitudes." In *Medicine and Society in France*, Selections from the *Annales* 6, edited by Robert Forster and Orest Ranum, pp. 137–176. Baltimore: Johns Hopkins University Press, 1980.

———. *Naissance. L'Accouchement avant l'âge de la clinique*. Paris: Seuil, 1982.

Lamotte, François. "Le Personnel médical féminin à la fin du 18e siècle: les sages-femmes de la Manche." In *Travail, métiers et professions en Normandie*, pp. 147–157. Nogent-sur-Marne: Société parisienne d'histoire et d'archéologie normandes, 1984.

Landes, Joan B. *Women and the Public Sphere in the Age of the French Revolution*. Ithaca: Cornell University Press, 1988.

Lefftz, J.-P. *L'Art des accouchements à Strasbourg de la Renaissance au siècle des lumières*. N.p., 1985.

Le Maguet, Paul-Emile. *Le Monde médical parisien sous le Grand Roi, suivi du porte-feuille de Vallant, Médecin de S. A. R. Madame de Guise et de Madame la Marquise de Sablé*. Paris, 1899; repr. Geneva: Slatkine, 1971.

Leymarie-Couturier, Jocelyne. "Histoire de la fondation de l'école de sages-femmes de Bordeaux." *Thèse*, University of Bordeaux II, 1987.

Lindemann, Mary. "Maternal Politics: The Principles and Practice of Maternity Care in Eighteenth-Century Hamburg." *Journal of Family History* 9, no. 1 (1984): 44–63.

Lingo, Alison Klairmont. "Empirics and Charlatans in Early Modern France:

The Genesis of the Classification of the 'Other' in Medical Practice." *Journal of Social History* 19, no. 4 (summer 1986): 583–603.

Lipinska, Melina. *Les Femmes et le progrès des sciences médicales*. Paris: Masson, 1930.

———. *Histoire des femmes médecins depuis l'antiquité jusqu'à nos jours*. Edited by G. Jacques. Paris, 1900.

Lipton, Eunice. *Alias Olympia: A Woman's Search for Manet's Notorious Model and Her Own Desire*. New York: Charles Scribner's Sons, 1992.

Loudon, Irvine. "Deaths in Childbed from the Eighteenth Century to 1935." *Medical History* 30 (1986): 1–41.

Lough, John. *France on the Eve of Revolution: British Travelers' Observations, 1763–88*. Chicago: Dorsey Press, 1987.

———. *Introduction to Eighteenth-Century France*. London: Longmans, 1961.

Mandell, Gail Porter. *Life Into Art: Conversations with Seven Contemporary Biographers*. Fayetteville: University of Arkansas Press, 1991.

Marion, Marcel. *Dictionnaire des institutions de la France aux XVIIe et XVIIIe siècles*. Paris: A. & J. Picard, 1984.

Marland, Hilary, ed. *The Art of Midwifery: Early Modern Midwives in Europe*. London: Routledge, 1993.

Maza, Sarah C. *Private Lives and Public Affairs*. Berkeley: University of California Press,1993.

———. *Servants and Masters in Eighteenth-Century France: The Uses of Loyalty*. Princeton: Princeton University Press, 1983.

McCloy, Shelby T. *Government Assistance in Eighteenth-Century France*. Durham, N.C.: Duke University Press, 1946.

McManners, John. *Death and the Enlightenment*. Oxford: Oxford University Press, 1985.

Ménétra, Jacques-Louis. *Journal of My Life*. With an introduction and commentary by Daniel Roche, foreword by Robert Darnton; trans. Arthur Goldhammer. New York: Columbia University Press, 1986.

Meynier, Georges. "Un cours provincial d'accouchements au 18e siècle (généralité de Soissons)." *Thèse de médecine*, University of Paris, 1899.

Monteiro, Lois A. "On Separate Roads: Florence Nightingale and Elizabeth Blackwell." *Signs* 9 (spring 1984): 520–533.

Morel, Marie-France. "City and Country in Eighteenth-Century Medical Discussions About Early Childhood." In *Medicine and Society in France*, Selections from the *Annales* 6, edited by Robert Foster and Orest Ranum, pp. 48–65. Baltimore: Johns Hopkins University Press, 1980.

———. "Théories et pratiques de l'allaitement en France au 18e siècle." *Annales de démographie historique*, 1977, pp. 393–426.

Morel, Pierre, and J.-M. Alasseur. "Mme le Boursier du Coudray et les prémices d'une education obstétricale populaire dans la généralité de Caen." In *Femme en Normandie*, pp. 239–251. Caen: Archives départementales du Calvados, 1986.

"Mother and Child Were Saved": The Memoirs (1693–1740) of the Frisian Midwife Catharina Schrader*. Trans. and annot. Hilary Marland. Amsterdam: Rodopi, 1987.

Nivet, V. *Note historique sur Mme du Coudray, maitresse sage-femme à Clermont Ferrand en 1756.* Clermont-Ferrand: Thibaud, 1879.

Ozouf, Mona. *Les Mots des femmes. Essai sur la singularité française.* Paris: Fayard, 1995.

Pachter, Marc, ed. *Telling Lives.* Washington, D.C.: New Republic Books, 1979.

Pardailhé-Galabrun, Annik. *La Naissance de l'intime. 3000 foyers parisiens aux 17e et 18e siècles.* Paris: PUF, 1988.

Pariset, François-Georges. *Bordeaux au 18e siècle.* Bordeaux: Fédération historique du Sud-Ouest, 1968.

Pecker, André. *La Médecine à Paris du 13e au 20e siècle.* Paris, 1984.

Perkins, Wendy. "Midwives Versus Doctors: The Case of Louise Bourgeois." *Seventeenth Century* 3 (1988): 135–157.

———. "The Relationship Between Midwife and Client in the Works of Louise Bourgeois." *Seventeenth-Century French Studies* 11 (1989): 28–45.

Pery, Georges. *Recherches historiques sur l'école d'accouchement, l'hospice de la maternité et la clinique d'accouchement de l'hôpital St. André de Bordeaux.* Bordeaux, n.d.

Pessard, Gustave. *Nouveau Dictionnaire historique de Paris.* Paris: Eugène Rey, 1904.

Petchesky, Rosalind Pollack. "Fetal Images: The Power of Visual Culture in the Politics of Reproduction." In *Reproductive Technologies: Gender, Motherhood, and Medicine,* edited by Michelle Stanworth, pp. 57–80. Minneapolis: University of Minnesota Press, 1987.

Pillement, P. "L'Enseignement de l'obstétrique en Lorraine au 18e siècle." *Revue médicale de l'est,* 1902, pp. 1–9.

Poovey, Mary. *Uneven Developments: The Ideological Work of Gender in Mid-Victorian England.* Chicago: University of Chicago Press, 1988.

Procès verbaux et rapports du comité de mendacité de la constituante 1790–1791, publiées, annotées par Camille Bloch et Alexandre Tuetey. Paris, 1911.

Prudhomme, Louis Marie. *Biographie universelle et historique des femmes célèbres.* 4 vols. Paris: Lebigre, 1830.

Railliet, A., and L. Moulé. *Histoire de l'Ecole d'Alfort.* Paris, 1908.

Ramsey, Matthew. *Professional and Popular Medicine in France, 1770–1830: The Social World of Medical Practice.* New York: Cambridge University Press, 1988.

Rich, Adrienne. *Of Woman Born: Motherhood as Experience and Institution.* New York: Bantam Books, 1977.

Rose, Phyllis. "Fact and Fiction in Biography." In *Writing of Women: Essays in a Renaissance,* pp. 64–81. Middletown, Conn.: Wesleyan University Press, 1985.

Rothney, John, ed. *The Brittany Affair and the Crisis of the Ancien Régime.* New York: Oxford University Press, 1969.

———. *Only Paradoxes to Offer: French Feminists and the Rights of Man.* Cambridge, Mass.: Harvard University Press, 1996.

Schama, Simon. *Dead Certainties (Unwarranted Speculations).* New York: Vintage Books, 1992.

Schelle, Gustave, ed. *Oeuvres de Turgot et documents le concernant avec biographie et notes.* 5 vols. Paris: F. Alcan, 1913–1923.

Scott, Joan Wallach. "Gender: A Useful Category of Historical Analysis." *American Historical Review* 91 (Dec. 1986): 1053–1075.

———. *Gender and the Politics of History.* New York: Columbia University Press, 1988.

Senior, Nancy. "Aspects of Infant Feeding in Eighteenth-Century France." *Eighteenth-Century Studies* 16 (summer 1983): 367–388.

Shorter, Edward. *A History of Women's Bodies.* New York: Basic Books, 1982.

Simons, Patricia. "Women in Frames: The Gaze, the Eye, the Profile in Renaissance Portraiture." *History Workshop,* no. 25 (spring 1988): 4–31.

Smith, Hilda. "Feminism and the Methodology of Women's History." In *Liberating Women's History,* edited by Berenice A. Carroll, pp. 368–384. Urbana: University of Illinois Press, 1976.

Smith, Sidonie. *A Poetics of Women's Autobiography: Marginality and the Fictions of Self-Representation.* Bloomington: Indiana University Press, 1987.

Spence, Jonathan D. *The Question of Hu.* New York: Vintage Books, 1989.

Stanley, Liz. *The Auto/Biographical I: The Theory and Practice of Feminist Autobiography.* Manchester: Manchester University Press, 1992.

Stofft, Henri. "Utilisation de la langue bretonne pour la formation professionnelle des sages-femmes au 18e siècle." *DALC HOMP SONJ! Revue historique bretonne,* no. 9 (1984): 11–17.

Sussman, George. *Selling Mother's Milk: The Wet Nursing Business in France, 1715–1914.* Urbana: University of Illinois Press, 1982.

Tackett, Timothy. *Priest and Parish in Eighteenth-Century France.* Princeton: Princeton University Press, 1977.

This, Bernard. *Naître.* Paris: Montaigne, 1972.

———. *La Requête des enfants à naître.* Paris: Seuil, 1982.

Thomachot, Marie-Andrée. "Chirurgie et chirurgiens parisiens au 18e siècle." *Thèse du 3e cycle,* University of Paris IV (Sorbonne), 1982.

Thompson, E. P. "Patrician Society, Plebeian Culture." *Journal of Social History* 7, no. 4 (summer 1974): 382–405.

Tocqueville, Alexis de. *The Old Regime and the French Revolution.* New York: Doubleday/Anchor Books, 1955.

Tomaselli, Sylvana. "The Enlightenment Debate on Women." *History Workshop,* no. 20 (autumn 1985): 101–124.

Tompkins, Jane. "Me and My Shadow." *New Literary History* 19, no. 1 (1987): 169–178.

Tormey, Alan. "Perception and Representation." In *Common Denominators in Art and Science,* edited by Martin Pollock, pp. 175–180. Aberdeen: Aberdeen University Press, 1983.

Towler, Jean, and Joan Bramall. *Midwives in History and Society.* London: Croom Helm, 1986.

Trenard, Louis. "De la Route royale à l'âge d'or des diligences." In *Les Routes de France depuis les origines jusqu'à nos jours,* pp. 101–132. Paris: André Chastel, 1959.

Ulrich, Laurel Thatcher. *A Midwife's Tale*. New York: Alfred A. Knopf, 1989.

Vanhamme. "Documents concernant l'enseignement de l'obstétrique et le problème de la maternité aux Pays Bas autrichiens." *Bulletin de la Commission royale d'histoire* 108 (1943): 41–59.

Vigarello, George. *Le Propre et le sale. L'Hygiène du corps depuis le Moyen Age.* Paris: Seuil, 1985.

Vissière, Isabelle. *Procès de femmes au temps des philosophes.* Paris: Des Femmes, 1985.

White, Hayden. *Tropics of Discourse: Essays in Cultural Criticism.* Baltimore: Johns Hopkins University Press, 1978.

Wiesner, Merry E. "Early Modern Midwifery: A Case Study." *International Journal of Women's Studies* 6 (1983): 26–43.

Wildenstein, George. "Jakob Christoffel LeBlon, ou Le Secret de peindre en gravant." *Gazette des beaux arts* 56 (1960): 91–100.

Williams, Alan. *The Police of Paris, 1718–1789.* Baton Rouge: Louisiana State University Press, 1979.

Wilson, Adrian. *The Making of Man Midwifery: Childbirth in England, 1660–1770.* London: UCL Press, 1995.

———. "Participant or Patient? Seventeenth-Century Childbirth from the Mother's Point of View." In *Patients and Practitioners: Lay Perceptions of Medicine in PreIndustrial Society,* edited by Roy Porter, pp. 129–144. Cambridge: Cambridge University Press, 1986.

Witkowski, Gustave J. *Accoucheurs et sages-femmes célèbres.* Paris: G. Steinheil, 1891.

———. *Histoire des accouchements chez tous les peuples.* Paris: G. Steinheil, 1887.

Yalom, Marilyn. *Blood Sisters: The French Revolution in Women's Memory.* New York: Basic Books, 1993.

Illustrations

Acknowledgments

This book could never have been done without the generous fellowships and grants I received over the past decade: a year of support from the American Council of Learned Societies, another from the National Endowment for the Humanities, and fellowships for shorter periods from the William Andrews Clark Library, the UCLA Center for Seventeenth- and Eighteenth-Century Studies, the Graves Foundation, and Occidental College. Also, a grant from the National Institutes of Health, LM 04384, awarded to me for a related project on eighteenth-century medical journalism, helped greatly with this one.

Many people assisted me at various stages of this project, some by reading parts or all of the manuscript, some by participating with me at conferences on related subjects, some by "just" sharing their good conversation, encouragement, and hospitality, some by explaining obstetrical maneuvers, some by taking photos and slides, some by translating Flemish, some by helping me get books and documents. These debts go back more than a decade. So thank you to Keith Baker, Roy Porter, Dorothy Porter, Alison Klairmont Lingo, Monica Green, Mary Lindemann, Colin Jones, Dena Goodman, Kate Norberg, Ruth Harris, Sara Maza, Gary Kates, Hilary Marland, Claude Maire, Sarah Hanley, John Brewer, Susan Staves, Karen Offen, Darlene Levy, Bonnie Smith, Bert Hansen, Isabel Hull, David Sabean, Steven Kaplan, Jan Goldstein, Peter Reill, Bob Frank, Dora Weiner, Toby Gelfand, Ludmilla Jordanova, Kathleen Wellman, Lloyd Moote, Joby Margadant, Ray Birn, Ellen DuBois, Alice Wexler, Robert Rosenstone, Vicky Steele, Cathy Donahue, Candy Waltz, Susan Glasser, Roger Boesche, Annabelle Rea, Bob Winter, Robijn Bruinsma, Theresia de Vroom, and Tim Pyatt. My editor at the University of California Press, Sheila Levine, believed in this book even before I did. Lynn Dumenil patiently got me over my computerphobia. Margery Proctor prepared the many drafts with matchless skill, inimitable humor, and generosity beyond the call of duty. Nancy Grubb helped graciously with all the finishing touches. In Europe I had the invaluable assistance of archivists and librarians far too numerous to list, and of Jean Content, Elsa Van Geyt, Bernard Chabaud, Marie-Lise Bonnet, Didier Roux, and Maurice Cren.

Our family cat, Judy, graced the manuscript by curling up on almost every page. My husband, Bill, and children, Eva and Matthew, supported me in their own ways, putting up with my prolonged absences in body and spirit. I dedicate this book with love and admiration to my parents, David and Henriette Rattner, two of the most special people in the world.

Index

Abelard, Peter, 101
Abortions, 68
Abrégé de l'art des accouchements (1759 edition, du Coudray): acquiescence of, to male authority, 76–77, 98–99; childbirth description in, 31–36, 290n1; comprehensible language of, 76, 77–78; cost-per-copy of, 72, 107; midwifery lessons of, 65–70, 295n1; mission statement on, 74–75; press coverage of, 78–79, 114; title page of, 73 fig.; validating impact of, 18, 74–75, 79; Verdier's "Observations" in, 49, 74, 77, 93
Abrégé de l'art des accouchements (1769 edition, du Coudray), 118, 302n5; anatomical engravings of, 129–32, 130 fig.; cleanliness focus of, 134; cost-per-copy of, 129, 136; du Coudray's portrait in, 4 fig., 129; on newborn's importance, 136–37, 138; rival manuals and, 150; Verdier's "Observations" in, 129; on wet nurses, 194, 195–96. *See also* Anatomical engravings
Abrégé de l'art des accouchements (1773 edition, du Coudray): distribution of, in Nancy, 172–73; Flemish edition of, 183, 184 fig., 308nn1,2; Le Roy on, 204; and rival manuals, 164, 187–88, 193, 194, 202, 309n5, 310n21
Abrégé de l'art des accouchements (1777 edition, du Coudray): cost-per-copy of, 214; press coverage of, 211–12; prize money for, 209, 214; royal credentials in, 205, 206 fig.
Abrégé de l'art des accouchements: sixth edition of, 248
"Accoucheuse" (Tarin), 57
Affiches, annonces et avis divers de Reims et de la généralité de Champagne, 164
Affiches de Poitou, 114
Affiches . . . du Dauphiné, 203
Afterbirth (placenta): delivery/use of, 34, 84

Agen, 138–40, 264
Aiguillon, d,' 133, 151, 153–54, 155
Alfort, 226, 227
Algalie (hollow tube), 32
Almanach royal, 39
American War for Independence, 249
Amiens, 176
L' Anarchie médecinale (Gilibert), 202
Anatomical engravings (*Abrégé*): cleanliness focus of, 134; cost of, 129; and Mme Coutanceau's manual, 280, 320n17; du Coudray on, 131; male midwifery texts *vs.*, 150, 229, 230–31 figs., 314n8; multichrome process of, 129–30, 130 fig., 302n13; representation of women and, 131–32
Anatomical models: of Mlle Bihéron, 49, 167; of Mme Coutanceau, 252; of Mme Lenfant, 167–68, 179, 306n6. *See also* Obstetrical mannequins
Anderson, Bonnie S., 301n1
Andouillé (royal surgeon), 246, 248
Angers, 221
Angoulême, 264
Annales typographiques, 78
Année littéraire, 78
Apprentice midwives: in du Coudray's entourage, 125; fees paid by, 46–47, 52; Hôtel Dieu's training of, 51–53; midwives' contracts with, 45–47, 292nn2,3. *See also* Provincial midwife students
Assignats (treasury notes), 261
Astruc, Jean, 41
Austrian Flanders. *See* Flanders
Authorship: and legitimation, 17–18
Autopsies, 41
Auvergne, 16, 55–59, 72, 74, 87, 94
Auxerre, 243
Avis au people sur la santé (Tissot), 202

Babies. *See* Newborns
Bailly, Mme (midwife), 55
Bairsin, Anne, 25, 26, 292n3

Compositor:	Prestige Typography
Text:	10/13 Palatino
Display:	Palatino
Printer and binder:	Edwards Brothers, Inc.